Christianities in the Trans-Atlantic World, 1500–1800

Series Editors

Crawford Gribben
School of History and Anthropology
Queen's University Belfast
Belfast, United Kingdom

Scott Spurlock
Department of Theology and Religious Studies
University of Glasgow
Glasgow, United Kingdom

Aim of the Series
Building upon the recent recovery of interest in religion in the early modern trans-Atlantic world, this series offers fresh, lively and inter-disciplinary perspectives on the broad view of its subject. Books in the series will work strategically and systematically to address major but under-studied or overly simplified themes in the religious and cultural history of the early modern trans-Atlantic.

More information about this series at
http://www.springer.com/series/14892

Andrew Crome
Editor

Prophecy and Eschatology in the Transatlantic World, 1550–1800

palgrave
macmillan

Editor
Andrew Crome
Manchester, United Kingdom

Christianities in the Trans-Atlantic World, 1500–1800
ISBN 978-1-137-52054-8 (hardcover)   ISBN 978-1-137-52055-5 (eBook)
ISBN 978-1-349-70514-6 (softcover)
DOI 10.1057/978-1-137-52055-5

Library of Congress Control Number: 2016952411

© The Editor(s) (if applicable) and The Author(s) 2016, First softcover printing 2018
The author(s) has/have asserted their right(s) to be identified as the author(s) of this work in accordance with the Copyright, Designs and Patents Act 1988.
This work is subject to copyright. All rights are solely and exclusively licensed by the Publisher, whether the whole or part of the material is concerned, specifically the rights of translation, reprinting, reuse of illustrations, recitation, broadcasting, reproduction on microfilms or in any other physical way, and transmission or information storage and retrieval, electronic adaptation, computer software, or by similar or dissimilar methodology now known or hereafter developed.
The use of general descriptive names, registered names, trademarks, service marks, etc. in this publication does not imply, even in the absence of a specific statement, that such names are exempt from the relevant protective laws and regulations and therefore free for general use.
The publisher, the authors and the editors are safe to assume that the advice and information in this book are believed to be true and accurate at the date of publication. Neither the publisher nor the authors or the editors give a warranty, express or implied, with respect to the material contained herein or for any errors or omissions that may have been made.

Cover image: Duvet, Jean (1485 - circa 1570), copper engraving from the series "Apocalypse". Lyon, France, 1561, Bibliotheque © INTERFOTO / Alamy Stock Photo

Printed on acid-free paper

This Palgrave Macmillan imprint is published by Springer Nature
The registered company is Macmillan Publishers Ltd. London

In memory of Arma Crome, 1923–2015

Acknowledgements

Any edited collection is an exercise in collaboration, and I have built up many debts of gratitude in the process of putting this book together. My thanks firstly to the contributors for their timeliness and enthusiasm for this project, which has made the editing process a pleasure. Jade Moulds, as Assistant Editor at Palgrave, has been a model of efficiency and organisation in her help with the book. The anonymous reader for Palgrave provided useful suggestions for a number of chapters which were gratefully received. I also extend my thanks to Crawford Gribben and Scott Spurlock as series editors; it was Crawford's suggestion that I might think about putting together something on this topic that was responsible for this volume's genesis. Thanks also to Jeffrey K. Jue, Ariel Hessayon, Geordan Hammond, and Philip Lockley who have discussed this collection at various points in its development.

I have been extremely lucky to be surrounded by supportive and dedicated colleagues at the University of Manchester, who have contributed to the congenial atmosphere in which this volume was put together. I have also been blessed with an array of incredible students who have thought through the complexities of the apocalypticism with me on a final year course I teach. I would also like to thank my new colleagues at Manchester Metropolitan University for affording me a warm welcome. Thanks also to my friends and family, who are surprisingly tolerant of listening to me bang on about my eclectic research interests, and continue to be a fantastic support. Special thanks to Jon Ainscough and Stef Elstub for their help in solving a cover design dilemma. My hope is that all who enjoy delving into the prophecies and predictions of 'dusty old books' (not to mention almanacs, sermons, pamphlets, and newspapers) will find something of interest here.

Contents

1 Introduction 1
  Andrew Crome

2 Between the New and the Old World: Iberian Prophecies
  and Imperial Projects in the Colonisation of the Early
  Modern Spanish and Portuguese Americas 33
  Luís Filipe Silvério Lima

3 Left Behind: George Herbert, Eschatology,
  and the Stuart Atlantic, 1606–1634 65
  John Kuhn

4 Bradstreet and Trans-Atlantic Non-Conformism
  in the American-Prophetic Mode 83
  Edward Simon

5 Antichrists, and Rumours of Antichrists: Radical
  Prophecy in the trans-Atlantic World, 1640–1660 105
  Chris Caughey

6   The Restoration of the Jews in Transatlantic Context,
    1600–1680   127
    Andrew Crome

7   Transatlantic Cunning: English Occult Practices
    in the British American Colonies   151
    Alexander Cummins

8   Eschatology and Radicalism after the Restoration:
    The English Context   187
    Warren Johnston

9   Reading Canticles in the Tradition of New England
    Millennialism: John Cotton and Cotton Mather's
    Commentaries on the Song of Songs   213
    Jan Stievermann

10 Prophecy and Revivalism in the Transatlantic
    World 1734–1745   239
    Jonathan Downing

11 Prophecy in the Age of Revolution   259
    Deborah Madden

Bibliography   283

Index   297

NOTES ON CONTRIBUTORS

Chris Caughey is an Adjunct Professor in Theology and History at William Jessup University in California, USA. He received his PhD from Trinity College Dublin, and his research interests focus on antinomianism and the development of Reformed covenant theology in the seventeenth century. In particular, he is interested in the theology of the Mosaic covenant and its wide-ranging effects on the faith and practice of early modern Reformed churches.

Andrew Crome is Lecturer in Early Modern History at Manchester Metropolitan University. He is the author of *The restoration of the Jews: Early modern hermeneutics, eschatology, and national identity in the works of Thomas Brightman* (Springer, 2014), and is currently working on a book on links between English national identity and ideas of Jewish restoration from 1600 to 1850. He also researches and writes on religion, popular culture, and media fandoms, and was co-editor (with James McGrath) of *Religion and Doctor Who* (2013).

Alexander Cummins received his doctorate in the history of early modern English magic and the emotions from the University of Bristol. His first book, *The starry rubric: Seventeenth-century English astrology and magic*, was published in 2012. His research interests include love magic, necromancy, grimoires, cunning-folk, and demonology, as well as how these concepts and practices intersected with early modern European and English-speaking culture, medicine, ontology, epistemology, and phenomenology. He is currently Reviews Editor for Sophia Centre Press.

Jonathan Downing is a Postdoctoral Research Associate at the University of Bristol, working on a project entitled 'Prophetic Inspiration and Scriptural Authority'. His research interests include the interplay between prophecy and biblical interpretation in modern and early-modern heterodox religious traditions.

Warren Johnston is an associate professor in the Department of History and Philosophy at Algoma University in Ontario, Canada. His area of interest is political and religious thought in Britain during the sixteenth, seventeenth, and eighteenth centuries. He has published a number of peer-reviewed articles and chapters on early modern English apocalyptic ideas. His book *Revelation restored: The Apocalypse in later seventeenth-century England* explains the importance of apocalyptic belief to political thought and culture during the Restoration. His current research examines the use of national thanksgiving celebrations to develop and represent ideas of Britishness from the late seventeenth century to the end of the Napoleonic wars.

John Kuhn is a doctoral candidate in English at Columbia University. His areas of interest include early modern drama, the disciplinary history of comparative religion, and the literatures of Atlantic expansion. He is completing a dissertation entitled 'Making Pagans: Non-Abrahamic Religions and the London Stage from Marlowe to Southerne', which explores English theatre's connections to ethnography and antiquarianism in the long seventeenth century. He is also the author of another article on Herbert, forthcoming in *English Literary Renaissance*.

Luís Filipe Silvério Lima is Senior Lecturer in Early Modern History at Federal University of São Paulo (Unifesp). The author of *Império dos sonhos: narrativas proféticas, sebastianismo e messianismo brigantino* (2010) and co-editor of *Facetas do Império na História* (2008), he is currently working on a study of the hopes of Fifth Monarchy and prophetic connections in the seventeenth-century Atlantic.

Deborah Madden is senior lecturer at the University of Brighton. She has written books and articles on eighteenth-century religion, medicine and culture. Her last monograph was an intellectual biography of the millenarian prophet, Richard Brothers, who became a cause célèbre during the 1790s. She is currently writing a book on Victorian cultures of life writing.

Edward Simon is a doctoral candidate in English at Lehigh University. He holds a Master's in Literary and Cultural Studies from Carnegie-Mellon University as well as a postgraduate certificate in Renaissance Studies from the University of Strathclyde. His research focuses on seventeenth-century Atlantic religion and literature, particularly non-conformist faith and the ways in which colonialism, geographic thinking, and Protestantism operated to form nascent American discourses. He is currently finishing his dissertation, 'The American Strand: Directional Poetics and the Apocalypse in the Early Modern Atlantic'. In addition to being published in several peer-reviewed academic journals and anthologies, he has also contributed widely to the public humanities in a variety of websites and magazines.

Jan Stievermann is Professor of the History of Christianity in North America at the University of Heidelberg, and director of the Jonathan Edwards Center, Germany. He has written and edited books and essays on a broad range of topics in the fields of American religious history and American literature, including a comprehensive study of the theology and aesthetics of Ralph Waldo Emerson. Most recently, he co-edited *A peculiar mixture: German-language cultures and identities in eighteenth-century North America* (2013) and *Religion and the marketplace in the United States* (2014). His edition of vol. 5 of Cotton Mather's *Biblia Americana* and a book-length study of this hitherto unpublished Puritan bible commentary are both forthcoming. For the *Biblia*-project as a whole (10 vols.) he also serves as the executive editor.

CHAPTER 1

Introduction

Andrew Crome

Early in the morning of 19 July 1591, two Puritan gentlemen, Edmund Coppinger and Henry Arthington, mounted a cart in Cheapside to announce that they had discovered the messiah. William Hackett, a Presbyterian of dubious moral character, had assumed 'the office and spirite of S. *Iohn Baptist*, affirming, that hee was sent thither by God, to prepare the way of the Lord before his second comming to iudgement'.[1] Arthington and Coppinger, viewing themselves as the two witnesses of God predicted in the Book of Revelation (Rev. 11:1–12), believed that Hackett had been sent to overthrow episcopacy and Elizabeth I, and inaugurate a new era of perfected church government on earth. The authorities were not amused, and Hackett was executed. Roughly two hundred years later, and several thousand miles to the west, an altogether more respectable New Jersey Presbyterian preacher, David Austin, predicted Christ's return for the fourth Sunday of May 1796. When the prophecy failed, Austin was not imprisoned or attacked by concerned authorities. Instead his flock (which included a number of politicians) humoured his preaching, until finally losing patience and dismissing him as minister

A. Crome (✉)
Department of History, Manchester Metropolitan University, Manchester, UK
e-mail: a.crome@mmu.ac.uk

as his prophecies continued unabated. Undeterred, the preacher fell to designing wharves and houses to prepare the Jews for their prophesied return to Palestine.[2]

These two examples, neatly bookending the period covered in this collection, might be taken as representative of the way in which interpretation of prophecy developed from the sixteenth until the late eighteenth centuries. What was seen as threatening and politically destabilising to Elizabethan politicians appeared eccentric, but largely harmless, to enlightened Americans on the cusp of the 1800s. Yet history never develops in such neat, sweeping, and clear-cut movements, despite what secularisation theory may seem to imply at times.[3] To problematise this narrative, two other stories might be considered. In 1587, the Puritan preacher William Perkins wrote *A Fruitfull Dialogue Concerning the End of the World*. Here, he was quick to condemn the sort of credulous acceptance of prophecy that led to Hackett's radical actions. In a dialogue between 'Christian' and 'Worldling', the latter betrays a popular interest and excitement in prophecy—finding prophecies hidden on stone walls, in popular ballads and breathless discussions with neighbours, as well as in books dedicated to the subject. 'Christian' is unimpressed: 'I make as little account of these verses as of *Merlin's* drunken prophecies, or the tales of *Robin Hood*.'[4] As the godly man reminds his credulous interlocutor, there are several signs that need to be fulfilled before the world will end—he should concentrate on holy living rather than prophetic speculation if he wants to be blessed.

Roughly two hundred years later and several thousand miles to the west in Rhode Island, Jemima Wilkinson arose from a serious illness reborn as the second coming of Christ, or the Publick Universal Friend. As the Friend she attracted significant attention from the press, who repeatedly slandered her, concerned at her refusal to accept any clear designation of gender or race, and speculating on her political and moral aims.[5] While Jemima was founding a community in New York State in the 1790s, across the Atlantic former naval officer Richard Brothers was declaring himself the 'nephew of the Almighty', and claiming that George III should surrender the crown in his favour. Against the backdrop of the French Revolution, Brothers's actions caused enough concern for the government to declare him criminally insane and imprison him in an asylum for some eleven years.[6]

These incidents are merely snapshots of events which need to be placed within a larger matrix of historical developments to fully make sense. But they serve as reminders that while a narrative of 'disenchantment' or secularisation might be read into the period 1500–1800, that in reality predictions, prophecies, and speculation about the end times cannot be slotted into neat historical boxes. As Perkins' work shows, Elizabethan writers might find prophecy as politically harmless and eccentric (albeit spiritually unhelpful) as those who dismissed Austin in late-eighteenth-century New Jersey; while governments and the press might be equally alarmed by the political dangers of the prophetic form in 1591 and 1795. While, as the anonymous 'Freethinker' bewailed in that year, it may be 'strange, that any man in his senses should, in this Enlightened age, be ambitious of the name and character of a prophet',[7] plenty continued to aspire to the title.

This book attempts to shed some light on why this was the case within a particular geographical and historical context. Taking as its frame the transatlantic world in the period 1500–1800, contributors explore the variety of ways in which prophetic discourse could be appropriated, transformed, and reworked as new lands and peoples were discovered, and unprecedented political revolutions were dealt with and debated. The aim of this introduction is therefore threefold. First, the choice of geographical focus will to be justified. The Atlantic paradigm has been both defended and heavily criticised in recent work, and it is important that the reader is aware of the benefits that adopting an Atlantic approach to examining prophecy can offer. At the same time, it would be remiss not to highlight continuing difficulties with the paradigm. Second, it introduces the reader to the importance of prophecy within this context. Starting from the 'discovery' of the Americas by Columbus, prophecy had an important role to play in shaping the way in which Europeans understood the new people groups, cultures, and landscapes they discovered. Prophecies of a future millennial kingdom and of a church in the wilderness motivated emigration; predictions of the discovery of the 'lost tribes' of Israel encouraged evangelisation of indigenous peoples; while prophecy might also be seen as playing an important part in encouraging rebellions and revolutions, as concerns relating to both Hackett and Brothers suggest. Finally, this introduction will lead the reader into the book itself, with a brief summary of each of the chapters. The book as a whole aims to provide an accessible but rigorous overview of the cultural, religious, and political impact of prophecy in the transatlantic world from 1500 to 1800. While it cannot claim to be exhaustive in scope, it aims to highlight important recent work in the field, suggest new approaches, and offer ways in which the study of prophecy might develop into the next decade of research.

1.1 Defining Key Concepts: Prophecy in the Atlantic

This book's title employs two related, but distinct, terms—prophecy and eschatology. Neither term is unproblematic. 'Prophecy' can refer, quite simply, to the statement of a prophet. As such, it implies inspiration from a deity, with the prophet speaking as their god's mouthpiece. The content of their discourse might highlight moral failings, offer predictions of the future, or be in a spiritual language which requires interpretation.[8] The primary role of the Old Testament prophets was often to engage in moral criticism of the society that surrounded them, calling God's people back into his service. In the early modern world, a number of different people might be described as (or describe themselves as) a prophet. These might be marginal figures such as Hackett, mythical prophets from the distant past such as Merlin, more detailed constructions from recent folklore such as Mother Shipton, or even someone as innocuous as the local Church of England minister. As one role of the prophet was to interpret the word of God, early modern Protestants sometimes described the regular exposition of the word as a form of prophecy.[9] In this sense, John Calvin has recently been described as a prophet.[10]

But prophecy, in a popular sense at least, could also refer to predictions. Prophecies relating to the future, whether to the outcome of events should the prophet's hearers not repent, or promises of ultimate redemption, were also part of both biblical and folk prophetic traditions. Here prophecy directly intersected with eschatology (the study of the 'last things'). Eschatology could be personal (as in the Catholic tradition of the four last things: death, judgement, hell, and heaven), or cosmic (as in the apocalyptic prophecies of Daniel and Revelation). When prophecy focused on its eschatological elements it became inherently politicised, as predictions of change could have alarming implications for authorities. At times of political turmoil, as the examples of Hackett and Wilkinson suggest, it could be subversive and used as a way of promoting rebellion—as seen in the predictions during the Pilgrimage of Grace which rose against Henry VIII in 1536–1537. Tudor governments therefore legislated against prophecy in 1541–1542, 1549–1550 and 1563. Yet at the same time, prophecy could be employed by those in power to support their positions, and to suggest divine endorsement of their rule; it remains 'a matter of conflicting interpretation … ever unstable and dynamic'.[11]

As this volume is focused on prophecy and eschatology, it is this more predictive sense of prophecy which predominates in this book. The precise form examined varies from author to author, with chapters moving between elite, popular, and radical contexts across religious traditions. Prophecy here is used to describe something more than a general sense of providence, although this remained an important part of prophetic speculation and an essential element in the shared worldview between Britain and America into the early nineteenth century.[12] In particular, many of the contributors focus on prophecies which might be described as millennial in nature. The term refers in the first instance to Revelation 20:1–6, in which Christ returns to earth and reigns with his saints for a period of a thousand years while Satan is bound. As a number of chapters in this collection highlight, the belief in the coming of the millennium was important across the Atlantic world in the early modern period. The precise nature that this millennium would take differed from group to group, and examinations of millennialism often break it down into three distinct forms: premillennialism (in which Christ returns *before* the millennium and thus inaugurates it supernaturally), postmillennialism (in which Christ returns *at the end* of the millennium, which has been inaugurated through a Christianisation of the world), and amillennialism (in which the millennium is not interpreted literally, but instead seen to refer to a spiritual state).[13] Although such clear-cut categories do not fully apply to pre-eighteenth-century eschatology, they remain a useful way of understanding the core of millennial debates.[14]

In attempting to comprehend the lands that were 'discovered' by Europeans in the late fifteenth century, the prophetic portions of scripture provided one way of situating the previously unknown portions of the world within existing maps of meaning. Columbus interpreted his voyages though the lens of the fulfilment of biblical prophecies, as well as those by twelfth-century abbot Joachim of Fiore and fourteenth-century astrologer Pierre d'Ailly, relating to what he believed would be a special role for the Spanish monarchy in rebuilding Jerusalem.[15] The natives that he discovered, he believed, were signs of a new age; marked by Edenic purity, their appearance presaged the return to a prelapsarian state.[16] While Columbus's position was not necessarily the mainstream view, neither was it unique. As a series of Friars arrived in America over the course of the sixteenth century, many read both the new lands and its inhabitants through the lens of prophecy.

This book therefore adopts a transatlantic approach to its study of prophecy and eschatology. At this point, it is necessary to justify the use of an Atlantic framework. As readers familiar with debates in Atlantic history may have ascertained, the term 'transatlantic' in this book's title makes use of one of David Armitage's three concepts of Atlantic history. In an important 2002 article, Armitage suggested that three approaches could be applied to the subject. 'Circum-Atlantic history' looks at the Atlantic as a whole, viewing it as a zone of 'exchange and interchange, circulation and transmission'.[17] 'Trans-Atlantic history' is a complementary, rather than contrasting, method to this. It is more concerned with comparison between different contexts than simply focusing on the Atlantic as a homogenous 'world'. It is therefore made possible by the assumptions of a circum-Atlantic approach, in that meaningful comparisons can be made and similarities and differences drawn 'because they already share some common features by virtue of being enmeshed within circum-Atlantic relationships'.[18] 'Cis-Atlantic' history therefore concentrates on the history of a particular location within both the broad Atlantic context, and the comparative approach promoted by a trans-Atlantic position. For Armitage, all of these approaches work together in order to ensure a rounded history of the Atlantic world which accepts both similarities and differences in particular geographical, political, and social contexts. By using the term 'transatlantic' this book does not therefore abandon a 'circum-Atlantic' or 'cis-Atlantic' approach. Rather it uses its transatlantic lens in order to draw out conclusions about the influence of both the wider Atlantic world on the prophetic and eschatological discourses it discusses, and the importance of local political and social conditions in shaping those prophetic positions in the first place.

At the outset, it is therefore important to set out a number of caveats about how this book will proceed. Much recent writing on the nature of Atlantic history has argued that abandonment, or at least a severe modification, of the paradigm is necessary. For example, Peter A. Coclanis has emphasised the way in which the Atlantic approach has 'blinded' historians to global developments in the period 1500–1800.[19] The concept could therefore be criticised for imposing an internationalist framework taken from the twenty-first-century world onto the early modern period. While Atlantic history first developed, in part, as a response to overly limited approaches to imperial history, it might also be thought to be recapitulating the forms of this discipline, in which the Atlantic world becomes a clearly delineated territorial area with its own distinct 'Atlantic' peoples and pseudo-empire.[20] Some have therefore recently claimed that the concept of the Atlantic world should be abandoned completely, in favour of focusing on relationships and causation without the quasi-national/imperial idea of a 'world' being employed.[21] Yet the idea of the Atlantic world as a sphere in which ideas could be exchanged and modified, as Janet L. Polansky has forcefully argued, still serves as a helpful lens for historians to use when examining those areas which bordered the Atlantic.[22] This is not to claim that a global approach is not also important, particularly in recognising connections with Asia that were developing over the early modern period. But it is to recognise, as Bernard Bailyn has argued, that the Atlantic world was unique in the way it was viewed and understood by early modern Europeans.[23] Neither is it to claim that the Atlantic world should be seen as some sort of pseudo-empire in and of itself—although as Philip D. Morgan and Jack P. Greene have noted, an Atlantic approach does allow an examination of imperial history which takes into account connections and interrelated developments that benefits both histories of empire and of the Atlantic more widely.[24] To avoid some of the difficulties that have been identified with the Atlantic world approach, it is therefore necessary to lay out precisely how the concept is used in this volume, particularly the way in which dangers of totalising explanatory paradigms are avoided, and local differences across the Atlantic emphasised.

It would certainly do this book's chances in the marketplace no harm were it to boldly claim that prophecy could operate as a total explanatory paradigm for all major developments within the Atlantic world in the period 1500–1800. As should be obvious, however, no such totalising claim can be made. Not only did the impacts of different forms of prophecy differ in the various contexts in which they were received, but prophecies (often *the same* biblical prophecies) generated very different reactions at different times. As Bailyn notes, Atlantic history must be viewed 'as process'.[25] By this he means that it is inherently fluid, and the contributors to this book have recognised this. Each of the authors has been alive to the particular challenges and historical contingencies in the contexts they examine, while recognising that previous developments in other parts of the Atlantic world helped to lead to change in the contexts they explore. This book therefore recognises the importance of the cross-cultural exchange of ideas from early in the history of Iberian exploration of the Americas.[26] From the sixteenth century onwards, a flow of both ideas and people can be seen between Spain, England, Africa, the Netherlands, and the Americas. The provenance of these ideas deserves some comment. By using the term 'transatlantic' in its title, this book highlights that it focuses primarily on comparative contexts. With the exception of Luís Filipe Silvério Lima's chapter, which concentrates particularly on the Iberian and Brazilian contexts of early exploration, the majority of chapters deal with what might be termed the British Atlantic—the interactions, ideas, and peoples which flowed between Britain, Ireland, and the American plantations (both continental and Caribbean). On one level, this focus might be seen as a limitation. However, contributors have been clear that a focus on the British Atlantic world does not mean ignoring the wider circum-Atlantic context in which it was situated. Iberian ideas and works had an important influence on developments in the British Atlantic.[27] Dutch and German biblical commentaries, as Jan Stievermann notes in his chapter, were important parts of prophetic thought in the British Atlantic well into the eighteenth century. As Alexander Cummins argues in his chapter, the importance of interactions with Africa (increasingly a part of the British Atlantic itself over this period) and indigenous Americans in shaping colonial beliefs should not be overlooked either. A focus on the British Atlantic world should not, therefore, be overly parochial, but instead embrace the wider contours of Atlantic thought. A further advantage of this approach is that it offers the reader the chance to see how ideas within one part of the Atlantic world could interact, change, and transform over time.

Such an approach also has advantages when tracing a particular theme, such as prophecy, over the *longue durée*. Of course, this can also raise serious issues. For example, Trevor Burnard has argued that historians should not conceive of the existence of a distinctively British Atlantic world until the eighteenth century.[28] Yet as several contributors to this book note, an argument can be made for adopting an Atlantic approach (to the anglophone world in particular) at a much earlier juncture. As Carla Gardina Pestana has argued, both the awareness of different religious forms in meetings with newly encountered people groups, and the practical challenges of trying to practice religion in new contexts, raised challenges for those of all persuasions in the Atlantic world.[29] In seeking to face these challenges, it is unsurprising that ministers, intellectuals, and ordinary people sought answers from a variety of sources, particularly those produced in other nations that had also wrestled with the same difficulties. For those in the British Atlantic, this meant an interaction with a range of Iberian and continental texts and explorers, and also demand in the growing print market for tales of newly discovered lands and peoples, stories of captivity, and news from the frontiers of empire. Thinking of prophecy in these terms is helpful, as Richard Connors and Andrew Colin Gow have argued, in that it enables us to see much more closely the connections between British and American thought, and the way in which events in one geographical arena impacted those in another.[30] Recognising these connections does not presume that the content of prophecy, or indeed its political aims, was the same in different areas. The temptation when writing about Atlantic history is to downplay very real differences which emerged, and ignore the way in which ideas, institutions, and individuals were transformed as they moved through Atlantic networks, a point emphasised recently by Jeremy Gregory.[31] As John Elliott has argued, it is important that historians make it clear not only where the Atlantic world was marked by shared ideas, but also where ideas differed.[32] It is therefore useful to remember Stephen A. Marini's point about the nature of millennialism as a flexible form that we should expect to transform into new and unexpected shapes: 'when one version of it has been employed by a religious or political group, it has invariably been answered by another version mounted by a rival movement. The opacity of millennial and eschatological symbols makes them the most contested of Christian images.'[33] In other words, we should not be surprised if prophecy changes as it moves from context to context. A helpful image for this process can be found in Kenneth Mills's appropriation of art historian George Kubler's metaphor of the lighthouse to explain religious change in the Atlantic world. Like a lighthouse's signal, religious ideas were relayed through official channels (for example, the Church of England, Massachusetts Bay ministers, or the Catholic Church). As they were shared, like the signal, these ideas could be appropriated and reflected by others; or increasingly transformed and take on new and unexpected aspects. Mills's point is that these new transmissions and appropriations of the signal should be 'accepted as equals' to the original, rather than as 'imitations, copies, satellites, or subsidiaries'. Such transformations therefore have the power to become more potent in new settings than the original form.[34] As with all metaphors, there are some problems with the image that is evoked here,[35] but Mills's central point is an important one: as contributors to this volume have recognised, the 'transformed' ideas should be taken seriously in their own right. In doing so, each author has recognised both the similarities between different parts of the Atlantic world, and the important differences between areas, people groups, and traditions as ideas have evolved. Crucially, however, they see the Atlantic context as vital in shaping these differences. As Susan Juster has noted, it is therefore 'still possible to speak of prophets ... as inhabiting a transatlantic world'.[36]

1.2 Prophecy and the Atlantic World

Understandings of prophecy have therefore been important to, and contested within, scholarship on the Atlantic for some time. Before coming to the contents of the book, it is helpful to provide a brief sketch of some of the key events in which prophecy was involved, and the major historiographical debates surrounding them. While many of these themes are explored more fully in the chapters that follow, a brief overview here will help to orientate readers on the prophetic map.

Some early accounts of the New World were what Jose Cañizares-Esguerra's described as 'Satanic epics' which detailed the way in which the land was under the dominion of the Devil, and saw the natives' religion as a parody of the true faith. This negative reading of America was increasingly questioned following the work of Dominican Bartolomé de las Casas (c. 1484–1566), which criticised the behaviour and attitude of the Conquistadors.[37] This represented a valorisation of the natives which returned to the sort of Edenic position adopted by Columbus. Comparatively successful missionary efforts also helped some to believe that they were on the cusp of the millennium, with some explanations of this falling foul of the authorities: for example, Franciscan Gerónimo de Mendeita (1525–1604), whose *Historia eclesiástica indiana* (1597) was banned by the Church for its overt Joachimite expectations.[38]

It is clear that the use of prophecy as an explanatory paradigm in the early modern Spanish Atlantic was therefore heavily contested. Columbus's use of prophecy could be controversial, but it could also offer a legitimation of Spanish imperial ambitions. As Linda Gregerson and Susan Juster have recently pointed out, 'biblical narratives of expulsion, salvation and the apocalypse were thus deeply embedded in early modern imperial projects'.[39] Yet the Bible's prophecies, in their appeals for the downtrodden and the despised alien, and proclamations of judgement against the rich and powerful, could also be employed as a powerfully subversive narrative. Prophecy, as a form of political legitimation, was a double-edged sword; it was a narrative which could be easily adopted by those on the margins, and redeployed to seek new political goals.

This sort of reworking of prophecy can be seen in its role in England's first colonial endeavours. Prophetic language could be used as a way of attempting to justify these overseas projects in terms of offering the potential to facilitate the end times conversions predicted in scripture. This could be directly contrasted with Spanish activities in America, demonstrating that England was engaging in conversion in a more humane way than the Spaniards, drawing on the 'black legend' of Spanish barbarity. The use of this trope in the promotional materials from English boosters for the endeavours in both Virginia and New England reveals something of the complex way in which ideas relating to prophecy could be exchanged in the early modern Atlantic world. Iberian works critical of Spanish actions in the Americas were often the source of these claims—and many of these contained Joachimite or other apocalyptic ideas.[40] The appeal of such texts could therefore develop in part through the shared prophetic interest in both England and Spain in the early seventeenth century, while also helping to maintain and further publicise it. From a more pragmatic point of view, as Beth Quitslund has shown in her work on the Virginia Company in the 1610s and 1620s, appealing to prophecy could also serve as a good way of raising capital.[41]

While Quitslund highlights the millennial appeal of the Virginia Company, perhaps the best-known link between prophecy and English overseas expansion has been the supposed millennial motivations behind the Puritan migration to New England in the 1620s and 1630s. This idea, which developed in the seminal work of Perry Miller, and was further expanded in Sacvan Bercovitch's research into New England Puritanism, has proved highly influential in research on both millennialism and the motivations of those who moved to New England in general. This position is often summed up in a phrase taken from John Winthrop's sermon 'A Model of Christian Charity', preached aboard the *Arbella* as it sailed to New England in 1630. Winthrop urged the migrants to consider that 'wee shall be as a citty upon a hill. The eies of all people are uppon us.'[42] To phrase this somewhat differently, those who fled to New England in search of the opportunity to worship as they believed God required, went on an 'errand to the wilderness', in which the aim was to construct and model the ideal godly society which would then spread across the globe. In this way, the errand could be seen as the fulfilment of the millennial prophecies of the Bible.[43] This reading of Miller has been questioned, and it is worth noting that he does not place as much emphasis on the 'city on the hill' motif as suggested in the works of some later historians.[44] Nonetheless, when combined with the concept of the 'elect nation' which developed from William Haller's work on national identity in late Elizabethan England,[45] the idea that New Englanders viewed themselves as a people set apart by God for a millennial mission could develop from Miller's work. Theodore Dwight Bozeman has heavily criticised the notion that New England's founders consciously intended to establish an exemplar colony, instead seeing them as focused on their own immediate religious interests.[46] This has found recent support in Susan Hardman Moore's work on the number of colonists who made a speedy return to Europe when the religious situation in England appeared to have improved.[47]

The millennial undertones of Miller's thesis were picked up by Sacvan Bercovitch in his work on the American jeremiad tradition. Bercovitch argued that the jeremiad was a key form of American cultural expression from the seventeenth to the nineteenth centuries. Rather than seeing it as an attack on the people's inability to live up to their special status under God, Bercovitch read the jeremiad as reaffirming a sense of eschatological calling which outlived the collapse of the New England Way to become a key part of American identity. A sense of eschatological mission from New England settlers thus became central to American self-conception.[48] Bozeman fiercely opposed this reading, arguing that the early settlers failed to tie distinct eschatological meaning to the particular territory they inhabited. Instead, Puritans tended to look backwards to the purity of the apostolic church.[49] While this historical controversy has rumbled on, with writers such as Avihu Zakai staunchly defending Bercovitch and the centrality of the millennial errand, and others such as Reiner Smolinski noting further difficulties with it,[50] increasingly nuanced positions have been adopted on the issue of late. Zachary McLeod Hutchins has recently suggested that the split between Bercovitch and Bozeman's position might be bridged by recognising the importance of the Edenic trope for early settlers—an image which could be both primitivist and millennial when employed in different contexts. As such, this concept points to the importance of considering the array of biblical images that could be used to form eschatological ideas, rather than limiting ourselves to those within specifically apocalyptic texts. Not only is it important to range outside of Revelation, Daniel, and Ezekiel when thinking about how prophecy was interpreted, but it is also helpful to think on a wider geographical, and even religious, scale. As Hutchins points out, the Edenic motif was active across Europe and the Iberian Atlantic, in discussions of creation, Christian life, and prophecy.[51] Its influence in New England was not therefore simply the adaptation of an existing European idea, but a concept which had been filtered through Spanish, Portuguese, New Spanish, French, Dutch, and indigenous American geographical contexts. Along the way, ideas from folklore, European magic, native religion, and Islam (in Iberia) all contributed to it. We should therefore be aware of the interconnected nature of prophecy in early modern New England. As Jeffrey K. Jue has noted, New England Puritans unquestionably looked to Europe, rather than America, for end times events to play out, but this does not mean that they felt that they could play no role in the forthcoming struggle with Antichrist.[52] As several contributors to this book highlight, the geo-politics of prophecy raised complex questions for those who tried to understand their place within the spiritual geography of the future.

Nonetheless, while ideas circulated across the Atlantic world, for linguistic reasons it is true that the majority of the early settlers looked back to their home countries for information, ideas, and guidance. While the home country was sometimes a site of stability in the turmoil of the difficult process of early colonisation, at other times events in Europe could raise problematic questions. This was particularly the case for New England, which had always had a complex relationship to the homeland due to its founders' attitudes towards the English authorities at the time of their departure. There is no doubt that some interpreted events through an eschatological lens, and were motivated to return by the opportunity to fight directly against Antichrist in the 1640s.[53] In England itself, the battle against Laudianism and Charles I was often interpreted directly in apocalyptic terms, as has long been established.[54] Apocalyptic discourse in the period in England was pervasive, and it is important to realise that it was not limited to the groups later historians have labelled as 'radicals', but was part of mainstream discourse. The influence of the writings of largely conformist divines such as Thomas Brightman (1562–1607) and Jospeh Mede (1586–1639), which were legally published for the first time in the 1640s, provided additional justification for what might be termed a mainstream apocalyptic approach, as well as justifying apocalyptic expectation around particular dates in the 1650s. As these writers had long been used by New England divines such as John Cotton, their renewed popularity in England could further strengthen transatlantic ties.[55] Neither should the important links with millenarians in the Holy Roman Empire, the Netherlands, or France be ignored. Protestant internationalism, combined with apocalyptic news networks which sometimes included Jewish as well as Christian writers, ensured that the study of the end times generally avoided becoming overly parochial.[56]

While this more conservative apocalyptic tradition was important in the mid-seventeenth century, it has often been the supposedly radical uses of prophecy that have caught both historians' and the public's imaginations. The Fifth Monarchy men, so named for their belief that they were called to bring about the final monarchy predicted in Daniel 2:44, were often viewed in the decades after the interregnum as evidence of the dangerous excesses that apocalypticism could lead to. Yet while important, they were far from representative of all of those who held apocalyptic beliefs—and indeed, were significantly less 'radical' than their enemies charged. Their belief that they would be called to act for Christ and fulfil the prophecies depended on a particular reading of providence, rather than a rash desire to fulfil prophecies.[57] As David Farr has recently pointed out, for the Major-General and regicide Thomas Harrison, this meant the bureaucratic engagements of government in the early 1650s, rather than leading a crusade against Rome.[58] Nonetheless, the interpretation of the Fifth Monarchists in the decades following the Interregnum again shows the importance of adopting an international approach to understandings of early modern prophecy. As Warren Johnston notes in his chapter in this volume, Fifth Monarchist activity was later interpreted through reference to the Anabaptist rising in the German city of Münster in 1534–1535. The polygamy, violence, starvation, and forced communalism of the millennial kingdom the Anabaptists tried to carve out coloured later interpretations of millennialism across the Atlantic world.[59] Memories of the regicide and of the desperate 1661 rising by Fifth Monarchist Thomas Venner seemed to cement this image of the danger of the apocalyptic, and proved somewhat embarrassing for New England.[60]

There is nonetheless a danger in overemphasising the conservative nature of prophecy in the period. In doing so, the potential for prophets to speak radically to the status quo can be drastically limited, and one of the major appeals of prophetic discourse—the potential to imagine change at a world historical-level—can be undermined. Figures such as Thomas Totney (TheaurauJohn Tany) in 1650s England, who saw himself as the Jewish High Priest and believed that he would lead the ten tribes back to Palestine, might appear eccentric, but his influences (drawing on Kabbalah, Jacob Boehme, alchemy, and astrology) demonstrate once again the importance of the international flow of ideas in the period. Similar points could be made about other prophets such as Joshua Garment, John Reeves, and

Lodowick Muggleton.[61] These prophets challenged the relatively tolerant faith of the Protectorate, as well as the more controlled situation in New England. Gerard Winstanley and the Diggers' well-known actions in creating a proto-millennial community at St. George's Hill in April 1649, for example, set up a visible challenge to the status quo and imagined an alternative society in a way that openly challenged the government. Likewise, the emergence of George Fox as a prophet within this milieu, and the subsequent Quaker movement, pushed the limits of toleration.[62] When James Nayler appeared to appropriate the mantle of Christ by riding into Bristol while followers threw their garments in his path, he was tried by parliament and narrowly escaped execution. Some Quaker prophets in New England were not so lucky—Mary Fisher and Anne Austin were deported from New England after preaching in Boston in 1656, while Mary Dyer was executed in 1660 for her repeated attempts at missionising. Neither was this limited to New England, as those Quakers who travelled as prophetic signs to New Amsterdam discovered.[63]

Given the excitement of the 1650s, and the prophetic hopes raised (and dashed) for a variety of groups by the Restoration, the period from 1660 to 1700 has often been seen as being marked by a trailing off of prophetic interest in the British Atlantic world. Yet as Warren Johnston's recent work has shown for England, this was far from the case: apocalyptic speculation may have been more conservative, and often even Royalist in nature, but it did not disappear from the landscape.[64] The international networks that had been developed over the course of the 1640s and 1650s continued to be used into the later period, with letters on apocalyptic themes moving between England, the Netherlands, and New England to spread information about figures such as the candidate for Jewish messiah Sabbatai Sevi and the armies of the lost tribes supposedly surrounding Mecca. As Brandon Marriott has emphasised, these ideas spread through Jews, Catholics, Protestants, and Conversos around both the Atlantic and Mediterranean worlds in the period.[65] Meanwhile, conservative uses of apocalyptic prophecy were increasingly seen in scientific work over the course of the later seventeenth century, whether in the studies of Increase Mather in New England (explored in Jan Stievermann's chapter), Cambridge Platonist Henry More, or in Isaac Newton's speculations on prophecy (both published and left in manuscript).[66] Yet explosions of prophetic excitement could nonetheless still occur, whether linked to the Glorious Revolution of 1688,[67] or to the uncertainty surrounding the Americas where wars and witch trials were often read through an apocalyptic lens. Neither did this interest in prophecy disappear at the start of the eighteenth century. The Camisard prophets who arrived in London in 1706 (and quickly attracted an English following), remained a *cause célèbre*. Their prediction that English follower Dr. Thomas Emes would rise from the dead in 1708 was proven wrong, but the movement itself continued into the later years of the century (with the Wesley brothers, amongst others, meeting prophets).[68] While it might be expected that such interests would fade as Enlightenment ideas of rationality become *de rigueur*, as recent scholarship has suggested, ideas of the miraculous and the seemingly 'irrational' did not disappear from the thought worlds of the majority of people in the eighteenth century.[69]

The clearest manifestations of the continued importance of religion in the eighteenth-century Atlantic world were the Evangelical revivals which began to sweep both Britain and America in the 1730s and 1740s. The rise of Evangelicalism was dependent, in part, on a variety of international networks, as W.R. Ward has convincingly shown. These networks did not just cross the Atlantic, but as Ward provocatively argues, can be seen in a wider global context.[70] His work also emphasises the importance of an eschatology which expected Christ's imminent return, but deferred it long enough to allow for genuine change to happen in the world.[71] This eschatology was passed across Atlantic networks of correspondence and shared religious interest, which tied believers together. Preachers such as George Whitefield, who proved popular both on frequent trips to America and in Britain, were figures around which wider communities could form.

It is not difficult to see why the revivals generated significant prophetic interest. Narratives of mass conversions and the sudden and radical changes that were seen in many individuals' lives, might seem to reflect the biblical promises that in the end times God's spirit would be poured out upon his people in a powerful way (Joel 2). Jonathan Edwards was open to the possibility that he was viewing the first signs of the millennium at points throughout his career—heavily influenced by the commentaries of Moses Lowman, his notebooks on the apocalypse combined newspaper clippings with the scripture they possibly fulfilled. For example, several articles from 1746 to 1758 were collected together under the heading of 'An Account of Events Probably Fulfilling the Sixth Vial on the River Euphrates' (Rev. 16:12–16).[72] As Stephen Stein has pointed out, however, Edwards was not vocal about his interest in prophecy: 'He kept conjectures to himself in the notebook… The millennium, a major subject of Edwards' private reflections, was noticeably absent as a leading topic in his early sermons, even on occasions when it would have served his announced ends.'[73] This once again raises the question of respectability and of whether apocalyptic speculation should be seen as conservative or radical. The fear of being seen as tending towards 'enthusiasm' remained a concern for Evangelicals, and a focus on prophecy could play into their opponents' hands. Indeed, Edwards complained in a 1744 letter to William McCulloch that it was 'slanderously reported ... that I have often said that the millennium was already begun, and that it began in Northampton', a charge he vehemently denied.[74]

Yet for all Edwards' denials, elements of the early revivals did often appear to have a prophetic hue. The transatlantic 'Concert of Prayer' movement, which explicitly linked American Evangelicals with their Scottish counterparts, was often promoted in terms of prophecy. Edwards's own sermon endorsing the 'Concert', *An Humble Attempt*, was subtitled 'For the Revival of *Religion* and the Advancement of *Christ's Kingdom* on Earth, pursuant to Scripture-Promises and Prophecies concerning the *last time*'.[75] The project thus served as a fascinating indication of the way in which believers on both sides of the Atlantic saw themselves as playing a key role in fulfilling the prophecies of the Bible.

The Revivals might therefore be helpfully seen as kairotic moments, as world-historical change and largescale conversions seemed possible due to the way in which events were being played out. Signs of a willingness to embrace the possibility of prophetic fulfilment in the period are even visible in John Wesley's reluctance to break from fellow preacher George Bell when he predicted the end of the world for 28 February 1763, due to Bell's claim to Christian Perfection.[76] Wesley himself accepted and reprinted parts of Johann Albrecht Bengel's millenarian commentaries on Revelation, and while Charles's interest in the subject has been overstated, he nonetheless shared some apocalyptic interests with his brother and other early Methodists.[77] As Jonathan Downing examines in his chapter in this volume, revivalism and prophecy could go hand in hand.

If revivalist prophecy was politically quietist, however, as the tumultuous events of the last quarter of the eighteenth century unfolded, eschatological interests once again showed their potential for inspiring controversy and justifying acts of rebellion. The importance of language drawn from the book of Revelation and other apocalyptic portions of the Bible has often been highlighted in examinations of the American War of Independence. This developed from its use in New England, where prophecy justifying God's providential destruction of antichristian enemies had been a regular part of explaining natural disasters such as earthquakes and conflicts from King Philip's War to the Seven Years' War.[78] Although there has been disagreement between historians as to how common apocalyptic rhetoric was in the lead up to the revolutionary war,[79] from 1776 onwards it became more prominent as Britain was increasingly viewed in the Manichean terms that had once been applied to the Catholic Church.[80] Prophecy was therefore seen as being fulfilled, and an independent America was imagined to serve a millennial role as an example to the world, and shelter for the oppressed. As Nathan O. Hatch has influentially argued, in this milieu ideas of a divine covenant and a millennial destiny could combine to produce a sense of 'civil millennialism': a combination of millennialism and eighteenth-century political theory which he saw as foundational to American political identity.[81] Even where this assertion has been questioned, it has been recognised that apocalyptic texts remained important as a justification for war.[82]

Where Hatch saw millennialism continuing throughout the post-revolutionary period, other scholars (including both Bloch and Miller) have noted a shift away from prophetic discourse post-1783. Stephen Marini has helpfully suggested that such a move may have been inevitable as moral and political failures among newly independent Americans led to the unavoidable conclusion that the millennium had not yet dawned. Yet, as he argues persuasively, millennial fascination continued to proliferate among those on the margins such as Quakers, Free Will Baptists, and Shakers.[83] Such groups, as with the Shakers, often had their origins in (or close links with) Europe, while transatlantic networks continued to move correspondence and religious ideas between the old and new worlds.[84] Prophets, such as Jemima Wilkinson mentioned at the start of this introduction, therefore presented an apocalyptic discourse at odds with the civil millennialism that Hatch has argued for. As Bloch noted, these transatlantic connections applied specifically to both apocalyptic and politically radical ideas, categories which often merged. International friendships between figures such as Joseph Priestley and Richard Price in England with Thomas Jefferson and Benjamin Franklin in America are important to note, not to mention Tom Paine's transatlantic interests.[85]

These revolutionary relationships did not go unnoticed in England, where events in America were followed with interest, and often formed part of a criticism of nascent imperial practices.[86] This condemnation could chime with that found in the apocalyptic portions of the Bible, demonstrating the continuing flexibility of prophecy as political critique.

Criticism of the institutions of slavery, imperialism, and the nature of British politics were therefore evident in a number of English prophets who arose in the aftermath of the French Revolution, responding to the increasing limits resulting from Pitt's 'reign of alarm'.[87] Most prominent of these was Richard Brothers (1757–1824), Prince of the Hebrews and 'nephew of the Almighty' who believed that he would restore the Jews to Palestine, be granted George III's crown, and rebuild Jerusalem.[88] In many ways, Brothers can be seen as the archetypal transatlantic prophet. Born in Newfoundland and serving in the British Navy in the American wars, Brothers's exploits were not only of interest in London. Indeed, his *Revealed Knowledge of the Prophecies and Times* (1795) went through eighteen editions in the United States, as compared to four in London, in addition to Dublin and Paris printings. As such, Brothers can be seen as part of what Deborah Madden has described as 'creative, visionary world' which saw events in France, America, and Britain as prophetically connected.[89]

Brother's title as the predominant English prophet was taken over by the Devonshire prophet Joanna Southcott (1750–1814), who saw herself as the 'woman clothed in the sun' (Rev. 12:1) and attracted international attention and a wide following until her death at the age of 64, supposedly pregnant with 'Shiloh', the predicted redeemer.[90] Southcott, as Deborah Madden discusses in her chapter in this volume, stole many of Brothers's followers, building on the existing interest in him as a way of establishing her own prophetic identity. She remains the most prominent of a number of female prophets in the late eighteenth and early nineteenth centuries, who used prophecy as a way of expressing their gender identity and responding to the challenges they faced in an industrialising society.[91] Yet Southcott's ministry also made canny use of the press and emerging public sphere. As Juster has argued, this led to an increased promotion for prophets across the Atlantic world, but it also raised serious problems for them. When prophecy assumed the language of reason, it could appear to be constructed and therefore inherently false; however, when this language was rejected, prophecy appeared as meaningless 'enthusiasm' to its detractors.[92]

This book ends its study with Southcott, but this should not be taken to imply that prophecy ceased to be important in the Atlantic world in the period after 1800. As Crawford Gribben has noted, the transatlantic pattern of prophecy can be traced into and beyond this period—through the growing interest in premillennialism in the early nineteenth century, to the use of prophecy as an explanatory paradigm for the US Civil War, to the incredible influence of British and Irish dispensationalism on American evangelicalism in the later nineteenth century.[93] As with any historical periodisation, an argument could be made for extending the period looked at in this book, and indeed for taking it forward as far as the present day where prophecy continues to beguile. 1800 is not a *terminus ad quem* for the topics examined in this book, then, and the curious reader is encouraged to continue to explore its themes into later periods.

1.3 The Book

Each contributor to this book therefore offers their own insights and impressions on the way in which prophecy developed in the transatlantic world. These contributors come from a range of disciplinary contexts (history, literature, religious studies) and from across the Atlantic world itself (Brazil, Ireland, Britain, the United States). Contributors were not asked to argue for any particular viewpoint on the role of prophecy, and some would disagree with the positions advocated by other authors. Nonetheless, each chapter highlights the importance of adopting a transatlantic approach when examining prophecy. While it is understandable that the reader will focus on those topics of particular interest, reading each of the chapters in turn will allow a greater appreciation of the sheer variety of transatlantic prophecy.

In the second chapter, Luis Filipe Silvério Lima explores a topic which has often been overlooked in anglophone studies of millenarianism—the development of apocalyptic thought in Iberia and South America in the sixteenth and seventeenth centuries. Lima offers a wide-ranging overview of the theme, demonstrating the way in which millenarian impulses could help solve some of the trickier questions raised by new discoveries, as well as driving both imperial expansion and native opposition to it in the period. The appeal of an empire fulfilling prophecies of the Fifth Monarchy is shown to have been a recurring idea in Spanish and Portuguese works, while at the same time ideas of apocalyptic election were applied by the 'Santidade do Jaguaipe' in their rebellion. A central theme of Lima's chapter is the way in which millennial ideas adapt freely to their wide ranging uses, both structuring and absorbing a variety of political and theological concerns. As he argues, they serve as 'the common grammar and vocabulary in the early modern Iberian world'.

John Kuhn's contribution examines a controversial and oft-debated portion of George Herbert's 'Church Militant'—the poet's discussion of religion's departure from England to America. While this passage may be well known, it is seldom located within its immediate context of Herbert's *The Temple*, or wider debates about Anglo-American eschatology. Kuhn manages to contextualise the poem within both of these, arguing persuasively that Herbert expresses a sense of frustration and of being 'left behind' by the movement of religion. This is not to claim that Herbert believed that the millennium would begin in America, although Kuhn argues that the poet was engaging with this position, but to express that all temporal religious institutions must ultimately fade away, with Christ returning to a world that would be as dark and faithless as that which he found at this first coming.

Edward Simon focuses on a different poet: the New England writer Anne Bradstreet and the millennial themes in her 1642 poem 'A Dialogue between Old England and New'. Simon argues that Bradstreet embraced a prophetic persona to condemn sin in England, with New England chastening her homeland for her sin and willingness to ignore her religious responsibilities. Nonetheless, this is not a poem about the translation of blessings from the old World to the New. Rather, Bradstreet sees a repentant England restored to a powerful position in which she will defeat Rome and the Ottoman Empire, and play a central role in converting the Jews. While Bradstreet is usually seen as a conservative figure, Simon argues that her thought displays similarities to the ideas which Fifth Monarchists and Anna Trapnell would promote in the 1650s. The blurred lines between radicals and conservatives, and the importance of viewing Bradstreet in the context of a wider Atlantic prophetic role claimed by many women, are two of the particularly helpful suggestions to emerge from Simon's work.

Chris Caughey's chapter moves to focus on radicalism. He looks at radical prophecy in the 1640s and 1650s through the figure of Antichrist. The description of a prophet as 'radical' very much depended on the political and religious position of the person assigning the label, and he demonstrates the way in which this caused problems both for the English parliament and for New England ministers. Where those who had fled to New England had departed so that they could practise what they saw as a pure form of Christianity, Caughey demonstrates the way in which religious change in England had a direct impact on the plantations, particularly as magistrates struggled to deal with Quaker prophets.

Andrew Crome looks at the way in which shifting understandings of the role that the Jews would play in end times events impacted upon eschatological debate on both sides of the Atlantic. An increasing focus on Palestine was part of a geographic turn in the study of prophecy. The restoration of the Jews to their ancient homeland was central to this, as commentators argued that prophecies of a Jewish return had not been fulfilled at the end of the Babylonian exile, and should not be applied spiritually to the Christian church. This fuelled an interest in finding the 'lost tribes' of Israel in America from some European Christians, but also the discovery of their own local geographic contexts encoded in Revelation. Ironically, while commentators argued that references to Jerusalem and Palestine had to be taken literally, at the same time they found typological allusions to Rome, Boston, and London as having key roles in the coming apocalyptic trials.

Moving into the later seventeenth century, Warren Johnston's chapter builds on his ground-breaking work on later seventeenth-century apocalypticism through an exploration of the way in which eschatology was linked to radicalism in the period. After the initial chaos of Venner's uprising in 1661 caused most dissenting groups to refuse its radical implications, apocalyptic symbolism and rhetoric revived in later years and was used as a way of condemning the Anglican hegemony. Johnston charts the way in which prophetic symbols from Daniel and Revelation could be used in a variety of contexts in order to defend non-conformity and attack supposed Catholic influences and plots. While focusing on England, Johnston's chapter nonetheless highlights the Atlantic networks sustaining prophetic speculation. Ideas developed in England, Scotland and in continental Europe, and he suggests that the use of prophecy by English groups was akin to the way in which it was then being employed in New England.

Outside of the world of theological debates, Alexander Cummins examines the ways in which English occult and alchemical traditions influenced popular prophecy in late seventeenth- and early eighteenth-century America. He finds a continual public demand for prophetic material in almanacs, which often adopted distinctly millennial positions. Yet prophecy is more than end times speculation, and he fruitfully explores instances of shifting conceptions of astrology, folk prediction, and divination as part of a general prophetic interest. This is placed against a backdrop of English debates on magic and 'cunning folk', New England fears of Satan, witch hunts, and changing scientific understanding. While contact with Native

Americans did change some of these English practices, settlers initially often ignored the prophetic and occult knowledge that might be gained from them. This changed as the eighteenth century progressed, leading to what Cummins describes as a 'melting cauldron' of occult, astrological, and prophetic beliefs by the turn of the nineteenth century.

Jan Stievermann's chapter makes use of his fascinating recent work on a scholarly edition of Cotton Mather's *Biblia Americana* to examine Mather's commentary on the Canticles (or Song of Songs) in depth for the first time. Stievermann offers a comparative reading in which Mather's work is compared to that of his grandfather, John Cotton. As is well known, Cotton held to a historicist reading of Canticles, in which it was seen to contain the history of Israel and the church in allegorical form. Although initially sceptical about this form of exegesis, Mather eventually came to follow it himself. However, where Cotton found the pattern of a Congregationalist millennium encoded in the book, his grandson was more sceptical about the potential for the gradual progression towards the millennium on earth. Although his thoughts on Canticles were heavily based of the work of continental millennialist Johannes Cocceius, he rejected the early commentator's optimism at the end of his commentary. Thus Stievermann argues that where John Cotton might be seen as a prototypical postmillennialist, Mather might serve as an important precursor to modern premillennialism.

Jonathan Downing takes up this theme by looking at the way in which a number of key figures during the first 'great awakening' understood prophecy. For preachers such as Jonathan Edwards, John Wesley, and George Whitefield, prophecy was both a powerful rhetorical form and a problematic discourse which could be linked back to the radicalism of the 1640s and 1650s. Downing therefore provides a fascinating overview of the way in which these preachers walked a fine line between claiming prophetic authority and straying into enthusiasm. This often led to ambivalence in the face of being proclaimed prophets by their auditors, but could also result in uncertainty over how to react to extreme manifestations of the Holy Spirit as a result of their preaching. This ambivalence continued into their views of the last days, with millennial language being used, but often directly disavowed to avoid charges of enthusiasm.

Deborah Madden closes the book with her examination of three key prophets of the 'Southcottian visitation': Richard Brothers, Joanna Southcott, and George Turner. While each had their differences, she places them in the context of the uncertainties and revolutionary tensions of the late eighteenth century, examining their approach to authority, theology, and Jerusalem. While Brothers emphasised an imperialistic physical return to Jerusalem with England's 'hidden Jews', Southcott viewed Jerusalem as a spiritual state, and was seemingly unconcerned with ideas of a literal return to Palestine. As Madden notes, Jerusalem represents an interesting imaginative arena in which issues of moral and spiritual geography, imperialism, and gender could all be imagined.

The contributors to this book do not claim to have offered the last word in the study of transatlantic prophecy and eschatology. Indeed, as noted above, many areas have been left unexamined. But the range of fascinating approaches demonstrated in the chapters that follow aim to encourage other historians to examine the questions of prophecy and eschatology in still greater depth in future, and to reiterate the importance of a transatlantic approach in doing so.

Notes

1. Richard Cosin, *Conspiracie, for pretended reformation viz. Presbyteriall discipline* (London, 1592), p. 7.
2. Ruth Bloch, *Visionary Republic: Millennial themes in American thought* (Cambridge, 1985), pp. 137–140.
3. For a recent defence of the secularisation thesis see Steve Bruce, *Secularization: In defence of an unfashionable theory* (Oxford, 2011).
4. William Perkins, 'A fruitfull dialogue concerning the end of the world' (1587), in *The vvorkes of that famovs and vvorthy minister of Christ in the Vniversitie of Cambridge, M. VVilliam Perkins. The third and last volume* (London, 1631), p. 467.
5. Susan Juster, *Doomsayers: Anglo-American prophecy in the Age of Revolution* (Philadelphia, PA, 2003), pp. 220–237.
6. See Deborah Madden, *The Paddington prophet: Richard Brothers's journey to Jerusalem* (Manchester, 2010).
7. A. Freethinker, *An enquiry into the pretensions of Richard Brothers in answer to Nathaniel Brassey Halhed* (London, 1795), p. 3.
8. Bertrand Taithe and Tim Thornton, 'The language of history: Past and future in prophecy', in Bertrand Taithe and Tim Thornton (eds), *Prophecy: The power of inspired language in history 1300–2000* (Stroud, 1997), pp. 1–16.
9. As in William Perkins's preaching manual *The arte of prophesying* (London, 1607). The fact that prophecy was described as a gift of the Spirit in 1 Cor. 14 meant that early modern interpreters had to address the question of prophecy's role in the wider church.

10. Jan Belserak, *John Calvin as sixteenth-century prophet* (Oxford, 2014). There is more to Belserak's argument than this. He convincingly argues that Calvin viewed the prophetic office in Old Testament terms as both speaking God's words, and as resisting and campaigning against idolatry. This prophetic identification led him to political involvement in potentially seditious schemes against the French crown.
11. Taithe and Thornton, 'The language of history', p. 11.
12. Nicholas Guyatt, *Providence and the invention of the United States, 1607–1876* (New York and Cambridge, 2007); Richard Connors and Andrew Colin Gow, 'Introduction', in Richard Connors and Andrew Colin Gow (eds), *Anglo-American millennialism, from Milton to the Millerites* (Leiden, 2004), pp. xi–xii.
13. Gribben, *Evangelical millennialism in the trans-Atlantic World, 1500–2000* (Basingstoke, 2011), pp. 11–12.
14. Andrew Crome, *The restoration of the Jews: Early modern hermeneutics, eschatology, and national identity in the works of Thomas Brightman* (Cham, 2014), pp. 11–12, n.51. For a discussion of the mishandling of these terms in early modern historiography see Crawford Gribben, *The Puritan millennium: Literature and theology, 1550–1682*, Second Edition (Milton Keynes, 2008), pp. 8–11.
15. Christopher Columbus, *The book of prophecies*, ed. Roberto Rusconi, trans. Blair Sullivan (Berkeley, CA, 1997). See also: Carol Delaney, 'Columbus's ultimate goal: Jerusalem', *Comparative Studies in Society and History* 48:2 (2006), pp. 260–292; Leonard I. Sweet, 'Christopher Columbus and the millennial vision of the New World', *Catholic Historical Review* 72:3 (1986), pp. 369–382; Pauline Moffitt Watts, 'Prophecy and discovery: On the spiritual origins of Christopher Columbus's "Enterprise of the Indies"', *American Historical Review* 90:1 (1985), pp. 73–102; Arthur Williamson, *Apocalypse then: Prophecy and the making of the modern world* (Westport, CT, 2008), pp. 71–78; Delno C. West, 'Christopher Columbus, lost biblical sites, and the last crusade', *Catholic Historical Review* 78:4 (1992), pp. 519–541.
16. Zachary McLeod Hutchins, *Inventing Eden: Primitivism, millennialism, and the making of New England* (Oxford and New York, 2014), pp. 13–14.
17. David Armitage, 'Three concepts of Atlantic history', in David Armitage and Michael J. Braddick (eds), *The British Atlantic world 1500–1800*, Second Edition (Basingstoke, 2009), p. 18.
18. Armitage, 'Three concepts', p. 21.
19. Peter A. Coclanis, 'Atlantic World or Atlantic/World?', *William and Mary Quarterly*, 3rd Series 63:4 (2006), pp. 725–742.
20. David Prior, 'After the revolution: An alternative future for Atlantic History', *History Compass* 12:3 (2014), p. 303.

21. Prior, 'After the revolution', pp. 300–309.
22. Janet L. Polasky, *Revolutions without borders* (New Haven, CT, 2015).
23. Bernard Bailyn, 'Introduction: Reflections on some major themes', in Bernard Bailyn and Patricia L. Denault (eds), *Soundings in Atlantic History: Latent structures and intellectual currents, 1500–1830* (Cambridge, MA, and London, 2009), pp. 1–43. Bailyn particularly emphasises the way in which colonisation, views of native peoples, and trade networks differed. He sees globalisation as anachronistic prior to the nineteenth, and perhaps even the late twentieth centuries.
24. Philip D. Morgan and Jack P. Greene, 'Introduction', in Philip D. Morgan and Jack P. Greene (eds), *Atlantic History: A critical appraisal* (New York and Oxford, 2009), pp. 9–10.
25. Bernard Bailyn, *Atlantic History: Concept and contours* (Cambridge, MA, 2005), p. 61.
26. Lisa Voigt, *Writing captivity in the early modern Atlantic: Circulations of knowledge and authority in the Iberian and English imperial worlds* (Chapel Hill, NC, 2009), pp. 255–263.
27. Jose Cañizares-Esguerra, *Puritan Conquistadors: Iberianizing the Atlantic* (Stanford, CA, 2006); Voigt, *Writing captivity*.
28. Trevor Burnard, 'The British Atlantic', in Jack P. Greene and Philip D. Morgan (eds), *Atlantic History: A critical approach* (Oxford, 2009), pp. 111–115.
29. Carla Gardina Pestana, 'Religion', in David Armitage and Michael J. Braddick (eds), *The British Atlantic World 1500–1800*, Second Edition (Basingstoke, 2009), pp. 71–91.
30. Connors and Gow, 'Introduction', p. x.
31. Jeremy Gregory, 'Transatlantic Anglican networks c.1680–c.1770: Transplanting, translating and transforming the Church of England', in Jeremy Gregory and Hugh McLeod (eds), *International religious networks* (Woodbridge, 2012), pp. 127–130. On this point see also Philip D. Morgan and Jack P. Greene, 'Introduction', in Philip D. Morgan and Jack P. Greene (eds), *Atlantic History: A critical appraisal* (New York and Oxford, 2009), pp. 10–12; Bailyn, *Atlantic History*, p. 62.
32. John Elliott, *Empires of the Atlantic world: Britain and Spain in America 1492–1830* (New Haven, CT, 2006), pp. xi–xx.
33. Stephen A. Marini, 'Uncertain dawn: Millennialism and political theology in Revolutionary America', in Richard Connors and Andrew Colin Gow (eds), *Anglo-American millennialism, from Milton to the Millerites* (Leiden, 2004), p. 163.
34. Kenneth Mills, 'Religion in the Atlantic World', in Nicholas Canny and Philip Morgan (eds), *The Oxford handbook of the Atlantic World* (Oxford, 2011), pp. 433–434.

35. The idea of religious ideas as 'transmissions', for example, might strike some readers as an overly hierarchical model for the way in which they are developed. Mills' appropriation of art history is helpful in suggesting ways in which historians might look to more contemporary art and media studies for models of cultural transmission.
36. Juster, *Doomsayers*, p. 10.
37. Cañizares-Esguerra, *Puritan Conquistadors*, pp. 35–82.
38. John Leddy Phelan, *The Millennial kingdom of the Franciscans in the New World: A study of the writings of Gerónimo de Mendieta (1525–1604)*, Revised Edition (Los Angeles, CA, 1970).
39. Linda Gregerson and Susan Juster, 'Introduction', in Linda Gregerson and Susan Juster (eds), *Empires of God: Religious encounters in the early modern Atlantic* (Philadelphia, PA, 2011), p. 5.
40. Cañizares-Esguerra, *Puritan Conquistadors*, pp. 1–33. See also Jose Cañizares-Esguerra, 'Typology in the Atlantic world: Early modern readings of colonization', in Bernard Bailyn and Patricia L. Denault (eds), *Soundings in Atlantic History: Latent structures and intellectual currents, 1500–1830* (Cambridge, MA and London, 2009), pp. 237–264.
41. Beth Quitslund, 'The Virginia Company, 1606–1624: Anglicanism's millennial adventure', in Richard Connors and Andrew Colin Gow (eds), *Anglo-American millennialism, from Milton to the Millerites* (Leiden, 2004), pp. 43–113. For a later example, on Thomas Thorowgood's use of prophecies of discovery of the lost tribes of Israel in New England as a way of funding John Eliot's missions in New England, see Kristina Bross, 'From London to Nonantum: Mission literature in the Transatlantic World', in Linda Gregerson and Susan Juster (eds), *Empires of God: Religious encounters in the early modern Atlantic* (Philadelphia, PA, 2011), pp. 123–142.
42. John Winthrop, 'A modell of Christian charity', Collections of the Massachusetts Historical Society, 3rd Series 7 (1838), pp. 31–48. Available online at https://history.hanover.edu/texts/winthmod.html
43. Perry Miller, *Errand into the wilderness* (Cambridge, MA, 1956).
44. See criticism from Theodore Dwight Bozeman, *To live ancient lives: The primitivist dimension in Puritanism* (Chapel Hill, NC and London, 1988), pp. 81–119.
45. William Haller, *Foxe's Book of Martyrs and the elect nation* (London, 1963).
46. Bozeman, *To live ancient lives*.
47. Susan Hardman Moore, *Pilgrims: New World settlers and the call of home* (New Haven, CT, and London, 2007).
48. Sacvan Bercovitch, *The American jeremiad* (Madison, WI, 1978). See also his *The Puritan origins of the American self* (New Haven, CT, and London, 1975).

49. Bozeman, *To live ancient lives*.
50. Reiner Smolinski, 'Israel redivivus: The eschatological limits of typology in New England', *New England Quarterly* 63:3 (1990), pp. 357–395; Avihu Zakai, *Exile and kingdom: History and apocalypse in the Puritan migration to America* (Cambridge, 1992).
51. Hutchins, *Inventing Eden*, pp. 14–18.
52. Jeffrey K. Jue, 'Puritan Millennialism in old and New England', in John Coffey and Paul C.H. Lim (eds), *The Cambridge Companion to Puritanism* (Cambridge, 2008), pp. 259–276.
53. Moore, *Pilgrims*, pp. 88–102.
54. The best general examination on the apocalyptic background and nature of the period 1630–1660 remains Crawford Gribben's seminal *The Puritan millennium*. For a briefer introduction see Jue, 'Puritan Millennialism', in Coffey and Lim (eds), *Cambridge Companion to Puritanism*, pp. 259–276. The following older works also remain valuable: Bryan W. Ball, *A great expectation: Eschatological thought in English Protestantism to 1660* (Leiden, 1975); Paul Christianson, *Reformers and Babylon: English apocalyptic visions from the Reformation to the eve of the Civil War* (Toronto, 1978); Katherine Firth, *The apocalyptic tradition in Reformation Britain 1530–1645* (Oxford, 1979); Tai Liu, *Discord in Zion: The Puritan divines and the Puritan revolution 1640–1660* (The Hague, 1973); Peter Toon (ed.), *The Puritans, The millennium, and the future of Israel* (Cambridge, 2002 [1970]).
55. On Brightman see Crome, *The restoration of the Jews*. On Mede see Jeffrey K. Jue, *Heaven upon earth: Joseph Mede (1586–1638) and the legacy of millenarianism* (Dordrecht, 2006).
56. Andrew Crome, 'The Jewish Indian theory and Protestant use of Catholic thought in the early modern Atlantic', in Crawford Gribben and Scott Spurlock (eds), *Puritans and Catholics in the trans-Atlantic world 1600–1800* (Basingstoke, 2015), pp. 112–130. See also Brandon Marriott, *Transnational networks and cross-religious exchange in the seventeenth-century Mediterranean and Atlantic Worlds: Sabbatai Sevi and the lost tribes of Israel* (Farnham, 2015) and Jason P. Rosenblatt, *Renaissance England's Chief Rabbi: John Selden* (Oxford, 2006).
57. Bernard Capp, *The Fifth Monarchy Men* (London, 1972).
58. David Farr, *Major-General Thomas Harrison: Millenarianism, Fifth Monarchism and the English Revolution 1616–1660* (Farnham, 2014).
59. Returning to Hackett, it is interesting that Cosin's attack specifically compares the later prophet with John of Leiden: 'And did not Hacket take vpon him to bee as great a Prophet, as Iohn Matthewe, or Iohn aLeiden his successor? […]Was not Coppinger likewise, as deeply bewitched as the people of Munster, when hee coulde not perceiue, that Hacket did but

dally with him, about particular intelligence of some treasons, supposed to bee plotted by some great persons?' (Cosin, *Conspiracie*, p. 98).
60. Yet as Farr points out, the Fifth Monarchists were only ever involved in two risings, both centring on the eccentric one-time New England resident Venner. See Farr, *Major-General Thomas Harrison*, pp. 251–256.
61. See Ariel Hessayon, *'Gold tried in fire': The prophet TheaurauJohn Tany and the English Revolution* (Aldershot, 2007).
62. On toleration see: John Coffey, *Persecution and toleration in Protestant England 1558–1689* (Harlow, 2000); Eliane Glaser (ed.), *Religious tolerance in the Atlantic World: Early modern and contemporary perspectives* (Basingstoke, 2014); Alexandra Walsham, *Charitable hatred: Tolerance and intolerance in England, 1500–1700* (Manchester, 2006).
63. On Quaker eschatology see Stephen W. Angell and Pink Dandelion (eds), *Early Quakers and their theological thought 1647–1723* (Cambridge, 2015)—particularly chapters by Douglas Gwyn, Carole Dale Spencer, Michael Birkel and Stephen W. Angell, Sally Bruyneel, Pink Dandelion and Frederick Martin, Michele Lise Tarter and Robynne Rogers Healey. Also: Sally Bruyneel, *Margaret Fell and the end of time: The theology of the mother of Quakerism* (Waco, TX, 2010), Gribben, *Puritan millennium*, pp. 215–219; Douglas Gwyn, 'Quakers, eschatology, and time', in Stephen W. Angell and Pink Dandelion (eds), *The Oxford handbook of Quaker studies* (Oxford, 2013), pp. 202–217; H. Larry Ingle, 'George Foxe, millenarian', *Albion* 24:2 (1992), pp. 261–278; Phyllis Mack, Visionary women: Ecstatic prophecy in seventeenth-century England (Berkley, CA, 1992); T.L. Underwood, 'Early Quaker eschatology', in Peter Toon (ed.), *Puritans, the millennium and the future of Israel* (Cambridge, 2002 [1970]), pp. 91–103.
64. Warren Johnston, *Revelation restored: The apocalypse in later seventeenth-century England* (Woodbridge, 2011).
65. Marriott, *Transnational networks*.
66. See James E. Force and Richard H. Popkin (eds), *Millenarianism and messianism in early modern European culture Vol. III: The millenarian turn: Millenarian contexts of science, politics, and everyday Anglo-American life in the seventeenth and eighteenth centuries* (Dordrecht, 2001); Sarah Hutton, 'More, Newton and the language of biblical prophecy', in James E. Force and Richard H. Popkin (eds), *The books of nature and scripture: Recent essays on natural philosophy, theology and biblical criticism in the Netherlands of Spinoza's time and the British Isles of Newton's time* (Dordrecht, Boston, MA, and London, 1994), pp. 39–54; Sarah Hutton, 'The seven trumpets and the seven vials: Apocalypticism and Christology in Newton's theological writings', in James E. Force and Richard H. Popkin (eds), *Newton and religion: Context, nature and influence*

(Dordrecht, 1999), pp. 165–178; Rob Iliffe, '"Making a shew": Apocalyptic hermeneutics and the sociology of Christian idolatry in the work of Isaac Newton and Henry More', in Force and Popkin (eds), *The books of nature and scripture*, pp. 55–88; Frank E. Manuel, *The religion of Isaac Newton* (Oxford, 1974); Michael Murrin, 'Newton's Apocalypse', in James E. Force and Richard H. Popkin (eds), *Newton and religion: Context, nature and influence* (Dordrecht, 1999), pp. 203–220; Reiner Smolinski, 'The logic of millennial thought: Sir Isaac Newton among his contemporaries', in Force and Popkin (eds), *Newton and religion*, pp. 259–289.

67. Johnston, *Revelation restored*, pp. 189–224; Kevin Sharpe, 'Reading revelations: Prophecy, hermeneutics and politics in early modern Britain', in Kevin Sharpe and Steven N. Zwicker (eds), *Reading, society and politics in early modern England* (Cambridge, 2003), pp. 122–163.

68. Lionel Laborie, *Enlightening enthusiasm: Prophecy and religious experience in early eighteenth-century England* (Manchester, 2015); Hillel Schwartz, *The French Prophets: The history of a millenarian group in eighteenth-century England* (Berkley, CA, 1980).

69. See Jeremy Gregory, 'Transforming the "age of reason" into "An age of faiths": Or, putting religions and beliefs (back) into the eighteenth century', *Journal for Eighteenth Century Studies* 32:3 (2009), pp. 287–305; Laborie, Enlightening enthusiasm; Phyllis Mack, *Heart religion in the British Enlightenment: Gender and emotion in early Methodism* (Cambridge, 2008); Phyllis Mack, 'The unbounded self: Dreaming and identity in the British Enlightenment', in Ann Marie Plane and Leslie Tuttle (eds), *Dreams, dreamers, and visions: The early modern Atlantic world* (Philadelphia, PA, 2013), pp. 207–225; Jane Shaw, *Miracles in Enlightenment England* (New Haven, CT, and London, 2006).

70. W.R. Ward, *The Protestant Evangelical awakening* (Cambridge, 1992). Further helpful overviews of the revivals, and their international nature can be found in Mark Noll, *The rise of Evangelicalism: The age of Edwards, Whitefield and the Wesleys* (Leicester, 2004). The key work on the specifically transatlantic elements of Evangelicalism is Susan O'Brien, 'A transatlantic community of saints: The Great Awakening and the first Evangelical network, 1735–1755', *American Historical Review* 91:4 (1986), pp. 811–832. See also Carla Gardina Pestana, *Protestant Empire: Religion and the Making of the British Atlantic World* (Philadelphia, PA, 2009), pp. 187–217.

71. W.R. Ward, *Early evangelicalism: A global intellectual history, 1670–1789* (Cambridge, 2010). Ward's dating of Evangelicalism as prior to the revivals has remained controversial, clashing with David Bebbington's assertion that the movement was novel and a product of distinct eighteenth-century

patterns of thought (Bebbington, *Evangelicalism in modern Britain: A history from the 1730s to the 1980s* (London: Routledge, 1989)). For an overview of the debate, although overly focused on links with Reformed theology, see Michael A.G. Haykin and Kenneth J. Stewart (eds), *The emergence of Evangelicalism: Exploring historical continuities* (Nottingham, 2008).
72. Jonathan Edwards, *Notes on the Apocalypse* (1723) in *Works: Apocalyptic writings* (WJE Online), ed. Stephen J. Stein, Vol. 5, pp. 254–285.
73. Stephen J. Stein, 'Introduction', in Jonathan Edwards, *Works: Apocalyptic Writings*, Vol. 5, p. 19.
74. Quoted in Stein, 'Introduction', p. 29.
75. Jonathan Edwards, *An humble attempt to promote explicit union of God's people in extraordinary prayer* (Boston, MA, 1747).
76. David Hempton, *Methodism: Empire of the Spirit* (New Haven, CT, and London, 2005), pp. 34–41. On Bell see Kenneth G.C. Newport, 'George Bell, prophet and enthusiast', *Methodist History* 35:2 (1997), pp. 95–105.
77. Much of the focus of Charles Wesley's apocalyptic interest rests on the interpretation of a letter dated 25 April 1754 in the Methodist Archive at the John Rylands Library Manchester, containing clear millennial predictions focusing on 1793 as the year of the millennium's consummation (see Kenneth G.C. Newport, *Apocalypse and millennium: Studies in biblical eisegesis* (Cambridge, 2000), pp. 119–149). However, this letter, while in Wesley's hand, is a transcription of parts of a 1754 pamphlet: *An account of the remarkable productions of Mr. David Imrie, minister of the gospel at St. Mungo in Annandale* (Edinburgh, 1754).
78. Bloch, *Visionary Republic*, pp. 3–21.
79. For arguments on the limit of apocalypticism in the period see Melvin B. Endy, 'Just war, holy war, and millennialism in Revolutionary America', *William and Mary Quarterly*, 3rd series 42:1 (1985), pp. 3–25; Harry Stout, *The New England Soul: Preaching and religious culture in colonial New England* (New York and Oxford, 1986), pp. 306–307.
80. Pestana, *Protestant Empire*, pp. 223–225; Bloch, *Visionary Republic*, pp. 53–74.
81. Nathan O. Hatch, *The sacred cause of liberty: Republican thought and the millennium in revolutionary New England* (New Haven, CT, 1977). For a counter argument see Gerald R. McDermott, 'Civil religion in the American Revolutionary period: An historiographical analysis', *Christian Scholar's Review* 18:4 (1989), pp. 346–362.
82. James P. Byrd, *Sacred scripture, sacred war: The Bible and the American Revolution* (Oxford, 2013), pp. 143–163.
83. Stephen A. Marini, 'Uncertain dawn: Millennialism and political theology in Revolutionary America', in Richard Connors and Andrew Colin Gow

(eds), *Anglo-American millennialism, from Milton to the Millerites* (Leiden, 2004), pp. 159–176.
84. David Hempton, 'International religious networks: Methodism and popular Protestantism, c.1750–1850', in Jeremy Gregory and Hugh McLeod (eds), *International religious networks* (Woodbridge, 2012), pp. 143–164.
85. Bloch, *Visionary Republic*, pp. 103–104.
86. Jack P. Greene, *Evaluating empire and confronting colonialism in eighteenth-century Britain* (Cambridge, 2013), pp. 200–233.
87. Kenneth R. Johnston, *Unusual suspects: Pitt's reign of alarm and the lost generation of the 1790s* (Oxford, 2013).
88. The best treatment of Brothers is Madden, *The Paddington prophet*. See also John Barrell, 'Imagining the king's death: The arrest of Richard Brothers', *History Workshop Journal* 37:1 (1994), pp. 1–32; Iain McCalman, *Radical underground: Prophets, revolutionaries and pornographers* (Cambridge, 1988), pp. 50–72 ; Jon Mee, *Dangerous enthusiasm: William Blake and the culture of radicalism in the 1790s* (Oxford, 1992), pp. 20–74.
89. Madden, *The Paddington prophet*, p. 107.
90. On Southcott see Francis Brown, *Joanna Southcott: The woman clothed in the sun* (Cambridge, 2002); Philip Lockley, *Visionary religion and radicalism in early industrial England: From Southcott to socialism* (Oxford, 2013); Matthew Niblett, *Prophecy and the politics of salvation in late Georgian England: The theology and apocalyptic vision of Joanna Southcott* (London, 2015).
91. Anna Clark, 'The sexual crisis and popular religion in London, 1770–1820', *International Labor and Working-Class History* 34 (1988), pp. 56–69.
92. Juster, *Doomsayers*. See especially pp. 1–20 and 216–259.
93. See Gribben, *Evangelical millennialism*. For an excellent recent examination of prophecy in the United States from the mid-nineteenth century to the present see Matthew Avery Sutton, American apocalypse: A history of modern Evangelicalism (Cambridge, MA, and London, 2014).

CHAPTER 2

Between the New and the Old World: Iberian Prophecies and Imperial Projects in the Colonisation of the Early Modern Spanish and Portuguese Americas

Luís Filipe Silvério Lima

When in 1500 the Portuguese commander Pedro Álvares Cabral, headed for India, landed at an uncharted coast in the South-western Atlantic, he and his crew claimed the land for the Portuguese king, Manuel I, and named it after the Holy Cross consecrating all with a mass. Bid by Cabral, the ship's scribe Pero Vaz de Caminha wrote a letter to the king announcing and describing their find and all their actions. The letter narrated the temperate weather, the abundance of trees and water, and also the possible existence of gold and silver. The soil was so rich that anything one tried to plant would most certainly flourish, he said. Caminha depicted the reddish-brown-skinned natives as innocent in their nudity, and wrote of their women showing their beautiful bodies as if they were unaware of the original sin.[1] The resemblance to Edenic motifs and *locus amoenus* topoi is evident, as is the overlapping between Christian faith and the royal maritime enterprise.[2] Decades later, the Land of Holy Cross, to the dismay of some

L.F.S. Lima (✉)
Department of History, Universidade Federal de São Paulo, São Paulo, Brazil

© The Author(s) 2016
A. Crome (ed.), *Prophecy and Eschatology in the Transatlantic World, 1550–1800*, Christianities in the Trans-Atlantic World, 1500–1800,
DOI 10.1057/978-1-137-52055-5_2

men of letters and of the cloth, had its name changed to Brazil, partially after the brazilwood tree ('Pau-Brasil') which produced red dye and was the first significant Portuguese American commodity. Authors like João de Barros, in 1554, saw in the naming a refusal to pursue an evident divine election and denounced it as the victory of mercantile and sinful actions over Christian mission. As such, the alteration to the new name denied the important role that the Portuguese kingdom and its new possession ought to take in God's plan.[3] A few years before the arrival of the Portuguese ship on the shores of future Brazil, Christopher Columbus found a land that he initially thought to be the Far East. The first and final destination of his endeavour supported by the Catholic kings of Spain, Columbus was trying to find a route to the East, as an alternative to that cut off by the fall of Constantinople, captured by the Ottomans. But when he realised that he was in an unheard of country of unknown peoples, he started to draw a prophetical plan based on pseudo-Joachimite writings in which the navigation and conquest of a New World would play a decisive part.[4]

The voyages of discovery and the conquest of the Spanish and Portuguese Americas were from the very start permeated by Edenic, biblical, and millenarian arguments, as much as by the pursuit of the wealthy and fabulous Far East which would provide the West with the resources to defeat the Ottoman and Moorish menace. Columbus's and Cabral's enterprises were pictured within a bigger Christian mission and a struggle against the enemies of the faith. Their financial gains should enrich the Iberian crowns, as their sponsors, but also fulfil Catholic providential expectations of their kings and courts. Those biblical-style remarks and prophetic hopes were part of a common language[5] that confirmed the maritime narratives' topics and common-places, and simultaneously were in a way the very reason for the voyages. The fifteenth- and sixteenth-century Portuguese and Spanish conceptions about the very foundations of their nations would implicate them in a concept of empire developed during the expansion. The Iberian monarchies' self-declared mission was founded on a messianic idea of the last empire and their election as the new chosen people. There was indeed a receptive climate for messianic and millenarian news, which echoed and reverberated in an apocalyptic perception of the end of the world. In the 1520s a certain David Reubeni, claiming to be the Messiah and descendent of the Lost Tribe of Reuben capable of defeating the Ottoman Empire, managed to be received by Pope Clement VII and, with his letter of recommendation, by John III of Portugal, leading to protests from the Spanish Inquisition.[6] At the same time, legends about the powerful and yet-to-be-discovered Prester John's mythical Christian kingdom in the middle of Africa and a military spirit derived from the 'Reconquista' wars were recurrent elements in the ultramarine enterprise's motives and representations.[7] Those elements justified and even organised the expansion of a 'Seaborn Empire', in parallel with more economic and material motives.[8] But beyond discussing the place of providential arguments as motors of Iberian expansion,[9] we could also inquire into how they impacted the process of the Iberian American conquest and on what levels this process changed the Spanish and Portuguese view of their own world.

This chapter therefore intends to analyse the role of prophecy and millenarian ideas in the colonisation of Iberian America and, conversely, the impact of information about a New World with new peoples in the eschatological projects of early modern Europe, namely for the Spanish and Portuguese empires. In the first part of the text, I will discuss on which level the so-called discovery of new lands and peoples posed problems to the former prophetical and millenarian Christian schemes. If the scriptures had foretold everything, how should one incorporate the Americas and their natives? Several concerns were raised by Spanish and Portuguese clergy about whether the discovery and conquest represented an evident sign of the end times or were only a necessary step towards the universal conversion of the globe. They likewise asked about the American Indians' origins, sometimes even assuming that the Native Americans were descendants of the Ten Lost Tribes. Similarly, the natives' origin and nature posed questions about not only their conversion's role in God's design, but also how it should be managed to fulfil whichever destiny was cast upon them. The effect of such inquiries was in some degree a reappraisal of Iberian (and European) theories of a universal and final monarchy, in which the New World would play a role, sometimes not only as the final frontier but as the centre of a Christian and global empire.

The second part will analyse the sixteenth- and seventeenth-century connections between politics and providentialism in the Spanish and Portuguese empires. Under the motto 'The kingdom where the sun never sets', the Spanish Hapsburgs designed an imperial project that took shape after the union of the Iberian Crowns in 1580, with Phillip II of Spain and then I of Portugal. Lords with domains in virtually all parts of the globe, Phillip II, and his descendants Phillip III and Phillip IV, staged a global dominion, following a path opened by Charles V.[10] This allegedly universal empire faced, of course, competitors amongst the foreign powers; however, more importantly here, it stimulated alternative prophetical and imperial proposals also within the Iberian empires. In Portugal, under the Hapsburg crown, the belief in a saviour 'Hidden king' or, more concretely, the return of Sebastian I after his loss in a battle in North Africa, produced the culturally lasting proposition of a Portugal-guided Fifth Monarchy. This messianic interpretation gained strength as a form of prophecy-based resistance during the union of the Iberian crowns, and it served as cement for a new dynasty and a renewed Portuguese empire after the restoration of Portugal in 1640. At this moment, the American domains played a crucial role, both in economic and military terms and also in the (re)construction of a millenarian project of a Fifth Monarchy or empire.

2.1 The Impact of the New World and the New Peoples on Iberian Prophetic and Missionary Discourse

I pointed out above the extent to which the prophetical and millenarian Iberian tradition influenced Portuguese and Spanish efforts in the fifteenth- and sixteenth-century conquests. However, that same cultural background by which ships were sailed in search of infinite riches and marvellous kingdoms to help defeat their ominous enemies was established around some principles that could not stand contradiction and had trouble assuming the possibility of the new. This section, therefore, addresses the question of how the so-called discoveries posed a problem to the founding tradition of Christian Europe.

The humanists' circles, in Italy or elsewhere, had already confronted some fundamental pillars of Western Christianity and the established intellectual system. Lorenzo Valla, for instance, tried to prove, by using methods of philological analysis derived from the systematic study of classical authors and his profound knowledge of rhetoric, that the 'Donation of Constantine' was a forgery.[11] However, Valla and other humanists were contrasting the 'modern' (meaning their contemporary) and the 'ancient' (meaning the classical tradition) in order to avoid the 'medieval' (the faded intermission between both).[12] They were renewing the old, in a way to distance themselves from their own present. But how could one deal with something which was not in the Bible and could not be found in Aristotle, Plato, Cicero, or even Lucretius? How could one relate to places and peoples that were not predicted or described either in sacred geography or in the increasingly important ancient cosmographies? Humanistic thinking and its heirs dealt with the problem in several different ways, even refounding the very notion of Humankind (as in Montaigne's *Essays* about the Brazilian natives), or by reaffirming the difference between free and the slave; therefore recovering and renewing Aristotle's principle of natural servitude as did Sepulveda in his academic disputes in Spain about the indigenous people in New Spain (Mexico, Central and part of North America).[13] From a millenarian and theological perspective, such paths were more uncertain.

As Carneiro da Cunha stated, the old world must recognise itself in the New, in order to understand the New.[14] In other words, the new discoveries had to be signified and comprehended, in one way or another, within an existing system of knowledge in order to be acknowledged. That process implied a reappraisal of the existing theories, in an attempt to adapt them in the face of the new information. Nevertheless, the foundations of early modern thinking, especially the Catholic foundations, were based on the principle of authoritative truth. The whole core of its philosophical, scientific, and overall theological interpretation took for granted pre-existent truth, given by the scriptures as well as by classical authority, and therefore feared novelty as a demonic element or even, at its limit, a logical impossibility. Hence the New World must be fitted to a former structure. But in doing so, the latter would also have to be adapted to accommodate the newly found. This is where the whole conundrum resided.

The thousand-year reign of the saints predicted in Revelation, or a Fifth and Ultimate kingdom (in Ezra and Daniel, among others), implied a necessary conception of history and geography. The interpretation of Nebuchadnezzar's dream of the statue (Dan. 2) and Daniel's dream of the beasts (Dan. 7) established the eventual historical consummation of a virtual sovereign power over the whole globe. This latent power was announced figuratively in the first ancient empires but it would only be completed in the last and universal one. However, the extension of the known world to be ruled and the addition of new peoples to be subjugated brought implications for the exegesis of how (and where) this last reign would be installed. The scriptures being God's word to humankind could not be wrong, so their former interpretation must have been equivocated to some extent. This posed a problem, especially for Catholics whose doctrine was firmly grounded on the Fathers and Doctors of the Church and scholastic readings of classical authors. How could one affirm that Augustine's cosmography was wrong even if Augustine had stated that the other hemispheres were not inhabitable due to, for example, the extreme heat of the 'torrid zone'?[15] The solution, far from abandoning the importance of scholasticism, was, on the contrary, to reinforce the scholastic method of questioning without ever surpassing and establishing a new truth. The truth, as a quality belonging to God alone, could be understood only through an analogical operation of a constant approximation among things and events. History, as well as the progressive human knowledge process, should be described as a provisional and analogical path to the final understanding beyond history at the end of time. Thus, Augustine was not wrong but equivocated due to the lack of accumulated lore at his time. Instead of surpassing him, one should only refute him in certain aspects, which were not completely disclosed at his time. In the Iberian theologians' neo-Thomistic interpretation, the human apprehension of the godly gift of knowledge operated in a similar space to that of the revelation of a prophecy, that is, through a figurative and analogical system. Through analogy and figuration, one could maintain the fundamental meaning of the Catholic eschatological message when facing new events.[16] Territorial expansion should be explained neither by a complete reappraisal of former theories nor by a denial of equivocated assumptions, but by an actualization of historical interpretations in the light of new events. It should be the development of a prior process that had allowed the apprehension of the New Testament and the Gospels as a prophetical and historical fulfilment of the Old. Through typological and analogical interpretation, everything could and should be contained in the scriptures, although at times readers lacked the necessary historical and empirical wisdom to interpret the truth. Daniel's and Nebuchadnezzar's dreams had to have predicted the New World as well as the conquest of natives and their conversion in a vision of an ultimate and universal kingdom. However, their former interpreters were not able to foresee it because in their time the necessary historical events were not fulfilled to allow a complete unveiling of the prophecy.

The question of the origin of Native Americans was one example of this troubling accommodation of the discoveries' outcomes within a biblical and prophetical explanation.[17] All humankind must have been generated from Adam and Eve,[18] and, according to late medieval and early modern cosmography, after the Flood the world's population were necessarily descendants of Noah's sons. Asia, Africa, and Europe, the three parts of the world known and described by medieval Christian geography, would each be populated by one of Noah's sons and their people, and therefore each continent's population must descend from and be identified with one of the brothers; for example, the Asians from Shem, the Europeans from Japhet, the Africans from Ham, with other possible combinations.

The increasing contact with Far Eastern populations from the thirteenth century, and the more constant expeditions, commerce and settlements in Sub-Saharan Africa, had already posed some problems to this explanatory scheme, but the discovery of new peoples in a completely unannounced continent brought new levels of complexity. While it was established that they were humans and that they had a soul (a long debate that took at least the first half of the sixteenth century) the question remained as to which branch of Noah's offspring they belonged. Some claimed that they were from the same side as the Africans, and thus bore the curse of Ham and his son, Canaan. Noah, after the Flood, planted a vineyard and, from the grapes, prepared some wine that he drank. He got himself drunk and stripped his clothes off. Ham saw it and went on to tell his brethren, instead of helping him, as Shem and Japheth did. Noah cursed his posterity to be servants of his brothers and thus bear a dark mark on the face as a sign of shame.[19] As Shem was, according to some interpretations, the firstborn, his progeny would be humanity's leader, and Japhet's would follow them. If the Native Americans came from Ham and Canaan, the sons of Japhet (the Europeans) could enslave them or put them to serfdom, although most importantly they had the obligation to save them from their own curse and barbarism through Christianity, as argued by the Portuguese Jesuit Manoel da Nóbrega in a 'Dialogue about the conversion of the Heathen', written in Brazil around 1556–7. As they were savages without any kind of religion and civility ('policia'), living almost in an animal state ('bestialidade'), the simple souls of Ham's descendents in America would be easier to convert than, for example, the full-of-stubbornness ('pertinacia') though polite and subtle grandsons of Shem, the Jews. Therefore, Nóbrega concluded the dialogue in favour of missionary work with the Indians:[20] 'simpler it is to convert an ignorant than a malicious and vainglorious one'.[21] But others stated that the American inhabitants could actually be Shem's offspring, either distantly or, more importantly in our case, through a more direct line as survivors of the Ten Lost Tribes of Israel.

This hypothesis was partly based on the book of 4 Ezra (or 2 Esdras). Although considered apocryphal and not recognised as a canonical book by the Council of Trent, 4 Ezra had wide acceptance among Catholic (as well as Protestant) writers, and its prophetical content was widely used as a source for Iberian messianic texts. As stated by the Jesuit Antônio Vieira, in his Fifth Empire project and his own defence (1666) written during the confinement ordered by the Portuguese Inquisition, the use of 4 Ezra was allowed by tradition and authority:

Despite being considered so, the apocryphal books or those with uncertain authority (that is the meaning of apocryphal) may have much of verity in them, as we follow from the doctrine and it is common practice of all the authors who quote them. And among all of the apocryphal books, there are not any with such huge authority, as the ones by Ezra, and as such they had been always (at least in many Bibles) placed with the others from the same author; and even after the Tridentine Council they have not been thrown out of the body or volume of the Bible, which is the most evident sign of respect and worship that one may have. And therefore the aforesaid books are referred to by many Fathers, and the very Church has selected from them many places for the ecclesiastical chants and prayers: beside, Saint John the Evangelist in his Book of Revelation alludes to the very same books, as noted by Cornelius A Lapide in his commentaries on the same Book of Revelation.[22]

Reasserting its authority despite being apocryphal, the Luso-Brazilian Jesuit, as many others, allowed himself to interpret 4 Ezra in order to identify the Ten Tribes' whereabouts and fulfil the gaps in the canonical biblical books about it.[23] According to 2 Kings (16:6–7, 22–3), the Ten Tribes were expelled from Israel by the Assyrians as God's punishment for their sins. No more than this is said about them in a few other biblical passages. However, in a dream of Ezra (4 Ezra 13:39–47), it was revealed that the Lost Tribes had crossed over the waters and gone to a distant and unheard of country, and that they would remain there until the 'latter time' when God would allow their return to Jerusalem to eventually be reunited with their kindred. This passage had been read as a prophecy about Jerusalem's reconquest, the reunion of the Tribes and the subsequent end of the world since the Middle Ages, but it gained new layers of interpretation with the discovery of new and unknown lands and the enlargement of the globe.[24] Vieira, for instance, identified in Ezra's passage the unequivocal necessity of maintaining Portuguese expansion and pursuing the Catholic mission. He recognised the possible validity of the theories about the Indian lineage of the Ten Lost Tribes, but he defended the existence of a yet unknown and austral land ('Terra Austral' or 'a Incógnita') populated by the Tribes' descendants, that would also be found in the 'torrid zone' beneath the Equator, which was formerly believed to be uninhabitable.[25]

Before Vieira, as he himself indicated, sixteenth- and seventeenth-century Catholic authors had sought in 4 Ezra the scriptural foundation to explain the origin of the Native Americans, identifying in the book the evidence of the migration through the seas from Israel as far as the new continent.[26] More than this, some of them saw in Ezra the justification for the necessary missionary action of converting the natives for their own salvation and reunion with the rest of humankind, and even – and more importantly – for the prominence of the Spaniards over the American Indians. The Indians as the Ten Tribes' posterity were doomed because of their forefathers' sins, therefore not only should they be saved but they should also obey the morally superior Catholic Spaniards. The Dominican Diego Durán, in his *History of the Indies of New Spain* (c. 1581), besides clearly affirming that the Indians were of Hebrew descent, and specifically from the Ten Lost Tribes, also argued that the defeat of the much more numerous native hordes by relatively few Spanish troops had been a result of their cowardice which marked their idolatry and abandonment by God. Less a definitive curse, this proved to be a blessing, because it allowed the Spaniards to conquer and brought them to the true faith.[27] The Spanish monarchy together with the Roman Church had therefore both the obligation and the right of subjugating and converting the natives in order to fulfil the prophecy announced by Ezra and complete God's design for the end times.

The acceptance of Jewish origin did not always imply the subjugation argument or even the intrinsic evilness of the savage people of America. Famous for the defence of the Indians' freedom (against Sepúlveda and others) and his cry about the Spanish destruction of the 'West Indies',[28] the sixteenth-century Spanish Dominican and Bishop of Chiapas Bartolomé de Las Casas was mentioned as one of the advocates of their Jewish origin by the Franciscan Juan de Torquemada in his *Monarchia Indiana* (1615).[29] Although recognising in Las Casas a source of great authority and wisdom ('mucha autoridad, y sabiduria'), Torquemada dismissed point by point the Jewish origin hypothesis defended in a 'testament' attributed to the Dominican – including the reliability of 4 Ezra. The Bishop of Chiapas had indeed believed in using – with caution – the apocryphal Ezra for historical analogies, and even prophetical approximations regarding the New World.[30] However, he had never fully accepted the Indians' Jewish ancestry, or even less had he entertained the notion of the Lost Tribes being the forefathers of Americas' indigenous populations in his writings.[31] The 'Testament' mentioned and refuted by Torquemada was not from Las Casas's hand. Most likely Torquemada was referring to a manuscript written by one 'Doctor Roldán' in the 1540s, which circulated in New Spain and Peru – possibly one of the main sources for the Jewish hypothesis in the Spanish America. Notwithstanding Torquemada's mistaken – but not necessarily unintentional – attribution,[32] and even Las Casas's apparent dismissal of the Jewish descent theory, this rapprochement between Las Casas's idyllic perception of the indigenous peoples, and a prophetical vision of their destiny within Christendom based (also) on their origin, is certainly noteworthy.[33]

Las Casas considered the Indians as gentle and pacific souls. As peaceful and pure, they should be separated from the Spaniard and creole colonists, set free from any kind of serfdom, and left to the care of the religious to ensure their salvation and incorporation into the Catholic Church.[34] From his perspective, there was a fierce fight between those who just wanted to exploit them and those such as himself, the priests and the Spanish kings, who wanted to save them.[35] At the same time, Las Casas was enthusiastic about Columbus's discovery of an uncharted continent and foresaw in his enterprise the manifest desire of God – he reinforced the literal meaning of Columbus' first name, Christopher, the 'bearer of Christ'. As Columbus did, he interpreted the discoveries as the fulfilment of both a Christian and Spanish mission, both reinforcing the conversion of the natives as a crucial and fundamental part of American colonisation and simultaneously the justification for the conquest of America by the Spaniards and Catholics.[36]

Influenced by Las Casas's ideas, another kind of reasoning likewise stressed conversion, but foresaw in the missionary work less the outcome of the Indians' good soul and prompt acceptance of Christian faith, and more the sign of the necessary conditions for the final kingdom. A reader and admirer of Las Casas, the Spanish Franciscan Gerónimo de Mendieta described conversion in New Spain, highlighting that the Indians' previous acceptance of the Word was disturbed by the bad influence of the greedy colonists. His *Historia Eclesiastica Indiana* (c. 1597) praised Catholic engagement among the natives, but above all described the millenarian actions and utopian plans of his order in the 'Indies'. This may have also been inspired, according to many authors, by the mysticism of the Franciscan Spirituals, Joachimite ideals and Thomas Morus' work.[37] Catholics were completing God's design in spreading the Gospel among people who had never heard of Him, as predicted in Isaiah (55:5), and bringing to Christianity several thousands of souls by ministering with ardour the Sacrament of Baptism. This was part of the path for founding a 'New Church' which would free Christendom of its corrupt portion. Mendieta was also inclined to consider the Jewish origin of the Indians, in spite of some sceptical remarks by Jesuit José de Acosta made a few years earlier. But more important than proving it beyond doubt was the possibility to consider and therefore validate it for the sake of his argument, because it could be a prophetic sign of the end of the world's proximity.[38] This apocalyptic tone had a twofold consequence in his writing. Firstly, it tried to align all Catholic and Spanish efforts, monarchic and religious activity, towards the same millenarian horizon, demonstrated by evidence (both human [the work] and divine [the miracles]) in the first century of colonisation. Secondly, it nonetheless indicated the problems with this project in his own time, when he perceived attacks in New Spain, lack of support from Madrid, and crisis in the empire.[39] The tone would mourn 'the fall of the Indian Jerusalem', as Phelan called Medieta's denunciation, but, at the same time, it would announce imminent destruction before the final judgement.[40] Perhaps due to this negative and critical apocalyptic tone, *Historia Eclesiastica* remained in manuscript until the nineteenth century, but more importantly, the disagreement with José de Acosta's perception reveals a dispute among the orders in terms of the significance of America's conquest.

Mendieta, echoing many other Franciscans in New Spain since the beginning of the sixteenth century, was certain of the proximity of the End, and the victory of a 'New Church' (and society) over a corrupted one. Moreover, the calamitous state of his time would only corroborate it in the same way as the natives' initial easy conversion had allegedly proved the election of the Franciscan mission and its evangelising fervour as tools for Christianising the Americas. The Indians' Jewish origin would reinforce the assumption that they were seeing the complete spread of the gospel throughout the globe which was necessary for the Second Coming and the millennial kingdom, as predicted in the Bible. But for authors like Acosta,[41] experiencing the Jesuit mission in Peru, the catechetical work had only started. They also understood from the recent decisions of Trent a more orthodox perspective. The Jesuits had witnessed or heard of several newly baptised natives that were still performing heathen 'idolatrous' rituals in secret (or even openly), showing that the initial preaching ardour had reached its limits. From that point of view, more efficacious than relying on the miraculous effect of baptism or dreaming of utopian cities of Indian Jerusalem, was the establishment of apostolic missions for converting at steadier pace. The hope of redemption and of the Devil's defeat should be based less on faith in the acts of the Holy Spirit, and more on a loving and charitable kind of work (the virtue of *Caritas*). The natives should be reduced (re-conducted to, through 'reducciones') within villages where they would be organised in an isolated civil and political entity (called 'aldeamentos' or 'aldeias', in Brazil and Maranhão), and kept apart from the influence of Portuguese and Spanish colonisers as well as from the still savages heathens. There they would be under a programmatic system of conversion, through regular and standardised confession and catechism, but at the same time adapted and reformulated (even linguistically) for each local environment and native culture.[42] Separated from the colonial world under Jesuit supervision, the Indians would also be protected from exploitation, although they should work hard both as a redemptive path to avoid the sin of 'acedia', and as a way of maintaining (and eventually feathering the nest of) the Society's missions.

Acosta therefore assumed an opposite position to Mendieta concerning the Jewish origin of Indians as well as the role of the Americas in the end times. In *Historia natural y moral de las Indias* (1590), he found it most unlikely that the natives were the Ten Tribes who had crossed the Euphrates as in the apocryphal Ezra.[43] And even if so, it should not be read as evidence of the inauguration of a millennial kingdom in the Americas. For him, the discovery of the New World and the spread of the gospel among the natives were only the initial signs of the fulfilment of apocalyptic prophecies. Long before the arrival of Doomsday, it would be necessary to convert all the newly discovered heathen and subjugate the recently charted strange lands. The 'mundo nuevo' should be considered infantile, even childish, because, in metaphorical terms, it was new, as if in its childhood. Hence there was the necessity of working even harder to bring it up to its maturity. More than this, he argued that it was implausible (and even unsafe for human knowledge) to be completely sure about the date of the Second Coming.[44]

As Prosperi points out, this way of seeing millenarian expectations may have also derived from his experience as inquisitor in Lima, Peru.[45] There, in the 1570s, Acosta participated as a qualifier in the trial of Spanish Dominican Francisco de La Cruz, who had been arrested as a follower of the Peruvian visionary María Pizarro. Incarcerated, the friar surpassed the initial scope of Pizarro's visions and started to defend the providential election of the New World and the condemnation of the old, echoing Las Casas' denouncement of the doom of Spain for its sins in Mexico. Not only did he strongly defend the Jewish ancestry of the Indians, but he also took it as a proof of the final conversion and redemption of the world. Most controversially, he proclaimed himself to be the father of the next saviour of the new kingdom to come, and therefore the new pope and king of Peru, and hence, of the globe.[46] Sentenced to death by fire in 1578, La Cruz's case certainly made an impression on Acosta, as he mentioned it in his *De temporibus novissimis* (1590) published in Rome.[47] Going beyond Medienta's and other Franciscans' utopian Jerusalem in the Americas, La Cruz and his attempts to confront local imperial authorities not only highlighted the importance of the Indians and the New World in God's plans, but also overthrew the centrality of Europe in his design, to the alarm of Acosta.

In Brazil, the transfer of the elected land to the Americas led to other steps when Christian prophecy met with native religiousness. During the 1580s a series of indigenous revolts occurred in Bahia, near the capital of Brazil, Salvador. They were organised around a millenarian sect known as 'Santidade do Jaguaripe' in which Catholic expectations, taught by the Jesuits to the indigenous populations, were merged with a Tupi-Guarani myth of 'The Land without Evil'. The leader of the 'Santidade', a former 'aldeado' - an inhabitant of an 'aldeia' - named Antonio, claimed to be a promised native god-hero as well the only true pope, and empowered as such, nominated bishops and priests. His wife was called Holy Mary Mother of God, and they adored, in their cults, a Holy Cross. Yet they maintained the Tupi rituals of chanting, smoking, and drinking, that Nóbrega had described with abhorrence in his 'Dialogue' as a mark of the natives' savagery. When eventually suppressed by the colonists following the governor of Brazil's orders in 1585, the Santidade had attracted the Tupi as well as African slaves, mestizos, and some Portuguese Christians. This reached such a level that when years later, in 1591, the first visitation of the Holy Office went to Bahia, the 'Visitador' discovered many traces of the Santidade in Brazilian religion, and filed charges against it.[48] The evangelistic experience in the Americas and the role of American Indians in it began to prove itself more radical than the dreams of utopian cities orderly organised as 'New Jerusalems'.

Mendieta and Acosta, both of them writing at the end of the sixteenth century, pointed out a divergent shift of positions towards the conquests' prophetical meaning also based on the ways of dealing with the loud alterations in Christianity.[49] Since the commencement of colonisation, the religious (as well as political) context in the New and the Old World had significantly changed – and not only by the news from the Americas and overseas. Criticism towards the Church had led to, on the one hand, the Reformation, and, on the other, to an institutional reform within Roman Catholicism, summed up in the Council of Trent. Rome after Trent (and the Reformation) was very suspicious of any sort of justification of the necessity of any Church modification, and concurrently, started huge efforts towards the systematisation and control of ecclesiastical functioning as well as of apostolic action in Christian Europe and in its dominions around the globe. A significant share of the task was entrusted to the recently founded Society of Jesus (1534), which provided in the late sixteenth century the most effective and widespread catechetical and educational program in Catholic Europe, and particularly in Iberian kingdoms and dominions. At the same time, the shift in the role of conversion was also pressed by the rejection of seeking a precise date for the end of the world. This was partially the result of a more cautious attitude towards millenarian and mystical movements. Part of this was the outcome of the Catholic response to the Reformation, or more precisely, a fear of any possibility of disruption or criticism in theological and institutional terms. Apocalyptic perspectives tended to criticise the *status quo* in order to show the decadence and upheaval prior to the time of justice and righteousness; and therefore they were sometimes read by the authorities as a menace to political and religious institutions – especially in times of crisis.

More concretely, the sixteenth-century Spanish crown and church faced several mystical and messianic movements arousing criticism towards both. The persecution of the 'Alumbrados' (Illuminated), influenced by Franciscan mystical practices and Erasmian ideals,[50] was certainly one of the most thorough campaigns of the sixteenth-century Spanish Inquisition, but the Holy Office and the monarchy were keen on pursuing several other cases in Spain and in the Americas. The revolts of 'Comunidades' in Castille or 'Germaníadas' in Valencia in the first years of Charles I of Spain (afterwards Emperor Charles V), although more circumscribed (1520–22), were also inspired by prophetical expectations and spiritual Franciscans' vision. In Valencia, the messianic figure of a 'Hidden One' ('Encubierto') represented a final resistance against the viceregal troops in the concluding months of the rebellion.[51] More importantly, the coming of a Hidden One was eventually transformed into a recurrent commonplace in Iberian Messianism, the 'Encubertismo', a belief in which a mysterious king would come to save an oppressed people or a kingdom in distress. The 'Encubertismo' (or 'Encobertismo' in Portuguese) was sustained and spread by several well-known prophecies, some apocryphally attributed to Isidore of Seville and the Joachimite friar Rocquettailade. This 'Encubertismo' and the prophecies related to him evolved from a more local based movement to projects within an imperial spectrum.

2.2 From Local Prophecies to Imperial Projects: Catholic Monarchy, the Iberian Union, and Restored Portugal in the Seventeenth Century

The end of the sixteenth and the first decades of the seventeenth century faced more than mystic millenarism or a regional messianism based on the Hidden One within the boundaries of Spanish kingdoms. Political upheavals and revolts appeared, several of them away from Madrid and Castile, and many against the imperial projects of Spanish Hapsburgs in

Europe and beyond.[52] For Milhou, those upheavals were influenced by the increasing criticism and disappointment with Madrid after the defeat of the Armada in 1588, as one could observe in Lucrezia de Leon's and Piedrola's dreams and visions.[53] Nevertheless, this widening of prophetical perspectives might be related to the changes in the Hapsburg dynasty.

After the abdication of Charles V (1555–6), the Hapsburg domains were split into two branches, the Austrian and Holy Empire, under the mandate of Charles's brother, Ferdinand II, and the Spanish, under the rule of his son and heir. Phillip II inherited not only the Spanish kingdoms but also the Netherlands, South and North Italy, and several other European regions, principalities, and duchies, but what is more important in our case, the overseas domains. In referring to all those possessions in the Spanish branch, the idea of a Catholic monarchy was increasingly transformed from a title given to the defenders of the Roman faith, as borne initially by Ferdinand of Aragon and Elizabeth of Castile, into an epithet of all the possessions throughout the globe which could imply a universal (the original meaning of 'Catholic') sovereignty over the world. From 1580–1, with the Iberian Union of Crowns, those boundaries were also spread to Portugal, India, Brazil, and the dominions in Africa and the Pacific (although not officially, as the Portuguese and Spanish kingdoms and overseas domains were never actually and *de jure* merged). With the acclamation of Philip II of Spain as Philip I of Portugal, an almost 60-year period of regency started, in which most of the decisions were taken in Madrid.[54] During this period, the Spanish crown thought it was eligible to claim, albeit metaphorically, the title of lords of all the world.[55] But at the same time, and probably due to its imperial ambitions, it faced several insurrections in the seventeenth century against its rule in Europe, from the Netherlands to Sicily, which not only contested its global aspirations but also heavily disturbed the delicate governance and power balance of the Catholic monarch.

As Serge Gruzinski, among others, stated, the Spanish monarchy's new global configuration changed millenarian and apocalyptic perception and prophetical movements in the Iberian sphere of influence.[56] The Spanish crown, far from abandoning the imperial tone with the separation from the Holy Empire, maintained and increasingly reinforced the notion of being God's elected kingdom, championing Catholicism in Europe, spreading the gospel, and conquering foreign nations and lands throughout the globe. As another side of the same coin, it increasingly faced prophetical revolts within the 'Spains' (all the Iberian realms) and in the imperial borders (within and out of Europe) which could have international implications. As the Spanish monarchy became progressively globalised both in its political-theological expectations and in its actual domains all over the world, so did the prophetical discourse and the millenarian and messianic beliefs and movements at the end of the sixteenth century and beginning of the seventeenth.

According to Michele Olivari, the aforementioned case of La Cruz and the attempt of a Limean upheaval should be placed in this context of contesting the Catholic monarchy.[57] More than that, La Cruz even tried to dispute and change the centre of the world, transferring it to the New World, and proclaiming himself pope and King of Peru. In a similar fashion, suggests Gruzinski, following Vainfas, the Santidade do Jaguaripe must be understood as an anti-colonialist revolt – and at the very beginning of the Iberian Union. He also stressed its hybrid aspect, mixing Catholic and indigenous religious expectations, and creating an alternative and conflicting millenarian project in and for the Brazilian territory.[58] Similar movements were to be found on the other side of the Atlantic too, in the European limits of the Spanish Empire.

In South Italy, Dominican friar Tommaso Campanella predicted the beginning of the Age of the Spirit for 1600, based on prophecies and astrological interpretations. Certain that an immense political change was about to happen, he was one of the leaders and conspirators in a Joachimite-inspired republican and communitarian plot against the Catholic monarchy's rule in Calabria. Denounced before it had even started, the plotters were severely persecuted by local authorities (with the knowledge of Philip III) and Campanella was incarcerated and spent 27 years in Naples' prisons.[59] Surprisingly, during his time as prisoner, he wrote and finished several treatises defending an absolute, final, and universal monarchy, and in one of them argued that Philip III, united with the pope, should be the emperor of the world, and that Spain was the ultimate kingdom prophesied in Daniel and Ezra. The former millenarian republican changed to a defender of a theocratic absolute monarchy, in which religion (in the pope) and civil power (in the Spanish kings), were bound together, and would continue the expansion of the Christian faith already in progress through the efforts of the Catholic monarchs. In his newer prophetic plan, the New World and the conversion of Indians were not only a sign of this, but also a necessary step in its fulfilment. More than an abstract millenarian utopia, his *Monarchia di Spagna* (as his more theological *Monarchia del Messia*) had aspects of a 'Mirror for Princes' too, avoiding and even combating any Machiavellian tone.[60] This indicated how the Spanish princes in collaboration with the papacy could conquer the globe. Although not printed in Italy at the time, his works were distributed, and were read by Spanish Catholics as well as his enemies, the Dutch and English Protestants. On the

Catholic side, the Spanish Friar Juan de Salazar borrowed, without quoting, several arguments and the core advice of Campanella's political-prophetical treatise in order to write a key work of Iberian imperial thought, *Politica Española* (1619).[61] On the Protestant side, printed in German in 1620s and also eventually in Latin in Amsterdam,[62] it was read as a 'papist' secret plan to destroy the Protestants. Translated into English in the 1650s, two decades after Campanella's death,[63] it was shown as evidence of a 'Plot of Jesuites' to overthrow England.[64] Some years later, the controversial polemist and lawyer William Prynne accused the Italian friar, ironically, of being a 'second Machiavel' whose advice to the king of Spain if followed would sever the Protestant world, namely his greatest enemies, England and the Netherlands, and lead him and Spain to a papist universal domain over the globe.[65]

Maybe the most interesting, but beyond doubt the most continuous, phenomenon arising during – and in opposition to – the Catholic monarchy was 'Sebastianism'. The belief in the return of King Sebastian of Portugal, and its several derivations and developments during the seventeenth century and beyond, were perhaps one of the longest-lasting messianic beliefs not strictly attached to a religion.[66] The young king was called the 'Desired One' ('O Desejado') from his birth (1554), and led to crusade-like desires of resuming the battles against the Moors by which the Portuguese kingdom had been founded. In the late 1570s he organised a fleet to invade Morocco and overcome the sultan, also inspired by the conquest of coastal African sites and strongholds that had started the Portuguese maritime expansion one century before. Missing in action during the Battle of Alcazar (El Ksar Kibir) in 1578, Sebastian I left no heirs, and after two years of intense expectation and dispute, his uncle Philip II was sworn king of Portugal. However, legends about Sebastian's disappearance (but not death) during the battle and his eventual flight started to spread immediately after the battle.[67] Until the end of the sixteenth century, several candidates for the returning Sebastian appeared in Portugal and Spain, with the most famous being Sebastian of Venice. Arrested in Venice in 1598, this Sicilian-born impostor managed to gather around him many exiled Portuguese noblemen, friars, and lettermen that apparently found in him the returned king that would free them from the Spaniards. Despite the support of these nobles, his destiny was rather grim, as he was condemned to the galleys and eventually delivered to the Spanish authorities, hanged and quartered.[68]

One fellow Portuguese in particular championed his cause: João de Castro. He transformed Sebastianism into an almost scholarly and systematised program.[69] A bastard son of a nobleman, Castro was named after his grandfather, a famous cartographer and Viceroy of the East Indies. When he first heard the news about Sebastian of Venice, he was an expatriate in Paris, where he had worked for one of the defeated contestants for the Portuguese throne, the late D. Antônio, Prior of Crato. He soon embraced the hope of the returning king, and went to Venice, as other of the former Prior's supporters did. More importantly, he started to incessantly write about Sebastian's return and also about the Fifth Monarchy to be led by the 'Desired king' and the Portuguese kingdom. After 22 manuscript volumes and three printed books and pamphlets, written from 1597 to 1626, he managed to marshal and arrange several prophetic traditions which had been circulating in Europe and cherished in the Iberian Peninsula, transforming all in the favour of Sebastian and the ultimate monarchy to come. In his writings he appropriated the manifest spirit of destiny that had justified Portuguese overseas expansion and assured Portugal of being an elect nation during the fifteenth and sixteenth centuries.

Part of this mix was already present in one of the central sources for Castro's messianic project, the *Trovas de Bandarra*. The verses, composed by a Portuguese cobbler named Bandarra, dealt with the 'Encobertismo' and with the dreams of a fifth kingdom to come in biblical books. In his dream vision, it was already the time for the arrival of the 'Desired one', as predicted in Daniel and Ezra.[70] Produced around the 1520–1530s, the verses exude the messianic expectations of the New-Christian communities (converted Jews and their descendents) intertwined with the ambitions of the Portuguese kingdom.[71] The visions had circulated in oral and manuscript versions throughout the sixteenth century, despite the fact that Bandarra was condemned in 1541 by the Inquisition and the inclusion of *Trovas* in the 1581 *Index*.[72] The text crossed Portuguese territorial frontiers and the Atlantic, being read in Spain and in Brazil.[73] Castro nonetheless was the first to compile different variants, organise them and, in 1603, had the verses printed accompanied by his explanations of their meaning – all pointing to the imminence of Sebastian's return and the Portuguese-led Fifth Monarchy.[74] More than this, he mingled the interpretation of the *Trovas* with the reading of the recently forged 'Oath of Afonso Henriques'. The oath was supposedly signed by the first Portuguese king, Alphonse I, as 'documental' proof of Portugal's miraculous foundation in 1139, in Ourique, by Christ himself. Here it was stated that the Portuguese kingdom had been chosen by God to spread the gospel to 'strange nations' in distant countries and to build for him an empire.[75] Allegedly discovered in the 1590s, this apocryphal source would retrospectively give prophetical grounds for the expansion throughout the seas and desire for a global empire, and combined with the *Trovas'* exegesis, allowed Castro to argue that a universal Fifth Monarchy would be necessarily Portuguese, as stated in his main prophetic sources.[76] Using those visions, he could adapt and rearrange the Joachimite tradition, the biblical prophecies, and commentaries, especially those about the five consecutive kingdoms, and other 'Encoberto' prophecies. Although anti-Jewish, he (albeit indirectly) drank in the messianic expectations which pervaded the New-Christian and Crypto-Jewish communities in Portugal, including some readings of Bandarra's *Trovas* themselves.

Although not unusual in early modern times, this assemblage of different visionary branches allowed Castro to build a theoretical body around the hope of the 'Desired One's' return, which, in consequence, started the establishment of a 'lettered Sebastianism'.[77] It responded at the same time to a previous imperial desire and to a need for rethinking the very core of what the Portuguese kingdom and nation were about. In a horizon of providential expectations, an answer was not abandoning the former desires of grandeur based on experiences of expansion and victories[78]; on the contrary, it relied on an actualisation of those hopes, provided that God's design never changed. Castro's proposition of a future Fifth Monarchy was one possible translation of this adaptation for his own troubling times. As a prophetic-based explanation, the fulfilment of Portugal's imperial destiny in the future was simultaneously its reason to exist in the present and the effect of its actions in the past, and vice-versa.

Assuming this Fifth Monarchy destiny, Sebastianism and subsequently Portuguese prophetical enterprises therefore gained an inextricably imperial, or even imperialistic, tone in explaining Portugal's history and ground for existence. To be fair, as we have seen, almost all of the prophecies were at the time interpreted in global and imperial terms, and not merely in terms of an abstract *Respublica Christiana* or in a Crusade-like spirit as before. Imperial and millenarian arguments turned into an inescapable political language and, as such, were used even by those who wanted to defeat the biggest and most menacing providential-thought empire at the time, the Catholic Monarchy.[79] However, for reasons too complex to explore fully here, the prophetical explanation was a core part of the Portuguese Empire's ideology and Sebastianism (and the idea of a Fifth Monarchy), a definitive aspect of their cultural and political life. The Restoration of Portugal, with the acclamation of John IV in 1640, far from diminishing this expectation, only strengthened it. The new king promptly incorporated the providential and imperial discourse as a way of legitimating himself and his dynasty, the Braganzas, and concurrently to attend and calm the Sebastianists' desires.[80]

The war of independence against Spain required material and diplomatic support as well as a political, theological, and rhetorical defence of Braganza's legitimacy to overcome the Spaniards – and per chance convince some reluctant Sebastianists.[81] The Jesuit Antônio Vieira was given this task. Born in Portugal, but raised, trained, and ordered in Salvador, Vieira was sent to Lisbon by the governor of Brazil with the colonial greeting committee for the newly restored monarch. Impressing the court with his wit and oratory skills, he found favour with John IV, and started to act as his personal advisor and eventually was nominated the royal preacher. Along with other supporters of the Braganza cause, he tried to establish a network in Europe to defend the Portuguese against Spain and its allies. Part of this network was interested in gathering funds and political approval, as well as opening connections with other millenarian and visionary thinkers, such as Mennaseh ben Israel, a well-known Dutch rabbi of Portuguese origin, in order to discuss their predictions and amass new sources for their political-prophetical campaigns.[82] Within this circle of supporters, providentialist thought, and financial and political aspects were bound together. For instance, Vieira and his circle defended the New-Christians against the Inquisition for both economic and providential reasons. They said that the seizure of their money would financially harm the crown's and colonial empire's revenues in severe times, but they also saw it as a strategy to regain confidence of the exiled Portuguese Jewish community abroad, especially in the Netherlands and France, in order to eventually convert them, as predicted in Ezra.[83] Likewise the Jesuit could preach in the Royal Chapel for the necessity of keeping the expansion as commanded by Christ to Alphonse I; and, concurrently, he could pragmatically advise the sale of Dutch-occupied north-east Brazil to an enemy, the heretical and Calvinist Netherlands, in order to avoid a conflict with the Dutch forces and an Atlantic war in times of dispute against a bigger (and common) enemy, Spain. He argued, in a letter known as 'Papel Forte' (Strong paper), that the sale would give the crown enough money to maintain the Empire and afterwards it could regain the lost territories, as one could deduce from the predictions.[84]

It was, however, only after the death of John IV in 1656 that Vieira began to more steadily delineate his plan of a Fifth Empire, as the Jesuit would call the last and ultimate earthly kingdom.[85] When back in South America, at the Maranhão State's Jesuit mission, he wrote a letter to comfort the widowed queen. Allegedly composed in a canoe on the Amazon in 1659, he commented on Bandarra's *Trovas* to show the providential need of John IV's resurrection to the end that all Portugal's predicted grandeur might be accomplished. The letter, entitled 'Hopes of Portugal', reached the Lisbon Inquisition and was taken as initial evidence to finally sue him. Summoned in 1663 and arrested for interrogation in Coimbra, Portugal, Vieira saw himself set apart from the world of disputes he was accustomed to. Isolated and pressed by the circumstances, he finally managed to elaborate his prophetical plan for the Portuguese Empire, as a part of his defence against the Holy Office.[86] In it, the Jesuit notion of conversion and missionary efforts, drawn, for example, in José de Acosta's writings, gained an explicitly prophetical dimension organised in Vieira's vision of the Fifth Empire.[87] The New World and the still to-be discovered lands were the final frontier to prepare the ultimate kingdom and reign of Christ on earth. Unlike Acosta's fear of dating the eschaton and closer to Acosta's rival, Mendieta,[88] Vieira kept continuously (regardless of previously failed attempts) assigning a specific time for this divine event. For instance, as with many others at the time, he was fascinated with the numerological and biblical implications of the 'fatal year' of 1666. When 1666 was over, realising that the world was the same (and that he was still arrested by the Inquisition), the Jesuit re-organised his predictions and set other future dates. He relentlessly transferred his hopes to subsequent Portuguese princes, certain of the fulfilment of his millenarian wishes. However, he lacked the support of his late king and his fellow Braganza millenarians, many of them dead. The long trial's outcome in 1668 was not especially favourable to him, although not disastrous, considering the charges. Accused of apostasy and Judaism, for believing in a messianic kingdom to come, he saw himself condemned to silence – a sentence he managed to eventually revoke in Rome, talking the pope himself into it. Free, but old and isolated from the Portuguese court, he eventually returned to Bahia in 1681 and, until his death in 1697, dedicated himself to preparing his sermons for printing and to write his most important prophetical treatise, *Clavis prophetarum*, which remained unfinished.

If the eventide of Vieira's life may be seen as rather gloomy, at the same time his fame as a preacher and visionary only increased in the late seventeenth century. His printed sermons, edited in Portugal and Spain, were read on both sides of the Atlantic, from Mexico to Madrid, from Salvador to Lisbon, and they were considered examples of oratory, wit, and good theological exposition. Any criticism towards them, as in the Mexican Sor Juana de La Cruz's *Carta Atenagorica*, could raise a myriad of responses from differents parts of the Spanish and Portuguese Empires.[89] Although none of Vieira's major messianic works had been printed in his lifetime, many circulated in copious manuscripts versions. They were read and discussed, and the Jesuit was repeatedly invoked to give authority for a plethora of other writings. In the late seventeenth century and throughout the eighteenth century, Vieira's readers transformed him into the epitome of prophecy, his name being even used for authoring apocryphal Sebastianist tracts. There were also several reappraisals of his Fifth Empire project in varied manners, even hermetic alchemical interpretations of the Portuguese destiny.[90] But for our discussion perhaps the most interesting appropriation was that made by Pedro de Rates Henequim.

The first half of the eighteenth century was marked by the richness derived from Minas Gerais' gold mines in central Brazil, which allowed long unseen opulence in the Portuguese court of John V, grandson of John IV. Engaged, as many others, in the gold rush that was taking place in Minas, Portuguese of Dutch origin Henequim came to Brazil in 1702 and discovered a completely different world. Reading Vieira's works along with other sources and blending them in a rich cultural-exchange ambiance in Minas, he managed to recreate the Jesuit's vision of the Fifth Empire giving an even more central role to the Americas. In a certain way, he combined the varied theories and positions towards the New World. He agreed on Vieira's imperial vision of the Portuguese Empire, and the central role of the Brazilian mission, but more radically, he transferred the stage of the last act of human history from Portugal (or the Iberian monarchies) to Brazil. The New World, Brazil in particular, would be the head of the Fifth Empire that would conquer the whole globe and convert all peoples to the Catholic faith. Besides, he showed evidence that would allegedly sustain it. For a start, as with Mendieta two centuries before, he was certain that the Lost Tribes resided in South America, as he also believed that their discovery and eventual conversion was a proof of America's part in the end of the world. But conversely, Henequim identified in Brazil the very beginning of human existence, since it would have been the original location of the biblical Paradise. Eden's river were actually great Brazilian rivers, Amazonas and São Francisco; the trees of Life and Knowledge were banana trees, in which leaves Adam inscribed messages to his progeny; the natives' redskin came from the tone of Adam's skin, red as theirs. The richness of Minas' goldmines – finally accomplishing Caminha's prediction in his letter of 1500 – could only corroborate Henequim's statement. In 1722, Henequim returned to Portugal to reveal his prophecies in the court, and in Lisbon he was listened to by crowds in the streets. With his recently acquired fame, he started to receive attention from more important ears, and eventually he managed to enter into the circle of the king's youngest brother, D. Manuel. The visionary then proposed that Manuel should rise up against his brother and flee to Brazil to start the Fifth Empire there, as Emperor of South America. We do not know if his plans were personally heeded by Manuel, who never had good relations with his elder sibling and might have enjoyed the notion of overcoming him; but we do know that they caused a great impression and, more dangerously, uproar in the colony and in the court. Without success, a riot was even planned in Minas to enthrone the new emperor. As a result, Henequim was arrested and eventually denounced to the Holy Office. Prosecuted as heretic, he was condemned to be burned in 1744.[91]

One could think that Henequim's case was a deviant and late episode of visionary delusion at the dawn of the Enlightenment or, on the contrary, should be read as proto-nationalistic Brazilian separatism.[92] In a less judgemental or anachronistic view, some authors have seen it as an episode of a particular and individual cosmographic interpretation that took place in colonial Brazil. There historical, philosophical, and prophetical readings were combined in an almost aleatory and peculiar fashion, entangled in the colonial reality and cultural connections, which can only be understood through the analytical lenses of Ginzburg-inspired micro-history.[93] However, we can also stress that he was part of a continuum of providential interpretation and dialogued with Iberian theological-rhetorical-prophetical thinking, as well as with an Edenic perception of the New World.[94] And, more importantly, his ideas did reverberate and had political implications. Even if we consider his prophecies' political appropriation as a mere opportunistic manoeuvre within a sibling's dispute for power, the fact remains that a visionary plan from Brazil had an interested reception by some eminent people in the Lisbon court as well as by the ordinary people on the streets. In the mid-eighteenth century, messianic grammar and language still moved audiences from different backgrounds.

2.3 Conclusion

If the chiliastic Dominican La Cruz and the more realistic Jesuit Acosta had been on opposite sides of the bench at the end of the sixteenth century, the lay visionary Henequim could base himself on pragmatic and messianic Jesuit Vieira. The idea of the Fifth Empire, transmuted in a congenial notion for the Portuguese Empire, united both.

The millenarian fervour of the Franciscan 'Indian Jerusalem'[95] might be understood by its anti-monarchic agenda, and the prophetic discourse as intrinsically radical or disruptive utopian dreams. However this conception leaves aside the fact that providential and millenarian ideas were the common grammar and vocabulary in the early modern Iberian world. Not only did the Spanish and, particularly, Portuguese concepts of empire absorb those providential dimensions but they also depended on them; and the American conquest augmented this relation. Throughout the sixteenth and seventeenth centuries, colonisation implied a broader perception of the limits of the world and the variety of the human race, and therefore changed the conception of the future of Christendom. Without abandoning biblical and eschatological thinking, the shift of perception resulted in a reappraisal of former millenarian projects and imperial desires. Far from representing their end, Catholic monarchical expansion and, moreover, the Iberian union, had on the contrary stimulated prophetic plans – even if to fight against Spanish dominion.[96] This is particularly evident in the Portuguese case, in which Sebastianism and a monarchic messianism gained a crucial role as a long-lasting identifying trait of their own historical explanation. However this did not mean a complete and safe acceptance of the sometimes 'heretical' prophetic ideas. The inquisitors, here and there, were keen to cut off any sort of possible apostasy and crime against faith – especially if they smelt the slightest possible scent of Judaism. On both sides of the Atlantic La Cruz, Vieira, Henequim, and many other who crossed the seas in both directions saw in the Americas and their peoples the confirming signs of a millennial kingdom to come. However, dreaming of its coming might have had consequences as faced by them before the bench of the Inquisition. Nevertheless, and despite all of the Holy Office's efforts, messianic expectations and prophetical visions prevailed as a core element of religious, cultural, and political life in the early modern Iberian world.

Notes

1. Pêro Vaz de Caminha, *La 'carta de achamento' di Pero Vaz de Caminha*, ed. Anna Unali (Milan, 1984).
2. On the Edenic motifs, see: Sérgio Buarque de Holanda, *Visão do paraíso* (São Paulo, 2010 [1959]), 'Prefácio'. On the letter: César Braga-Pinto, *As promessas da história. Discursos proféticos e assimilação no Brasil Colonial (1500–1700)* (São Paulo, 2003), chap. 1; Luís Adão da Fonseca, 'O sentido da novidade na carta de Pêro Vaz de Caminha' *Revista USP*, 45 (2000), pp. 38–47.
3. Laura de Mello e Souza, 'O nome do Brasil', *Revista de História* 145 (2001), pp. 68–78.
4. Christopher Columbus, *Libro de las profecías*, ed. Juan Fernández Valverde (Madrid, 1992). See also: Alain Milhou, *Colón y su mentalidad mesiánica en el ambiente franciscanista español* (Valladolid, 1989).

5. For the notion of language, see: J.G.A Pocock, *Politics, language, and time* Second edition (Chicago, 1971), esp. chap. 1; Stuart Clark, 'French historians and early modern popular culture' *Past and Present*, 100 (1983), pp. 62–99; Stuart Clark, *Thinking with demons. The idea of witchcraft in early modern Europe* (Oxford, 1997).
6. Matt Goldish, *The Sabbatean prophets* (Cambridge, 2004), pp. 43–4.
7. Giuseppe Marcocci, 'Prism of empire: The shifting image of Ethiopia in renaissance Portugal (1500–1570)' in Maria Berbara and Karl A.E. Enenkel (eds), *Portuguese humanism and the republic of letters* (Leiden, 2012), pp. 447–65; Luís Filipe Thomaz, 'A ideia imperial manuelina' in Andreá Doré et al (eds), *Facetas do império na história* (São Paulo, 2008), pp. 65–72.
8. Charles Boxer, *The Portuguese seaborne empire* Second Edition (London, 1993), ch. 1; John H. Elliott, *Empires of the Atlantic world* (New Haven, CT, 2007), pp. 16–20.
9. This has been a particularly important question in Portuguese historiography around the motivations that led the Iberian kingdoms to start the ultramarine voyages. For a reappraisal of the question, see the debate between Sanjay Subrahmanyam and Francisco Bethencourt in the *Annales*: Sanjay Subrahmanyam, 'Du Tage au Gange au XVIe siècle: une conjoncture millénariste à l'échelle eurasiatique'. *AHSS*. 56 (2001), pp. 51–84 (Extended version in English: 'Sixteenth-Century millenarianism from the Tagus to the Ganges', in *Explorations in connected history: from the Tagus to the Ganges* [Oxford, Oxford University Press, 2005]); Francisco Bethencourt, 'Le millénarisme: idéologie de l'impérialisme eurasiatique?', *AHSS*, 57 (2002) pp. 189–94; Sanjay Subrahmanyam, 'Ceci n'est pas un débat…' *AHSS*. 57 (2002), pp. 195–201.
10. John H. Elliott, *Empires of the Atlantic world*, p. 23.
11. Carlo Ginzburg, 'Lorenzo Valla and the Donation of Constantine' in *History, rhetoric, and proof* (Hanover, NH, 1999), pp. 56–8.
12. Quentin Skinner, *The foundations of modern political thought: Volume 1, The Renaissance* (Cambridge, 1978), pp. 85–8.
13. Anthony Pagden, *The fall of natural man* (Cambridge, 1986), chap. 5.
14. Manuela Carneiro da Cunha, 'Imagens de Índios no Século XVI', *Estudos Avançados*, 4:10 (1991), pp. 101–4. See also: Stephen Greenblatt, *Marvellous possessions: The wonder of the New World* (Oxford, 1992), p. 88; César Braga-Pinto, *As promessas da história*, pp. 27, 30, 42.
15. Pablo de Felipe, 'The antipodeans and science-faith relations: The rise, fall and vindication of Augustine,' in Karla Pollman and Meredith Gill (eds), *Augustine beyond the book: Intermediality, transmediality and reception* (Leiden, 2012), pp. 305–7.
16. João Adolfo Hansen, 'Vieira: Tempo, alegoria, história', *Broteria* 145 (1997), pp. 541–56. See also Erich Auerbach, 'Figura' in *Scenes from the drama of European literature* (Minneapolis, MN., 1984).

17. See Marcel Bataillon, 'Novo Mundo e fim do mundo', *Revista de História* 18 (1954), pp. 343–5.
18. An alternative theory, and a much contested one, stated that the Gentiles did not come from Adam, only the Jews. About the Pre-Adamite theory, see: Richard Popkin, *Isaac La Peyrère (1596–1676): His life, work, and influence* (Leiden, 1987), chap. 3.
19. Benjamin Braude, 'The sons of Noah and the construction of ethnic and geographical identities in the medieval and early modern periods', *William and Mary Quarterly*, 54:1 (1997), pp. 103–42. For a very thorough narrative and extensive consideration about the existent arguments of the Native Americans' dark colour in an early seventeenth-century source, see: Juan de Torquemada, *Segunda Parte de Los veinte i un libros rituales i Monarchia Indiana, con el origen y guerras de los Indios occidentales, de sus poblaçones, descubrimiento, conquista, conversion y otras cosas* Second edition (Madrid, 1723 [1st ed. 1615]), lib. 14, cap. XVIII–XIX, pp. 567–571.
20. The term 'Indians' here and throughout this text follows the original sources.
21. Manuel da Nóbrega, 'Diálogo da conversão do gentio' (1556-7) in *Cartas do Brasil e mais escritos do Manuel da Nóbrega (Opera Omnia)* (Coimbra, 1955), pp. 240–1 (in the original: 'Mais facil hé de converter hum ignorante do que hum malicioso e soberbo'). For decades after the 'Dialogue' and throughout the seventeenth century, this vision about the Brazilian Indians' easy conversion changed to a more sceptical and negative view. The Natives' soul rather than be described as a white sheet should be more accurately perceived as inconstant as the form of 'myrtle' bushes. About this discussion, see: Eduardo Viveiros de Castro, *A inconstância da alma do selvagem*, (São Paulo, 2002), ch. 3 (English translation: *The Inconstancy of the Indian Soul. The encounter of Catholics and cannibals in 16th-century Brazil* [Chicago, IL., 2011]). For a general view of the Brazilian slavery question and a comparative analysis of Nóbrega's Dialogue within the Jesuit mission debate in Brazil, see José Carlos Sebe Bom Meihy, 'A ética colonial e a questão jesuítica dos cativeiros índio e negro', *Afro-Ásia*, 23 (1999), pp. 7–25.
22. Antônio Vieira, *Defesa perante o tribunal do Santo Ofício*, edited by Hêrnani Cidade (Salvador, 1957) v. 1, 'Representação primeira', § 200 (p. 123, § 201, in Ana Paula Banza's Edition). (Original: 'Quanto mais que os livros apócrifos ou de incerta autoridade (que isso quer dizer apócrifos) nem por serem tais deixam de poder ter muitas verdades, como é doutrina recebida e praxi de todos os escritores que os alegam. E entre todos os livros apócrifos, nenhuns há de tão grande autoridade, como os de Esdras: e como tais andaram sempre (ao menos em muitas Bíblias) insertos com os outros do mesmo autor: e ainda depois do Concílio Tridentino não foram lançados fora do corpo ou tomo da Bíblia; que é o

maior sinal de respeito e veneração que pode ser. E por isso são os ditos livros alegados de muitos Padres, e a mesma Igreja tomou deles vários lugares para o canto e rezo eclesiástico: e o que é mais, S. João Evangelista no seu Apocalipse alude aos mesmos livros, como nota Cornélio Alápide nos Comentários do mesmo Apocalipse.')

23. Vieira, *Defesa*, 'Representação segunda', § 352–355.
24. See for a broader context of Ezra interpretations: Alastair Hamilton, *The apocryphal apocalypse: The reception of the Second Book of Esdras (4 Ezra) from the Renaissance to the Enlightenment* (Oxford, 1999). This discussion is based on chapter 9.
25. Antônio Vieira, *Defesa*, 'Representação segunda', §355.
26. See: Lee Eldridge Huddleston, *Origins of the American Indians: European concepts 1492–1729* (Austin, TX, 2015 [1967]), pp. 33–47; Florentino García Martínez, 'La Autoridad de 4 Esdras y el Origen Judío de los Indios Americanos', *Fortvnatae*, 22 (2011), pp. 41–54.
27. Diego Durán, 'Historia de las Indias de Nueva–España y islas de Tierra Firme', Vitr/26/11, f. 2v–3v, Biblioteca Nacional de España, http://bdh-rd.bne.es/viewer.vm?id=0000169486&page=1. Last accessed 11 November, 2014. For an English edition, see: Diego Durán, *The history of the Indies of New Spain*, trans. Doris Heyden (Norman, OK., 1994), pp. 4–5.
28. See Pagden, *Fall of Natural Man*, chap. 6.
29. Torquemada, *Monarchia Indiana*, 'Libro Primeiro', p. 24.
30. García Martínez, 'La autoridad de 4 Esdras y el origen Judió de los Indios Americanos', p. 52.
31. Huddleston, *Origins of the American Indians*, p. 34.
32. García Martínez, 'La Autoridad', pp. 45–6, 48, 51.
33. See: Richard H. Popkin, 'The rise and fall of the Jewish Indian theory' in Yosef Kaplan, Richard H. Popkin, Henry Méchoulan (ed), *Menasseh Ben Israel and His World* (Leiden, 1989), pp. 64–65.
34. Bartolomé de Las Casas, '(…) Veinte razones, por las cuales prueba no deberse das los indios a los españoles en encomienda ni en feudo ni en vasallaje ni de otra manera, si su Majestad, como desea, quiera librarlos de la tiranía y perdición que padecen (…)' in: 2nd Tome of *Tratados de Bartolomé de Las Casas* (Mexico, 1997), p. 647–667.
35. Bataillon, 'Novo mundo e fim de mundo', p. 346.
36. Daniel Castro, *Another face of empire: Bartolomé de Las Casas, indigenous rights, and ecclesiastical imperialism* (Durham, NC., 2007), p. 38.
37. On Mendieta's millenarianism, see John Leddy Phelan, *The millennial kingdom of the Franciscans in the New World* (Los Angeles, CA., 1970), 104–7 passim. For a critical view of Joachimite centrality, see: Josep I. Saranyana, Ana de Zaballa, *Joaquín de Fiore y América* (Pamplona,

1995); Ana de Zaballa, Josep I. Saranyana, 'La discusión sobre el joaquinismo novohispano en el siglo XV en la historiografla reciente', *Quinto centenario*, 16 (1990), pp. 173–89.
38. Gerónimo de Mendieta, *Historia eclesiástica indiana* (Alicante, 1999), Libro Cuarto, chap. XXI, XL, XLII, http://www.cervantesvirtual.com/servlet/SirveObras/12038305328923728654435/p0000004.htm. Last accessed 21 August 2015.
39. For similar coeval perceptions, but in Spain, see: Maria Jordan, *Soñar la historia. Vida y textos de Lucrecia de León en la España del Siglo de Oro* (Madrid, 2007).
40. Phelan, *The millennial kingdom*, p. 103.
41. For a general view on Acosta's works and remarks about the Natives, see: Pagden, *Fall of natural man*, chap. 7.
42. Cristina Pompa, 'O lugar da utopia: os jesuítas e a catequese indígena', *Novos Estudos (Cebrap)*, 64 (2002), pp. 84–90.
43. Acosta, *Historia*, b. 1, chap. XXIII.
44. Adriano Prosperi, 'America e apocalisse' in *America e apocalisse e altri saggi* (Pisa, 1999), pp. 16–18.
45. Prosperi, 'America e apocalisse', pp.17–18.
46. Michele Olivari, 'Milenarismo y política a fines del quinientos: notas sobre algunos complots y conjuras en la monarquía hispánica' in Adeline Rucquoi et. al (eds), *En pos del tercer milenio* (Salamanca, 1999), pp. 146–50. For a comprehensive yet brief account of the trial and a keen analysis of the importance of the case for the Jesuit order and its missionary activities, see: Stefania Pastore, 'Mozas Criollas and new Government: Francis Borgia, Prophetism, and the spiritual exercises in Spain and Peru', in Luís Filipe Silvério Lima and Ana Paula Torres Megiani (eds) *Visions, prophecies and divinations: Early modern messianism and millenarianism in Iberian America, Spain and Portugal* (Leiden and Boston, 2016), pp. 59–73. The trial proceedings were published in *Francisco de la Cruz, Inquisición, Actas* (Madrid, 1996).
47. Prosperi, 'America e apocalisse', p. 18.
48. The main study about the Santidade is still Ronaldo Vainfas' *Heresias dos Índios* Second Edition (São Paulo, 1995). An abridged version of his ideas can be read in Ronaldo Vainfas 'Do milenarismo idolátrico ao sabá tropical: a demonização das santidades brasílicas nos escritos jesuíticos' in Lucía Helena Costigan (ed.), *Diálogos da conversão* (Campinas, 2005), pp. 45–82.
49. Pompa, 'O lugar da utopia', pp. 83–85.
50. Bataillon, *Erasmo y la España* (Mexico City, 1996), chap. IV; Augusta E. Foley, 'El alumbradismo y sus posibles orígenes', in *Actas del VIII Congreso de la Associación Internacional de Hispanistas* 1 (1983) pp. 527–32.
51. Sarah Nalle, 'El Encubierto revisited: Navigating between visions of Heaven and Hell on earth', in Kathryn A. Edwards (ed.), *Werewolves,*

witches, and wandering spirits (Kirksville, Mo., 2002), pp. 77–92, Sarah Nalle, 'The millennial moment: Revolution and radical religion in sixteenth-century Spain', in Peter Schäfer and Mark Cohens (eds), *Toward the Millennium: Messianic expectations from the Bible to Waco* (Leiden, 1998), pp. 153–73; Ricardo Garcia Cárcel, 'Las Germanias de Valencia y la actitud revolucionária de los Gremios', *Estudis*, 2 (1973), pp. 97–154; Pablo Pérez García and Jorge Antonio Catalá Sanz, *Epígonos del encubertismo. Proceso contra los agermanados de 1541* (Valencia, 2000).
52. Nalle, 'The millennial moment'; Alain Milhou, 'Panorama de la prophétie messianique en Espagne (1482–1614)' in Augustin Redondo (ed.), *La prophétie comme arme de guerre des pouvoirs, XVe–XVIIe siècles* (Paris, 2001).
53. Milhou, 'Panorama de la prophétie messianique en Espagne', p. 22. For Lucrezia and Piedrola cases, see: Jordan, *Soñar la historia*; Richard Kagan, *Lucrecia's Dreams. Politics and prophecy in sixteenth-century Spain* (Los Angeles, CA, 2011).
54. This was only ended by the 1640 insurrection of the Portuguese nobles against the rule of Philip III of Portugal, IV of Spain, grandson of Philip II, in favour of the Duke of Braganza, the future John IV
55. For a general view, see: Anthony Pagden, *Lords of all the world: Ideologies of empire in Spain, Britain and France c.1500–c.1800* (New Haven, CT, 1998).
56. Serge Gruzinski, 'From *The Matrix* to Campanella: cultural hybrids and globalization', *European Review*, 14:1 (2006), p. 121; Serge Gruzinski, *Las cuatro partes del mundo* (Mexico City, 2010), 'Epílogo'; Olivari, 'Milenarismo y politica a fines del quinientos'. We will now roughly follow Gruzinski's and Olivari's arguments, also in our selection of La Cruz, Campanella and Sebastianism as a messianic response developed within the imperial and millenarian projects of the Hapsburgs.
57. Olivari, 'Milenarismo', pp. 138–9.
58. Gruzinski, 'From *The Matrix* to Campanella', p. 120; Vainfas, *Heresia dos índios*.
59. Olivari, 'Milenarismo', pp. 150–2.
60. John A. Marino, 'An anti-campanellan vision of the Spanish Monarchy and the crisis of 1595', in John A. Marino and Thomas Kuehn (eds), *A Renaissance of conflicts: visions and revisions of law and society in Italy and Spain* (Toronto, 2004), pp. 367–94.
61. Juan de Salazar, *Politica Española* (Logroño, 1619); Martim de Albuquerque, *Campanella e Portugal.* (Lisbon, 2009), p. 50.
62. Luigi Firpo, *Bibliografia degli scritti di Tommaso Campanella* (Turin, 1940) pp. 56–67; Luigi Guerrini, 'Schede delle antiche stampe campanelliane e della biografia di Cyprianus', in Eugenio Canone (ed.), *Tommaso Campanella. L'iconografia, le opere e la fortuna della «Città del Sole»* (Milan, 2001), pp. 43–4.

63. Tommaso Campanella, *A discourse touching the Spanish monarchy*, (London, [1653]).
64. *The plots of Jesuites: (viz. of Robert Parsons an English-man, Adam Contzen a Moguntine, Tho. Campanella a Spaniard, &c.) how to bring England to the Romane religion without tumult. Translated out of the original copies* (London, 1653).
65. Tommaso Campanella, *Thomas Campanella an Italian friar and second Machiavel. His advice to the King of Spain for attaining the universal monarchy of the world. (...) With an admonitorie preface by William Prynne of Lincolnes-Inne, Esquire* (London, 1660).
66. For an overview, the reference work is still João Lucio de Azevedo, *A evolução do Sebastianismo* (Lisbon, 1918).
67. For the battle and its developments, see: Lucette Valensi, *Fables de la mémoire : la glorieuse bataille des trois rois* (Paris, 1992).
68. For the fake Sebastian cases, see, among others: Jacqueline Hermann, *No reino do desejado* (São Paulo: Companhia das Letras, 1999), chap. 5; Eric Olsen, *The Calabrian charlatan, 1580–1603: Messianic nationalism in early modern Europe* (New York, 2003); Ruth Mackay, *The baker who pretended to be King of Portugal* (Chicago, IL 2012).
69. Hermann, *No Reino do Desejado*, pp. 189–207; João Carlos Serafim, 'João de Castro, "O sebastianista"' (Unpublished PhD Thesis, FLUP, 2004).
70. Gonçalo Annes Bandarra, *Trovas do Bandarra* (Nantes, 1644), pp. 49, 54, 56, 63.
71. See: Maria Ferro Tavares, 'O messianismo judaico em Portugal (la metade do seculo XVI)'. *Luso-Brazilian Review*, 28 (1991), pp. 141–51.
72. 'Processo de Gonçalo Annes Bandarra' IAN/TT, Inq. Lisbon, proc. n. 7197, pasta 8 (facsimile edition in: Arnaldo da Soledade (ed.), *Processo de Gonçalo Annes Bandarra* [Trancoso, 1996]); Jesus Martinez de Bujanda, *Index de l'Inquisition portugaise: 1547, 1551, 1561, 1564, 158* (Quebec, 1995), pp. 501, 680.
73. Juan de Horozco y Covarrubias, *Tratado de la Verdadera e falsa prophecia* (Segovia, 1588), pp. 38–9; Capistrano de Abreu (ed.), *Primeira Visitação Santo Officio ás Partes do Brasil* (São Paulo, 1925), pp. 317–9. See also: Jacqueline Hermann, 'O sebastianismo atravessa o Atlântico: análise de um documento da primeira visitação do Santo Ofício no Brasil' In: *49 CONGRESSO INTERNACIONAL DEL AMERICANISTAS (ICA)* (Ecuador, 1997), http://www.equiponaya.com.ar/congresos/contenido/49CAI/Hermann.htm. Last accessed 3 September 2015.
74. João de Castro, *Paraphrase et concordancia de Algvas Propheçias de Bandarra, çapateiro de Trancoso*, [1603] facsimile ed. (Porto, 1942).
75. Carlos Coelho Maurício, 'Entre o silêncio e o ouro – sondando o milagre de Ourique na cultura Portuguesa', *Ler História*, 20 (1990); Luís Filipe Silvério Lima, *Império dos sonhos* (São Paulo, 2010), chap. 3.

76. See, for example, his *Aurora da Quinta Monarquia*, ed. João Carlos Serafim (Porto, 2011).
77. Hermann, *No reino do Desejado*, p. 219.
78. Cf. Reinhardt Koselleck, *Futuro passado* (Rio de Janeiro, 2006), pp. 29, 32, 57, 315–6.
79. David Armitage 'The Cromwellian protectorate and the languages of empire', *The Historical Journal*, 35:3 (1992), pp. 531–55; Geoffrey Parker, 'The place of Tudor England in the messianic vision of Philip II of Spain', *Transactions of the Royal Historical Society*, 12 (2002), pp. 167–221. Cf. Arthur H. Williamson, 'An Empire to end empire: The dynamic of early modern British expansion', *Huntington Library Quarterly*, 68 (2005), pp. 227–56.
80. Eduardo d'Oliveira França, *Portugal na época da Restauração* (São Paulo, 1997), pt. 3, chap. 1; Lauri Tähtinen, 'The intellectual construction of the Fifth Empire: Legitimating the Braganza restoration', *History of European Ideas* 38:3 (2012), pp. 413–25
81. See Luís Reis Torgal, *Ideologia política e teoria do Estado na Restauração* (Coimbra, 1981–1982), 2v.
82. António José Saraiva, 'António Vieira, Menasseh ben Israel e o Quinto Império' in *História e utopia* (Lisbon, 1992), pp. 75–107; Natalia Muchnik, 'Antonio Vieira y la diáspora sefardí en el siglo XVII' in Pedro Cardim and Gaetano Sabatini (eds), *António Vieira, Roma e o Universalismo das Monarquias Portuguesa e Espanhola* (Lisbon, 2011), pp. 97–120.
83. Alcir Pécora, 'Vieira, a inquisição e o capital', *Topoi*, 1 (2000), pp. 189–193.
84. Antonio Vieira 'Papel que fez o Padre Antonio Vieira a favor da entrega de Pernambuco aos Holandeses (Papel Forte)' [1648] in Alcir Pécora (ed.), *Escritos Históricos e Políticos* (São Paulo, 1995).
85. For a broader view of Vieira's theory of Fifth Empire within the apocalyptical tradition, see Maria Ana Valdez, *Historical interpretations of the 'fifth empire'* (Leiden, 2011). About the differences between the concepts 'Fifth Monarchy' and 'Fifth Empire' in early modern Portuguese messianism, see: Luís Filipe Silvério Lima, *Império dos Sonhos: Narrativas Oníricas, Sebastianismo e Messianismo Brigantino* (São Paulo, 2010), chap. 5.
86. Adma Muhana, 'O processo inquisitorial de Vieira: aspectos profético-argumentativos' *Semear*, 2 (1997). For an edition of the letter and the trial proceedings, see *Autos do processo de Vieira*, edited by Adma Muhana (São Paulo, 2008).
87. Pompa, 'O lugar da utopia', 87–8; Thomas Cohen, 'Millenarian themes in the writing of Antonio Vieira', *Luso-Brazilian Review*, 28 (1991); Thomas Cohen, *The fire of tongues: Antônio Vieira and the missionary church in Brazil and Portugal* (Stanford, 1998).
88. Luisa Trias Folch considers Mendieta an exponent of the late medieval millenarian desires and expectations which were fulfilled with the discovery of

the New World and the spread of the gospel for natives. Hence she sees Mendieta as an exponent (and survival) of late medieval and Iberian Joachimism then translated into an American millennial project. The Joachimite vision had an Iberian interpretation, which was the base of Portuguese messianism, even in Brazil, as in Vieira's case. Although uniting them in the same Iberian Joachimite tradition, she separates Vieira's Fifth Empire from Mendieta's millennial kingdom, stating that the difference between them is mainly because of Vieira's patriotism. I tend to disagree. Luisa Trias Folch, 'El Joaquinismo en el Nuevo Mundo: Jerónimo de Mendieta y Antonio Vieira' in Juan Paredes (ed.), *Medievo y literatura. Actas del V Congreso de la Asociación Hispánica de Literatura Medieval* (Granada, 1995), vol. IV.

89. Robert Ricard, "Antonio Vieira y Sor Juana Inés de la Cruz", *Revista de Indias*, 11, 43–44 (1951), pp. 61–87; Luisa Trias Folch, 'A obra do Padre António Vieira em Espanha', *Oceanos*, 30/31 (1997), pp. 82–8; Luisa Trias Folch, 'Novos documentos sobre a controvérsia de Sor Juana Inés de la Cruz e o padre António Vieira' *Limite*, 5 (2011), pp. 75–89.

90. Anselmo Caetano Castello-Branco, *Ennoea ou aplicação do entendimento sobre a pedra filosofal*, [1732] facsimile ed. (Lisbon, 1987).

91. Most of the information about Henequim is in his trial: 'Processo de Pedro de Rates Henequim', IAN/TT, Inq. Lisbon, proc. n. 4864, http://digitarq.dgarq.gov.pt/details?id=2304862. Accessed 15 January 2015. The Holy Office sentence, along with a study of the case, was published in: Pedro Vilas-Boas Tavares, *Pedro Henequim. Proto-mártir da separação (1744)* (Lisbon, 2011), pp. 73–119. Part of his writings were edited by Plinio Gomes Freire in his book, *Um herege vai ao Paraíso* (São Paulo, 1997), pp. 154–71. The definitive study is still: Adriana Romeiro, *Um visionário na corte de D. João V: Milenarismo e revoltas nas Minas setecentistas* (Belo Horizonte, 2001).

92. See Pedro Vilas-Boas Tavares, *Pedro Henequim*.

93. See Plinio Gomes Freire, *Um Herege vai ao Paraíso*.

94. Sérgio Buarque de Holanda, *Visão do paraíso*.

95. Phelan, *The millennial kingdom*, pp. 104–7.

96. I disagree with Popkin and Katz who affirmed that prophetic thought and movements diminished in the Iberian Peninsula after a peek with the discovery of America and a renaissance of the philo-semitic enviroment, due to decades of Inquisition, Jewish persecution and Tridentine orthodoxy. David S. Katz and Richard H. Popkin, *Messianic revolution* (New York, 1999).

CHAPTER 3

Left Behind: George Herbert, Eschatology, and the Stuart Atlantic, 1606–1634

John Kuhn

> *I have always observed the thread of life to be like other threads or skeins of silk, full of snarles and incumbrances. Happy is he, whose bottom is wound up, and laid ready for work in the New Jerusalem.*
>
> George Herbert, letter to Magdalen Herbert, 1622[1]

The poet and divine George Herbert wrote this letter to his mother, thanking her for a previous communication that brought him 'earthly preferment'. Though it is unclear what favour Herbert is referring to (there are a number of possibilities, including his selection as Cambridge University Orator in 1620), the letter has a tone of twinned disappointment and gratitude, as the writer expresses his desire to 'change' whatever favour he has received for the opportunity to engage in actual 'work in the New Jerusalem'. Though it would be easy to read this passage as simply a metaphoric elevation of heavenly concerns over earthly ones, this chapter will suggest instead that Herbert's desire to work in 'New Jerusalem' was anything but figurative. New Jerusalem—the city in which the godly would reign on earth for a thousand years—was a practical goal for many

---

J. Kuhn (✉)
Department of English, Columbia University, New York, NY, USA
e-mail: jmk2187@columbia.edu

© The Author(s) 2016
A. Crome (ed.), *Prophecy and Eschatology in the Transatlantic World, 1550–1800*, Christianities in the Trans-Atlantic World, 1500–1800,
DOI 10.1057/978-1-137-52055-5_3

of Herbert's Protestant contemporaries in Caroline England, a literal interpretation of scripture that was fuelled by the widespread suggestion that the New World of the English colonies might eventually be the site of the new world of the godly.

By suggesting this, I hope to re-contextualise Herbert's writings, particularly his long and critically-neglected apocalyptic poem 'The Church Militant', amid a stew of millenarian and colonial interests that were emerging in England in the 1620s and 1630s. The poem's publication helped further stir an already-fevered debate among colonists, theologians, and lawmakers over the respective roles that would be played by England and its colonies in the eagerly anticipated end-times. These early readings of Herbert's poem were largely citational and fragmentary, anticipating the modern critical tendency for reading portions of the poem for polemical content rather than attending to the whole. I argue that Herbert's apocalypticism is both more pessimistic and less sectarian than these local, polemical readings of it by both early modern zealots and modern critics might suggest. Herbert's poetry rejects sectarian models of millennial geography, asking us instead to imagine the condition of being 'left behind' as God's moving mandate abandons religious institutions. Herbert relies on two types of speaker to explore this experience of abandonment: the Jew, an exemplar for him of a religious culture that has survived past its divine mandate, and the elegiac speaker, who appears in 'Church-rents and Schisms' and Herbert's elegies for his mother. In these poems, Herbert attempts to develop a lyric vocabulary for the experience of apocalyptic abandonment or loss, an ambitious generic experiment that fuses eschatological doubt with elegy in an attempt to mourn, so to speak, the missed boat of apocalyptic history.

Scholars have long been uncomfortable with 'The Church Militant', the extended verse history of the rise and fall of national churches that concludes Herbert's posthumously published magnum opus *The Temple*. A series of editors have characterised the poem as an 'early' or immature work; Herbert's nineteenth-century editor Alexander Grosart underscored this characterisation by physically separating 'The Church Militant' from 'The Church Porch' and 'The Church' and placing it in another volume, alongside Herbert's earlier Latin poetry. Other editors, though they have not physically separated the text as Grosart did, have nonetheless still gone out of their way to characterise it as juvenilia. F.E. Hutchinson, a major twentieth-century editor of the works, noted that the poem's 'anti-Roman animus is characteristic of Herbert's early and more controversial mind'.[2] Even the most recent collected edition of Herbert's poems, magisterially edited by Helen Wilcox, notes of the poem that 'like *The Church Porch*, it is an early poem that underwent significant revision'.³ One scholar has even gone so far as to characterise the poem as entirely unrelated to *The Temple*, as a mere 'earlier work included there [at the end] for convenience' by an editorial hand rather than by Herbert himself.⁴

Despite the frequent scholarly characterisation of Herbert's poem as 'early' relative to the rest of his work, little hard evidence exists to support this claim. Wilcox cites its inclusion in the Williams manuscript of Herbert's poetry as evidence of its early composition, though all attempts to date that manuscript—sometimes characterised as an 'early draft' of *The Temple*—have proven fruitless.⁵ Beyond this and some vague internal references to Spain and France that could have been produced at any time during the early seventeenth century, the most common piece of evidence offered by scholars for dating 'The Church Militant' is that the adult Herbert would not indulge in controversy or polemic. This justification derives from a desire to see Herbert's career as progressing from a concern with the this-worldly politics of religious controversy into a saintly 'maturity' characterised by retreat, moderation, and the internal scrutiny of 'heart-work'. This tendency is subtly visible in Wilcox's recent edition: though she goes out of the way to designate 'The Church Militant' as an early poem, she does not characterise other, more introspective poems that also appear in the Williams manuscript as juvenilia, like 'Love (III)', the Anglican lyric *par excellence*.⁶

But although the poem has been marginalised as immature work in modern accounts of Herbert's writing and religious thought because of its engagement with polemic, evidence of its seventeenth-century reception suggests that it was one of Herbert's most popular works and that contemporary readers valued the poem for precisely the polemic engagements with religious politics that have troubled later editors. Robert Ray has shown that only 'The Church Porch' was more often quoted than 'The Church Militant' by Herbert's seventeenth-century readers.⁷ Likewise, Henry Vaughan, in his introduction to *The Mount of Olives* (1652), described Herbert as skilled at writing 'incomparable prophetick Poems', citing 'The Church Militant', 'Church-rents and schismes', and 'Church Musick' as exceptional examples of this 'prophetick' vein.⁸ Vaughan's list of poems shows us how at least one seventeenth-century reader valued Herbert for his future-oriented writing about church history, rather than for the more meditative, inward-looking lyrics so prized by contemporary scholars.

'The Church Militant' offered readers like Vaughan a sweeping vision of the history of the 'true church' from its inception to its apocalyptic future, a history that was satisfyingly full of polemic content. The poem, though its first two sections chart the move of 'true religion' as it creeps west, shifts to a discussion of how religion's progress has been dogged by 'Sin', which moves behind and gradually replaces her, bringing the polytheistic/animist worship of 'gardens of Gods' (108) to Egypt; shrines, oracles, and seductive but empty poetry to Greece (124–138); and an obsession with 'glorie' (temporal power) and 'pleasure' (140–150) to Rome. The fourth section deals extensively with the arrival of Sin in Rome, and the fifth section claims similar corruption has begun to work inside the English church, predicting that God's presence in it 'shall ev'ry yeare decrease and fade' (229): a pronouncement that, in the Williams manuscript version, is rendered even more pessimistically as 'ev'ry day'. The poem goes on to make the inflammatory claim that 'religion stands on tip-toe in our land/Ready to pass to the American strand' (235–236), before narrating the future progress of religion westward around the globe until it reaches its original site in Jerusalem.

The arguments about the Atlantic colonies made in 'The Church Militant' must be understood in two linked but distinct transatlantic contexts. Herbert's millenarian ideas almost certainly *initially* emerged from his childhood exposure to the Virginia Company. As Beth Quitslund has shown, the Company deployed stridently millenarian rhetoric in the first decades of the seventeenth century, connecting a promised colonial emphasis on the conversion of Native Americans to the coming millennium in the slew of sermons and pamphlets they produced for English audiences.[9] The young Herbert would have been exposed to this rhetoric through his family's tight links to the more 'godly' members of the Virginia Company. Herbert's mother Magdalen invested heavily in the organisation and in 1608, when George was fifteen, she married Sir John Danvers, another prominent investor and close friend of George Sandys, the leader of the Company's so-called 'godly' faction. The Herbert family had close ties to other members of the Virginia Company as well, including John Ferrar, his brother Nicholas, and Arthur Woodenoth, all of whom continued to be involved in colonial ventures even after the Company's dissolution in 1624.[10] George kept these contacts throughout his life; on his deathbed he entrusted the manuscript of *The Country Parson* to Wodenoth and that of *The Temple* to Nicholas Ferrar. The Ferrars, particularly, seem to have been both tightly connected to the Herberts and specifically invested in the colony as a conversion mission. Nicholas Ferrar Sr's will, executed in 1619, sets aside the exorbitant amount of 300 pounds for the construction and maintenance of a 'College' 'for the conversion of infidels' children unto Christian religion' in Virginia.[11]

But the Virginia Company collapsed in 1624, well before the print publication of *The Temple*, and though Herbert's ideas about the New World and its role in the coming millennium may have emerged originally out of a familial commitment to the conversion of natives in Virginia in the first decade of the century, his work would be read in a different Atlantic context by the time of his death and *The Temple*'s publication in 1633. Three responses to Herbert's poem, all written in 1634, testify that a later generation of readers understood the 'The Church Militant' as part of a new debate about the relationship between separatist Atlantic Puritanism and the coming apocalypse. Published just years after the formation of the Massachusetts Bay Colony and at the height of English fears about the consequences of Puritan separatism and Atlantic migration, 'The Church Militant' exemplified a particular polemic position for its early readers: that the Church of England was theologically bankrupt and that the Puritan migration to America was a necessary step in the establishment of New Jerusalem and the ushering in of the millennium.

The Temple immediately raised hackles in the Church of England because of the colonial material in 'The Church Militant'. Izaak Walton tells us in his *Life of Herbert* that the 'two so much noted Verses' containing the 'tiptoe' section about the flight of true religion from England were censored by the ecclesiastical licenser at Cambridge during *The Temple*'s printing.[12] These 'much noted' verses seem to have perfectly encapsulated the threat posed by separatism and migration for church officials, and they would crop up again, just months later, in an ecclesiastical inquest aimed at the separatist minister Samuel Ward, who preached at Ipswich, the biggest port of embarkation for New England-bound Puritans. Samuel's brother Nathaniel—a figure who has become well known to scholars of early America as an important lawmaker and clergyman in Massachusetts—was excommunicated by Laud in 1631 and had left England for New England in 1633. In 1634, Samuel would also come under fire from English ecclesiastical authorities, when he was brought before Laud and charged with 43 articles that ranged from small doctrinal irregularities to the larger issue of inciting separatism and migration in his ministry. The questions that the court asked Ward are not extant, but his responses to the inquest do survive, and they record that the separatist minister 'expressly sayd he was not of soe melancholly a spiritt, nor looked throughe soe blacke spectacles as he that wrote that Religion stands on the Tiptoe in this land, looking westwards nor feared their feare that feared an imminent departure of the Gospell'.[13] Ward here seems to be responding to a question containing a direct citation of Herbert's 'The Church Militant', and his response shows him attempting to distance himself from the 'melancholly' belief that 'Religion stands ...Tiptoe' ready to leave England. In doing so, the court and Ward both posthumously portray Herbert as a 'melancholly' spirit who believes God's divine mandate has already left England, describing the poet's ideas as one cause for the ongoing migration of separatist Puritans westward.

Another ecclesiastical figure would engage at length with Herbert's ideas in the context of transatlantic Puritan separatism in 1634: Joseph Mede, who was a Hebraist and Biblical scholar working at Christ's College, Cambridge from 1603 to 1638, a period of time coincident with Herbert's tenure at Trinity (1609–1628). Mede was well known and respected for his forays into Biblical exegesis, particularly his examinations of the apocalyptic books of Daniel and Revelation. First published in 1627, though probably circulated privately much earlier, his *Clavis Apocalyptica* went into two Latin editions and an English translation before 1650, and established him as the leading millenarian thinker of his day.[14] In 1634, Mede's friend and frequent correspondent William Twisse wrote to the theologian asking for clarification about the role of Puritan separatism in the coming apocalypse. Twisse tells Mede that he had formerly wondered why the 'English Plantations' may not 'be the place of New Jerusalem', considering the 'opinion of many grave divines concerning the Gospel's fleeting Westward'. Twisse does not directly cite Herbert in the manner of the Ward trial, but there are suggestive parallels in phrasing between his description of the church 'fleeting westward' and Herbert's text, which describes the church's continual tendency to 'westward flie' and predicts that 'then shall Religion to America flee' (271, 283). Far from subscribing to these ideas, however, Twisse claims to be 'handsomely and fully clear'd' of such 'odd conceits' by Mede, but still wonders what the fate of the colony will be, asking if Mede believes that the American colonists will 'degenerate' and join themselves with 'Gog and Magog' (the armies of Satan, which Mede, in *Clavis*, had predicted would arise in the New World). Mede's response is lengthy and telling:

> And where did the Devil ever reign more *absolutely* and without controll, since mankind fell first under his clutches? And here it is to be noted, that the story of the *Mexican* Kingdom (which was not founded above 400 years before ours came thither) relates out of their own memorials and traditions, that they came to that place from the *North*; whence their God *Vitzliliputzli* led them, going in an *Ark* before them: and after divers years travel and

many stations (like enough after some generations) they came to the place which the Sign he had given them at their first setting forth pointed out, where they were to finish their travels, build themselves a City, and their God a Temple; which is the place where *Mexico* was built. Now if the Devil were God's ape in this; why might he not be so likewise in bringing the first Colony of men into that world out of ours?[15]

Mede, here and elsewhere, posits that the natives were led to America by the Devil in his bid to create a kingdom that would compete against Christ's. He cites Mexican history (here, he seems to be drawing on José Acosta's description, in *La Historia Natural y Moral de las Indias*, of the natives' inability to mark past time beyond 400 years), claiming that they received a 'sign' from Satan to build themselves a 'city, and their God a Temple'.[16] Though Mede subsequently suggests that the English colonial project will perhaps productively strip away worshippers from Satan, he also worries that settlers might 'degenerate ... as to come in that Army of Gog and Magog against the Kingdom of Christ'. Here, Mede dodges the question of the location of New Jerusalem, but decisively denies that it is located in New England, praying instead that the colonists be 'translated thither' (that is, back to the 'Kingdom of Christ' *from* America) before the 'Devil be loosed'.[17]

Herbert's poem would be posthumously deployed in yet another spat about Atlantic Puritan separatism in 1634, as we can see in a unique manuscript translation of 'The Church Militant' into Latin that currently resides at the Durham Cathedral Library. The document, dated 1634, was prepared by a Cambridge undergraduate named Jacob Leeke and is fulsomely dedicated to John Coke, one of Charles I's Privy Councillors. Coke was in the process of adjudicating a messy challenge to the Massachusetts Bay Colony's charter in the early and mid-1630s by a group of non-Puritan settlers who sought to break the colony's hold on the region. Seeking royal intervention, the group attacked the Massachusetts Bay Colony in England by emphasising their separatist religious tendencies and especially the heterodoxy of their millenarian beliefs.[18] Emmanuel Downing, a spokesman for the Massachusetts colony and John Winthrop's cousin, would carefully rebut these charges in a letter to John Coke, in which he emphasised that the colony's primary mission was the conversion of Native Americans, 'that the fulnes of the Gentiles might come in before the Jewes shalbe recalled'.[19] Downing provides a soothing countervision to rumours of millenarian separatism, one in which the English church expands across two continents without snapping, and New and old England work together to bring in a transatlantic New Jerusalem.[20] Downing's letter was just one part of a deluge of petitions, correspondence, and publications generated by the charter controversy, many of which were aimed directly at John Coke, and the presence of a custom-dedicated translation of 'The Church Militant' amongst these documents suggests that Herbert's poem had become entangled in another argument about Puritan colonial separatism and the apocalypse, though the precise political goals of the translation are difficult to discern.

These immediate posthumous uses of Herbert show us that early readers of the poet saw 'The Church Militant' as primarily a sectarian volley, a rejection of the Church of England in favour of an embrace of New-World-bound 'hot' Protestantism. These readings are narrowly citational, focusing on the 'tip-toe' lines (Ward) or the description of the church 'fleeting Westward' from England (Twisse) and isolating this episode from the larger poem. The small handful of modern scholars who have attended to the 'The Church Militant' at all have often followed in the footsteps of these early modern readers, focusing on small parts of the poem, typically Herbert's indictment of Catholicism or his prediction of religion's flight to America. These scholars cite these passages as proof of Herbert's attitudes toward specific devotional or colonial organisations without contextualising these bits as part of the poem's broader structure.[21] I will suggest that both early sectarian readers and modern commentators on 'The Church Militant' have underestimated the poem's pessimism about institutional religion writ large, overlooking, in the process, Herbert's most interesting aesthetic contributions to seventeenth-century arguments about the progress of the true church toward the millennium. The final poem of *The Temple* offers us not a triumphal story of the Atlantic Puritan mission but a darker vision of history, almost antinomian in its tenor, in which all individuals must eventually come to grips with the slow drip of God's divine mandate out of the ephemeral corporate religious bodies they occupy.

It is easy to see why 'The Church Militant' has been interpreted as a document of conventional polemic: its opening account of the regions east of England would be, for Herbert's readers, a fairly standard narrative of election, one that cast the Protestant church as the true inheritor and *telos* of the Christian tradition, Judaism, and the Catholic Church as having lost their divine mandate. But the poem eventually veers away from this history, shifting from its critique of Catholicism in order to devote significant time describing the moral bankruptcy of the English church, a critique that, as Sidney Gottlieb has shown, was sharp enough in the manuscript versions to require softening in the published version of *The Temple*.[22] In Herbert's words:

> The second Temple could not reach the first:
> And the late reformation never durst
> Compare with ancient times and purer yeares;
> But in the Jews and us deserveth tears.
> Nay, it shall ev'ry yeare decrease and fade;
> Till such a darknesse do the world invade
> At Christs last coming, as his first did finde: (225–231)

The reference to the failure of the 'late reformation' brings Herbert's satire home to seventeenth-century England, and the use of the first-person plural pronoun evokes the moment of *The Temple*'s publication itself. The 'second Temple' refers here not just to the English church, but to Herbert's volume itself, and it serves to confront readers who have just moved through the portions of the collection that model the physical manifestations of the church ('The Church-Porch' and 'The Church') with the despairing recognition of the ultimate inadequacy of the material and organisational instantiations of English religion. Herbert articulates, in the collection's final poem, a recognition that the objects of Laudian worship—stained glass windows, marble floors—and Herbert's own celebratory paeans to their lovely materiality are, in the end, merely insufficient or transient forms that shall 'decrease and fade'.

The poem subsequently argues that God's mandate has migrated to the New World. In Herbert's vision of the *immediate* future of the godly church, she flees England for America. Yet, the poem is quick to reject the colonial landscape as the ultimate location of New Jerusalem:

> Yet as the Church shall thither westward flie,
> So Sinne shall trace and dog her instantly:
> They have their period also and set times
> Both for their vertuous actions and their crimes.
> And where of old the Empire and the Arts
> Usher'd the Gospel ever in mens hearts,
> Spain hath done one; when Arts perform the other,
> The Church shall come, & Sinne the Church shall smother: (259–266)

The imminent arrival of 'Empire and Arts' in America and the conversion they entail is here described in language perhaps linked to the Ferrars. Herbert's separation of 'Arts' from the 'Gospel' indicates that he is speaking here of the role of secular education in the new colony, perhaps the 'College' at Henrico so generously supported by Nicholas Sr. But the poem, though it paints this effort as an immediate gain for America (who, after all, would not want to be in the new historical location of the sunshine of 'true religion'?), reminds the reader that 'Sinne' will 'trace and dog' the progress of conversion, ultimately consuming the colonies just as it has England. The final lines of the poem depict Sin and the church proceeding westward until they, paradoxically, arrive in the east at their 'first and ancient sound', the site of Old Jerusalem (268).[23] This moment in the poem, crucially, is *not* allied with a national or religious organisation; Sin has moved through and beyond the Americas, and no other worldly church or sect is mentioned in connection with the final arrival of the apocalypse.

There are two ways to read this vision of the loss of God's mandate by a series of religious institutions. Raymond Anselment has argued for an optimistic reading, characterising Herbert's vision of history as broadly Augustinian, and claiming that a 'devout seventeenth-century Anglican can accept the flight of religion from his own nation as well as from others, because he finds a more fundamental meaning in the passage of time ... Although glimmerings of its apostolic purity appear to shine in some areas, the essence can only be preserved in the universal church.'[24] But Anselment's assessment of the poem, which tacitly approves of and emphasises this 'universalism', ignores the darker affects of despair and abandonment that are generated by this bankruptcy of faith in individual religious organisations and which seem to have fascinated Herbert. 'The Church Militant' teasingly enumerates the successive triumph of religious organisations, leading its reader to hope for a satisfyingly sectarian or polemical conclusion (one that many seventeenth-century and contemporary readers, as we have seen, have happily found by segmenting the poem and citing it in fragments). But Herbert's poem focuses the bulk of its narrative not on these local triumphs or, indeed, the triumphant transcendence of a universal church, but rather on the progressive, ever-encroaching experience of being left behind.

Throughout his works, Herbert urges his readers to identify with the figure of the Jew as the exemplar of the experience of divine abandonment, explicitly inviting the implied English (or colonial) reader to understand the Jewish experience as a version of the church's immediate future. 'The Church Militant' cites Ezra 3:12, in which older Jews wept to see the diminishment of the second temple upon its construction.

That 'the second Temple could not reach the first' merits tears from *both* 'the Jews and us', an exhortation that conflates the Jewish and English experience of loss. 'The Church Militant' thus links the undoing of the material and organisational practices of the English church to the destruction of Jerusalem and the exodus of the Jews, a movement echoed in the poem by the Protestant diaspora westward. The exhibition of the Jews as a reminder of the contingency of divine approval crops up elsewhere in Herbert's works, including in his pastoral manual *A Priest to the Temple*, where the Jews appear as God's 'proof', a leftover people doomed to wander the earth for the 'exciting of others', a sign that God's grace can and will abandon religious organisations.[25]

This comparison is also made in the first stanza of Herbert's short poem 'The Jews', one of the lyrics in 'The Church' section of *The Temple*:

> Poore nation, whose sweet sap and juice
> Our cyens have purloin'd, and left you drie:
> Whose streams we got by the Apostles sluce,
> And use in baptisme, while ye pine and die:
> Who by not keeping once, became a debter;
> And now by keeping lose the letter: (1–6)

Commentators have linked this poem to the broader millennial enthusiasm for Jewish conversion and readmission projects in the mid-seventeenth century, but Herbert attempts something different here, focusing not on future Jewish conversion (widely believed to be a precondition of the millennium) but instead dwelling on their experience of abandonment.[26] The history related in 'The Jews' resembles that found in 'The Church Militant', where true religion moves slowly from nation to nation, 'letting, while one foot stept, the other stay'. In the latter poem, this slow, graded transition is imagined as the slowly growing and fading light of a moving sun, which lingers and 'listens behind him, and allows some light, till all depart'. The imagery used to represent the process of divine abandonment in 'The Jews' shares an emphasis on slow, graded transitions. The poem first likens the loss of God's grace to a host being slowly sucked 'drie' by a new-grafted shoot. The poem immediately turns to a second image of slow drainage to describe this process, imagining it as a river that is drained gradually by the 'sluice' of the Apostles. Reading 'The Jews' alongside 'The Church Militant', we can see Herbert describing the historical experience of the loss of divine grace in ways that suggestively link the affective experience of Jewish abandonment to the immediate future condition of Herbert's English readership.

Elsewhere in *The Temple*, Herbert turns to another formal strategy to express the emotional intensity of apocalyptic loss, drawing on the generic resources of elegy. The short poem 'Church rents and schisms', which Henry Vaughan linked to 'The Church Militant' as another example of 'prophetick' Herbert, deals with the same issues of divine abandonment as the longer poem. But rather than couching this experience of loss in the epic sweep of historical narrative, Herbert here registers eschatological doubt through the more immediate and personal conventions of elegy. The poem opens with the speaker addressing a 'brave rose' that 'didst lately so triumph and shine', but has since vanished, consumed by a 'worm' (2). The vision of the worm-eaten rose gives way to a consideration as to whether this prophetic vision applies to the English church. Addressing the church as 'my Mother', the speaker initially doubts whether this figure applies to the church, before concluding in despair that she, like the rose, has already been 'unloosed' and destroyed by 'schisms and rents'.

Stanza three extends this metaphor in a way that turns this seemingly simple satire of church problems into a mournful meditation on the role of the Atlantic in apocalyptic history. New, more severe internal discords within the rose/church result in her dissolution and death:

> Then did your sev'rall parts unloose and start:
> Which when your neighbours saw, like a north-winde,
> They rushed in, and cast them in the dirt
> Where Pagans tread. (20–24)

The rose dissolves into unspecified 'parts', which are tossed 'by the north-winde' into 'the dirt/where Pagans tread'.[27] Scholars have seen in this extended address to the rose a nostalgia for the Jacobean and Elizabethan church, as well as an indictment of the 'schisms' ripping apart the Caroline church.[28] But if one takes seriously the vision of history articulated in 'The Church Militant', these lines resonate in a broader Atlantic apocalyptic framework, giving new meaning to the complaint that parts of the church have been 'cast' abroad to 'the dirt where Pagans tread': America. Though the speaker laments the destruction of the mother church, there is a note of hope here. The 'parts' of the rose are not specified, but in combination with the 'dirt' in line 23, the poem indirectly suggests the possibility of eventual germination here, a hint that a new blossom might grow abroad.

But the poem immediately moves away from this hope in the stanza's second half, just as the 'The Church Militant' moves on from its temporary description of the new growth of the true church in America. The speaker turns from his bitter yet matter-of-fact description of the colonial religious project's causes to a pronounced state of sorrow:

> ... O Mother deare and kinde,
> Where shall I get me eyes enough to weep,
> As many eyes as starres? since it is night,
> And much of Asia and Europe fast asleep,
> And ev'n all Africk; would at least I might
> With these two poore ones lick up all the dew,
> Which falls by night, and poure it out for you! (25–30)

Rather than dwelling on the possibility of new growth abroad, the speaker instead returns to a state of mourning and the language of elegy. In the wake of the rose's destruction, night has fallen, a night that reigns over 'much of Asia and Europe', and 'ev'n all Africk' and has, finally, arrived in Britain. Herbert describes this chronology—the church moving West through her history, with Sin following—in 'The Church Militant', but 'Church-rents and schisms' stages this history with an important difference, dwelling even more intensely on the embodied experience of despair through the elegiac form. Herbert's speaker mourns the church as a *mother*, finding in elegy a smaller-scale lyric language to express the intensity of despair at the progress of God's mandate beyond the English church.

In 'The Church Militant', 'The Jews', and 'Church-rents', Herbert dwells on the affective experience of being left behind, and perhaps it is no coincidence that the elegiac moments found in these poems strongly resemble his poetic monuments to his mother, herself an enthusiast of the godly mission of the Virginia colonies. Herbert had written *Memoriae Matris Sacrum* [In Sacred Memory of My Mother], a series of nineteen elegiac Latin poems, after Magdalen Herbert's death in 1627. The final lines of 'Church-rents' share much in common with this earlier work. For example, consider the opening lines of the first poem in *Memoriae*[29]:

> Ah Mater, quo te deplorem fonte? Dolores
> Quae guttae poterunt enumerare meos?
>
> Ah Mother, with what fountain could I mourn you?
> What [portion of] drops could reckon up my sorrows?

Here the elegiac speaker dwells on the insufficiency of his tears, questioning their ability to express the sorrow he feels at his mother's passing. This is similar both in tone and content to the final stanza of 'Churchrents', in which the speaker doubts his capacity to find enough tears to mourn another 'mother', asking 'O Mother deare and kinde,/Where shall I get me eyes enough to weep,/As many eyes as starres?' These declarations of the insufficiency of tears to express the severity of loss are conventional in elegy, but the resemblance of these two moments nonetheless resonates with what we know of Herbert's life. In Herbert's despairing speakers—left behind on earth, left behind like the Jews, left behind in England—we might see something of his family biography: the son who wrote to his mother of a life 'snarled' with a frustrated desire to help bring about New Jerusalem, the scion of a family obsessed with New World conversion projects who missed the boat. But Herbert's 'melancholly' view through 'blacke glasses', to borrow Samuel Ward's term, was nonetheless enormously aesthetically productive, generating an almost deistic or antinomian poetics of abandonment and despair that rendered the epic sweep of eschatological history in the intensely personal, small-scale terms of elegy. For Herbert, as perhaps for other members of the godly who unwillingly remained behind in England in the early seventeenth century, the Atlantic mission was less a symbol of the triumph of the true church as it was a provocative reminder of the inevitable decay of all temporal religious institutions in the longer scheme of history.

Notes

1. Reprinted in Walton's *Life of Herbert*, a full-text version of which has been made available through Project Canterbury and can be found at http://anglicanhistory.org/walton/herbert.html. Last accessed 21 August 2015.
2. George Herbert, *The English poems of George Herbert*, ed. Helen Wilcox (Cambridge, 2007), pp. 181–182. All citations to Herbert's poetry will appear in-line and refer to this edition.
3. Wilcox, *English poems*, p. 664.
4. Annabel M. Endicott, 'The structure of George Herbert's *Temple*: A reconsideration', *University of Toronto Quarterly* 34:3 (1965), p. 236.
5. All attempts to date the Williams manuscript and the poems within it should be treated as, at best, spirited guesswork. Nothing is known about the manuscript's early provenance, forcing critics to date the poems largely by internal reference, a strategy that is highly speculative outside of the context of occasional poetry and *especially* in the case of this manuscript, which appears to be

a copy intended to collect, preserve, and organise lyrics that were composed at different times. Dating attempts for the Williams MS have mostly ignored two key and very inconvenient facts about the manuscript: a) no *terminus ad quem* for the date of the copying of the manuscript's lyrics can be established besides Herbert's death and b) given that the manuscript is a collection and re-copying of lyrics produced earlier, a *terminus a quo* can only be conclusively established for a limited number of explicitly occasional poems (the satires on Pope Urban and the poems to Elizabeth of Bohemia). This means, unfortunately, that any non-occasional poems in the collection could have dates ranging from 1610 to the early 1630s. The highly speculative nature of internal dating strategies is particularly apparent in reference to the 'The Church Militant'. Scholars have variously suggested that its emphasis on colonial triumph suggests that it was written before 1618 'because of its sanguine prophecy of the progress of religion to America' (Charles), between 1619 and 1622 because of its 'movement away from a career at court' (Powers-Beck), or between 1618 and 1619 with no reason given (Hodgkins). Amy Charles, *Life of George Herbert* (Ithaca, NY, 1977), p. 82; Jeffrey Powers-Beck, *Writing the flesh: The Herbert Family dialogue* (Pittsburgh, PA, 1998), p. 192; Christopher Hodgkins, *Reforming empire: Protestant colonialism and conscience in British literature* (Columbia, MI, 2002), p. 152.

6. Wilcox, *English poems*, pp. 658–659.
7. Robert Ray, 'Herbert's seventeenth-century reputation: A summary and new considerations', *George Herbert Journal* 9 (1986), pp. 1–14.
8. See Henry Vaughan, *The Mount of Olives* (London, 1652), p. 119.
9. Beth Quitslund, 'The Virginia Company, 1606–1624: Anglicanism's millennial adventure', in Richard Connors and Andrew Colin Gow (eds), *Anglo-American Millennialism, from Milton to the Millerites* (Leiden, 2004), pp. 43–113.
10. For a more comprehensive treatment of the Herbert family's extensive entanglements with the Virginia Company see Powers-Beck, *Writing the flesh*, pp. 189–221.
11. John Ferrar and Dr. Jebb, *Nicholas Ferrar: Two lives* (London, 1855), p. 340.
12. Izaak Walton, *The lives of Dr. John Donne, Sir Henry Wotton, Mr. Richard Hooker, Mr. George Herbert* (London, 1670), p. 75.
13. National Archives, SP 16/278 f.140.
14. Christopher Hill suggests that the delayed publication was to avoid Laud's wrath; this seems likely, given the government disapproval Mede's contemporaries Thomas Brightman and Henry Finch had received for similar eschatologically-oriented projects. See the discussion in Christopher Hill, 'Radical prose in 17th century England: From Marprelate to the Levellers', *Essays in Criticism* 32:2 (1982), p. 98. The fullest treatment of Mede and his milieu can be found in Jeffrey Jue, *Heaven upon earth: Joseph Mede (1586–1638) and the legacy of millenarianism* (Dordrecht, 2006). For an abbreviated life, see

Bryan W. Ball, 'Mede, Joseph (1586–1638)', *Oxford Dictionary of National Biography*, Oxford University Press, 2004; online edition, Jan 2008, http://www.oxforddnb.com/view/article/18465. Last accessed 10 May 2011.
15. Twisse's letter dates from 1634, but does not survive in manuscript. It comes down to us, instead, from a print collection of Mede's correspondence produced later in the seventeenth century. Joseph Mede, *The works of the pious and profoundly-learned Joseph Mede, B.D., sometime fellow of Christ's Colledge in Cambridg* (London, 1672), pp. 800–801.
16. Acosta had been translated into English in 1604, and Mede seems to take his testimony—that native peoples could only date their own history back 400 years—as evidence that they must have arrived in the New World at that time. Acosta: 'Some learned men write, that all which the Indians make mention of, is not above 400. yeeres old, and whatsoever they speake of former ages, is but a confusion full of obscuritie, wherein we find no truth. The which may not seeme strange, they having no use of books, or writing; in steede whereof, they use counting with their Quipocamayes, the which is peculiar unto them. But which reckoning all they can report is not past 400. yeeres.' Jose Acosta, *The naturall and morall histories of the East and West Indies* (London, 1604), p. 80.
17. Jue has examined the links between Mede and Protestant irenicists like Samuel Hartlib and John Dury, who envisioned a broader, transnational Protestant reconciliation before the apocalypse, a vision which Mede seems to have been reluctant to endorse. See Jue, *Heaven*, pp. 65–84. Andrew Crome, on the other hand, has pointed out that Mede's apocalypticism has suggestive links to the more nationalist apocalyptic visions in the work of Thomas Brightman, a key forerunner to Mede in English millenarian theology, though Mede is less stridently nationalist than Brightman. See Andrew Crome, *The restoration of the Jews: Early modern hermeneutics, eschatology, and national identity in the works of Thomas Brightman* (Cham, 2014), esp. pp. 160–161. My point here, however, is not to characterise Mede as either a nationalist or pan-European irenicist figure, but rather to demonstrate the way he responded to separatist migration in the mid-1630s by denying the millennial centrality of New England.
18. For an exhaustive, blow-by-blow history of Gorges' smear campaign on the Massachusetts Bay Colony, see the dated but still-definitive documentary account in Charles McLean Andrews, *The colonial period of American history, Volume 1* (New Haven, CT, 1934), pp. 400–429. For a shorter, livelier version of the same affair, see Francis J. Bremer, *John Winthrop: America's forgotten founding father* (Oxford, 2005), pp. 232–236.
19. Reprinted in *Proceedings of the Massachusetts Historical Society, Volume 28* (Boston, 1894), p. 383.
20. Whether or not Massachusetts Puritans were driven to migrate westward by an exclusively American-centric vision of New Jerusalem has been the subject

of lively debate among historians ever since Perry Miller's famous analysis of John Winthrop's 1630 'city on a hill' sermon. A fuller examination of the theological convictions that drove migration is outside the scope of this chapter, but Herbert's writings and Twisse's letter clearly show that at least some English thinkers entertained the idea that New England was contiguous with New Jerusalem. For a general overview of the historiography surrounding this issue from Miller onward, see Jeffrey Jue's recent discussion in his monograph on Joseph Mede. Jue completely rejects millenarianism as a motive for migration, but nonetheless provides a helpful overview of the historiography surrounding the issue in *Heaven upon earth*, pp. 175–208.

21. For reading that casts the poem as an anti-Catholic text, see Sidney Gottlieb, 'The social and political backgrounds of George Herbert's poetry', in *"The muse's common-weale": Poetry and politics in the seventeenth century* (Columbia, MO, 1988), p. 116. An example of a narrowly citational reading practice can be found in Christina Malcolmson's chapter 'Religion and enterprise', which draws broad conclusions about Herbert's colonial attitudes by examining only eight of the poem's 279 lines in *Heartwork: George Herbert and the Protestant ethic* (Stanford, CA, 1999), Chap. 7.
22. See Gottlieb, 'Social and political backgrounds'.
23. This conceit echoes that found in Donne's 'Good Friday, 1613. Riding Westward', a poem that narrates—perhaps significantly—Donne's ride to visit Herbert's older brother Edward.
24. Raymond A. Anselment, 'The Church Militant: George Herbert and the metamorphoses of Christian history', *Huntington Library Quarterly* 41:4 (1978), p. 315.
25. All references to *A priest to the temple, or The country parson* will hereafter appear in-text and are to George Herbert, 'The country parson', in *The works of George Herbert*, ed. F.E. Hutchinson (Oxford, 1959). Reference here at p. 282.
26. Nabil Matar, 'George Herbert, Henry Vaughan, and the conversion of the Jews', *Studies in English Literature* 30:1 (1990), pp. 79–92.
27. Wilcox notes an oblique reference to Scottish Presbyterianism in Herbert's evocation of 'neighbours' and 'north-winde', but does not comment on the mention of paganism two lines later. Wilcox, *English poems*, p. 391.
28. See review of scholarship in Wilcox, *English poems*, pp. 391–394.
29. Latin text taken from George Herbert, *Works*, ed. F.E. Hutchinson (Oxford, 1970), p. 422. Translations are my own.

CHAPTER 4

Bradstreet and Trans-Atlantic Non-Conformism in the American-Prophetic Mode

Edward Simon

In the spring of 1654 a woman named Anna Trapnel found herself arrested and jailed at Bridewell by parliamentary forces. Months before she had held a trance-like vigil for just under two weeks, with followers recording her prophecies related to the new Commonwealth government and especially regarding the Lord Protector Oliver Cromwell. At turns ecstatic and mystical, gnomic, and revelatory, Trapnel concerned herself with issues of eschatology, politics, government, and apocalypse.[1] Trapnel functioned as a popular female prophet, indeed she was so popular that she was released from imprisonment by virtue of her own defence only a few months after her arrest.[2] Over the course of her life she promulgated her visionary theology in works like *Strange and Wonderful News from White-Hall, A Report and Plea, The Cry of a Stone*, and *A Legacy for Saints*.[3] It is a testament to both her power and attitudes towards the prophetic in the period that she was able to avoid long-term imprisonment, prosecution, and punishment, especially as she enthusiastically spoke out against the state.[4] In a prose style not uncharacteristic of the vibrant non-conformists and dissenters that wrote and published during the Interregnum, Trapnel commented on the key political and religious controversies of her day.[5]

E. Simon (✉)
Department of English, Lehigh University, Bethlehem, PA, USA
e-mail: ens310@lehigh.edu

© The Author(s) 2016
A. Crome (ed.), *Prophecy and Eschatology in the Transatlantic World, 1550–1800*, Christianities in the Trans-Atlantic World, 1500–1800,
DOI 10.1057/978-1-137-52055-5_4

Central to her vision was her association with the Fifth Monarchy Men. The group were a perhaps surprisingly strategically successful millenarian party; they subscribed to a teleological view of history based upon their own readings of Daniel and Revelation.[6] They awaited the arrival of 'King Jesus', and, contrary to the conservative Augustinianism of normative Christianity (be it Catholic or Protestant), they saw the enactment of this millennial goal as being the responsibility of humans living within and participating in history. For them apocalypse was an explicitly political goal, and society was to be redrawn according to it.[7] Increasingly mutually distrustful of Cromwell, the Fifth Monarchy Men would eventually see him as a pseudo-monarchical replacement for kingly tyranny, no better than Charles whose regicide they had championed. It is in this chaotic and fractured context that Anna Trapnel preached her utopian gospel of the coming fall of Cromwell, the return of Christ, and the mystical equivalence of men and women. For Trapnel it was a new and future England that was to be the site of this future Fifth Monarchy, the final and godly kingdom to rule for Christ's return.[8]

More than 3000 miles to the west a different Anne was producing her own writings. Only four years before Trapnel's imprisonment, a frontier poet named Anne Bradstreet had her first book of writings, *The Tenth Muse Lately Sprung up in America*, published in London.[9] The book of verse marked the first time that poetry had been published in English by an explicitly American poet, and indeed in the centuries since, whether her critical stock has risen or fallen, Bradstreet has been taken as the genesis of American letters.[10] Bradstreet has been championed as the mother of American literature separate from its British antecedents, and as an example of celebrated Puritan ingenuity and rugged individualistic American values.[11] She has often been conceptualised as a pioneer woman raising her family and supporting her beloved husband Simon, who was himself a sometime governor of Massachusetts. In her lifetime she was honoured as an example of feminine poetic genius, being given the pagan-orphic appellation of the 'tenth muse' by her brother-in-law Rev. John Woodbridge.[12] Yet in the nineteenth century she was dismissed and relegated with the rest of early American Puritan literature to a place of insignificance, as an embarrassing and primitive relic of America's stern, austere, repressed Calvinist roots.[13] In the twentieth century she was reformed and rehabilitated by second-wave feminist critics and poets like Wendy Martin and Adrienne Rich, who interpreted Bradstreet as being a woman who, despite the necessarily marginal position she was forced to hold in her society, was able to not just independently write verse but to also become the progenitor, that is, the mythic founding-mother of all American poetry and literature which was to follow.[14] With this new understanding of Bradstreet her poetry became canonical, anthologised not just in the *Oxford Anthology of American Literature* but, indeed, in seeming deference to a Lincolnshire childhood, in the *Oxford Anthology of British Literature* as well. As early modernists scoured the record to find potential candidates to be the figurative 'Shakespeare's sister' of Virginia Woolf's *A Room of One's Own*,[15] Anne Bradstreet stood tall next to authors as varied as Mary Sidney, Mary Wroth, Amelia Lanyer, Margaret Cavendish, and Aphra Behn.[16] But where English authors had a tendency to be submerged within the traditional patriarchal canon of Renaissance English writers, overshadowed by figures such as Shakespeare, Marlowe, Donne, Jonson, Spenser, and Milton, Bradstreet remained unequivocally the most talented, important, and influential of seventeenth-century American writers.[17] Not just feminist criticism of the second half of the twentieth century, but indeed American Studies as a discipline, celebrated the seeming singularity of Bradstreet's achievement.[18] And yet, despite the appropriation of Bradstreet as an early American proponent for women's voices, the picture of her still remained steadfastly conservative. Her most celebrated verse, presented as self-evidentially superior to her other writings, remained the domestic lyrics she wrote later in life, such as 'Before the Birth of One of Her Children', 'For Deliverance from a Fever', 'Verses Upon the Burning of Our House', and 'To Her Dear and Loving Husband', all of which are later poems.[19] And living during a time of incredible theological tumult in New England during the high days of Anne Hutchinson's Antinomian controversy, Bradstreet with her husband was seen as in opposition to the more liberal views of her one-time minister John Cotton who had taken to defending the soon to be exiled Hutchinson.[20] In our current historical view Bradstreet may be celebrated as a trail-blazing female poet, but paradoxically the understanding of her which we have inherited is of a woman who is still no radical.[21]

So it would seem that our two Anns—Trapnel and Bradstreet—did not have much in common other than being women united in religious fervency and writing in English, albeit on different sides of the Atlantic Ocean. Yet it is my contention that the two have far more in common than may be supposed, and that Bradstreet as a poet needs to be read within not just the context of Atlantic women's prophetic writings, but that she needs to be acknowledged for her unique 'American' contribution to seventeenth-century millennial thought. While Bradstreet has been virtually canonised as the matriarch of American literature, Trapnel is largely unknown among literary scholars. Despite this, I argue that both women are representative of the same phenomenon emerging at the time, a newly emboldened sense of free speech and the possibilities of women contributing not just to religious discourse, but indeed to the radical re-evaluation of religious discourse. This is a shift from the more aristocratic environs of seventeenth-century women's patronage poetry that the academy has rediscovered in the last generation. While coming from the semi-aristocratic Dudley family (and indeed a distant relation of both Philip and Mary Sidney and thus the Herberts as well), Bradstreet might from a literary perspective be expected to have more in common with Mary Sidney than she does with a more proletarian radical like Trapnel. Yet I argue that Bradstreet can be placed within a radical eschatological and political camp, one that has more in common with the working class radicals discussed by Christopher Hill[22] than royalist women writers like Aphra Behn and Margaret Cavendish of a few decades later. And while Bradstreet's non-conforming Puritanism may seem the obvious point of reclamation for placing her in the category of religious and political radical, I would argue that what she shares with Trapnel (and indeed later female prophets) is a sense of the radical possibilities of womanhood being directly related to the providential and chiliastic project (in Trapnel's case the Fifth Monarchy; in Bradstreet's New England). The seventeenth-century flowering of English non-conformist thought included such groups as the Levellers, the Diggers, the Ranters, the Muggletonians, the Baptists, the Quakers and, of course, the Fifth Monarchy Men. A similar affinity for radicalism is not absent from the orthodox Reformed Calvinism of Bradstreet, despite her silence during the antinomian affair and her personal relationships to the prosecution against Hutchinson. As Rosemond Rosenmeir has pointed out, a strong strain of hermeticism inherited from the Renaissance interests of the Dudleys permeates her writings (and indeed that same influence can be seen in the occult writings of none other than John Winthrop Jr).[23] Central to this is the presence of Wisdom, a feminine gendered quality which Trapnel and Bradstreet see as central to the movements and transitions of empires, and which is crucial to the emergence of an apocalyptic polity which brings about the post-millennial kingdom of Christ.

Broadly my argument about Bradstreet will be structured in the following way: first, while readings of Bradstreet have gone through various critical permutations (largely interpreting her either in light of Puritanism or through a feminist critical lens), another perspective exists that more properly situates her within the wider world of women's prophetic and religious writings in both the British Isles and New England. Under such a rubric she has less in common with more conservative and traditional authors she may have been grouped with before (such as Mary Sidney, for example), and can instead be read as part of the same milieu that produced writers such as Trapnel and Jane Lead.[24] To that end, while I will not engage in a close reading of Trapnel, I will nonetheless use her as a rhetorical foil with which to compare and contrast the discourses of women's prophetic writings at this time period in relation to Bradstreet. Second, I argue that Bradstreet's political vision is specifically one that engages what the philosopher Carl Schmidt popularised as 'political theology'.[25] It is an ostensibly theocratic[26] (though still radical) political worldview that marries a millennial political theology to a perspective with imperialist overtones. Thirdly, I argue that despite her inclusion (for all intents and purposes) in the canon over the past century and a half, and despite the understanding of her as a political and religious moderate, elements of her thought show a surprising affinity to the 'radical' positions that would later emerge with the Fifth Monarchy Men. Her poem 'A Dialogue between Old and New England' can be seen as a specifically 'American' millennial interpretation of ideas that would be used by these groups in the 1640s and 1650s.

I will not argue that Bradstreet saw herself as anything other than an Englishwoman (it would not be until a generation later that her grandnephew Cotton Mather was able to conceptualise the 'American' as something separate from his European progenitors)[27] but I do argue—in opposition to much traditional critical commentary about Bradstreet—that she finds a specific and explicitly millennial role for America within the providential history of British Christianity.[28] Central to this is a conception of having to recover Bradstreet in a radical tradition, both in terms of her hermeneutics and her understanding of women's roles, which are of course related to one another. Finally, I would like to place Bradstreet's political theology within the burgeoning confines of what could be thought of as an explicitly theological conception of American significance which secularises itself into many of the tropes and themes of American canonical literature, an understanding of national literature and genre classification which I will elaborate on in my conclusion and which I refer to as 'the American Prophetic Mode'.

In situating Bradstreet within these different arguments I will be focusing on a close reading of one poem, 'A Dialogue between Old England and New', which was included in the 1650 printing of *The Tenth Muse, Lately Sprung up in America*. This poem best exhibits the prophetic quality that I am ascribing to her. There are certainly other Bradstreet poems that a reading could focus on, including her epic quaternion 'The Four Monarchies' which explicitly engages eschatological imagery from Daniel, and especially her remarkable poem 'In Honour of that High and Mighty Princess, Queen Elizabeth'.[29] Both of these texts engage a similar prophetic mode in advocating for the potentially particularly American qualities of the millennium. What makes 'A Dialogue between Old England and New' so crucial however, is that in this particular poem we see Bradstreet explicitly forging a 'New English' identity which is conceptualised in opposition to old England. This serves to problematise more traditional interpretations of Bradstreet's relationship to her home country. As such, my argument concerns situating Bradstreet, and in particular her early poetry, within this collection of trans-Atlantic prophetic discourses, not a historicist re-evaluation of those discourses themselves.

While aesthetic arguments are not my focus here, 'A Dialogue' has often been ignored in favour of her later more domestic works (not just in spite of feminist criticism but often times because of it).[30] Implicit in my wider argument is the more subjective position that those poems often ignored by literary scholars are worthy of greater critical attention, not just for historical but also for aesthetic reasons. As such, it is worth briefly justifying the importance of a literary critical method in situating Bradstreet within the wider currents of trans-Atlantic female prophecy during the seventeenth century. My argument is one of critical and methodological categorisation. I am not claiming that Bradstreet necessarily influenced or was influenced by larger currents of non-conformist political thought occurring during the English civil wars. My argument should not be read as historical, or theological, but rather as tracing the issue of understanding the ways in which 'prophecy' sometimes manifested itself as a specifically literary phenomenon in the seventeenth century. A close reading of a representative though under-read early political poem demonstrates that in terms of literary mode and rhetoric that Bradstreet bares similarities to these wider theological discourses, and that in our contemporary conversation about Bradstreet it may make sense to speak of at least her earlier career in terms of those prophetic and literary modes. I argue that this will reorient our generic classification of Bradstreet, allowing for readings of her in light of other women writers such as Trapnel and Lead who are rarely discussed in the context of literary studies.

'A Dialogue between Old England and New; concerning their present troubles, Anno 1642' appears in the first printing of Bradstreet's only anthology, released in 1650. Given the speed with which the situation could change during the civil wars, it is interesting, though often difficult, to read these texts as autobiographical accounts of Bradstreet's own political opinions. When first written by Bradstreet the idea of Charles I's death was arguably unthinkable; by the time the poem found its readership, the execution had already happened. As I will demonstrate over the course of my close reading of the poem, and as is to be expected of a New England Puritan, Bradstreet's political sympathies are clearly parliamentarian. But as the last chaotic years of the revolution unfolded, and indeed especially during the Interregnum through to the Restoration, most thinking people had complicated political opinions that often changed allegiances, or allowed for a degree of subtlety that they need to be given credit for.[31] As an object of critical attention the poem is occasionally anthologised and taught, but generally not written about as much as her latter poems such as 'To my Dear and Loving Husband' and 'Upon the Burning of my House'.[32] While not as obscure as her Quaternions, the subject of 'A Dialogue between Old England and New' is the current political climate surrounding the English civil wars, and some critics have had a tendency to relegate this text to juvenilia, along with many of her other early poems which take complex political, cultural, scientific, historical, and theological issues as their subject matter.[33] This position, that classifies Bradstreet's earlier poems as incompetent and pretentious as opposed to the more technically proficient and mature domestic poems, has resulted in minimising comparisons between Bradstreet and female prophets, both of whom were emerging out of the environment of religious non-conformity in the anglophonic Atlantic world.[34] This poem in particular embodies many of the aspects that can be seen as central to the American Prophetic Mode, if written during a time period where a more contemporary understanding of 'America' had yet to fully emerge. But perhaps more importantly to the broader argument of placing Bradstreet within this contemporary movement of women's prophetic writings, 'A Dialogue between Old England and New' is by all definitions prophetic—in that it castigates modern England for the presence of sin while also predicting the future—and that it utilises a specifically feminine language marshalled towards a particularly millennial conclusion.

The text is structured as a dialogue poem, and within it is recorded a conversation between Old and New England. Both characters are personified as female, and indeed the relationship between them is best characterised as that between a mother and a daughter. It is notable, although not novel, that Bradstreet has chosen to personify both nations in the form of women. This is a venerable tradition: for example, Spenser's celebration of Elizabeth as 'Gloriana' in *The Faerie Queen*. Bradstreet embraces a particular vision of women's mysticism that she was able to absorb from books that she was likely to have been familiar with in both her father Thomas Dudley's and her husband Simon Bradstreet's libraries. Still, while the personification of feminine nationhood does not preclude the existence of a form of women's mysticism within the poem, its presence within a wider cultural (and often very conservative tradition) does not necessitate it either.

The poem begins with New England asking 'Alas, dear mother, fairest queen and best, / With honour, wealth, and peace, happy and blest; / What ails thee hang they head and cross thine arms …' (1) The maternal relationship between the two is literally stated within the prefatory dedication which also, to an extent, functions as an evocation of the muse, with the mother that is Old England fulfilling this role. Written in 1642, this poem is drafted the same year as the earliest major skirmishes of the first civil war. This period sees the Bishops' Wars, Scottish incursion into the north of England, and the beginning of pitched battles between Royalists and Parliamentarians. The executions of Archbishop Laud and Charles were respectively still three and seven years away. As such, at this time, with England, Scotland, and Ireland not yet completely scorched over, New England could ask her mother naively 'With honour, wealth, and peace, happy and blest' why Old England should 'hang thy head and cross thine arms'(2)? It is worth considering that with the difficult endeavour of crossing the Atlantic Ocean being around two months in the mid-seventeenth century that current events in the British Isles were disseminated slowly in the colonies. New England's seeming naivety at her mother's despair can therefore be read as a fairly literal representation of the average New Englander's lack of knowledge of contemporary events—as all information was delayed, it is unsurprising that New England was surprised at the state of her mother. And while 'cross thine arms' can be simply read as the crossing of arms in indignation, one could also read it as Old England taking on an implied cruciform position. With her head hanging and her arms crucially in a 'cross' the body-politic has become conflated with the body of Christ. Despite the femininity of Old England, she is not in the Marian posture of the Pieta but rather in Christ's posture on the cross.

Old England seems to feign surprise at New England's ignorance of her state, and indeed, it is worth entertaining the possibility that despite New England's initial naivety that she is not in some sense also fully aware of the political tribulations her mother is going through. Old England asks, starting at line nine 'Art ignorant indeed of these my woes? / Or must my forced tongues these griefs disclose?/And must myself dissect my tattered state, / Which 'mazed Christendom stands wond'ring at?' (9–12). There is lack of dignity in Old England having to explain the state that she is in. With all of her trials, it seems that the mother being forced to explain her fallenness and shame to the daughter New England is but another indignity. Yet Bradstreet implies that this is an indignity that may be deserved, and as the poem progresses it becomes clear that though Old England's fallen state is not one that is to be permanent, it is one that for the time-being is justified. It is in this section of Old England's dialogue that we see indication of Bradstreet's utilisation of the American Prophetic Mode. As a poet, Bradstreet has often been labelled only as American insomuch as a mistake of biography. As noted above, she is included in the *Oxford Anthology of British Literature* precisely because she is so often categorised as a British author who simply happened to be in America; no less a poet-critic than Adrienne Rich argued that there was nothing distinctly American about Bradstreet.[35] I argue that this poem proves such an evaluation to be unequivocally wrong. Bradstreet is not just interested in themes which would become characteristically American, but she fully embraces this particular mode which might be seen as characteristic in much of canonical American literature. Old England rhetorically asks at 'If I decease, doth think thou shalt survive? Or by my wasting state dost think to thrive' (19)? Bradstreet and New England do not answer the question. The answer to the question itself—What does New England think will happen if Old England is not restored?—is mute. But then that question—What will happen to New England if Old England is not restored?—also has a mute answer. The question itself belies certain implications: if Old England should 'decease' that New England may not only 'survive' but indeed 'thrive'. Of course the presence of such a sentiment in Bradstreet's poem does not imply that such a belief was universal in the colony, though it does suggest that it was perhaps one current of thought. Here we have the language of *translatio studii et imperii*, the Renaissance belief that empires transitioned or translated one into another and that this course often was geographically westward.[36] If by Old England's 'wasting' New England is to 'thrive', it can be read as part of that tradition that has world empires transitioning one into another on an east–west axis. Indeed *translatio studii et imperii* is a classical trope that finds its justification in the four monarchies predicted in the Book of Daniel, and elaborated on by many different millennialist groups, obviously including the Fifth Monarchy Men. Crucially, Bradstreet wrote about these monarchies concurrently to this text in her quaternion 'The Four Monarchies'.

New England begins to hypothesise the various causes for Old England's tattered state. She enquires whether Old England's present deprivations are caused by 'that Saxon stout' (28) and asks 'hath Canutus, that brave valiant Dane' (31) been responsible for the current usurpations of power in England? She continues with 'Or is't a Norman, whose victorious hand/With English blood bedews thy conquered land' (33)? New England conjures these historical invaders to make the civil strife within England appear unique when Old England finally reveals the exact form of her bedevilment. Two things are notable in Bradstreet conjuring the outside threats of Saxon, Dane, and Norman. First, in explicitly stating that the Saxons are an outside threat she seems to be discussing English national identity and making it equivalent to another ethnic group, as was historically done when the Saxons were invoked by the Britons. This was not an uncommon rhetorical manoeuvre during the reign of the Welsh Tudors, particularly Elizabeth who often conflated herself with a Celtic Arthuriana.[37] By the mid-seventeenth century, however, increasing religious and political problems with Celtic peoples in Cornwall, Wales, Ireland, and Scotland saw a diminishment in the English-as-Britons narrative in favour of seeing the English as strongly Saxon.[38] Indeed the internal contradiction in this passage is that after first mentioning the Saxons as an outside invader, she moves to the Normans as a possible threat. Yet much as the Saxons were characterised as the oppressors of the Britons, the Normans were often characterised as the oppressors of the Saxons, especially in mid-seventeenth-century politically radical writings that emerged from the newly emboldened English working class, particularly among groups like the Diggers.[39] For example, in Gerrard Winstanley's pamphlets written for the Diggers, the ancient rights of the Saxons are often portrayed as a type of prelapsarian, egalitarian, utopian commonwealth in contrast to contemporary political and economic systems.[40] Again, it is important to emphasise that Bradstreet did not identify with either the Fifth Monarchy Men, or certainly the Diggers; rather she engaged rhetoric common enough to them that it is worth rethinking the ways in which she has been critically and generically classified. It is also important to remember that this is not to suggest that Bradstreet's historical understanding was confused or incomplete. Devoted reader of Raleigh and Du Bartas that she was, Bradstreet had a thorough understanding of historical complexity.[41] Rather, within this individual literary text, Bradstreet purposefully conflates and confuses historical particularities so as to suggest that the broad archetypal narrative of oppressor and oppressed is more important than the ever changing vagaries of individualised historical particularities.

New England now changes her questioning. The cause of England's sufferings may not be foreign powers, but rather 'intestine wars' internal to the nation of England itself. While this is more correct, New England's apparent contemporary awareness still does not allow for the full possibility of the radicalism of the coming English civil wars. Bradstreet writes 'Do barons rise and side against their king? ... Must Edward be deposed? ... that second Richard must be clept in th' tower? ... Must Richmond's aid, the nobles now implore to come and break the tushes of the boar?' (37) New England's accurate understanding of medieval English strife is that when it is internal it is not between the populace and their king but rather between the king and his aristocratic equals. It is a traditional understanding where no commonwealth can rise against the monarch, but rather that 'barons [can] rise and side against their king', as Bradstreet writes. But there is still the spectre of regicide (although the poem was written several years before Charles I's execution, it was not published until a year after it) where 'Edward' can 'be deposed' and 'second Richard ... clept in th' tower' and where Henry VII can be enlisted to 'break the tushes of the boar' by defeating Richard III at the battle of Bosworth Field.

Finally, New England brings up the possibility of more contemporary foreign powers threatening Old England. The Saxon, Dane, and Norman belong to a distant past, the internal War of the Roses to a more recent yet still medieval past. Now, only a few decades after the events that she comes to mention, New England asks if her mother does 'fear Spain's bragging Armado?/Doth your ally, fair France, conspire your wrack, Or do the Scots play false behind your back?/Doth Holland quit you ill for all your love?' (46). New England has moved her line of questioning closer and closer to the chronological present. Hapsburg Spain threatened England's coast only a generation before, the politics of the Netherlands were confused with Charles giving limited aid to the most moderate of Protestant factions in the Eighty Years War there (and allowing for the southern Netherlands to remain Catholic and under Spanish control), and Scotland had actually invaded northern England only a year before the poem's composition.[42] With her extensive knowledge of history, New England's rhetoric seems purposefully naïve; one wonders if she is attempting to goad her mother who is made decrepit through sin into an honest accounting of her own failings, one in which the events of the civil wars are part of a long history of conflict. 'Whence is the storm, from earth or heaven above?' New England talks in tricolons of 'drought,' 'famine,' and 'pestilence.' With the verses before recounting war we are only the horseman of death away from completing the apocalyptic quartet from Revelation.

Old England responds to her daughter's inquiries with 'But foreign foe, nor feigned friend I fear' (59). Written in perfect Anglo-Saxon alliterative metre (with the comma acting as the required caesura),[43] the mother harkens back to traditional English values which have been abandoned but which shall be redeemed (at least by the end of the poem). It is fascinating (though outside of the purview of this chapter) to examine how aware of Anglo-Saxon verse Bradstreet may have been. Though the vast majority of it was lost with Henry VIII's dissolution of the monasteries (that which survived often remaining to be rediscovered by philologists in the nineteenth and twentieth centuries), it is still notable that in a poem that has so centrally to do with English national identity Bradstreet suddenly employs the archaic yet traditional verse structures of the English people. It is crucial for the answer that she is to give to New England's entreaties as to whether Old England is beleaguered outside or within, for she is actually threatened by both. The foreign pollution of popery, of sin moving from east to west, threatens England in the form of Laudianism, yet it is English figures (like William Laud himself) who are encouraging the arrival of such impurity. Indeed in reference to the Lancaster–York wars of the fourteenth and fifteenth centuries, Old England says 'None know which is the red, or which the white' (72). Old England has made clear that while England has experienced civil war before, this is internal strife of an entirely different sort. When one reads some of Bradstreet's later poems, also included in the 1650 printing (such as her lamentation on Saul written in testimony to the execution of Charles I), it is clear that Bradstreet saw the newest civil wars in England not in terms of past English history, but rather in terms of biblical typology. For Bradstreet, this is divine history as well as temporal. We have left the arena of mere British chronicle and are entering the realm of contemporary biblical-prophetical politics.

Old England continues the explanation of her contemporary woe by clarifying, starting at line 89, that 'Before I tell th' effect, I'll show the cause/Which are my sins, the breach of sacred laws, / Idolatry, supplanter of a nation, / With foolish superstitious adoration, / Are liked and countenanced by men of might, / The Gospel trodden down and hath no right; / Church offices were sold and bought for gain, / That Pope had hope to find Rome here again' (89–96). Accusing the current Church of England of engaging in idolatry, superstition, and simony, it should be clear that even if she is not explicitly condemning Charles himself for the current English Babylonian captivity, she is certainly implying his close-counsellors. Archbishop Laud is the obvious figure of her derision and blame for the implementation of Church reforms (and the feared imposition of actual Catholic influence), but even the Catholic Queen Henrietta Maria, who sanctioned the private practice of Mass for herself and her French countrymen within the royal grounds, is seen as a threat that allows for the pollution of pure English religious identity.[44] Old England says with the American Prophetic Mode seeming central, 'And thou, poor soul, were jeered among the rest, / Thy flying for the truth was made a jest' (103). As directed to her daughter this seems to be an explicit reference to the actual New England—the word 'flying' conjures the escape of *translatio*. It is not a stretch to read this flight to New England as referencing the second mass wave of the Puritan Great Migration to America in 1630, that of the Puritans (as opposed to the schismatics) who composed the core of the initial Massachusetts Bay Colony and first arrived on the *Arbella* and her attendant ships. This is the armada associated with John Winthrop and his celebrated *Model of Christian Charity* sermon, best known for its quoting of Matthew and its declaration of the American project to serve as a 'city upon a hill'.[45] If delivered on the *Arbella* as has long been claimed, one of the many listeners on board would have been Anne Bradstreet.

Old England continues tracing the arrival of sin and destruction working its way from the east to the west in the standard spatial movement of *translatio*. She says 'I mocked the preachers, put it far away; / The sermons yet upon record do stand/That cried destruction to my wicked land' (124). She seems to evoke the genre of sermon that would become so intrinsic to early American identity, that of the jeremiad. An apostate England jeers the warnings of preachers, which predict her wickedness and fall. But to the east lay examples of where such apostasy would lead. She continues with 'Nor took I warning by my neighbor's falls./I saw Germany's dismantled walls,/I saw her people famished, nobles slain,/Her fruitful land, a barren heath remain' (137–141). Germany and the Protestant principalities of the Holy Roman Empire held a privileged place in Reformation historiography as being the birthplace of reform. Yet Germany was in an especially ambivalent position for English Protestants, where the church and state could often appear intrinsically intertwined in an understanding of national election, as well as Calvinist Puritanism's vexed relationship to German Lutheranism (especially in terms of Eucharistic controversies).[46] Here Old England references the brutal violence of the Thirty Years' War, and also England's tepid response in the defence of her Protestant coreligionists on the continent.[47] As a result, Old England claims that 'Now sip I of that cup, and just't may be/The bottom dregs reserved are for me' (128).

Old England may have been sober and dramatic in her appraisal and analysis of her current situation, but she is still enigmatic, allegorical, inexact, and abstract. New England demands a clearer and more literal explanation of why Old England finds herself in the tattered state that she is in. Here we reach the relevant crux of the poem to Bradstreet and her contemporaries. Old England declares 'Well to the matter then, there's grown of late/"Twixt king and peers a question of state,/Which is the chief, the law, or else the king,/One said, "It's he," the other no such thing' (158–161). This is a simple explanation of the causes of the civil wars—disagreement as to the origin and legitimacy of state sovereignty and with whom state power should reside. It is also ambiguous as to who the 'correct' side is, with Bradstreet hedging her bets, obviously approving of the broad political and religious arguments of parliament while seemingly still believing in some degree of monarchical authority. If truly written in 1642 then the lines where she writes 'I that no wars so many years have known,/Am now destroyed and slught'red by mine own;/But could the field alone this strife decide,/One battle two or three I might abide,/But these may be beginning of more woe' (188–192) become especially poignant as indeed much more woe was to come. In these lines the poem almost seems to not just be literary but literally prophetic.

The conclusion of the poem involves New England not only reassuring Old England that this present state of degradation is a period of repentant cleansing that will lead to a new era of holiness within Old England as well as in New, but that Old England will reassert a Christian greatness with explicitly millennial expectations. Bradstreet writes 'To see those latter days of hoped for good,/Though now beclouded all with tears and blood./After dark Popery the day did clear,/But now the sun's brightness shall appear./Blest be the nobles of thy noble land,/With ventured lives for truth's defence that stand. Blest be they commons, who for common good, / And they infringed laws have boldly stood' (214–221). New England and by extension Bradstreet make no explicit claim to support either political side in the civil wars, both nobles and the commons are called as authentic Christian versions of Englishness, but rather there is a greater spiritual war over the fate of England. It is not a question of monarch versus parliament, but a question of the Godly on either side defeating the un-Christian. Again the radicalism of the poem is tempered. The king and his nobles may not be marked as un-Christian, but the implications that many of his associates, particularly Laud and other Arminian bishops within the Church, are to be considered as such is certainly there. New England continues: 'These are the days the Church's foes to crush, / To root out Popelings head, tail, branch, and rush; / Let's bring Baal's vestments forth to make a fire, / Their miters, surplices, and all their tire, / Copes, rochets, crosiers, and such empty trash, / And let their names consume, but let the flash/Light Christendom, and all the world to see/ We hate Rome's whore with all her trumpery' (230–237). In an evocation of the most radical iconoclastic acts of the Edwardian Reformation but also various continental permutations of iconoclastic Protestant fury, Bradstreet continues with the classical conflation of Catholicism with a satanic paganism. All of the accoutrements, relics, and rituals of High Church Christianity, equally associated with Papal Catholicism as with Laudianism, are to be consumed in a bonfire of the vanities. New England prophesies that with a newly repentant and Christian Old England, revitalised in her Protestant faith, that a new millennial era will emerge, to echo Trapnel, a Fifth Monarchy. We are told that English armies will 'sack proud Rome and all her vassals rout' (267) and that with 'This done, with brandished swords to Turkey go' (278). With military victories over Catholic Rome and the Islamic East, Bradstreet writes that the Jews will soon convert to Reformed Christianity, a necessary precursor for the second coming of Christ, completing her poem with 'Farwell, dear Mother, rightest cause prevail,/And in a while, you'll tell another tale' (294).

Bradstreet's closing stanza, with its invocation of Rome destroyed and the Ottomans defeated, with the Jews converted and Christ triumphant, is the prophetic crescendo of her poem. This portion of the poem is where Bradstreet taking on the literary conceit of being a prophet is most clearly demonstrated. In ignoring Bradstreet's earlier poetry for her later domestic poems we have critically ignored the trans-Atlantic traditions of writing in the prophetic mode which she is categorisable under. Again, I am not arguing that Bradstreet was herself Fifth Monarchist (though she was certainly a millennialist), but I am arguing that the critical pairing of Bradstreet's works alongside Fifth Monarchists such as Trapnel is not inappropriate. My argument particularly applies to literary scholars, who should reorient the questions they ask about Bradstreet, and the ways in which they classify her, so as to place her within the wider historical and cultural context of seventeenth-century millenarianism and religious non-conformism.

In poems like 'A Dialogue between Old England and New England' among others by Bradstreet, we see the development of a voice that, as powerful as it was unique, was also indebted to currents of women's prophetic thinking that were gaining prominence on both sides of the Atlantic. Bradstreet has been given her due as a poet for generations, but in the development of a particular voice that is sometimes categorised and taught as quintessentially American, even as it borrowed from English non-conformist thought.[48] What then do we do with the relationship between our two Anns—Bradstreet and Trapnel? I do not wish to suggest that Bradstreet was an influence on Trapnel, though it is certainly possible that as popular as Bradstreet's book of verse was in London that the prophet may have been aware of her Atlantic contemporary. Nor do I wish to imply that Bradstreet was a crypto-Fifth Monarchist.[49] As such, this is not a historian's argument about literal chains of influence, but rather a literary theorist's argument about generic classification and canonicity. Whether Bradstreet and Trapnel knew of each other or influenced each other is irrelevant to the fact that they are both classifiable as being distinctly female prophetic voices, and that Bradstreet's language, rhetoric, tropes, thought, and narrative are all more similar to and more characteristic of the sorts of arguments made by Trapnel than she is categorisable with more traditional women poets of the time period.

Notes

1. See Elaine Hobby, *Virtue of necessity: English women's writing 1649–88* (Ann Arbor, MI, 1989); Stephanie Hodgson Wright, *Women's writings of the early modern period 1588–1688* (Edinburgh, 2002); Maria Magro, 'Spiritual biography and radical sectarian women's discourse: Anna Trapnel and the bad

girls of the English revolution', *Journal of Medieval and Early Modern Studies* 34:2 (2004), pp. 405–437, and Phyllis Mack, *Visionary women: Ecstatic prophecy in seventeenth-century England* (Oxford, 1992).
2. See Brian Levack, *The witch-hunt in early modern Europe* (London, 2006).
3. It is important to mention that although she was the author of these works, they were printed and promoted mostly by men in the movement. For more information consult Wright, *Women's writings*.
4. This was not necessarily unusual. See the government consultation with prophet Elizabeth Poole in 1648–1649 over the Agreement of the People as detailed in Carolyn Polizzotto, 'Speaking truth to power: The problem of authority in the Whitehall Debates of 1648–9', *English Historical Review* 131 (2016), pp. 31–63.
5. Consult Andrew Bradstock, *Radical religion in Cromwell's England: A concise history from the English Civil War to the end of the Commonwealth* (London, 2012).
6. To get a sense of the diversity of non-conformist thought during this period it is helpful to investigate other contemporary millenarians in comparison to Trapnel. An excellent source is Ariel Hessayon, *'Gold Tried in Fire': The Prophet TheauraJohn Tany and the English Revolution* (Aldershot, 2007). See also Ariel Hessayon, 'Totney, Thomas [later Theaurau John Tany] (bap. 1608, d. 1659?)', *Oxford Dictionary of National Biography* (Oxford, 2004).
7. This is, of course, a broad simplification of Fifth Monarchist ideology. They were a diverse group with a multitude of political and theological positions. For a sense of the diversity of opinion within the movement, consult Bernard Capp, *The Fifth Monarchy men: A study in seventeenth-century English Millenarianism* (London, 2011). For a recent analysis of a specific Fifth Monarchist, consult David Farr, *Major-General Thomas Harrison: Millenarianism, Fifth Monarchism and the English Revolution 1616–1660* (Burlington, VT, 2014).
8. For more on western millennialism see Norman Cohn, *The pursuit of the millennium* (Oxford, 1970), and for more specifically on the Fifth Monarchy Men consult Capp, *Fifth Monarchy Men*.
9. All poetry is quoted from the Jeannine Hensley edition of *The works of Anne Bradstreet* (Cambridge, MA, 2010).
10. For example, her recovery starts in the mid-nineteenth century in Ruffus Griswold, *Gems from American female poets* (Philadelphia, PA, 1842), where the prominent critic listed her as the first American poet, but did not include any of her verse. More than a century later, and F.O. Mathieson, who was central to the development of American Studies as an independent discipline, described Bradstreet as 'our first American poet,' (xv–xvi) in *The Oxford book of American verse* (Oxford, 1950). Enthusiasm for Bradstreet as the genesis of American letters has not waned. In David Lehman's anthology *The Oxford book of American poetry* (Oxford, 2006), Bradstreet and Phylis Wheatly are

the only women poets listed below Emily Dickinson. Lehman uncomplicatedly refers to Bradstreet as simply 'the first American poet'. In American higher education she is frequently presented in literature survey courses as the first American poet, even though there are potential candidates for that title writing before her.
11. Bradstreet's critical and educational status as the first American poet in large part derives from both the development of American Studies as a distinctive discipline, as well as the migration of American literary studies from U.S. history departments to English departments in the 1970s and 1980s. See William Spengemann, *A new world of words: Redefining early American literature* (New Haven, CT, 1984) for a thorough explanation of the critical and generic difficulties in classifying Bradstreet as 'American', and also for an account of how she was ultimately categorised as such. For a sense of the continued ambiguities in designating her nationality, see Christopher Ricks (ed.), *The Oxford book of English verse* (Oxford, 1999). Bradstreet (alongside T.S. Eliot and W.H. Auden) is one of the few poets to appear in both this volume and in Lehman, *Oxford book of American poetry*.
12. As recounted in Heidi Nichols, *Anne Bradstreet: A guided tour of the life and thought of a Puritan poet* (Phillipsburg, NJ, 2006), p. 36.
13. Rosemond Rosenmeier, *Anne Bradstreet revisited* (Woodbridge, 1991) is an excellent source for information both biographical and critical on Bradstreet.
14. Wendy Martin, *An American triptych* (Chapel Hill, NC, 1984) is the standard source here.
15. Virgina Woolf, *A Room of One's Own, and Three Guineas* (Oxford, 1998).
16. For example, both Bradstreet and Cavendish share a chapter (surprisingly alongside John Milton) in Michael Schmidt, *Lives of the poets* (New York, 2000). Sidney, Wrote, Lanyer, Cavendish, Behn, and Bradstreet all appear in Sandra Gilbert and Susan Gubar (eds), *The Norton anthology of literature by women* (New York, 2007), which is frequently taught in undergraduate classrooms. An excellent account of the process of establishing this canon of women's literature is Margaret J.M. Ezell, 'The myth of Judith Shakespeare: Creating the canon of women's literature', *New Literary History* 21:3 (1990), pp. 579–592.
17. Attitudes to this can be seen when we examine the differences in seventeenth-century poetry in Ricks, *Oxford book of English verse* compared to Lehman, *Oxford book of American poetry*. The previously mentioned English women poets comprise a relatively small number of page numbers when compared to the more canonical male authors in the first anthology, however Bradstreet has the largest number of pages devoted to her in the Lehman anthology.
18. In the Lehman anthology; in Paul Lauter and Richard Yarborough (eds), *The Heath anthology of American literature* (Belmont, CA, 2013); and Nina Baym and Robert S. Levine (eds), *The Norton anthology of American literature*

(New York, 2011). The only other seventeenth-century American poets to approach Bradstreet in space devoted to her within any of these anthologies are Michael Wigglesworth and Edward Taylor. I argue that in analysing the composition of anthologies that are in common circulation we can establish our common contemporary attitudes surrounding the poet.

19. For examples of this sort of celebration, consult Kenneth A. Requa, 'Anne Bradstreet's poetic voices', *Early American Literature* 9:1 (1974), pp. 3–18; Abram Van Engen. 'Advertising the domestic: Anne Bradstreet's sentimental poetics', *Legacy* 28:1 (2011), pp. 47–68, and Allison Giffen '"Let no man know": Negotiating the gendered discourse of affliction in Anne Bradstreet's "Here follows some verses upon the burning of our house, July 10th, 1666"', *Legacy* 27:1 (2010), pp. 1–22. The most representative example of this sort of exultation of the later poems at the expense of her youthful attempts is Adrienne Riches' introduction to *The works of Anne Bradstreet* (Cambridge, MA, 2010).
20. As recounted in Nichols, *Anne Bradstreet: A guided tour*, p. 35.
21. An example of recent work which takes a more heterodox view of Bradstreet, one which is not dissimilar to my own perspective on the poet, can be found in Zach Hutchins, 'The wisdom of Anne Bradstreet: Eschewing Eve and emulating Elizabeth', *Modern Language Studies* 40:1 (2010), pp. 38–59.
22. Almost any of Christopher Hill's works are intensely illuminating, but *The world turned upside down* (New York, 1984) is perhaps the most influential.
23. Consult Rosenmeir, *Anne Bradstreet revisited* as well as Walter W. Woodward, *Prospero's America* (Williamsburg, VA, 2013).
24. For more on Lead the standard reference is Julie Hirst, *Jane Lead: Biography of a seventeenth-century mystic* (Farnham, 2005). See also Ariel Hessayon (ed.), *Jane Lead and her transnational legacy* (Basingstoke, 2016).
25. Carl Schmidt, *Political theology: Four chapters on the concept of sovereignty* (Chicago, IL, 2006).
26. I would argue that this broadly secularises in the context of American civil religion. See Robert Bellah, *The broken covenant: American civil religion in a time of trial* (Chicago, IL, 1992).
27. See Robert Middlekauf, *The Mathers* (Los Angeles, CA, 1999).
28. This assessment is based in large part on Adrienne Rich's introduction to *The works of Anne Bradstreet* (Cambridge, MA, 2010); in which the critic argues that there is absolutely nothing distinctively 'American' about Bradstreet's verse, and that it would make more sense to classify her as an English poet.
29. Both poems appear in *The Works of Anne Bradstreet* (Cambridge, MA, 2010).
30. For the standard approach to Bradstreet's domestic poems being celebrated as examples of particularly feminine agency at the expense of her earlier verse consult Wendy Martin, *An American triptych: Anne Bradstreet, Emily Dickinson, Adrienne Rich* (Chapel Hill, NC, 1984).

31. For a summary of some of the key political debates see Peter Lake, 'Post-Reformation Politics, or on not looking for the long-term causes of the English civil war', in Michael Braddick (ed.), *The Oxford handbook of the English revolution* (Oxford, 2015), pp. 21–39 and John Walter, 'Crowd and popular politics in the English revolution' on pp. 330–346 of the same volume. For their linkage to explicitly millenarian themes, see Crawford Gribben, *The Puritan millennium: Literature and theology, 1550–1682* (Milton Keynes, 2008).
32. For a sense of this see, Raymond F. Dolle, 'The new Canaan, the old canon, and the new world in American literature anthologies', *College Literature* 17:2/3 (1990), pp. 196–208.
33. Again, this tendency is apparent in such works as Wendy Martin, *An American Triptych*, as well as Adrienne Rich's introduction to the Belknap edition of Bradstreet's poems.
34. Again, this hesitancy to read Bradstreet in this way may have to do with the particular administrative evolution of American departments of English. For more on this subject, consult Consult Spengemann, *A new world of words*.
35. Adrienne Rich, 'Foreword', in Anne Bradstreet, *The works of Anne Bradstreet*, ed. Jeannine Hensley (Cambridge, MA: Belknap, 1981), p. xiv.
36. For more on the western nature of *translatio studii et imperii* consult Nicholas Guyatt, *Providence and the invention of the United States, 1607–1876* (Cambridge, 2007); Jan Willem Schulte Nordholt, *The myth of the west: America as the last empire* (Grand Rapids, MI, 1995); Richard Slotkin, *Regeneration through violence: The mythology of the American frontier, 1600–1860* (Oklahoma City, OK, 2000); Yi-Fun Tuan, *Space and place: The perspective of experience* (Minneapolis, MN, 2001) and Wayne Cristaudo, 'History, theology and the relevance of the *translatio imperii*', *Thesis Eleven* 116:1 (2013), pp. 5–18. See also John Kuhn's chapter in this volume.
37. See Stewart Mottram, '"An empire of itself": Arthur as icon of an English empire, 1509–1547', *Arthurian Literature* 25 (2015), pp. 153–174 and James P. Carley, 'Polydore Vergil and John Leland on King Arthur: The battle of the books', *Interpretations* 15:2 (1984), pp. 86–100.
38. See Colin Kidd, *Identities before nationalism: Ethnicity and nationhood in the Atlantic world, 1600–1800* (Cambridge, 2006).
39. The standard source here is Hill, *The world turned upside down*. Also consult Nigel Smith, *Literature and revolution in England, 1640–1660* (New Haven, CT, 1987).
40. Consult Tony Benn's edition of Winstanley's *A common treasury* (London, 2006).
41. For information on the influence Raleigh, Du Bartas, and others had on Bradstreet's writing, see Kenneth A. Requa, 'Anne Bradstreet's poetic voices', *Early American Literature* 9:1 (1974), pp. 3–18; Robert Richardson, 'The

puritan poetry of Anne Bradstreet', *Texas Studies in Literature and Language* 9:3 (1967), pp. 317–331 and Alfred Owen Aldridge, *Early American literature: A comparatist approach* (Princeton, NJ, 1982).

42. Consult Michael Braddick, *God's fury, England's fire: A new history of the English civil wars* (New York, 2009) for information on the English civil wars.
43. See Mark C. Amodio, *The Anglo-Saxon literature handbook* (Hobokon, NJ, 2013).
44. See both Braddick, *God's fury, England's fire* and *The Oxford handbook of the English revolution*.
45. Consult Perry Miller, *The New England mind: The seventeenth century* (Cambridge, MA, 1983), as well as his *Errand into the wilderness* (Cambridge, MA, 1956). Also Sacvan Bercovitch, *The puritan origins of the American self* (New Haven, CT, 2011).
46. See, for example, Richard Allen, *An antidote against heresy: Or a preservative for Protestants against the poyson of Papists, Anabaptists, Arrians, Arminians, &c.* (London, 1648) who described consubstantiation as 'invented by some to shun the absurdities of the former opinion, fell into worse' and taken up by Luther, which 'gave occasion to continue the bowing and cringing that was lately used to the Communion table' (pp. 127–128). Thomas Brightman had concluded that Rev. 3 contained a prediction of Germany's fall due to their dalliance with this sin. As a pamphlet popularisation of Brightman noted in 1641: 'Germanie ... still retained manie errors ... Consubstantiation of the Lords Supper, and about free-will, justification, good works, &c. by which [Brightman] foreseeing the miserie since come upon them, admonished the *Germans* to consider of it before hand, and to prevent these impending judgements by reformation and timely repentance' (*Brightmans predictions and prophecies written 46 yeares since* (London, 1641), p. 3.
47. Consult Jayne E.E. Boys, *London's news press and the Thirty Years War* (Woodbridge, 2014).
48. My argument and intervention can be read in light of the particular institutional development of the university English department within the United States. As William Spengemann makes clear in *A new world of words*, U.S. literature departments were initially wary of teaching American literature, and so it was originally history and later American Studies departments which defined the contours of the discipline. It is within this context that Bradstreet was initially canonised as the primogenitor of American poetry, while in English departments she was understood as a minor English poet working on the periphery of seventeenth-century literature. From this particular theoretical orientation emerged two broadly contradictory understandings of the poet—that she was somehow the first American poet, while not being particularly 'American'. My intervention broadly inverts that older conception; I claim that Bradstreet must be read in light of these broader Atlantic currents

concerning women's prophecy in the seventeenth century, but that her rhetoric is individually 'American' in theme, content, and rhetoric in a manner that is identifiable in later American literature.

49. The aristocratic one-term governor of Massachusetts (and advocate for religious toleration) Sir Henry Vane was a supporter of the Fifth Monarchists, and through Atlantic connections such as these Bradstreet may have been surprisingly aware of schismatic non-conformist religious groups in Britain. However it should be emphasised that Vane was on the opposite side to her husband when it came to the Antinomian controversy. See Margaret Judson, *The political thought of Sir Henry Vane, the younger* (Philadelphia, PA, 1969).

CHAPTER 5

Antichrists, and Rumours of Antichrists: Radical Prophecy in the trans-Atlantic World, 1640–1660

Chris Caughey

When the congregation of the church at Kendal met toward the end of December in 1652, they were likely prepared only for their regular worship service. So when the wife of Edmund Nubye entered the church wearing only a shirt, her prophetic sign surely received its intended attention.[1] Quakers were known to 'go naked as a sign' in the manner of the Old Testament prophet, Isaiah, in order to signify the sinfulness of all who saw them. Just as the usually religious audiences saw the nakedness of these Quakers, so those same audiences could not conceal their sin and hypocrisy from God. Thus, such Quakers wrote and spoke as though nakedness as a prophetic sign was completely appropriate. However, to those who witnessed this behaviour, it certainly appeared radical.

The sea change in the political atmosphere during the years of the civil wars and the interregnum at once created the conditions which made Quakerism possible, and simultaneously marginalised it. When the Long

---

C. Caughey (✉)
Department of English, William Jessup University, Rocklin, CA, USA
e-mail: caugheyc@tcd.ie

Parliament dissolved the courts of High Commission and Star Chamber in 1641, religious sects that had once been too afraid of violent persecution to make their presences known were now much more free to teach openly. The fact that many sectarians had enlisted in Cromwell's army must have also been encouraging to radical groups. Though Quakers would not have enlisted by conviction, George Fox, the founder of Quakerism, had more than one friendly encounter with Cromwell.

Of course, using the term 'radical' to describe anything from the seventeenth century, including prophecy of any stripe, presents challenges. Ariel Hessayon and David Finnegan have addressed the inherent anachronism of such an endeavour.[2] They note that since George Gooch's work, *The History of English Democratic Ideas in the Seventeenth Century* (1898), the term 'radicalism' has been used with ever-greater frequency, such that there appears to be no going back. However, some observations about the use of the term only underscore the problems associated with its use. Near the turn of the twentieth century, P. Brooks defined radicalism as simply an interest in returning to the roots of things.[3] Thus, radicalism was like conservatism, recognising the goodness of existing institutions, and building upon the good roots established by preceding generations. But a few decades later, Horace Kallen defined it as being akin to modern progressivism: the calculated move to destroy those things which have come to be hated, and the replacement of them with what can be 'logically demonstrated as true and good and beautiful and just'.[4]

John Owen's sermon before the House of Commons on 31 January 1649 problematises both of these definitions simultaneously. Charles I had been beheaded by Owen's theological compatriots just the day before, and parliament had asked him to preach in light of the momentous and solemn occasion. Owen and many other Puritans saw themselves as conserving the best of the church and continuing the trajectory of the Protestant Reformation out of the roots of the Church Fathers. Yet few things could have been more revolutionary than the unprecedented regicide. In his sermon, Owen interpreted the history and politics of England in light of the biblical conflict between Christ and Antichrist. The heirs of the Reformation in early modern England were on the side of Christ, whom Owen not accidentally referenced as the Lord of lords, and the King of kings. Without naming Charles I specifically, Owen mentions the Pope and the kings of the earth who give their power to another figure of the Antichrist, namely the Beast (Rev. 19:19).[5] The implication seems clear: those earthly kings who are allied with the purposes of the Antichrist ought to perish like the Beast of Revelation.

To Roman Catholics and Anglicans in early modern England, not only the regicide, but Owen's sermon must have appeared radical. The English monarchy was one of the oldest institutions in the land. Furthermore, one of the lasting effects of the Constantinian revolution was the conviction that magistrates shared some important religious responsibilities with ecclesiastical officers. Magistrates were to enforce membership in the established church, and conformity to its faith and practice—which included punishing heretics and sectarians such as radical prophets. Given these historical circumstances, it was not unimportant that Henry VIII's solution to his lineal challenge was to become the head of the Church of England. So to participants in the English religious establishment, the irony must have been bitter when Owen preached his January 1649 sermon which, in part, justified the execution of the head of their church.

All of this means that the 'radicalness' of prophecies during the English Civil Wars and the Interregnum was largely in the eye of the beholder. To the extent that it is meaningful to speak of Puritanism, that community of the 'hotter sort of Protestants' was an unstable system. There was anything but homeostasis among Puritans who accused some of their fellow believers of antinomianism, and suspected others of legalism; who were willing to condemn each other over principles of church government—and whether those principles should be Presbyterian or Independent and Congregational; who disagreed vehemently over the nature and proper recipients of the sacraments (or ordinances); and who subscribed mutually exclusive confessional documents—or subscribed the same confessional documents while engaging in war against each other (e.g., the London Parliament and the Scots during the second civil war, 1648–1649). It was not uncommon for one Puritan to view another Puritan's prophetic message for England as radical. To most Anglicans, messages worthy of the name of Puritan tended to be messages that were radical. To Roman Catholics, even Anglicans who might have been sympathetic to Rome were radical in light of the machinations of Henry VIII. And to true atheists—even incorrigible citizens like the Earl of Rochester and Lord Audeley, Earl of Castlehaven—all prophecies were likely viewed as radical, whether Christian or not.

This essay will survey radical prophecy in the transatlantic world from 1640 to 1660. The figure of the Antichrist will provide a way into the variegated prophecies in which different sects participated. Specifically, the theme of radical prophecy about the Antichrist will be traced from the community of Puritans broadly considered, to antinomians more narrowly considered, finally concluding with the Quakers. The survey will begin broadly with prophecies about institutions and prominent world leaders, and will conclude with more subjective and esoteric messages. One particular relationship that will feature prominently here is that between the Parliament, the radical prophets, and their prophecies. In fact, it is one of the great ironies of the seventeenth century that as Puritan interests assumed control of the magistracy, and as they liberated non-established churches, non-Anglican Protestantism tended to lose its composure. Thus, radical prophecy is one of the unintended consequences of at least the elision of cult and culture, if not of Erastianism.

5.1 Radical Prophesying Among the Godly

The term 'prophecy' may conjure up images of bearded heralds with esoteric messages based on dreams or visions. But from the time of the Reformation, Protestants had begun to refer to the careful exposition of the Bible in a particular manner. This is exemplified in the way the Second Helvetic Confession (1566) treats preaching: 'Wherefore when this Word of God is now preached in the church by preachers lawfully called, we believe that the very Word of God is proclaimed and received by the faithful.'[6] In other words, preaching was the Word of God. Thus, the last entry for prophecy in the Oxford English Dictionary is an older Protestant usage: 'A meeting or debate held for the systematic exposition of scripture'; or 'the interpretation and expounding of the Bible'. No less a figure than the paradigmatic Puritan, William Perkins, interpreted the spiritual gift of prophecy in 1 Corinthians 14 as both the preaching of the Bible, and public prayer. Thus, prophesying was 'a publique and solemne speech of the Prophet, pertaining to the worship of God and the salvation of [his] neighbour'. On such words, many Puritans were trained for pastoral ministry.[7]

With the impeachment of Archbishop Laud in 1640 and the dissolution of the Courts of High Commission and Star Chamber in 1641, the historical record swelled with examples of radical prophecies. One Puritan who went to print with messages of eschatological foreboding earlier than most during this period was John Milton. In 1641, he wrote two treatises on church government.[8] These read like works written by someone who saw himself in league with Presbyterianism against the forces of the Antichrist. The Antichristianity against which he wrote was that which was free to do anything in worship that was not forbidden in the Bible. However, Milton echoed the Presbyterian regulative principle, namely, that the Church may only do in worship what is expressly commanded in the Bible. One of the clear implications that Milton drew from this was that the Pope was Antichrist, and the Roman Catholic Church was the kingdom and seat of that beast. Indeed, Milton wrote that even the Catholic form of government—'Prelaty'—was 'more Antichristian then Antichrist himselfe'.[9] Yet in addition to his criticism of Rome, he found fault with the Church of England for spending so much of England's treasury in order 'exquisitely to out-vie the Papists' because such mammon gave birth to the Antichrist.[10]

During this same time, Henry Burton preached that Roman Catholics were not Christians, but were disciples of Antichrist, instead.[11] This was not remarkable for Puritans. But Burton was an early pioneer of a new practice: he took his radical prophecy to the floor of one of England's representative magisterial bodies. Many had preached for the king and for parliament before. But prior to the 1640s, those sermons tended to be occasional, affirmative and approving—at least with regard to the religion of the current monarch and the Church of England. Yet on 20 June 1641, Burton preached a sermon about England's spiritual bondage, and its only hope of deliverance, before MPs at St Margaret's in Westminster. Borrowing from Luther's metaphor of Israel's captivity in Babylon to describe the condition of Christians under Roman Catholicism, he proclaimed that England had been under an 'Ecclesiasticall bondage' to Antichrist.[12] This bondage, he claimed, was to the hierarchy of prelacy because it replaced a spiritual government and bound the consciences of Christians.[13]

Burton was joined in this new practice by William Bridge, who preached before the House of Commons at Westminster in 1641. His prophecy echoed Burton's, but Bridge saw the Antichrist as magisterial rather than ministerial.[14] Thus, he saw parliament as the place where the man of sin would appear, and the battleground where he would be fought. Yet he also sounded the eschatologically triumphant note that the 'Antichristian Roman Babylon' would most certainly fall.[15] Likewise, Edmund Calamy had an audience before the Commons on both 23 February and 22 December 1641. Appealing to England's unique ecclesiastical establishment, Calamy interpreted Henry VIII as opposing Antichrist by his politico-religious machinations; and he praised James I as the first English monarch to recognise the Pope as Antichrist in print.[16] He also saw Antichrist's fingerprints on the political upheaval threatening Ireland and England.[17] The year before parliament called the Westminster Assembly, they heard more Puritan prophecies regarding the ultimate antagonist. Thomas Goodwin preached before the House of Commons on 27 April

1642, identifying the Antichrist with Rome and extra-biblical worship practices.[18]

But the year that the Westminster Assembly began their work of confessional deliberation toward a Puritan settlement, radical prophecies before parliament accelerated in frequency and intensity. Robert Baillie proclaimed that priests were inherently Antichristian because they regressed to the types and shadows of a Mosaic institution, thereby discarding the antitype of Christ himself.[19] John Lightfoot warned the elected officials that the Antichrist had added external trappings to the Christian religion, and that there could be no communion between Christ and Antichristian Rome.[20] Both the House of Lords and the House of Commons heard Thomas Hill prophesy that the fight against the Roman Catholic Church should be waged with preaching because Rome was the tool of the Devil and his angels.[21] After all, Satan was seeking to besiege England through Papists who wanted to leave the Church with half a sacrament, antinomians who wanted to leave them with half a Bible, and universities that wanted to place all kinds of stumbling blocks before them.[22] In September, Anthony Burgess prophesied that the Church needed to be even more diligent than unbelievers—who were living to make straight the way for the Antichrist—by making the way straight for Christ in England.[23]

The English Parliament heard many more prophecies from Puritans over the course of the next sixteen years. Most of the sermons continued to warn against the dangers of Popery and prelacy.[24] In fact, as Anthony Milton has observed, something like an 'apocalyptic nationalism' developed in light of the doctrine that the Pope was Antichrist. This complemented well the largely Puritan notion that England was an antitypical, if not eschatological Israel.[25] Yet some were concerned that potentates were the peril that threatened England, and ultimately, the world.[26] A few were content to simply prophesy to the Parliament about the Antichrist using the vocabulary of Protestant theology and the New Testament.[27]

Across the Atlantic, the prophesying that took place in New England Puritan communions during the decade leading up to the Long Parliament and the Civil Wars prepared the way for radical prophecy. It did so in perhaps an ironic way; though it may appear to most students of Puritanism that the godly took sin exceedingly seriously, at least in New England in the 1630s, perhaps they did not take it as seriously as Protestants had on the continent during the previous century. If Luther, Calvin, and other continental reformers from the sixteenth century were correct about original sin, it affected humanity so completely that not only was the guilt of

Adam's sin imputed to everyone born of natural means, but the corruption from that sin was embedded in every facet of what it meant to be human. Such sin, they believed, could not be removed by sinners, no matter how diligently they applied themselves to the task. Yet, as Philip Gura has observed, if sinners could never be inherently good enough to earn God's acceptance, New England Puritan churches tended to act as though sinners could become good enough to be members of a local church. New England Puritans had developed conditions for church membership that went beyond giving a credible profession of faith. They taught that candidates for church membership were also required to give evidence of God's grace in their lives. Election had to be proven according to something like empirical methods.[28]

The result of this type of prophecy and its attendant practice was not that the godly increased in godliness, or in number. Instead, 'only 1700 of 20,000 residents of Massachusetts' were worthy of membership in Puritan churches there in 1643.[29] This provoked Puritans like Robert Stansby, on the other side of the Atlantic, to criticise their New England brethren for being so strict about the criteria for church membership that more than half of the population was excluded from the churches.[30] In fact, New England's own Peter Bulkeley was sceptical of the genuineness of the piety of these Massachusetts church members. He accused them of contenting themselves with outward conformity, such that 'they may seeme cleane before men; but they harbour many corrupt lusts within, which they does not seek to cast forth'.[31] Thus New England Puritans believed that members of their churches should have assurance of salvation; yet few seemed confirmed by the church in that assurance, and even those who did were suspected of hypocrisy by some of the Puritan ministers. Such messages contributed to what Theodore Dwight Bozeman calls 'antinomian backlash'.[32]

New England minister John Cotton, who had managed to sidestep charges of antinomianism in the controversy surrounding Anne Hutchinson, had his own radical prophecies. In the records of a 1646 conference Cotton had with the elders of New England, he laboured the point that theology and practices of the Roman Catholic Church were in league with Antichrist. Of course, this was not radical in the sense that the idea that the Pope was Antichrist was being increasingly worked into Protestant confessions since the inception of the Reformation.[33] Therefore, by the time of this conference, Puritan preoccupation with the Antichrist was well established. Yet even a few years later, Cotton caused fear and suspicion in the Presbyterian Robert Baillie. Baillie was not only concerned that Cotton was an antinomian because he had written in support of Congregational church polity, but also worried that he was therefore an agent of Antichrist. In England, Baillie published his condemnation of Cotton in *Anabaptism, the True Fountaine of Independency, Brownisme, Antinomy, Familisme, and Most of the Other Errours, Which For the Time Due Trouble the Church of England* (1647). Once Cotton received a copy in New England, he responded in *The Way of Congregational Churches Cleared* (1648). In this way radical prophetic discourse crisscrossed the Atlantic.

Back in England, there was still more prophesying about the Antichrist taking place, even if not before an audience of magistrates. Thomas Goodwin preached a sermon designed to exonerate the Fifth Monarchists, in which, like Foxe's *Acts and Monuments*, he admitted that the Pope may not be the Antichrist: the Antichrist may be the Islamic religion.[34] Jeremiah Burroughs tried to encourage the godly with the notion that the Antichrist would only attack the pious.[35] Thus, those who were committed to 'the name and profession of Religion alone', like Anglicans and Roman Catholics, would escape persecution; but only because they were allied with dark forces. Similarly, Edmund Calamy warned that the Antichrist would only imitate godliness in order to better deceive the world.[36] And using a somewhat common Protestant strategy, Anthony Burgess, in a sermon preached to the church of Sutton-Coldfield in Warwickshire, quoted Pope Gregory I (590–604) as having said that '*Whosoever should arrogate to himself the Title of Universal Bishop, he was the Forerunner of Antichrist.*'[37]

Such prophecies were not unique to old or New England. Even in Ireland, the godly sounded the alarm about the Antichrist. In a sermon given at Christ-Church in Dublin, for a military interment, Faithful Teate told believers that the Antichrist would try to convince the world that religion was not something for which it was worth fighting.[38] This piece of prophecy was a call to arms to Christian soldiers (metaphorical and civil) to be ready, willing, and able to go to war against the Antichrist. Archbishop of Armagh, James Ussher preached scathing sermons against the Pope, citing Catholic and Anglican prelates, as well as Protestant theologians—including Jacob Arminius—who identified the pontiff as the Antichrist.[39] Ussher also acknowledged how common it was for ordained ministers of his time to be called the Antichrist. But he urged his hearers to use moderation and to 'consider who deserves the Title, whether those that observe the *rule of Christ*' or those who are '*a law unto themselves*'.[40]

Christopher Hill also notes that Ussher was critical of 'men fathering upon Antichrist whatsoever in church matters did not suit with their humours'.[41]

Both individual and corporate notions of the Antichrist were invoked in radical Puritan prophecies. Indeed, the pre-eminent Puritan confession produced by the Westminster Assembly identified the Pope as the Man of Sin. Yet even in such cases, the Pope could stand in for the whole institution of the Roman Catholic Church by way of synecdoche. In fact, on the whole, a close reading of the prophecies referenced above will bear this out.

There was, then, no shortage of concern about the Antichrist among Puritans. While Puritans tended to focus their fears on the Pope and the Roman Catholic Church, they could not help but suspect some in their own community. Perhaps an Independent, Congregationalist, or nonconformist minister would turn out to be the Antichrist. Perhaps some prophet with a 'legal spirit' would be revealed as the biblical man of lawlessness. Or perhaps a notorious antinomian would ascend to that office, as Samuel Rutherford opined in his work, *A survey of the spirituall antichrist* (1648).

5.2 Radical Prophecies of Antinomians

One term of abuse that was used almost synonymously with at least 'radical', if not 'Antichrist', in the seventeenth century was 'antinomian'. Just as the godly harboured concerns that the Antichrist might be in pulpit, pew, or parsonage, so that same community tended to nurture concerns that too many of their peers were antinomians. Accusations of antinomianism were abundant and pervasive, such that even men like John Owen and John Bunyan were labelled as antinomians by vocal anti-antinomians such as Richard Baxter.

The Welshman Walter Cradock was one such preacher who was suspected of antinomianism. He prophesied about the Antichrist in a sermon on the verse: 'All things are lawful for me, but all things are not expedient' (1 Cor. 10:23). Although he did associate Popery with the Antichrist, he added some unique insights. He situated his language about Antichrist in the context of general unbelief.[42] He even claimed that the binding of consciences about extra-biblical matters was an identifying mark of the Antichrist.[43] Strangely, however, Cradock urged caution in applying the terms 'Antichrist' or 'Antichristian' to people. Perhaps this was a result of his own experiences of having been marginalised by being labelled an antinomian. Though this was not at all a radical move, Cradock was concerned that an injudicious use of the term 'Antichrist' was not winsome.[44]

The infamy of William Dell's antinomianism was much more widespread than Cradock's. At least some of his prophecies about the Antichrist were personal. For example, an unnamed member of the Westminster Assembly was alleged to have said, '*If the Parliament approved Mr. Dells Sermon, it were no blasphemy to say, They were no Parliament.*' Dell replied:

> If the Assembly (which I hope they will not) should condemne that Doctrine of the Gospel for the substance of it, delivered then by Mr. Dell; it will be no blasphemy to say, *They are enemies of the truth of Christ: And (I hope) the last prop of Antichrist in the Kingdome.*[45]

But outside of that repartee, Dell, like Cradock, brought unique insight to his prophecies about the Antichrist. In *The Building and Glory of the Truely Christian and Spiritual Church* (1646), Dell proclaimed that the idea of established churches, in which all citizens of a given nation were members of the national church, was one that came from the Antichrist.[46] In the age of Constantinian ecclesiology, such a prophecy stood out sufficiently to appear radical. Dell buttressed this claim about national membership in established churches with the argument that magistrates and ministers lent each other their power or authority—and that the result was not the power of God, but the power of the Antichrist.[47] Furthermore, though unity was Christian, uniformity was antichristian.[48] But Dell had hope regarding the future and God's promises against the Antichrist; he prophesied that Christ would destroy the Antichrist 'by the Spirit of his mouth, and the brightness of his coming'.[49]

In contrast to both Cradock and Dell, John Saltmarsh read the events of his day through the interpretive lens of the biblical prophecies regarding the Antichrist. He prophesied that the current wars in Germany, Denmark, Italy, Ireland and England were 'preparatories' for the battle of Armageddon.[50] He claimed that the Antichrist would come with the same signs and wonders as the sorcerers of Egypt against Moses.[51] Inside the Church, it was the Antichrist who had confused or elided the Old and New Testaments, the law and the gospel, and 'the two covenants'.[52] Saltmarsh also claimed that Antichrist could dwell within believers.[53] As Saltmarsh put it, 'this Antichrist thus described is found in man, or the spirit of meer man, in al his departure or falling away from God'.[54] This was unusual, in that it sounded more mystical than Cradock, Dell, or even most of the rest of Saltmarsh's own writings.

David R. Como has observed a qualitative difference between seventeenth-century antinomians. Cradock, Dell, and Saltmarsh fall into his first category of 'imputative antinomians'. These antinomians tended to focus on the Protestant doctrine of justification, and thus they understood Christ's righteousness as alien, outside of themselves, yet also for themselves. Anti-antinomians such as Richard Baxter, Samuel Rutherford, Anthony Burgess, and Robert Baillie described Como's imputative antinomians as radical because it was thought that they had made justification to swallow up sanctification—and that they had made Christ's perfect obedience to abolish any need for Christian obedience. Thus, this kind of antinomian was working with legal categories, because he or she was alleged to believe that Christ's righteousness, imputed to believers, was all that was needed—to the exclusion of believers' good works.[55] Como's other category of antinomian is either 'perfectionist' or 'inherentist' antinomians. Unlike the imputative antinomians, this latter category of antinomians involved people who believed that not only Christ's righteousness, but both Christ and God, were inside the godly. Rather than Christ doing everything *for* someone, these antinomians prophesied Christ doing everything *in* someone.[56] One popular idea attributed to perfectionist or inherentist antinomians by anti-antinomians was that a person could be 'Godded with god, and Christed with Christ'.[57] This was renovative prophecy, which advocated direct encounters between God and the human soul. Thus, the emphasis, instead of legal, was introspective, mystical, and ultimately, radical.

Fewer historical specimens actually fit this latter category of antinomianism than the imputative antinomians. Yet one English minister did stand out in this regard. John Everard, a minister from Kensington, who had the ears of Henry Rich the Earl of Holland, and Edmund Sheffield the Earl of Mulgrave, was a radical prophet of the mystical sort. Though he died in 1641, a collection of Everard's sermons was published in 1657, entitled *The Gospel treasury opened*. Like other Puritans, he identified the Pope as the Antichrist.[58] But frequently, he employed a list of terms to describe evil and malevolent forces in the world, forces that were arrayed against God and his purposes. Though the list varied in different sermons, it tended to include the likes of the natural man, the strongman, the old man, sin, the Devil, Satan, Lucifer, and Antichrist.[59] All of these were biblical terms, but Everard's use of them was unusual, especially among Puritans. Not only by listing them together, but also by referring to them collectively in the singular (e.g., 'this *Enemy* of ours'), he made them identical; and that was a strange move to make amidst theologians who excelled at making distinctions.[60]

Everard had moments of apparent orthodoxy: he affirmed both the Lord's Prayer,[61] and the Apostles' Creed[62]—the corporate recitations of which would connect him and his congregation to the Roman church. But even his use of these elements in worship seemed duplicitous. On the one hand, he acknowledged that the second article of the Creed was something that the Antichrist could not confess: that Jesus Christ had come in the flesh. But on the other hand, this gave him occasion to ask his congregation whether the historical events mentioned in the Creed had happened inside each of them, individually:

> But I would ask thee, Is Jesus Christ come into the flesh with thee? Is he come into thy flesh? That Christ is born in thee, risen in thee, that he is glorified in thy members? Then thou art no Antichrist: but if he be not, thou needest not go far to find Antichrist.[63]

The unusual, mystical and allegorical understanding of the relationship of the seventeenth-century individual to the historical events of Christ's life, death, and resurrection was therefore just the beginning. Everard also understood the Antichrist in the same way. In Everard's radical prophecies, the Man of Lawlessness was in each person.[64] This was, by far, the most common way for him to refer to the apocalyptic figure. In light of this ontological, rather than ethical, way of understanding the Antichrist, it should not be surprising that he proclaimed that the Antichrist was everywhere, and in everything.[65] Those who did not believe so were like sceptics who did not believe in 'Spirits and Hobgoblings'.[66]

Antinomians, whether of the imputationist or perfectionist and inherentist varieties, contributed to radical prophecy in the decades of the English Civil Wars and the Interregnum. Their sermons indicate that the Antichrist was a matter of concern for them as much as it was for the rest of the community of Puritans. No matter whether their ultimate interests were in divine justice, sin, grace, and redemption, or matters of ontology and the close union of divine and creaturely essences, they understood the Antichrist to be a true and present danger—especially to believers in Jesus.

5.3 The Society of Prophetic Friends

If all Puritans did not share the same understanding of what it meant to do all things 'decently and in order,' (1 Cor. 14:40), most at least agreed that they should 'suffer not a woman to teach' (1 Tim. 2:12). So when Quakers made a regular practice of sending prophetesses out into the world—female preachers who would sometimes bring apocalyptic messages—they could not avoid the charge of radicalism. Even within the Quakers' own ranks, there was dissention over the propriety of women preaching, prophesying, and pontificating.[67] In any case, this cut against the grain of the gender roles in the patriarchal cultures of the early modern, transatlantic world. These often itinerant, female preachers would frequently travel by ship with fellow female Quakers, usually across the Atlantic, to the New World.

Some of the first Quaker prophets to go to America were Elizabeth Harris, Mary Fisher, and Ann Austin.[68] In fact, Fisher and Austin left England for New England, after enduring much corporal punishment for their prophecies. But it did not take long for the Boston colony to banish them to Barbados; and after prophesying for a while there, they eventually traversed the Atlantic again in order to return to England.[69] This was another way that radical prophecy passed back and forth across the Atlantic; in this case, in the persons of female prophets. Another Quaker prophet, Mary Tompkins, prophesied to a Boston magistrate that she held his honour under her foot after he ordered her to remove her hat, and she had stomped on it.[70] Mary Dyer also assumed this office, using the Old Testament story of Esther to shame Boston magistrates for not repenting of being kept from shedding blood—and that shaming was intensified because it was done by a woman.[71]

Whether in the old World or the New, on either side of the Atlantic, Quakers inhabited a tension in the discursive space between metaphysical gender, the physicality of their prophecies, and their theology of prophecy. On the one hand, they tended to use their bodies quite frequently in their prophesying. In fact, the Quaker body often formed the medium of the prophecy itself: from 'going naked as a sign', to wearing unusual items in public, to enduring grotesque and torturous corporal punishment.[72] In a very important sense, then, matter mattered to Quakers with regard to their prophecy. Yet when it came to prophecy, gender was a matter of interpretation and spiritual discernment. Richard Farnsworth claimed that when the Spirit of God was manifested in a person, the man Christ was speaking, regardless of the gender of the person in whom the Spirit was manifested.[73] Edward Burrough explained that Christ was the man who may speak in church, and so any 'Male & Female-man' who wished to preach or prophesy must do so 'in *thy Head*, and *the Head* of every man is *Christ Jesus*'.[74] Metaphysical gender, then, was reinterpreted in light of the man Jesus Christ, who, apparently, swallowed up the gendered bodies of believers in himself. Thus, some Quakers found a way to justify female prophets by claiming that only men could prophesy, because it was the man Jesus Christ who prophesied through believers. In this way, some Quakers even wrote that women were forbidden to teach; and even fallen males were spiritual women.[75]

Of course, Quaker men prophesied, too, when God impressed their consciences with the duty to say or do something in God's stead. No less than the first Quaker, George Fox, prophesied a great deal about the Antichrist. While he agreed that the Pope was Antichrist, and the doctrines and practices of the Roman Catholic Church were Antichristian, Fox also had distinctive ideas about the man of lawlessness.[76] The Quaker leader had pointed messages for Protestant ministers: not only were they Antichrists, but their church buildings were also Antichristian.[77] The prophecy that the Antichrist preaches Christ in form, but not in power, was likely intended for all ministers in traditional, institutional churches.[78] And since many confessional Protestants and Catholics tended to support at least corporal, if not capital punishment for Quakers, Fox also proclaimed that anyone who killed God's people (e.g., Quakers) was the Antichrist.[79] Similarly, the man of sin was any false Christ who used force to compel people to worship him.[80]

But Fox was also like John Everard, in that he tended to see the Antichrist everywhere and in everything. Deceivers and false prophets were the Antichrist, and there were many of those in the world.[81] But so was anyone who opposed the light of Christ, or could not see the light of Christ.[82] That not only included all professing non-Christians, but it also involved more ambiguous criteria. Moving even farther in this direction, Fox prophesied that anyone who denied that a person who claims to be Christ truly was Christ—or who denied that Christ's disciples truly were his disciples—was the Antichrist.[83] Anyone who opposed the scriptures as the Quakers understood them, was the Antichrist[84]; as was anyone who opposed the Spirit in Quaker prophecy.[85] But only Fox himself could detect the Spirit of Antichrist in certain people.[86]

Quakers generally did not develop networks with civil magistrates, and so they were also not asked to preach before parliament or other magisterial bodies. Theology accounts for this to some extent, but temperament was also a contributing factor. Simply because Quakers were not invited to preach for the civil government, did not mean that such preaching did not take place. But when Quakers did preach or prophesy before the authorities, it was usually in the mode of confrontation.

5.4 Conclusion

Alexandra Walsham has argued persuasively that it is too simplistic to trace a social or political move in the seventeenth century from 'persecution to toleration' because the interrelationships between ideologies, public policies, and the 'tolerance of practical rationality' defy easy explanations. Individuals are often quixotic and change their minds; policies have unintended consequences; and even the most zealous religionists wanted to avoid annihilation or extinction.[87] Certainly there is appeal, and truth, in the story of toleration as the grandchild of the Enlightenment, and its offspring, secularism. But history is rarely as tidy as the stories we tell ourselves.

Magistrates and radical prophets had an uneasy relationship during the troubled decades of the English civil wars and interregnum. For one thing, it is not clear whether the English Parliament invited prophetic utterances on radical themes such as the Antichrist, or whether such prophecies were sufficiently known in the culture that they had piqued the Parliament's interest. If the former is the case, then it appears that parliament could not stop the stream of radical prophecy once it opened the door. In a sense, they would have been responsible for radical prophecies insofar as they had eliminated the politico-religious institutions of restraint, and invited prophets into the halls of power. It would have been ironic, indeed, for parliament to attempt to discriminate between radical prophecies, approving some, and censuring others after the fact. This theory seems to ring true. For example, Edward Fisher, who was considered a dangerous radical under Laud's oversight, was given the imprimatur of Parliament for his controversial work *The Marrow of Modern Divinity* (1646).[88] Stephen Dobranski has recently chronicled such changes in the use of censorial powers.[89] However, if parliament were only responding to a widespread cultural phenomenon, that could indicate that the theological climate was already out of control—even as the Westminster Assembly was being called to articulate some measure of authority.

Antinomian prophets must have been particularly troubling to parliament. On the one hand some of the men they had selected to participate in the Westminster Assembly were some of the most outspoken anti-antinomians of the seventeenth century. But on the other hand, the leader of the parliamentary cavalry, Oliver Cromwell, had commanded a variety of antinomians who had enlisted in the New Model Army. Thus, while some commissioners to the Westminster Assembly were busy writing and prophesying against antinomianism, the new face of English law enforcement was giving quarter to the same antinomians. Cromwell himself spoke to the Governor of Edinburgh Castle and parliament, on different occasions, regarding the Antichrist—yet he sounded more measured and collected than either the antinomians or their antagonists.[90]

Quakers were a different story in that they were theologically proscribed from involvement in the violent activities of the State, such as war. Thus, their relationship with magistrates and the parliament was not one of ironic entanglement, but of confrontation and rebuke. Quakers seemed to be unafraid to offend officials in the hopes that their magisterial consciences might be pricked, so that they might repent and become Quakers themselves. Many magistrates were offended, and some responded violently, causing severe physical damage or death to Quaker prophets. But eyewitnesses also told stories of magistrates who tried to be creative and lenient in dealing with Quakers, but who eventually had no choice but to have them arrested and jailed.[91]

In all of these cases, radical prophets in the seventeenth century were the unpaid debts incurred by a parliament that wanted to enforce the Reformation wherever its power and authority went. In the New World, Puritans attempted to exercise their new politico-religious liberty to prophesy freely and with clear consciences. Yet the antinomians among them were eager to exercise that same liberty. Quakers had also hoped to benefit from a post-Laudian regime, making the Atlantic trek only to discover that Puritan magistrates could be equally as cruel as the late Archbishop and his courts. Walsham has observed that, while individual Puritans tended to live in certain places and ways in order to contribute to the enforcement of Reformation, there were also ways in which civil and ecclesiastical authorities could provide leniency discreetely.[92] In the old World, parliament may have heard radical prophecies in their chambers, but they were less than prepared to tolerate the variety of prophesying that ensued. Liberty for the parliament's kind of Puritans, then, simultaneously meant tyranny for those who believed and worshiped differently. Thus, if the Antichrist could not be defeated by parliamentary policies and laws, neither could a Puritan establishment or the ultimate kingdom of God be inaugurated by the same means.

Notes

1. Thomas Weld, *A further discovery of that generation of men called Qvakers* (London, 1654), p. 84.
2. Ariel Hessayon and David Finnegan, 'Introduction: Reappraising early modern radicals and radicalisms', in Ariel Hessayon and David Finnegan (eds), *Varieties of seventeenth- and early eighteenth-century English radicalism in context* (Burlington, VT, 2011), pp. 1–29.
3. P. Brooks, quoted in J.E. Shea, 'Radicalism and reform', *Proceedings of the American Political Science Association* 3 (1906), p. 167.
4. Horace Kallen, 'Radicalism', in E. Seligman (ed.), *Encyclopaedia of the Social Sciences* (15 vols., New York, 1930–1934), vol. 13, pp. 51–54.
5. John Owen, *A sermon preached to the honourable House of Commons, in Parliament assembled: On January 31. A day of solemne humiliation* (London, 1649), pp. 61, 76.
6. Philip Schaff, 'The Second Helvetic Confession in English', in *Bibliotheca symbolica ecclesiæ universalis. The creeds of Christendom, with a history and critical notes* (New York, 1919), p. 832.
7. William Perkins, *The arte of prophecying* (London, 1607), pp. 1–4. See also Charles Broxholme, *The good old way, or, Perkins improved in a plain exposition and sound application of those depths of divinity briefly comprized in his Six principles* (London, 1653); John Robinson, *An appendix to Mr. Perkins his six principles of Christian religion* (London, 1641); Anonymous, *The practise of Christianity containiug* [sic] *a briefe of Christian instructions gathered out of holy Scripture, in Perkins, and other learned writers* (London, 1634); Teresa Toulouse, 'The art of prophesying: John Cotton and the rhetoric of election', *Early American Literature* 19:3 (1984); Francis J. Bremer and Tom Webster, *Puritans and Puritanism in Europe and America* (Santa Barbara, CA, 2006), pp. 279–299; 416, 479, 490, 494–496.
8. John Milton, *Of reformation touching church-discipline in England* (London, 1641); and *The reason of church-government urg'd against prelaty* (London, 1641).
9. Milton, *The reason of church-government*, p. 59.
10. Milton, *Of reformation*, pp. 61–62.
11. Henry Burton, *A most godly sermon preached at St. Albons in Woodstreet on Sunday last being the 10 of October, 1641* (London, 1641), sig. A5.
12. Henry Burton, *Englands bondage and hope of deliverance* (London, 1641), p. 20.
13. Burton, *Englands bondage*, p. 24.
14. William Bridge, *Babylons downfall a sermon lately preached at Westminster before sundry of the honourable House of Commons* (London, 1641), p. 9.
15. Bridge, *Babylons downfall*, pp. 3, 28.

16. Edmund Calamy, *Gods free mercy to England presented as a pretious and powerful motive to humiliation: In a sermon preached before the honourable House of Commons at their late solemne fast, February 23, 1641* (London, 1642), p. 4.
17. Edmund Calamy, *Englands looking-glasse presented in a sermon preached before the Honorable House of Commons at their late solemne fast, December 22, 1641* (London, 1642), p. 10.
18. Thomas Goodwin, *Zerubbabels encouragement to finish the temple. A sermon preached before the honourable House of Commons, at their late solemne fast, April 27, 1642* (London, 1642), pp. 12–13, 17–18, 39.
19. Robert Baillie, *Satan the leader in chief to all who resist the reparation of Sion. As it was cleared in a sermon to the honourable House of Commons at their late solemn fast, February 28, 1643* (London, 1643), pp. 15–16.
20. John Lightfoot, *Elias redivivus: A sermon preached before the honorable House of Commons, in the parish of Saint Margarets Westminster, at the publike fast, March 29, 1643* (London, 1643), p. 21, 40.
21. Thomas Hill, *The militant church triumphant over the dragon and his angels presented in a sermon preached to both Houses of Parliament assembled on Friday the 21 of July 1643* (London, 1643), pp. 19–20.
22. Hill, *The militant church*, p. 23.
23. Anthony Burgess, *The difficulty of and the encouragements to a reformation a sermon preached before the honourable House of Commons at the publick fast, September 27, 1643* (London, 1643), p. 24.
24. Samuel Rutherford, *A sermon preached to the Honourable House of Commons at their late solemne fast, Wednesday, January 31, 1644* (Edinburgh, 1644); Henry Hall, *Heaven ravished: Or A glorious prize, atchieved by an heroicall enterprize: As it was lately presented in a sermon to the honourable House of Commons, at their solemn fast, May 29, 1644* (London, 1644); John Owen, *A vision of vnchangeable free mercy, in sending the means of grace to undeserved sinners* (London, 1646); *A sermon preached to the Honourable House of Commons, in Parliament assembled: On January 31* (London, 1649); *Ouranon Ourania, the shaking and translating of heaven and earth a sermon preached to the Honourable House of Commons in Parliament assembled on April 19, a day set apart for extraordinary humiliation by John Owen* (London, 1649); William Strong, *A voice from heaven, calling the people of God to a perfect separation from mystical Babylon as it was delivered in a sermon at Pauls before the right honorable the Lord Major and Aldermen of the city of London, on November 5, 1653* (London, 1653); Peter Sterry, *The way of God with his people in these nations opened in a thanksgiving sermon, preached on the 5th of November, 1656, before the Right honorable the High Court of Parliament* (London, 1657); Richard Baxter, *The vain religion of the formal hypocrite, and the mischief of an unbridled tongue (as against religion, rulers, or dissenters) described, in several sermons, preached at the Abby in Westminster, before many members of the Honourable House of Commons, 1660* (London, 1660).

25. Anthony Milton, *Catholic and reformed: The Roman and Protestant churches in English Protestant thought, 1600–1640* (Cambridge, 1995), p. 101.
26. George Gillespie, *A sermon preached before the Honourable House of Commons at their late solemne fast Wednesday, March 27, 1644* (London, 1644); Roger Williams, *The blovdy tenent, of persecution, for cause of conscience, discussed, in a conference betweene trvth and peace vvho, in all tender affection, present to the high court of Parliament, as the result of their discourse, these, amongst other passages, of highest consideration* (London, 1644); John Lightfoot, *A sermon preached before the Honorable House of Commons: At Margarets Westminster, upon the 26th day of August 1645* (London, 1645); John Arrowsmith, *A great wonder in heaven, or, A lively picture of the militant church drawn by a divine pencill: Revel. 12, 1, 2: discoursed on in a sermon preached before the honourable House of Commons, at Margarets, Westminster, on the last monthly fast-day, January 27, 1646* (London, 1647); Thomas Manton, *Meate out of the eater, or, Hopes of unity in and by divided and distracted times. Discovered in a sermon preached before the honourable House of Commons at Margarets Westminster on their solemne day of fast, June 30, 1647* (London, 1647); *Englands spirituall languishing; with the causes and cure: Discovered in a sermon preached before the honorable House of Commons, on their solemn day of fast, at Margarets Westminster, June 28, 1648* (London, 1648).
27. John Owen, *A sermon preached to the Parliament, October 13, 1652. A day of solemne humiliation. Concerning the kingdome of Christ, and the power of the civile magistrate about the things of the worship of God* (Oxford, 1652); John Gauden, *Megaleia theou, Gods great demonstrations and demands of iustice, mercy, and humility set forth in a sermon preached before the honourable House of Commons, at their solemn fast, before their first sitting, April 30, 1660* (London, 1660).
28. Philip Gura, *A glimpse of Sion's glory: Puritan radicalism in New England, 1620–1660* (Middletown, CT, 1984), pp. 162–163.
29. Gura, *Glimpse*, p. 166.
30. Gura, *Glimpse*, quoted from the Winthrop Papers (4:151), p. 165.
31. Peter Bulkley, *The Gospel-covenant; or The covenant of grace opened* (London, 1646), p. 256.
32. Theodore Dwight Bozeman, *The precisianist strain* (Chapel Hill, NC, 2004).
33. Lutherans confessed this in 'A treatise on the power and primacy of the Pope—Treatise compiled by the theologians assembled at Smalcald 1537', articles 39, 41, 42, 57; and The Smalcald Articles (1537), 'Of the Invocation of Saints', II.II.XXV, 'Of the Papacy', II.IV.X, XII, and 'Of the Marriage of Priests', III.XI.I. See Paul Timothy McCain, W.H.T. Dau, and F. Bente, *Concordia: The Lutheran confessions: A reader's edition of the Book of Concord* (St. Louis, MO, 2006). See also 'The Second Scotch Confession of Faith' (1580); 'The Irish Articles' (1615), pp. 79, 80; the preface to 'The Canons of Dort' (1618–1619); and 'The Westminster Confession of Faith' (1647) XXV.VI in Philip Schaff,

Bibliotheca symbolica ecclesiae universalis: The creeds of Christendom, with a history and critical notes, Vol. 3 (New York, 1877), pp. 481, 484, 540, 550, 658–659, respectively. This only reflects confessional references to the Pope as Antichrist. The data from individual Protestant theologians is far more voluminous.

34. Thomas Goodwin, *A sermon of the fifth monarchy. Proving by invincible arguments, that the saints shall have a kingdom here on earth, which is yet to come, after the fourth monarchy is destroy'd by the sword of the saints, the followers of the lamb* (London, 1654), pp. 12, 20. Compare John Foxe, *Actes and Monuments* (London, 1583), pp. 769, 773.
35. Jeremiah Burroughs, *Moses his choice with his eye fixed upon Heaven, discovering the happy condition of a self-denying heart, delivered in a treatise upon Hebrews II, 25, 26* (London, 1650), pp. 15–16, 472.
36. Edmund Calamy, *The monster of sinful self-seeking, anatomized together with a description of the heavenly and blessed selfe-seeking* (London, 1655), p. 26.
37. Anthony Burgess, *CXLV expository sermons upon the whole 17th chapter of the Gospel according to St. John* (London, 1656), p. 98. Italics in original.
38. Faithful Teate, *The souldiers commission, charge, & reward both of the deceitful and negligent, and the faithful & diligent in the Lords work* (London, 1658), p. 6.
39. James Ussher, *Certain discourses, viz. of Babylon (Rev. 18. 4.) being the present See of Rome (with a sermon of Bishop Bedels upon the same words)* (London, 1659), pp. 119–123, 126–129, 131–135, 139–142.
40. Ussher, *Certain discourses*, p. 210.
41. Christopher Hill, *Antichrist in seventeenth-century England* (Oxford, 1971), p. 132.
42. Walter Cradock, *Gospel-libertie in the extensions limitations of it* (London, 1648), pp. 149–150.
43. Craddock, *Gospel-libertie*, sig. A6.
44. Craddock, *Gospell libertie*, pp. 144, 155.
45. William Dell, *Right reformation* (London, 1646), sigs. B2–B3. Italics in original.
46. William Dell, *The building and glory of the truely Christian and spiritual church* (London, 1646), p. 15. See also Hill, *Antichrist in seventeenth-century England*, p. 127.
47. Dell, *Right reformation*, pp. A4–A5.
48. William Dell, *Uniformity examined whether it be found in the Gospel or in the practice of the churches of Christ* (London, 1646), sig. A7.
49. William Dell, *Several sermons and discourses of William Dell minister of the gospel* (London, 1651), pp. 122–123.
50. John Saltmarsh, *Dawnings of light* (London, 1646), sigs. A15–A16.
51. John Saltmarsh, *The smoke in the temple* (London, 1646), p. 17.
52. John Saltmarsh, *Free grace* (London, 1646), p. 40.
53. John Saltmarsh, *Sparkles of glory* (London, 1647), pp. 24–25.

54. Saltmarsh, *Sparkles*, pp. 217, 279.
55. David R. Como, *Blown by the Spirit: Puritanism and the emergence of an Antinomian underground in pre-Civil War England* (Stanford, CA, 2004), pp. 40, 176–218.
56. Como, *Blown by the Spirit*, pp. 38–40, 219–324.
57. See, for example, Henry More, *Enthusiasmus triumphatus* (London, 1656), pp. 160, 299.
58. John Everard, *The Gospel treasury opened* (London, 1657), pp. 95, 178, 180.
59. Everard, *Gospel treasury*, pp. 80, 149, 152–153, 169–170, 179–180, 187, 207, 222.
60. Everard, *Gospel treasury*, p. 81.
61. Everard, *Gospel treasury*, p. 179.
62. Everard, *Gospel treasury*, p. 178.
63. Everard, *Gospel treasury*, p. 178. See also p. 169, where Everard uses language which the gospels use about Jesus, to describe seventeenth-century sermon-goers: 'Now when a Christian begins but to set his face toward *Ierusalem* ...'.
64. Everard, *Gospel treasury*, pp. 80, 95, 149, 152–153, 169, 178–180, 187, 207, 222, 359, 389, 407, 460.
65. Everard, *Gospel treasury*, pp. 179–180.
66. Everard, *Gospel treasury*, p. 161.
67. Catie Gill, '"Ministering confusion": Rebellious Quaker women (1650–1660)', *Quaker Studies* 9:1 (2004), p. 18.
68. Phyllis Mack, *Visionary women: Ecstatic prophecy in seventeenth-century England* (Berkeley, 1992), p. 131.
69. Mack, *Visionary women*, p. 169.
70. Mack, *Visionary women*, p. 166.
71. Mack, *Visionary women*, p. 172.
72. Mack, *Visionary women*, pp. 138, 167–168, 193, 201, 208, 266; See also, Amanda Herbert, 'Companions in preaching and suffering: Itinerant female Quakers in the seventeenth- and eighteenth-century British Atlantic world', *Early American Studies* 1 (2011), pp. 73–113.
73. Richard Farnworth, *A Woman forbidden to speak in the Church* (London, 1654), pp. 2–8. None of the editions of this work which are listed in the ESTC spell Farnsworth's name the way other Quakers spell it. Note Lodowick Muggleton's *The neck of the Quakers broken ... in a letter to Richard Farnsworth, Quaker* (Amsterdam [London], 1663).
74. Edward Burrough, *An alarm to all flesh with an invitation to the true seeker* (London, 1660), p. 8.
75. Priscilla Cotton, *To the priests and people of England, we discharge our consciences, and give them warning* (London, 1655), pp. 7–8.
76. George Fox, *The papists strength, principles, and doctrines* (London, 1658), pp. 15, 18, 20, 32, 34, 41, 47, 58.

77. George Fox, *Truth's defence against the refined subtilty of the serpent held forth in divers answers to severall queries made by men (called ministers) in the North* (York, 1653), pp. 91–92, 95; also, George Fox, *To all the ignorant people, the word of the Lord, who are under the blind guides the priests* (London, 1655), p. 1.
78. George Fox, *Several papers some of them given forth by George Fox* (London, 1654), p. 9.
79. Fox, *The papists*, pp. 18, 20.
80. Fox, *The papists*, p. 2.
81. Fox, *The papists*, pp. 35, 38–40, 61–62, 64–65, 69–70, 81–84, 87.
82. George Fox, *The unmasking and discovering of Anti-Christ* (London, 1653), 2–7; also Fox, *Truth's defence*, p. 67.
83. Fox, *Truth's defence*, p. 65.
84. Fox, *Truth's defence*, pp. 34–36, 39, 64. Compare Hill, *Antichrist in seventeenth-century England*, p. 133.
85. Fox, *Truth's defence*, p. 11, 13, 16, 97, 104.
86. Fox, *Truth's defence*, p. 60.
87. Alexandra Walsham, *Charitable hatred: Tolerance and intolerance in England, 1500–1700* (Manchester, 2006), p. 231.
88. See Como, *Blown by the Spirit*, pp. 1–9. See also Edward Fisher, *The marrow of modern divinity* (London, 1646), page opposite the title page, sigs. A3, A4.
89. Stephen Dobranski, 'Principle and politics in Milton's *Areopagitica*', in Laura Lunger Knoppers (ed.), *The Oxford handbook of literature and the English revolution* (Oxford, 2012), pp. 190–205.
90. Oliver Cromwell, *Severall letters and passages between His Excellency, the Lord Generall Cromwell, and William Dundas, governour of Edinburgh Castle, and the ministers therein* (York, 1650), p. 5; see also *His Highnesse the Lord Protector's two speeches to the Parliament in the Painted Chamber the one on Monday the 4. of September; the other on Tuesday the 12. of September, 1654* (London, 1654), pp. 6–7.
91. Mack, *Visionary women*, p. 167.
92. Walsham, *Charitable hatred*, pp. 228–328.

CHAPTER 6

The Restoration of the Jews in Transatlantic Context, 1600–1680

Andrew Crome

Writing in 1615 from Harwich in Essex, Church of England minister Thomas Draxe was drawn to consider the future of the Jewish people. Would the Jews, he wondered, 'bee restored into their countrey'? Considering the theological and logistical challenges of such a restoration, Draxe concluded that 'It is very probable. First, all the Prophets seeme to speak of this returne. Secondly, they shall no longer bee in bondage. Thirdly, God having for so many ages forsaken his people shall the more notably shew them mercy.'[1] For Draxe, the literal restoration of the Jews to their ancient homeland of Palestine was based on God's mercy and justice, but most importantly on the stable foundation of unfulfilled Old Testament prophecy.

This focus on the importance of a literal fulfilment of prophecy might be taken to suggest that Draxe was far from conventional in his thinking, marking his views as a signpost towards radical interpretations of biblical prophecy in mid-seventeenth-century England.[2] Yet Draxe remained resolutely conformist in his thought. Two years after he wrote about Jewish restoration, he penned an open appeal to 'those of the Separation

---

A. Crome (✉)
Department of History,
Manchester Metropolitan University, Manchester, UK
e-mail: a.crome@mmu.ac.uk

© The Author(s) 2016
A. Crome (ed.), *Prophecy and Eschatology in the Transatlantic World, 1550–1800*, Christianities in the Trans-Atlantic World, 1500–1800,
DOI 10.1057/978-1-137-52055-5_6

(or *English Donatists*)'. If they could not be reconciled to the Church of England, Draxe suggested that 'for the avoiding of scandall, and in expectance of some prosperous successe' they 'remove into *Virginia*, and make a plantation there, in hope to convert infidels to Christianitie'.[3] Given that Harwich was at the time the home port of *The Mayflower*, Draxe's words, for all their orthodoxy, had ironically prophetic overtones.

Draxe offers a helpful introduction to the important role that the idea of Jewish restoration played in a transatlantic context. For while his mind moved towards Palestine to look for the fulfilment of prophecy, his focus on America initially appeared purely financial and practical. Virginia might be a useful dumping ground for unrepentant separatists, but it was also a place of economic opportunity and Christian flourishing.[4] His hope that separatists might convert 'infidels' in the New World suggests that Draxe could still conceive of a role for radicals in fulfilling God's prophetic plans. For Draxe, the conversion of the Jews was to be intimately linked to the conversion of those 'infidels' he imagined Separatists evangelising: 'why may not (specially after the generall calling and conuersion of the Iewes …) the Americans, West Indians, and other Nations; yea even in the Turkes Dominions, be enlightned?'.[5]

The central aim of the chapter is to unpack this hope for conversion which linked North America, England, and imaginings of the Holy Land in the early modern period. It therefore attempts to provide an overview of the process through which the idea of Jewish restoration linked into wider prophetic speculation in the British Atlantic world. While an exhaustive examination of the theme across the period 1500–1800 is impossible due to issues of space, its influence will be broadly outlined and a number of writers analysed in greater detail. Jewish restorationism can be examined with particular reference to the way in which it impacted upon ideas of the other, national mission, and the prophetic geography of the Bible's apocalyptic books. Each element will form part of this chapter's exploration of the theme.

6.1 Jewish Restoration in Context

The idea that there would be a large-scale conversion of the Jewish people to Christ prior to the end times had long been a part of Christian eschatological belief. Romans 9–11, particularly Paul's confident statement in Romans 11:26 that 'all Israel' would eventually be saved, was the most important biblical support, but the promise of an end-time conversion could be found across scripture. Unfulfilled prophecy relating to the reunification of the ten lost tribes of Israel with the two remaining tribes of Judah (Ezk. 37) and the sealing of '144,000 of all the tribes of the children of Israel' (Rev. 7:4) could be taken as implying that conversion was to be expected. On the Day of Judgement, wrote Augustine, 'even the Jews will certainly repent, even those Jews who are to receive "the spirit of grace and mercy"'.[6]

While Luther and Calvin notably denied the likelihood of a mass Jewish conversion, the belief remained strong in reformation Europe and flourished in England. As John Bale noted in his 1545 commentary on Revelation, *The Image of Both Churches*, 'he that hath dispersed Israell, shall bringe him againe to his folde'.[7] The marginal notations in the 1560 Geneva Bible promised a great end-times Jewish conversion based upon Romans 11: 'He sheweth that the time shal come that the whole nation of ye Jewes thogh [*sic*] not every one particularly, shalbe joined to the church of Christ.'[8] John Foxe similarly claimed that God would 'vouchsafe to reduce [Jews] againe into his owne familie, with his elect Saints, and make [them] partakers of his gladsome Gospell'.[9] These beliefs were very different from claiming that there would be a restoration of the Jews to Palestine. As Foxe noted, such hopes were a 'shew of a false shadow ... a fantasticall hope of a terrene kingdome, whereof they [the Jews] had never any one word promised by God'.[10]

Yet ideas of restoration might find their way into Christian discourse through radicals such as Roger Edwards, who wrote to John Dee and Bishop Cooper of Lincoln in the 1580s regarding his conviction that he would lead the Jews back to Palestine, or Ralph Durden who shared a similar belief.[11] The minister Francis Kett, executed as a heretic in 1589, included in his list of aberrant beliefs the idea that Jesus had physically returned to Palestine and was preparing to gather the Jews there.[12]

Regardless of these controversial links, ideas of a restoration of the Jews to Palestine began to become more mainstream over the early seventeenth century. The seeds of this can be seen in the work of former Brownist Henoch Clapham, who in his 1596 *Briefe of the Bible* suggested that Jews 'dreamed that *Israel* should have restored to them a Kingdome not onely spirituall, such a dreame cannot be infringed: nay, reade the Prophets attentively, and they insinuate a Kingdome not onely spirituall'.[13] A more influential figure was Bedfordshire minister and biblical commentator Thomas Brightman (1562–1607), whose commentaries on Revelation, Daniel, and Song of Songs focused upon a physical restoration of the Jews that would see them granted dominion over the world after Christ had defeated the Satanic forces of Pope and Turk. 'What, shall they return to *Jerusalem* againe?', asked Brightman, 'There is nothing more certaine, the Prophets do every where directly confirme it and beat upon it.'[14] Draxe's own shift from a denial of Jewish restoration to his belief in its literal fulfilment is attributable to Brightman's influence, and his book generated considerable interest despite being banned from being printed in England until the 1640s.[15]

Brightman's influence, which grew among puritans in the 1630s thanks to his assertion that the Church of England was the 'lukewarm' Church of Laodicea referred to in Revelation 3, had a transatlantic impact. Combined with his suggestion that the Jewish return to Palestine would begin in 1656, his work seemed particularly well suited to the times (as well as offering a useful justification for those leaving England).[16] After his arrival in Boston, John Cotton made extensive use of Brightman in sermons on Revelation and the Song of Songs to suggest that Jewish restoration was imminent, looking forward to a time when the Jews would convert and return to a gloriously restored Jerusalem.[17] Likewise, fellow New England minister Peter Bulkeley anticipated that 'all nations must be gathered to *Jerusalem*, to joyne with the Church of the *Jewes* in the worship of God'.[18] A form of Judeo-centric eschatology was of central importance in the New England plantation.[19] Ephraim Huit tied a rejection of Jewish restorationism to the false theology of the Laudian regime, and wrote in his commentary on Daniel of 'the Iewes ... to be restablished into their former kingdome with greate glory and large command'.[20] As Increase Mather's 1669 *Mystery of Israel's Salvation* suggested, the idea of a Jewish restoration to the Holy Land should be seen as part of established belief in New England.[21]

At the same time, the belief found renewed popularity in England. Amidst the eschatological excitement of the 1640s and 1650s on both sides of the Atlantic, the idea that the Jews might be preparing to return to Palestine was driven by both contemporary events and the growing freedom which accompanied the collapse of the Star Chamber and press censorship.[22] These speculations were not limited to one political or religious group, covering instead the full spectrum of opinions. The idea worked itself out in the preaching of luminaries such as John Owen and Jeremiah Burroughs, who preached on the return to 'the very land of Canaan itself'.[23] Independent minister William Strong told his congregation that the Jews 'shall be brought into their own land, and they shall dwell there, they shall dwell in their owne citie as in days of old'.[24] Meanwhile, Fifth Monarchists such as John Tillinghast could look forward to the pouring of the sixth vial of God's judgement upon the Euphrates, at which point 'the Jews ... shall return to their own land and convert to Christ'.[25] Some, such as Thomas Totney (who renamed himself TheaurauJohn Tany in response to his divine visions) took things further. In publications with titles such as *I Proclaime from the Lord of Hosts the Returne of the Jewes from their Captivity* (1650), Tany saw himself as a new Jewish High Priest, who would lead his people back to Palestine.[26]

By the middle of the seventeenth century, a concept of Jewish restoration to Palestine was therefore an established part of eschatology in both England and New England. But as the variety of figures that made use of it suggests, it was also an idea that could have particularly powerful political and theological implications. It is tempting to view the growth of English speculation on the eschatological role of the Jews as a response to the chaos of the wars that raged in the three kingdoms in the 1640s. However, to do so would be to ignore the important international, and particularly transatlantic, dimension of the nature of debates on Jewish restoration. Instead, it is more profitable to examine the question through taking a wider geographical perspective which incorporates the entire transatlantic world.

A first reason for taking an Atlantic approach to the question of Jewish restoration is obvious, but has nonetheless often been overlooked. The debate about Jewish restoration was not limited to England, or indeed, to the British Atlantic world. Discussions of restoration relied on reports from America of natives who might be Jews,[27] on Spanish speculation on the role of *conversos* and Jewish ancestry of Indians,[28] while English, German and Dutch writers were in regular correspondence on the nature of prophecy.[29] This correspondence involved not only Protestant and Catholic writers, but also Jews. The transatlantic network that connected New England minister John Eliot with London-based divine John Dury and Amsterdam rabbi Menasseh ben Israel in the 1650s was only the most obvious example of these interactions.[30] These networks have been examined elsewhere recently in both my own work and in an excellent study by Brandon Marriott, and they will not be the focus of the remainder of this chapter.[31]

Second, a focus on Jewish restoration raised questions of space and spiritual geography. Broadly speaking, the Reformation had been desacralising in terms of its attitude towards sacred spaces.[32] Shrines and other pilgrimage sites were no longer to be revered, as God was to be sought in his word rather than the externals of the world. Yet as Alexandra Walsham has recently shown, the landscape continued to have sacred connections for both Protestants and the remaining Catholic population in England during the seventeenth century. Biblical prophecy was one of the elements that could drive a re-sacralisation of the landscape, and concentrate on particular areas as uniquely holy.[33] While the basis of God's restoration of the Jews might be seen to be the land covenant he made with Abraham, he was nonetheless specific as to where that land would be: Palestine. The debate on Jewish restoration therefore raised questions of the geographic arena in which apocalyptic prophecies might play out, and suggested God's concern for one area over all others.

This leads to a final reason for adopting a less-localised view. Ironically, at the same time as some writers were insisting that promises to the Jews had to relate to specific areas of land in the Middle East, the tendency to read the geography of their own local surroundings into prophecy began to emerge. The 'great city, which spiritually is called Sodom or Egypt' (Rev. 11:8) could just as easily be Paris or London as it could be Rome or Constantinople. This focus on spiritual geography raised questions of the role that different parts of the world would be expected to play in the end-times script of Daniel and Revelation. In turn, this could raise anxiety. Had England lost its chance to be involved in God's plans to destroy Rome and restore the Jews? What part could the American plantations be expected to play? In other words, how did conceptions of land and territory from scripture's apocalyptic texts relate to understandings of 'land' in the Atlantic world, and what did these say to interpretations of 'the land' in Palestine? Where Walsham has written about the way in which an understanding of space rather than time was the more important category for the early modern mind, prophecy offered an opportunity to combine both space and time as a way of exploring future geographies.[34]

Of course, these international networks and concerns should not suggest that early modern thought on these questions was not also influenced by national (or indeed local) events. For example, the antinomian controversy in New England could be placed alongside the tumultuous events in Europe as dual signs of the coming fall of Antichrist.[35] However, ideas of Palestine as a distinctly 'special' place, finding one's own land coded in biblical apocalypse, and international eschatological networks combined to raise important questions of nationhood and identity.

6.2 The Centrality of Palestine

Palestine had a particularly strong hold over the English imagination. As Eva Holmberg has recently highlighted, it was one of the most popular areas for early modern writers to discuss. Descriptions tended to merge two tropes: pity for the state of the land, which was seen to have been judged and rejected by God, combined with awareness and sometimes even grim celebration that God had punished the Jews for their deicide.[36] In Thomas Fuller's evocative phrasing: 'The stump indeed stands still, but the branches are withered; the *Skeleton* remains, but the favour and flesh thereof is consumed. *Iudea* is, and is not, what it was before; the same in bulk, not blessing; for fashion, not fruitfulness; the old Instrument is the same, but it is neither strung with stock, nor plaid upon with the hand of skilfull husbandry. The *Rose of Sharon* is faded, her leaves lost, and now nothing but the prickles thereof to be seen.'[37] Such descriptions of Palestine also included an attack on the Ottomans, considered incapable of keeping the land in an acceptable condition.

The idea that Palestine itself was to be the site of the excitement of Armageddon and the New Jerusalem was one that was familiar to writers producing works about the land. Fuller raised this as one of the imagined objections to his decision to discuss geography in his 1650 *Pisgah-sight of Palestine*: 'describing this Countrey is but disturbing it, it being better to let it sleep quietly, intombed in its owne ashes. The rather, because the *New Ierusalem* is now daily expected to come down, and these corporall (not to say carnall) studies of this terrestriall *Canaan*, begin to grow out of fashion, with the more knowing sort of Christians.'[38] The quotation is revealing in what it suggests about attitudes towards the land as rejected and abandoned, memorialised only through its deadened ashes. Richard Baxter suggested that for most Jews a return to Palestine 'instead of an exaltation, it would be a banishment' describing the land as 'very full of mountains, rocks and deserts, oft infested with famines'.[39]

Yet Palestine could still capture the imagination, and travel narratives and geographical studies emphasised the nature of the land and its connection with the early days of Christianity. Fuller argued that his work was designed to act as an aid to theological reflection, with geography serving as an imaginative tool through which seventeenth-century readers could better appreciate scriptural texts.[40] Samuel Purchas may have explained his description as part of a process of mapping out unfamiliar cultures and landscapes, but he also recognised that any reflection on the nature of Jews and Judaism also had an eschatological element—he apologised that his extensive relation of Jewish customs must necessarily be expanded by a discussion of the conversion of the Jews as per Romans 11.[41] Fuller, writing at a period when eschatological speculation was a more common part of daily discourse, was even more explicit, dedicating a section of his work to 'Of the Jews, their repossessing their native countrey'.[42]

An increased interest in the land and ancient customs was a natural corollary of a detailed focus on the Old Testament and increasing willingness to use it as a model for faith, practice, and personal experience. A side-effect of this was that commentators such as Brightman, Draxe, and Cotton were willing to question the idea that prophecies of a restoration to Palestine in the Hebrew Bible should be applied spiritually to the Gentile church or to Christ's first coming. Combined with a developing interest in interpreting the text in a way that would have made sense to the original readers, this meant that when prophecies suggested that there would be a restored Jewish nation, that was exactly what they meant. As Joseph Mede wrote, when scholars 'wrest the plaine prophesies touching things which shall be at his second coming of Christ to his first, the Iewes laugh at us, and they are hardened in their infidelitie.'[43]

This concern over providing a consistent hermeneutic therefore emerged repeatedly in the writings of figures on both sides of the Atlantic. This was at its strongest in the 1640s and 1650s, but continued into the later seventeenth and eighteenth century. Neither was this new—it had its roots in Brightman's work, where he had reminded readers tempted to allegorise prophecies of restoration that they 'must not start from the naturall signification but where there is necessitie of the figurative here nothing inforceth [*sic*] to leave the proper: but contrariwise there is a necessitie to reteine it'.[44] As Jeremiah Burroughs argued, such prophecies had not been fulfilled in the past, so were 'yet certainly to come, when the fulnesse of the Gentiles shall come in, & the Jews be converted'.[45] Preaching to parliament in 1645, William Gouge argued that '*the recalling of the Jewes* is most literally and plentifully fore-told by the prophets. Many apply sundry prophecies that tend that way to the delivery of the Jews from the *Babylonish* captivity; and others to the spirituall *Israel*, consisting of *Gentiles*. But assuredly, such prophecies as foretell the re-uniting of *Judah* and *Ephraim* together, have especiall reference to the fore-said *recalling of the Jews.*'[46] While Jews and Gentiles were equal in God's sight, the prophecies pointed to fact that 'God will have a very glorious church there, specially in Jerusalem before the end of the world come.'[47] William Strong thus argued that the Fifth Monarchy would be instituted by the Jews in Palestine: 'who are every where called the holy people, not of the Gentiles, *Dan* 8.24 and 12.7 and therefore it is they must take the kingdome and possesse it, and it shall be given to them'.[48] As Edmund Hall wrote, it would be nonsensical should the prophecies not be applied to the Jews. Given that those Jews who initially heard the prophecies presumed that they related to a restoration to the land, it was ridiculous, he argued, to interpret them any differently:

> If these prophecies do nothing concern the restauration of the Jewes in these latter dayes, then to what purpose did God send his prophets to sing songs in their ears, if it nothing concerned them? Certainly these prophecies were prophesied amongst them to no purpose; if all those prophecies belong to the Gentiles, then certainly God would have sent his prophets amongst them, but they principally concerned the Jewes, and therefore they were prophesied amongst them, and to them, to whom they belonged.[49]

This hermeneutic basis was repeatedly given as a reason for a focus on the land by American writers as well. As Huit wrote in his *Whole Prophecie of Daniel Explained* (1644), by mistakenly applying prophecies of Jewish restoration to the first coming of Christ, commentators fundamentally misunderstood prophecy in its literal sense.[50] Bulkeley argued that such prophecies had to be applied to Palestine: 'let those scriptures be examined which speake of their conversion, and it will appear, that they speake ... punctually concerning their inhabiting owne land, and their building and dwelling in their own cities'.[51] Preaching in 1666, Increase Mather went so far as to claim that the Spirit 'more frequently useth these literal expressions, that so a mystical interpretation might not be looked upon as sufficient'.[52] The geography of restoration was therefore extremely important:

> 'We should let the Lord have no rest in heaven, till *Jerusalem be made a praise in the earth*? [*sic*] And when will that be? Verily when *Jerusalem* shall be inhabited again in her own place, even in *Jerusalem*.'[53]

This approach took the complex prophecies which had often been applied as spiritual allegories, and returned them instead to the world of politics and geography. A focus on the land of Palestine as a contemporary geographical reality therefore became an inevitability. This instituted one of the most important debates on the topic, as Richard Baxter and Increase Mather responded to one another across the Atlantic in the later seventeenth century. Baxter, who had always been uncertain of apocalyptic speculation, came to the subject late and was angered by what he saw as an overly-literal approach.[54] Those who argued for a literal millennium at Jerusalem were 'the grossest feigners of all the rest, well did *Jerom* [*sic*] say, that the millenaries fetch their errour from the Jews, and would set up Judaism by it'.[55] Such misinterpretation failed to realise that Romans 11 had been fulfilled in the adoption of all believers as children of Abraham and that Judea was little better than the Isle of Man.[56]

Baxter chose to dedicate his book on the subject to Mather due to the American minister's learned nature. For those who supposed that millenarians should be equated with the Independent (and possibly radical) Thomas Beverley, who Baxter also attacked in the work, the puritan elder gave an important reminder that 'the chief writers for the millennium are conformists (and men of greatest learning and piety among them)'.[57] Mather was pleased at the dedication, although he was less happy with the contents of Baxter's work—having sent 'three thousand miles to obtain it' he was left disappointed in its denial of the millennium and Jewish restoration.[58] Baxter's failure was once again hermeneutic. Building on this to defend his interpretation of the first resurrection as literal, an exasperated Mather asked 'How can a man then take a passage of so plain, and ordinarily expressed words … in any other sense than the usual and literal?'[59] The use of the literal sense meant that a focus on Jerusalem became a central element of biblical prophecy. This necessitated that writers had to work out how the Jews were going to get there, and what was going to happen to the Ottomans who currently possessed the land when they did.

This usually resulted in a twofold response which managed to simultaneously ignore and demonise the current inhabitants of the Holy Land. For most commentators, Palestine was treated as if it had been left abandoned, awaiting the restoration of the Jews since Roman times. As Baxter noted in exasperation, 'must all that now possess [the land] be robbed of their habitations and estates, to make room for our Jews?'[60] This was combined with a much more active geopolitical awareness of the requirements for a Jewish return. As Nabil Matar has noted, the restored Jews often played a key role in destroying the Ottomans in Judeo-centric works. This was to continue a long pattern of associating the fall of the Ottomans with the end times, but added a distinctly Judeo-centric twist in viewing Jews as the people through whom God would work. Brightman had seen the Jews as the 'Kings of the East' who would cross the Euphrates at the pouring out of the sixth vial of God's judgement.[61] The geography, however, could range further afield. In 1651, John Dury was imagining converted Jews marching through Egypt, and avenging themselves on both the Ottomans and the Inquisition who 'kept [them] out of the Holy Land and their beloved city *Jerusalem*'.[62] Huit hinted that they might be involved in the downfall of the Roman Church.[63] Matar has seen this focus on the Jews as agents for achieving Protestant aims as a symptom of orientalism and emerging colonialism, and it was certainly the case that the Jewish action against the Ottomans was seen as a way of explaining how the Muslim empire might be defeated.[64] Nonetheless, as Richard Cogley has noted, this sort of criticism fails to recognise that the majority of Judeo-centrists viewed the restored Jewish state in Palestine as being functionally superior to the West, rather than a colonial outpost.[65] Strong therefore emphasised that the Jews would be above all other authorities and Christ 'shall in more special manner be … *King of the Jews*'.[66] As Mather wrote, 'the *Israelitish* nation shall then be acknowledged and respected in the world above any other nation or people'.[67]

This focus on the Jews therefore established Palestine as a special area of God's focus, and highlighted the extent to which God was still intimately concerned with geography. An emphasis on the 'literal' reading of scripture guaranteed this. Yet at the same time, and somewhat ironically, this highlighted a tension—if God was concerned with particular locations, then what did this have to say to writers in England and America, and God's relationship to them?

6.3 Geographical Tensions

While interest in Jewish restoration may have focused upon Palestine, it would be wrong to claim that this meant that the prophecies of Daniel and Revelation were simply seen as being concerned with the Holy Land. Eschatology formed one of the important lenses through which to view the new discoveries in America, and the plantations established there. Columbus's focus on the role of prophecy in his discoveries and the links he made to the liberation of Jerusalem have been well documented,[68] but the question of Jewish return to Palestine raised new geographical issues which could be linked to the new world.

Where were the Jews going to return from? Brightman's belief that the Euphrates would be dried to allow them passage suggested that their pilgrimage would be from the East, a view based on the apocryphal book of 2 Esdras. Here he was drawing on a strand of Jewish tradition linked to the discovery of the 'lost' tribes of Israel. In c. 722 BCE, the ten tribes that made up the northern kingdom of Israel (in contrast to the southern kingdom of Judah) had been exiled following the Assyrian conquest. Their fate was a mystery. As Zvi Ben-Dor Benite has recently documented, the possible location of the tribes had fascinated both Jewish and Christian writers from the early church onwards, and often led to opportunities for dialogue between them.[69] As Brandon Marriott argues, these eschatological ideas connected to the tribes explicitly allowed for dialogue across both the Mediterranean and Atlantic worlds.[70]

The majority of writers argued that the lost tribes were located somewhere in Asia, perhaps amongst the Tartar tribes, a view held by the Elizabethan ambassador to Russia, Giles Fletcher, and circulated in manuscript until finally published by his grandson in 1677.[71] Some, however, were willing to go so far as to suggest that the discovery of America was a providential act through which the true location of the tribes would be revealed. This was a suggestion that had been found in a number of Iberian works, which had noted supposed cultural and linguistic similarities between Jews and American Indians.[72] The Norwich minister and Westminster divine Thomas Thorowgood's enthusiastic exposition of this so-called 'Jewish Indian theory' resulted in two books over the course of a decade, confusingly both titled *Jews in America*, despite their different content.

The use of this theory was important in an Atlantic context for two reasons. First, it served as a way of dismissing an eschatological interpretation in which the Americas were seen as a demonic territory breeding the forces of Gog and Magog that would be involved in a Satanic rebellion at the millennium's conclusion. This concept had Iberian roots, particularly in the work of the Franciscan Juan de Torquemada, who suggested that the Devil had led the Americans to the new world in a Satanic parody of the Christian story. The history of South Americans, and the at once familiar but uncanny difference in their religious rites and histories, suggested a deliberate inversion of Christianity.[73] Joseph Mede had espoused a version of this thesis when he responded to William Twisse's question of whether America might be the site of the New Jerusalem. Satan had led heathen nations into America with the express purpose of being 'God's ape' in setting up a kingdom out of the reach of the word of Christ. His purposes had been frustrated when the Spaniards had come, and might be further dashed by the New England colonists, even if their aim of conversion of natives was fanciful: 'though we make no Christians there, yet to bring some thither to disturb and vex him [Satan]'.[74] Locating the lost tribes in America would not only answer eschatological criticism of the type offered by Mede, but on a more practical level it might also generate financial support for the plantations, while also giving hope to the evangelistic efforts of the colonists. This was especially important given that the evangelical potential of the New England settlements was one of their key justifications.

A second use of the theory came in the way in which it supported a trend for identifying one's own nation in the apocalyptic sections of scripture, something that appears frequently in the work of Judeo-centric writers in the period. Again, this can be traced back to Brightman. While focusing on the literal return of the Jews to Palestine, at the same time he had emphasised the distinctly English fulfilments of some parts of the text. Baxter had referred to Brightman's commentaries despairingly, seeing the earlier commentator as responsible for the deluded claim that 'almost half the *Revelation* spake of *England*'.[75] While this was undoubtedly an exaggeration, Brightman did adopt a looser interpretation of geography than his insistence on a literal interpretation of the land of Israel might initially suggest. The winepress of Revelation 14, which overflowed with blood for 1600 furlongs, was thus equated with the flow of goods taken from monasteries by the English government in the Henrician reformation. Geographically this led Brightman into difficulties, for as he acknowledged, 1600 furlongs equated to roughly 200 miles, which fell somewhat short of the length of England. The solution, he suggested, was to remove the north from the calculation as it 'is more desert, and unmanured neer the borders, which ... *their crue of religious Monks, Fryars and Nunnes*, was afraid of, as being in a colder aire, then that they could endure it, who delight in the most champion and pleasant places of the Land; We shall see a marvellous consent even in this circumstance also'.[76]

This sort of approach might initially appear to offer a strained reading of the text, but it can also be seen as the natural counterpoint to the renewed geographical focus that writers were placing upon Jerusalem and Palestine. On the one hand, none of this was entirely new. A historicist interpretation of prophecy always encouraged specific identification with particular territories and historical figures as writers worked through the narrative. It was common, for example, to find the ten kings who initially support the Beast (Rev. 12, 13) connected to their specific geographical locations.

Yet the Judeo-centric focus on Palestine threatened to focus the entire book on the Levant, and leave little room for gentile involvement in the narrative of prophecy. Brightman's work thus moved away from the literal interpretation of geography—the land that was plagued by blood became England rather than Palestine. Confusingly, prophetic geography was relatively malleable and could be read in a variety of contexts when applied to the past, but was usually literal when applied to the near future. In England, this led a number of writers to promote a distinctly English interpretation of many of Daniel and Revelation's prophecies, while at the same time focusing upon Jewish restoration to Palestine. Much of this was driven by the chaotic events of the 1640s and 1650s, which seemed to place England at the centre of efforts to destroy the power of Antichrist.[77] Enemies of Cromwell such as Edmund Hall made similar claims, but with different political implications: thus the slaying of the two witnesses was the destruction of 'a lawful magistracy and ministry', the name 'Oliver Cromwell' could be calculated as 666, while the sixth vial referred to a literal restoration of Jews to Palestine.[78] Here again, the tension between the literal geography of Palestine and the imagined geography of the apocalypse in England came into play. On the one hand, as has already been shown, Hall argued that the prophecies of restoration must be literal: 'If these prophecies do nothing concern the restauration of the Jewes in these latter dayes, then to what purpose did God send his prophets to sing songs in their ears?'[79] On the other, he claimed that Christ's return to the Mount of Olives should be read as referring to England and Scotland, which would be reunited at Cromwell's future fall, an event he dated (somewhat optimistically) to 1651.[80]

The discussion of geography in these works often also led to contemplation on the prophetic role of New England. Hall, for example, suggested that New England was now experiencing an evangelistic success that was denied to England itself. This could be seen as part of a *translatio imperii*: 'God ... is now calling his ministers away to some greater harvest ... In New England the harvest begins to increase upon those few labourers hands ... And here in old England men despise the ministers ... really, I much fear 'tis evening with England'.[81] This sense of political shift was driven in part by his belief in the Jewish Indian theory.[82] Thorowgood showed a similar enthusiasm in connecting the restoration of the Jews with a providential role for New England. Arguing that the English, while Jutes and Angles in ancient Germany, had originally received their faith from the Jews, he claimed that God had arranged things so that the favour was returned: 'from this second *England* [i.e., old England] God hath so disposed the hearts of many in the third, New *England*, that they have done more in these last few yeares towards their [the natives'] conversion, then hath been effected by all other nations and people that have planted there since they were first known to the habitable world'.[83]

While these writers found a distinct apocalyptic role for New England, in terms of seeing the plantations as key in bringing about the conversion (and thus promoting the restoration) of the Jewish people, New England writers often expressed a distinct sense of unease about their role in fulfilling prophecy. As Susan Hardman-Moore has noted, the sense that prophetic events were unfolding back in Europe was both depleting the population and raising difficult questions about New England's purpose.[84] John Cotton's 1642 sermon on the resurrection of the churches linked this longed for event with the 'calling home of the Jewes', tying it in with the pure church state in New England.[85] Bulkeley skilfully tied together events in England with developments in New England and the restoration of the Jews. Turning to England first, he congratulated his brethren and warned that 'the light is now coming, and the glory of the Lord is now rising upon thee ... make much of it'. New England, rather than looking jealously at England should remember that they were more richly blessed than any other people: 'thou enjoyest many faithfull witnesses ... thou hast many bright starres in thy firmament... the Lord looks for more from thee, then [*sic*] from any other people'. Part of this process of faithfulness in both locations would be to hasten the fall of Rome, an event necessary for the return of the Jews to Palestine. Thus both New England and old were called to be faithful not just in active opposition to the Devil, but also in prayer for Jewish conversion and restoration: 'If it were but our enemies beast, we were bound to helpe it out, how much more these that have been the people of God, and have such promises made unto them?'[86]

Increase Mather similarly argued that the American plantations had to have some part in the fulfilment of prophecy. While Brightman had found England's geography detailed in the prophecy, Mather found suggestive references to New England's role in Robert Parker's *Exposition of the Powring Out of the Fourth Vial*, written at some point in the 1610s, but unpublished until 1650. Parker, who was revered in New England as a trail-blazing Congregationalist, had written against Brightman's interpretation of the vial as judgement on Rome. Instead, he argued that the vial represented a form of judgement on a Protestant prince or state, which would suffer burning before going on to attack Rome as the judgement of the fifth vial.[87] This prince or state, suggested Parker, would be in a state of wilderness before God used it: '*John* is placed in a wildernesse to see *Romes* ruine; it is a signe that *Romes* ruine shall arise out of some Countrey reduced to a wildernesse.' Significantly, he tied this wilderness state to the restoration of the Jews: 'so when *John* is to see the beauty of the *Jewish* Church, he is carried to a great high mountain to see it, *Apoc.* 21.10 to wit, because this Church shall be set on high like a mountain, *Isaiah* 2.2'.[88]

The implication of this in 1650 was that England represented this state, although the paratextual material in Parker's work, in the form of an end note probably written by Thomas Gataker, warned against taking political action in response to a belief that the prophecies were being fulfilled.[89] Mather carefully reworked this. The country burned with fire and reduced to a wilderness could easily be England, as he noted by referring to the Great Fire of London which was then recent news to those who heard his sermons. Yet the nature of the 'wilderness' also invited comparisons to New England: 'God hath led us into a wilderness ... who knoweth but that he may send down his Spirit upon us here, if we continue faithful before him? These then are motives to stir us to search into these mysterious truths.'[90] Mather therefore imagined a compound identity, in which New England could become the force driving apocalyptic events—not through direct actions, but through prayer. Like John, who had been taken into the wilderness to witness Rome's fall, so New Englanders could expect a role in apocalyptic events through being brought into a wilderness to see and support European Protestants through prayer and study of the Bible. 'What a solemn charge is here', he concluded, 'that we should pray continually every night and every day, and that we should let the Lord have no rest in heaven, till *Jerusalem be made a praise in the Earth.*'[91] Mather's rhetorical work allowed him to have things both ways. England's geography was found within Revelation as the state damaged by burning and purging, while New England took the position of John, watching on from the wilderness while God achieved his purposes in Europe and Asia. Prayer became a way for New Englanders to contribute both to developments in England and to the restoration of the Jews. This echoed a theme with an established history in the plantation. It recalled, for example, William Hooke's 1645 assertion that New England's churches acted as 'regiments or bands of souldiers lying in ambush here under the fearn and brushet of the Wildernes ... to come upon God's enemies with deadly fastings and prayers, murtherers that will kill point blanke from one end of the world to the other'.[92]

The sort of exegesis offered by Mather therefore offered a way of preserving the apocalyptic geography of the old world, while also reading New England into the biblical text. Given this interest, it might appear surprising that few New England commentators supported the Jewish Indian theory. Those pushing it tended to be boosters of the plantations publishing in England, while it gained little traction in the plantations themselves. Thus the series of tracts publicising New England evangelisation of natives issued by the New England Company from 1649 onwards often referred to the theory, as did Thorowgood in his volumes dedicated to the claims of Jewish-Indian ancestry. At the same time in New England, John Cotton suggested that the lost tribes were in China.[93] Although 'apostle to the Indians' John Eliot held hopes that those he preached to might be of Jewish extraction, he appears to have abandoned this belief by 1656, writing to Thorowgood that 'your labours and letters have drawn me forth further that way, than otherwise I should have gone ... give me leave to hear and observe in silence, what the Lord will teach others to say in this matter'.[94] The reasons for this reticence to embrace the theory may stem from a variety of causes, including a desire to keep apocalyptic events focused on Rome and Jerusalem, fear of the implications of recognising Native Americans as a 'superior' Jewish power, and a familiarity with the natives which made their Jewish ancestry appear unlikely.[95] Yet New England's backers recognised the potential financial value of keeping the theory alive. As Kristina Bross has recognised, ministers in New England allowed such publications to 'feed the religious fantasies of metropolitan supporters' even when 'openly skeptical about the Christian Indians' Jewish origins'.[96]

6.4 Conclusion

The idea of Jewish restoration to Palestine can be seen as rooted in a self-consciously 'literal' interpretation of prophecy, and linking a diverse range of eschatological positions. Tied to a political and hermeneutical moment when readers were attempting to find their own geographical surroundings in the Bible's apocalyptic sections, it might be seen as part of a geographical turn in apocalyptic interpretation that took place during the early modern period. This had two, seemingly contradictory, elements. First, a firm focus on Palestine and a constant reminder that when God said 'Jerusalem' he meant 'Jerusalem' in prophecy. Second, however, commentators found their own nations encoded under other names and places in these same books of scripture. The Mount of Olives might be England and Scotland, the land of 1600 furlongs England with its 'northern parts' cut off, and the wilderness of Revelation 12 New England. Given this setting, it is unsurprising that writers in both England and New England were interested in the apocalyptic implications of the New World.

Yet this was not necessarily as the sort of millennial errand that Perry Miller identified.[97] Instead, the Judeo-centric prophecy that was shared by writers in both old and New England meant that the central apocalyptic focus remained on the Holy Land. While William Twisse may have speculated that New England could be the location of the New Jerusalem, the majority of writers in the early plantation largely eschewed such thoughts. As Mather wrote, prophecy would never be fulfilled until '*Jerusalem* shall be inhabited again in her own place, even in *Jerusalem*'.[98] Regardless, the expectation of Jewish conversion offered a shared structure of prophetic speculation that could be used by writers on both sides of the Atlantic to understand the role of the New England in the coming conversion of the Jews: whether this was (for English writers) in the conversion of Native Americans who might be secret Jews, or for New Englanders in supporting Jewish restoration through prayer and fasting.

This interaction reveals the complex dynamic play of geography and transoceanic relationships involved in early modern prophetic discourse, and helps to explain the continuing confusion over interpreting references to land in apocalyptic texts in literal or allegorical forms. This contextual battle continued later, for example in Jonathan Edwards' work. In his *Notes* on the apocalypse, Edwards wrestled with a belief that God would act 'that nothing might hinder the Israelites returning to their God and their land'[99] and an argument that America might find itself described in the Book of Revelation.[100] The temptation to look back to the old world and see Revelation as referring to the Holy Land, clashed with the desire to find familiar local geographical markers described in prophecy. This was not unique to Edwards—it is an issue which continues to the present day, with contemporary dispensationalists focusing on Palestine while simultaneously asking about America's role in prophecy.[101] This is not to claim a direct link between the early modern beliefs discussed here and contemporary eschatological speculation, but it is to highlight that discourses of discovery, geography, and Jewish restoration continue to raise questions that were already being addressed in the transatlantic prophetic discourse of the seventeenth century.

Notes

1. Thomas Draxe, *An alarum to the last iudgement* (London, 1615), p. 81.
2. On this see Crawford Gribben, *The Puritan millennium: Literature and theology 1550–1682*, Revised edition (Milton Keynes, 2008) and Ariel Hessayon, '*Gold tried in fire': The prophet TheauraJohn Tany and the English Revolution* (Aldershot, 2007).
3. Thomas Draxe, *Ten counter-demaunds propounded to those of the separation, (or English Donatists) to be directly, and distinctly answered* (London, 1617), sig. A2^{ii}r.
4. This might be seen as part of the millennialist marketing of Virginia traced by Beth Quitslund. See 'The Virginia Company, 1606–1624: Anglicanism's millennial adventure', in Richard Connors and Andrew Colin Gow (eds), *Anglo-American millennialism, from Milton to the Millerites* (Leiden, 2004), pp. 43–113.
5. Draxe, *Alarum*, p. 29.
6. Augustine, *City of God*, trans. H. Bettenson (Harmondsworth, 1972), p. 960 (XX.30). See also Jeremy Cohen, 'The mystery of Israel's salvation: Romans 11:25–26 in patristic and medieval exegesis', *Harvard Theological Review* 98:3 (2005), pp. 247–281.
7. John Bale, *The image of both churches* (London, 1570), I.142. See also I.96–99.
8. *The Geneva Bible: A facsimile of the 1560 edition* (Madison, WI, 1969), New Testament, f. 75.
9. John Foxe, *A sermon preached at the christening of a certaine Iew* (London, 1578), sig. M1r.
10. Foxe, *Sermon*, sig. C1v.
11. British Library MS 353, ff.192–230. See also James Shapiro, *Shakespeare and the Jews* (New York, 1996), pp. 142–145; Richard W. Cogley, '"The most vile and barbarous nation of all the world": Giles Fletcher the Elder's *The Tartars Or, Ten Tribes* (ca. 1610)', *Renaissance Quarterly* 58:3 (2005), p. 785.
12. Robert O. Smith. *More desired than our owne salvation: The roots of Christian Zionism* (Oxford, 2013), pp. 65–66. See also Dewey D. Wallace, Jr., 'From eschatology to Arian heresy: The case of Francis Kett (d.1589)', *Harvard Theological Review* 67 (1974), pp. 459–473.
13. Henoch Clapham, *A briefe of the Bible drawne first into English poesy, and then illustrated by apte annotations* (Edinburgh, 1596), pp. 182–183.
14. Thomas Brightman, *A revelation of the Revelation* (London, 1644), p. 544. For more on Brightman see Andrew Crome, *The restoration of the Jews: Eschatology, hermeneutics and early modern national identity in the works of Thomas Brightman* (Cham, 2014).
15. See Crome, *Restoration*, pp. 131–165.

16. In arguing that the Church of England was the Church of Laodicea in Rev. 3, Christ's warning that he was about to 'spew thee out of my mouth' (Rev. 3:1) could be applied directly to impending judgement.
17. John Cotton, *A brief exposition of the whole book of Canticles* (London, 1642), pp. 195–262.
18. Peter Bulkeley, *The gospel covenant or the covenant of grace opened* (London, 1646), p. 6.
19. Richard W. Cogley, 'The fall of the Ottoman Empire and the restoration of Israel in the "Judeo-Centric" strand of Puritan millenarianism', *Church History* 72 (2003), pp. 304–322; Smith, *More desired*, pp. 117–140.
20. Ephraim Huit, *The whole prophecie of Daniel explained, by a paraphrase, analysis and briefe comment* (London, 1644), p. 63.
21. Increase Mather, *The mystery of Israel's salvation* (n.p., 1669). Of course, the fact that Mather felt the need to write shows that the theory was not universally accepted. Indeed, he admits that for some it was viewed as a 'seeming novelism' (sig. C4̇v).
22. Gribben, *Puritan millennium*, pp. 49–58.
23. Jeremiah Burroughs, *An exposition of the prophesie of Hosea* (London, 1643), p. 117.
24. William Strong, *XXXI select sermons, preached on special occasions* (London, 1656), p. 286.
25. John Tillinghast, *Generation work* (London, 1655), Part II, p. 38.
26. For more on Tany see Hessayon, *'Gold tried in fire'*.
27. Zvi Ben-Dor Benite, *The ten tribes: A world history* (Oxford, 2009).
28. Jorge Cañizares-Esguerra, *Puritan Conquistadors: Iberianizing the Atlantic, 1550–1700* (Stanford, CA, 2006).
29. Johannes Van den Berg, 'Joseph Mede and the Dutch millenarian Daniel Van Laren', in Michael Wilks (ed.), *Prophecy and eschatology* (Oxford, 1994), pp. 111–122.
30. For full discussions of the circumstances surrounding the conference see Andrew Crome, 'English national identity and the readmission of the Jews, 1650–1656', *Journal of Ecclesiastical History* 66:2 (2015), pp. 280–301; Todd M. Endelman, *The Jews of Britain, 1656–2000* (Berkeley, CA, 2002), pp. 15–27; David S. Katz, *Philo-Semitism and the readmission of the Jews to England 1603–1655* (Oxford, 1982) ; David S. Katz, *The Jews in the history of England* (Oxford, 1994), pp. 107–144; David S. Katz, 'English redemption and Jewish readmission in 1656', *Journal of Jewish Studies* 34 (1983), pp. 73–91; Shapiro, *Shakespeare and the Jews*, pp. 55–62, 167–194.
31. Andrew Crome, 'The "Jewish Indian" theory and Catholic/Protestant intellectual networks in the early modern Atlantic world', in Crawford Gribben and Scott Spurlock (eds), *Puritans and Catholics in the trans-Atlantic world, 1600–1800* (Basingstoke, 2015), pp. 112–130 and Brandon Marriott, *Transnational networks and cross-religious exchange in the seven-*

teenth-century Mediterranean and Atlantic worlds: Sabbatai Sevi and the lost tribes of Israel (Farnham, 2015).
32. Carlos M.N. Eire, *War against the idols: The Reformation of worship from Erasmus to Calvin* (Cambridge, 1986).
33. Alexandra Walsham, *The reformation of the landscape: Religion, identity and memory in early modern Britain and Ireland* (Oxford, 2011).
34. Walsham, *Reformation of the landscape*, p. 7.
35. Karyn Valerius, '"So manifest a signe from heaven": Monstrosity and heresy in the Antinomian controversy', *New England Quarterly* 83:2 (2010), pp. 179–199.
36. Eva Johanna Holmberg, *Jews in the early modern English Imagination* (Aldershot, 2011).
37. Thomas Fuller, *A Pisgah-sight of Palestine* (London, 1650), p. 16.
38. Fuller, *Pisgah-sight*, p. 3.
39. Richard Baxter, *The glorious Kingdom of Christ described and clearly vindicated* (London, 1691), p. 69.
40. Fuller, *Pisgah-sight*, p. 3.
41. Samuel Purchas, *Purchas his pilgrimage. Or relations of the world and the religions observed in all ages and places discouered, from the creation vnto this present* (London, 1613), p. 183.
42. Fuller, *Pisgah-sight*, p. 194.
43. Joseph Mede, *The key of the revelation* (London, 1643), II, p. 135.
44. Thomas Brightman, *A most comfortable exposition of the last and most difficult part of the prophecie of Daniel* (Amsterdam, 1635), pp. 64–65.
45. Burroughs, *Prophesie of Hosea*, p. 105.
46. William Gouge, *The progresse of divine providence* (London, 1645), p. 29.
47. Burroughs, *Prophesie of Hosea*, p. 117
48. Strong, *Sermons*, p. 288.
49. [Edmund Hall], *Lingua testium* (London, 1651), pp. 6–7.
50. Huit, *Whole prophecie of Daniel*, pp. 196–200.
51. Bulkeley, *Gospel covenant*, p. 16.
52. Mather, *Mystery*, p. 128.
53. Mather, *Mystery*, p. 180.
54. William Lamont, *Richard Baxter and the millennium: Protestant imperialism and the English Revolution* (London, 1979), esp. pp. 27–75.
55. Baxter, *Glorious kingdom*, p. 9.
56. Baxter, *Glorious kingdom*, pp. 58–60.
57. Baxter, *Glorious kingdom*, sig. A2v. Baxter had been imprisoned with Beverley and the two wrote against one another civilly. Beverley's *The thousand years kingdom of Christ* (1691) and *The universal Christian doctrine of the Day of Judgment* (1691) contained answers to Baxter's *Glorious kingdom* and *A reply to Mr. Tho. Beverley's answer* (1691).

58. Increase Mather, *A dissertation concerning the future conversion of the Jewish nation* (London, 1709), p. 7.
59. Mather, *Dissertation*, p. 19.
60. Baxter, *Glorious kingdom*, p. 61.
61. Brightman, *Revelation*, pp. 542–558.
62. John Dury in Thomas Thorowgood, *Iewes in America* (London, 1650), sigs. E3ⁱr-E3ⁱv.
63. Huit, *Whole prophecie of Daniel*, p. 63.
64. Nabil Matar, *Islam in Britain 1558–1685* (Cambridge, 1998), pp. 167–183.
65. Cogley, 'The fall of the Ottoman Empire', p. 331.
66. Strong, *XXXI select sermons*, p. 281.
67. Mather, *Dissertation*, p. 58.
68. See Christopher Columbus, *The book of prophecies*, ed. Roberto Rusconi, trans. Blair Sullivan (Berkeley, CA, 1997).
69. Zvi Ben-Dor Benite, *The ten lost tribes: A world history* (Oxford, 2009). See also Tudor Parfitt, *The lost tribes of Israel: The history of a myth* (London, 2002), pp. 1–25.
70. Marriott, *Transnational networks*, pp. 19–36.
71. This is printed in Samuel Lee, *Israel redux: Or The restauration of Israel, 2 treatises* (London, 1677).
72. This theme was explored by writers such as Joannes Fredericus Lumnius, Peter Martyr d'Anghiera, and Gilbert Genebrard. See Amy Sturgis, 'Prophesies and politics: Millenarians, rabbis, and the Jewish Indian theory', *Seventeenth Century* 14 (1999), pp. 15–23. However, Lee Earnest Huddleston argues that Martyr did not fully espouse the theory (*Origins of the American Indians: European concepts, 1492–1729* [Austin, TX, and London, 1967], p. 33). See also Luís Filipe Silvério Lima's chapter in this volume.
73. See Cañizares-Esguerra, *Puritan Conquistadors*, pp. 35–82.
74. This is laid out in a letter to William Twisse of 23 March 1634/5. See Joseph Mede, *The works of the pious and profoundly learned Joseph Mede* (London, 1672), pp. 798–803. On Torquemada's influence see Cañizares-Esguerra, *Puritan Conquistadors*, pp. 100–104.
75. Richard Baxter, *A paraphrase of the New Testament* (London, 1685), f. 292v.
76. Brightman, *Revelation*, p. 503.
77. See Gribben, *Puritan millennium*; Paul Christianson, *Reformers and Babylon: English apocalyptic visions from the Reformation to the eve of the Civil Wars* (Toronto, 1978); Katherine R. Firth, *The apocalyptic tradition in Reformation Britain, 1530–1645* (Oxford, 1979).
78. Edmund Hall, *Manus testium movens, or a presbyteriall glosse upon many of those obscure prophetick Texts* (London, 1651), pp. 27–45.
79. Edmund Hall, *Lingua Testium, Wherein Monarchy is Proved 1. To be Jure Divino 2. To be Successive in the Church* (London, 1651), pp. 6–7.
80. Hall, *Manus testium movens*, p. 81 [misl. 77].

81. Hall, *Manus tesitum movens*, p. 89 [misl. 85].
82. Hall, *Lingua Testium*, p. 8.
83. Thorowgood, *Jews in America* (1650), sig. b2r.
84. Susan Hardman-Moore, *Pilgrims: New World settlers and the call of home* (New Haven, CT, and London, 2007).
85. John Cotton, *The churches resurrection* (London, 1642), p. 8.
86. Bulkeley, *Gospel covenant*, pp. 14–19.
87. Robert Parker, *An exposition of the powring out of the fourth vial mentioned in the sixteenth of the Revelation* (London, 1650), pp. 7–9.
88. Parker, *Exposition*, p. 9.
89. Gataker wrote the preface here, and it seems possible that he also contributed the closing 'annotations'. As the annotator notes: 'it is not safe for any men, to ground any action upon presumption or confidence that now the time is come when things shall be fulfilled, and that it doth belong to them to execute the Wrath of God against *Papists* or any others, whom they imagine to be designed by the Holy Ghost' Parker, *Exposition*, p. 15.
90. Mather, *Mystery*, p. 164.
91. Mather, *Mystery*, p. 178.
92. William Hooke, *New-Englands sence of Old-England and Irelands sorrowes* (London, 1645), p. 19.
93. John Cotton, "The Sixth Vial" in *The Powring Out of the Seven Vials: Or an exposition, of the 16. chapter of the Revelation, with an application of it to the times* (London, 1642), p. 21. Note the pagination of this work often resets after the explication of each vial.
94. Eliot, quoted in Thorowgood, *Jews in America* (1660), p. 34. However, Marriott argues that Eliot's interest in the tribes was reinvigorated through news of Sabbatai Sevi in 1666 (see Marriott, *Transnational networks*, pp. 34–36).
95. Claire Jowitt, 'Radical identities? Native Americans, Jews and the English Commonwealth', *Seventeenth Century* 10:1 (1995), pp. 101–119; Sturgis, 'Prophesies and politics', pp. 15–23.
96. Kristina Bross, 'From London to Nonantum: Mission literature in the Transatlantic World', in Susan Juster and Linda Gregerson (eds), *Empires of God: Religious encounters in the early modern Atlantic* (Philadelphia, PA, 2011), p. 136.
97. Perry Miller, *Errand into the Wilderness* (Cambridge, MA, 1956).
98. Mather, *Mystery*, p. 180.
99. Jonathan Edwards, *Notes on the Apocalypse* (1723) in *Works*, Vol. 5, p. 116.
100. Stephen J. Stein, 'Introduction', in Jonathan Edwards, *Works: Apocalyptic Writings* (WJE Online), ed. Stephen J. Stein, Vol. 5, p. 26.
101. See, for example, Mark Hitchcock, *101 Answers to the Most Asked Questions about the End Times* (Sisters, OR, 2001), pp. 31–35.

CHAPTER 7

Transatlantic Cunning: English Occult Practices in the British American Colonies

Alexander Cummins

Jon Butler's examination of 'the survival of European occult or magical practices in the American colonies, especially astrology, divination, and witchcraft' highlighted that, in spite of a lack of orthodoxy, 'American colonists were indeed religious, but many resorted to occult and magical practices'.[1] Refining this notion, David D. Hall has suggested that 'we do better if we perceive an accommodation between magic and religion than if we regard magic as somehow the substance of a different tradition'.[2] Predictive divination and religious prophecy combined with cosmological and environmental dimensions of eschatology in the thought and methodologies of those crossing the Atlantic to a so-called New World. A new Eden beckoned, often in expressly eschatological and soteriological terms: 'Eden was the ideal to which colonial ministers looked as a pattern of ancient purity and a model of coming perfection in the seventeenth and eighteenth centuries.'[3]

A. Cummins (✉)
Sophia Centre for the Study of Cosmology in Culture,
University of Wales: Trinity Saint David, Lampeter, UK
e-mail: bellweather@hotmail.com

To understand how colonisation was framed in terms of the end of days, we must understand that 'a millenarian prophecy of particular importance to English Puritan intellectuals'—including those who emigrated to the North American colonies—'was the belief in a Great Instauration, a rapid increase in learning that, in the days before the Second Coming of Christ, would restore the dominion man lost over nature at Adam's fall'.[4] This recovery of Adamic knowledge was part of the historicist activism necessary to perfect the world prior to the millennium of Christ's benevolent rule that would itself presage the end of the universe. Francis Bacon is perhaps the best remembered advocate for this eschatological reformism, and indeed Bacon framed it expressly in terms of intellectual endeavours catching up to the discovery of the New World:

> it would be disgraceful to mankind if the regions of the Material Globe, i.e. of land and sea, and of the stars, should be immensely laid open and illustrated, while the limits of the Intellectual Globe were bounded by the discoveries and narrowness of the Ancients.[5]

Tracing the occult philosophy and magical activity conducted in the early colonies provides a rich context for fruitful analysis of prophetic and eschatological practices. So it is that this essay concerns what early modern English occult practitioners brought with them as they immigrated: not simply their books, but their skills, practices, and especially their outlooks and expectations. It will examine what news and reports they might have had in mind on embarking concerning the spiritual practices of indigenous Americans, how some of those were met or challenged upon arrival and contact, what kinds of English occult practices were worked on American soil, and what kind of magical opportunities and crises can be analysed. It seeks to follow English threads of prophecy and eschatology into the Americas via the works of astrologers and almanac-makers, even as their familiar stars hung somewhat crooked. Although clearly a related field, this is not a work on the colonial witch-hunts or trials themselves, but rather on the contexts of witch- and cunning-craft as social, religious, and magical practices of the English-speaking parts of the early British American colonies.[6] Following these threads of English transmission and development equips us with better context to analyse distinct characteristics of and wider influences upon later American occult philosophy, magical activity, and spirituality.

7.1 Prejudices

The first thing English practitioners brought with them to the American colonies were their expectations. Gleaned from travel writings, geographical surveys, and even early ethnographies of the inhabitants of the (so-called) New World, various early modern English texts—perhaps most notably Iberian translations such as that of José de Acosta, S.J. ('a best-seller in several languages')[7]—adumbrated the Americas and the Americans for the curious. Not only were such works frequently printed and sold by the same booksellers as occult works, some even advertised new works of seventeenth-century occult philosophy themselves.[8]

George Alsop's 'Relation of the Customs, Manners, Absurdities, and Religion of the Susquehanock Indians in and near Mary-Land' is a typical framing of such reports, which often peppered colonialist infantilisation with good old fashioned sensationalism.[9] Faced with such accounts of the 'blind errors' of indigenous Americans, the duty of good early modern Christians was clear: 'the servants of God which labour to draw them to salvation, ought not to contemne these *follies and childishnesse*, being sufficient to plunge these poore abused creatures into eternall perdition; but they ought with good and cleere reasons, to drawe them from so great ignorance'.[10] Infantilisation could even extend to emphasising a base, even bestial, nature of natives in an elision of habitat and inhabitants, as in (the English translation of) Acosta's report: 'for that they are the workes of nature, as of freewill; which are the deedes and customes of men, the which hath caused mee to name it the Naturall and Morall Historie of the Indies'.[11]

Many texts relayed accounts of indigenous magic.[12] At the turn of the seventeenth century, for instance, Richard Hakluyt published compendia of sailors' accounts of their travels which included various references to 'Indian sorcery'. Several historians have noted that the services of occult practitioners were especially popular with seamen—usually electing suitable times to set sail, but including protective charms—and it is at least likely some would have actually heard, as well as read, such tales.[13] We can identify two specific foci of colonial English interest in and condemnation of native American magic, both of which were consistent concerns in wider European moral and intellectual discourses on magic: necromancy and images.

It seems popular to have noted 'the Indians Idolatries towards the deceased', such as images of dead kings at certain important times being carried 'to obtaine victorie, and raine, and they made diuers sacrifices vnto them'.[14] Acosta lays out a necromantic (or perhaps simply mournful) aetiology of idolatry—the wish to keep the departed in mind in some manner: 'for when a father mourned heavily for the death of his miserable sonne, he made for his consolation, an Image of the dead man, and beganne to worshippe him as a god, who a little before had ended his daies like a mortall man, commanding his servants to make ceremonies & sacrifices in remembrance of him'.'[15] Indeed, there is a sense that this was common behaviour for peoples outside of earshot of the good news of Christianity, for 'we find that among other Nations they had in great estimation and reverence the bodies of their predecessors, and did likewise worship their Images'.[16] There seems a general—even natural—tendency ascribed to indigenous peoples to worship the dead, especially through images.

This tendency was extended to past civilisations, and frequent efforts were made to compare the Greeks and other ancient cultures with the indigenous peoples of the Americas; further solidifying a positivism framing Christian Europeans as spearheading civilisation, and natives of the 'New' World as primitive or under-developed. Sacrificing servants and women was 'a maner generall throughout all the Indies', just as 'before the Englishmen were converted to the Gospel, they had the same custome, to kill men to accompany and serve the dead'.[17] Likewise, the tradition of setting 'meate and drinke vpon the grave of the dead, imagining they did feede thereon ... hath likewise beene an error amongst the Ancients, as saint Augustine writes'.[18] There is a homogenising component to such analysis: *all* unchristian peoples behave according to the same principles, defined by the absence of Christ as much as the particularities of their cultures. This was arguably also a humanising factor, albeit a patronising one—poorly-raised children could not be blamed too harshly for their ungodly manners, provided they changed their ways after being properly educated.

The assertion that an absence of Christianity allows or even encourages necromancy would not have surprised an early modern English reader. The semantics of 'nigromancy' as non-specific black magic led to necromancy, like witchcraft, being generally 'aligned with the suspicious practices of others'.[19] The seventeenth-century physician and sceptic Thomas Ady even asked rhetorically: 'how then can this distinction hold, that VVitchcraft differeth from *Necromancy?*[20] One dictionary opined 'the difference between *Necromancers* and *Witches* King *James* (in his *Demonologie*) hath taught in a word; the one (in a sort) command, the other obey the Devil'.[21] Necromancers were dangerous indeed.

Necromancy was also especially theologically controversial since Protestantism had done away with purgatory, on the grounds that only

God could return souls to earth. Any supposedly ghostly appearances contradicted the power of the Almighty, and the notion of holding spiritual authority to actually call up a ghost may have seemed especially hubristic. Swiss Reformed pastor Ludwig Lavater attempted to dismiss ghost sightings themselves using a variety of explanations: fakes, tricks of the light, and—perhaps most significantly—spirits pretending to be the dead, chiefly demons or even the Devil himself.[22] Thus, necromancers could be considered both powerful in their own right, and—like English witches— unwitting loci of manipulative diabolical forces.[23] This combination of necromancy's danger and ignorance (not to mention heresy) was clearly an important context for the reports of indigenous American customs and practices concerning the dead.

Wider concerns with idolatry and images underlay this focus on necromancy. Images and iconoclasm were major points of intellectual and moral debate in post-Reformation Europe, and various revisions and developments of the older medieval faculty psychology placed the imagination and its evocative powers of endopsychic image-making in new and potentially dangerous contexts.[24] Image magic itself—the construction and deployment of marked objects by occult principles—was a longstanding popular practice.[25] It was also a tradition undergoing considerable early modern questioning; chiefly, whether the inscription of magical words and names could still be justified by both theological and natural philosophical principles, or if it too was rather more based upon infernal engineering.[26]

Acosta presents four categories of idolatry, bifurcated along a natural– artificial dichotomy.[27] Charges of general 'nature worship' also covered particular stars afforded names and earthly influence. Indeed, it was even granted that 'it seemed they approached somewhat neere the propositions of Platoes Idees'.[28] Acosta mentions a few instances of these stars being worshipped and offered sacrifice to gain particular favours, such as 'to preserve their cattell'.[29] The stars as sources of powerful (as well as specific) protection by occult sympathy and apotropaic warding were clearly recognisable to English-speaking occultists. The translations of alchemist and medical researcher Robert Turner[30] and Agrippa's 1651 'Englished' *Occult Philosophy*, not to mention the manuscript forms of the manual of Arabic astrological magic *Picatrix* that circulated between English practitioners in this period,[31] all featured specific manners in which the stars could be employed to perform similar actions.[32] Indeed, the stars—or their angels, at least—were the very 'Secundarian Intelligences' before the throne of God which imbued all physical matter with occult virtue in the first place.[33]

Much of the criticism of the veneration of 'the Sunne, Moone, Starres, and Elements' mentions their 'power and authoritie to doe good or harme to men'.[34] This in itself was not necessarily idolatry. After all, astrology also employed the wondrous effects of such natural resources as occult 'vertues'. Rather, the issue was that 'although God hath created all these things for the vse of man, yet hath he [that is, native man] so much forgotte himselfe, as to rise vp against him. Moreover, he hath imbased himselfe to creatures that are inferiour vnto himselfe, worshiping and calling vpon their workes'.[35] The proper use of images and various counterparted anxieties over man's idolatry and 'forsaking his Creator' also mark early modern European discourses on astrological magic.[36]

Yet despite debate about the dangers of astral sorcery, the extent to which European star-lore was deemed not only acceptable but culturally embedded knowledge can also be evidenced in various texts informing the expectations of travelling occult philosophers and practitioners, such as Thomas Tryon's 'brief Treatise of the most principal Fruits and Herbs that grow in the East & West Indies; giving an Account of their respective Vertues both for Food and Physick, and what Planet and Sign they are under'.[37] It was far from unusual for books on dietary health to contain astrological, and certainly humoural, material.[38] Diet was an important 'non-natural' principle whereby health could be regulated.[39] The right sort of star-lore was clearly considered a useful tool for colonists to march on their stomachs.

At worst, the native Americans were considered to 'haue no knowledge of God, nor of any religion, sauing of that which they see, as the Sunne and the Moone'. Yet there is a clear occult and medical tension between natural philosophy and operative sorcery present—'they haue their Priests to whom they giue great credit, because they are great magicians great soothsayers, and callers vpon diuels'.[40] In this assessment, it is difficult not to see the parallels and prejudices of early modern European debates over licit and illicit practices of natural and demonic magic in the old World as well as the New.[41]

Various apparent tensions, such as that between acceptable Christian astrology and idolatrous heathen starlore, were often unaddressed by most reporters on Americas—largely because such writers were expected to simply report, and not to draw conclusions about what they saw. Bacon's *The Advancement of Learning* (1605) and *New Atlantis* (1627) both extolled the virtues of observers handing over their observations to analytical specialists, and that 'the secrets of nature would thus be unlocked in a prescribed order in which the eyewitness would surrender his first-hand observations to the detached "speculator" to be refined into the "true axioms" of modern knowledge'.[42] Zachary McLeod Hutchins refers to this as a paradigm that 'divided responsibilities between colonial observers and imperial interpreters of the natural world'.[43] Thus we see, in yet another dimension of settlement, the attitude that the New World was something to survey, enclose, refine, and submit to a distant authority. Reports of New England's flora, fauna, and landscape thus also present a fascinating example of certain kinds of epistemological colonisation and imperialism—once again, emerging and propelled by an impulse to reform, to refine, and to be pure. Such purity must be at least partly understood in contemporary millenarian and eschatological contexts.

Far from travel broadening the mind and correcting misunderstandings of American beliefs, 'closer contact with Native Americans did little to correct such misconceptions'.[44] Rather, reports of satanic blood libel and human sacrifice were now apparently confirmed, from those seeing—but not understanding—native American ceremonies. While Edward Winslow reported such child sacrifices in 1624, Alfred Cave judges Winslow 'misinterpreted descriptions of Algonquian puberty rites and concluded that the Indians sometimes sacrificed their own children to the Devil'.[45] Preconceptions coloured contact. Indeed, this supposed devilish core of Indian customs meant detailed study of native American practices itself might even be considered sinful, as when Protestant theologian Roger Williams (who spoke some Algonquian dialects) refused to 'bee an eye witness ... lest I should have been a partaker of Sathan's Inventions and Worships, contrary to Ephes[ians] 5.14'.[46]

Not only was the Devil ultimately responsible for their heathen practices, indigenous priests were described—in a popularly reprinted account of 1613 by a Virginia minister—as 'no other, but such as our English witches are'.[47] And yet, few if any actual reports of *maleficium* (sorcery to harm or destroy) appear to emerge from contact.[48] A horrified Winslow described a healing ceremony in diabolical terms, yet 'despite his use of sinister terminology evocative of English fears of Satanism, Winslow's account offers no concrete evidence of *maleficium*'; similarly, many other reports 'relied upon verbal characterizations of their practices as bizarre, grotesque, and irrational ... diverted the readers' attention from the essentially benevolent purpose of the ritual he had described'.[49]

Again, the uncertain labelling of native medical and spiritual practices may remind us of European concerns and debate over demonic sources for the healing powers of even benign cunning folk. Daniel Gookin,

Superintendent of Indian Affairs for Massachusetts Bay Colony, defined Indian powwows as 'partly wizards and witches, holding familiarity with Satan … and partly … physicians … sent for by the sick and wounded … by their diabolical spells, mutterings, exorcisms, they seem to do wonders'.[50] John Josselyn, visiting New England in 1674, defined powwows as folk who had consorted with the Devil to gain 'their Diabolical Art in curing of Diseases, which is performed with rude ceremonies'.[51] The key difference between the considerations of European and American practitioners seems to be how explicit this demonic consorting was considered to have been. Crucially, 'Puritan observers generally portrayed powwows as equivalent, not to the sinister witches of the popular imagination, but to the English "cunning people" who practiced a benign form of folk magic.'[52] Whether Euro-American cunning practitioners agreed with this comparison is somewhat less clear.

Thus while indigenous peoples were conceived of as infantile or primitive 'works of nature', they were also considered to have access to powerful, diabolic power. Here was a further emphasis on a white man's burden to re-educate these savages as good Christians, to remove dangerous things from the hands of spiritually feral children. Here, indeed, was the work necessary to aright the pre-lapsarian Garden from the unspoiled but primitive wildernesses of the heathens.

German-British polymath Samuel Hartlib's efforts to bring about the new spiritual millennium of Christ's benevolent rule included, for instance, printing various works on tree-husbandry, acting from a soteriological rationale 'that the earth had to be cultivated to reverse both the curse occasioned by the Fall and the subsequent injury to the land caused by the Flood'.[53] There were cosmological and eschatological meanings to economic toil and political ownership of the New Eden. Untended land was more widely considered a general affront to God's plan, and therefore another reason—as presented by John Locke *inter alia*—to colonise the New World: for had not man's 'God and his Reason commanded him to subdue the Earth'?[54]

Of course, there were earlier endeavours to link piety and colonisation with occult philosophical inquiry, 'putting greater emphasis on alchemical knowledge and the relationship between world reform and Christian service'.[55] Woodward draws attention to the Brotherhood of the Rosy Cross' call for a 'Universal and General Reformation of the whole wide world', and shows how the Brotherhood's first tract, the *Fama Fraternitatis*, emphasised natural magic, alchemy, and Kabbalah as means to perfect nature in line with this early modern European eschatology.[56] As we shall see, Rosicrucianism seems to have influenced certain circles of important early settlers whose occult philosophy informed their colonialism.

Such notions of combining soteriology with practical, even proto-scientific, experimentation with land and materials were also supported by many Baconian reformists, whose ideal:

> was for natural philosophers to adopt the utilitarian, craft-oriented approach of Adam, the first man. Adam was viewed as a hands-on, practical scholar, a gardener, and naturalist who knew entirely the secrets of the natural world. Importantly, among the highest attainments ascribed to Adam by contemporaries were mining and metalworking: he was even credited with knowing the secret of transmutation. Through arduous and pious effort, natural philosophers could recover Adamic knowledge and improve the world.[57]

A return to pre-lapsarian methodologies to rediscover and further develop pre-lapsarian knowledge and skills must also be expressly contextualised in terms of early modern millenarianism. If the new stars of 1604—appearing in the constellations of Cygnus and Serpentarius and signalling to many 'the onset of the millennium'[58]—demonstrated the importance of paying attention to new expressions of the natural world, certainly exhortations to explore, settle, and refine a New World were taken in similar eschatological terms.

7.2 Texts and Techniques

Once occult practitioners arrived in America there were several kinds of opportunities available to them to practise their crafts. Let us focus our assessment on print and services—that is, occult texts and cunning-craft—for 'a wide range of occult ideas and practices—alchemical practitioners, the availability of occult books, occult notions in colonial almanacs, and even a few self-announced cunning persons—were evident in the colonies between 1650 and 1720'.[59] Cotton Mather lamented the 'gateway drug' of folk magic leading colonists to witchcraft: 'in some Towns, it has been an usual Thing for People to Cure Hurts with spells, or to use Detestable Conjurations, with Sieves, & Keyes, and Pease, and Nails and Horse-Shoes … to Learn the Things', insisting ''Tis in the Devils name', and that we must 'be duely Watchful against all the Steps Leading thereunto'.[60] He considered the 'Phamphlets of such Idle, Futil, Trifling Star-gazers' a particular threat.

Alchemists such as Robert Child and George Stirk were known to have practised their art on both sides of the Atlantic in the mid-seventeenth-century, and men such as John Winthrop Jr. brought substantial collections of alchemical texts to the colonies. Some historians have suggested Winthrop the younger may have even penned the alchemical treatises of 'Eirenaeus Philaletha'.[61] Butler considers the author 'someone who spent considerable time in the colonies, even if the claim for Winthrop's authorship is put aside, it seems likely that Americans not only read sophisticated occult literature but contributed to it as well'.[62] Winthrop certainly 'maintained contacts with a wide circle of men with similar hermetic interests, corresponding with the likes of Samuel Hartlib in England and sending books and encouragement to Jonathan Brewster Jr., a trader on the Pequot coast at what would become New London, Connecticut, who was attempting to distill the 'red elixer"'.[63]

Alchemical perpectives on the perfection of nature, operationalised ideologically by the humanism of the Renaissance and spurred on methodologically by the nascent scientific endeavours of inductive logic and experimental methodology, sought a new laboratory and found it in the Americas. There were also both geographical and empirical drives to search the world. An alchemist's journey to perfection—whether of self, nature, or the self-arising-from-nature—was often suggested to be as much a literal as a metaphorical journey: 'mastering alchemy often involved physical pilgrimage'.[64] These travels would allow the adept to gather knowledge and experience of the natural world, and practise the skills needed to operate upon and within it. So it was that Danish Paracelsian alchemist Peter Severinus extolled would-be-alchemists to 'buy yourselves stout shoes, travel to the mountains, search the valleys, the deserts, the shores of the sea, and the deepest depressions of the earth; note with care the distinctions between animals, the differences of plants, the various kinds of minerals, the properties and mode of origin of everything that exists'.[65] It appears precisely by this logic that the 21-year-old Winthrop attempted to travel to Turkey. He arrived at La Rochelle in 1627, before setting off on what ended up being a fourteen-month roundtrip expedition to Constantinople and back, taking in such intellectual centres as Venice, Padua, and Amsterdam.[66] Around 1630, 'Winthrop began to display a special affinity for the English alchemist John Dee', who had 'given instruction and advice to pilots and navigators conducting exploratory voyages to North America' as well as conjuring angels 'to ask them of the success of a colony he proposed to establish there'.[67] To visit new lands was to expand one's sample sets, collect more data points, and refine one's craft in refining nature herself. Moreover, there was an express and direct influence upon some English occult philosophers to journey to the Americas we can trace to Dr. Dee's scrying, apocalyptic angelology, and heavily alchemically-inflected natural philosophical.

7.2.1 Almanacs

By far the most popular format for colonial American occult material was the almanac. Sara Gronim considers that 'up through the 1750s almanacs were the most important expression of beliefs in British colonial New York about the nature of the universe'.[68] Furthermore, 'American historians have often observed that almanacs outsold the Bible and were the most popular book publications in the colonies.'[69] Most typically, American almanacs contained ephemerides with 'Rectifyed' latitudes and longitudes for American astrologers needing American data,[70] and calendrical tables of planetary aspects. Some, such as Atkins', offered additional observations for each month such as 'The 30th day at 6 in the morning the [Moon] is near Mars.'[71] Others predicted the monthly behaviour of the tides.[72] Although arguably increasingly vaguely applied, the majority of almanacs 'continued to assert that the positions of the planets influenced the material natural world throughout the entire British colonial period'.[73]

Beyond their time-keeping calendrical functions of sun rises, moon phases, and zodiacal revolutions, almanacs contained astrological physic. Nicholas Campion has suggested these were 'quite popular—even necessary as medical aids'.[74] Trained and experienced physicians and laypeople alike already 'consulted the heavens to determine appropriate times to let blood, perform surgery, and administer medicines'.[75] Of all an almanac's supporting tables and reference diagrams, the zodiacal Man of Signs proved the most popular.[76] The Man demonstrated *melothesia* (correspondences of astrological signs to parts of the human body) employed to diagnose and treat the humoural subject.[77] Horrocks summarises that 'along with the Anatomy and weather predictions'—which were also expressly astrological and very popular—'almanacs issued from the 1690s through the 1750s offered advice about the appropriate times for gathering herbs, clearing land, and cutting trees and seasonal instructions for bleeding and purging'.[78] Divination—especially astrological knowledge—was not exclusively about simply decoding personal destiny; it also ordered time and space to allot a season for all things. Combining these two endeavours, occult epistemologies could produce etiological diagnosis in any number of spheres of interrelation between self and environment: such as disease, nutrition, agriculture, and healing.

If there was any doubt, as Butler notes, the popularity of almanacs often depended directly upon their occult contents.[79] One popular occult field beyond astrological physic and natural magic was prophecy. Partly founded upon 'the conviction that the natural universe and the moral universe reflected each other',[80] this reflection could have obvious connections with almanacs' other material.

Astrology offered both cosmology and theology, and colonial almanac makers and readers observed and considered 'an active universe of a powerful and sometimes wrathful God, a God who wrote in the sky commands to repent and reform'.[81] Indeed, a direct link has been proposed between growing evangelical ministry and declining belief in astrological prophecy.[82] Nevertheless, 'in New York public prophesising did not disappear until the 1750s', and Gronim locates its continuance in 'the fact that none of the prophecies had clear political content (aside from the general and occasional "woe-will-come-to-great-men" prophecy) and no connections were drawn between the content of almanacs and social conflicts within the province'.[83]

Clearly there was a deeper shift of focus in popular conceptions of prophecy, from natural magical investigative endeavours of accurate prediction of the future—of which astrology offered the most obvious examples, from medical to agricultural and even expressly political utilities—to prophecy as preaching rectitude from insightful visions of the present. We might consider a move away from political content and towards the more straightforwardly religious, but a fairer assessment of this turn might be from quantitative to qualitative ways of knowing. The Church of England back home had, since the Reformation, taken 'the view that Christians now had all the revelation they needed, but others felt that the possibility of further messages from God could not be entirely ruled out'.[84] A theological tension emerged between this older notion of the end of prophecy after Christ and St Paul's reference to prophecy as an active gift of the Holy Spirit that should operate all the time within any fully Christian congregation as attested in 1 Corinthians 12–14. The favoured resolution of this tension, at least across New England (albeit in regionally distinct degrees) was that 'prophesying', after Christ's coming, meant the free inspired speech of any Christian within a congregation during worship, which should bear more on the present than on any somewhat distant future.[85]

Furthermore, Phyllis Mack has pointed out how many radicals, such as Quakers, 'preaching during the chaos of the Civil War period... expressed [their] principles by adopting the language of angry Old Testament prophets, chastising the moral laziness of their neighbours'.[86] This was especially common for the heterodox milieu of English revolutionary radicals referred to as the Ranters.[87] Abiezer Coppe, one of the most infamous Ranters, is certainly judged to have written 'as if he were re-enacting the social critique of the biblical prophets and his voice... is deliberately fashioned as an echo of the biblical context'.[88] We should consider an underlying soteriological drive in the employment of prediction in the language of the prophets which—as one contemporary writing on the proper use of prophecy put it—'doe mingle the doctrine of repentance, and doe almost alwaies vse consolations in Christ to them that doe repent'.[89] Attention to the body politic turned to the body spiritual; understandable from a perspective which held that, come the Day of Judgement, the latter would far outlive the former. Finally, along with bringing to bear scriptural authority, such echoing of the prophets—such identification of self and circumstances with biblical proverbs and parables—further enforced a notion of a certain eternal mythic present, that the struggles faced in these end-times had real cosmological bearing on the unfolding destiny of the moral universe. They played a part in 'imbuing time with an eschatological pulse'.[90]

This clarification about the lack of prediction in some 'prophesying' should not necessarily suggest a declining interest in the future. John Seller's Virginia almanac for 1685 continued a long folk-prophetic tradition of listing unlucky 'Dogg days' ('so called because of the influence of those stars called the Dog [Sirius, the Dog-Star]' often 'beginning about the 20th day of July, and ending the 17th of August')[91] along with saints' feasts and other calendar notables.[92] The most common approach in England was to recommend moderation during this dangerous period, as the dog days were often associated with disease. Conversely, it was thought a particularly bad idea to take medicine of any kind during this period, or, indeed, to engage in sexual activity.[93] But such particular conditions exacerbated by dog days and the means of their avoidance were usually not specified in the American almanacs. Colonists seemed more interested in the practical calendrical information than an authoritative interpretation.

One particularly famous millenarian almanac maker (and, indeed, occult philosopher) was Daniel Leeds. Emigrating as a Quaker to New Jersey in the 1680s, Leeds had 'a theological falling out with his fellow Quakers and rejoined the Church of England, though his theology continued to be distinctly millenarian'.[94] Butler notes that Leeds was proficient in the works of German mystic, Jacob Boehme, as well as quoting legendary magician-priest Hermes Trismegistus, summarising England's most famous early modern astrologer William Lilly, advocating Paracelsian medicine ('at a time when its influence had waned dramatically', no less), and 'quoted Psalms 78:49 to support the notion that the "first Cause" (who used angels as agents) also used stars as "second Causes of Effects upon Mankind"'.[95]

It should be noted that Leeds also recommended practices consistent with English astrologer-physicians and cunning-folk, such as advising readers to gather herbs 'when the Planets that govern them are dignified and friendly aspected'.[96] The astrological-medical basis for gathering plants at particular times lay in the effort to harvest ingredients when their innate occult virtues were waxing most potent and useful. Leeds' advice echoes that of astrologer-physicians ranging from famed translator and physician Nicholas Culpeper to Joseph Blagrave, whose own *Physick* detailed instructions for astrological sigils, herb charms, and exorcisms.[97] While astrology's magical applications were wide, Leeds had also grown up during the period of English astrological reform in which 'many of the arcane details and complicated decoding of previous centuries were stripped away, resulting in a simpler astrology that claimed to be closer to what actually happened in the skies'; certainly 'Leeds presented his skills as a straightforward matter of knowledge and experience.'[98] Although more complicated computational astrology fell out of favour, folk magical and medical applications of naked-eye star-lore persisted, as did demand for such knowledge and services in the colonies.

Leeds frequently included 'A Breviate of some Astrological Predictions' in his almanacs, which might be general warnings, as when 'many wonderful Mutations or Revolutions … shall shortly be effected'.[99] He also offered more details on particular events. When 'there hath lately appeared a prodigious and amazing Comet', he cited the comet interpretation of William Lilly in 1680 ('its appearance hath been universal, so also will its direful effects be, as great Wars, Quarrels, Discords, Contentions, Division, Confution &c'), and John Hollwell of 1682 ('it doth declare Wars and Devastations to the World, with abundance of Unhappiness towards Mankind').[100] His almanac of 1696 offered astrological details and (generally gloomy) interpretations of two upcoming eclipses.[101]

Beyond almanacs, Leeds' *Temple of Wisdom for the Little World* demonstrates his particularly theologically-inflected occult philosophy. Topics ranged from free will to the Philosopher's Stone, and from 'the Serpent that deceived Adam' to a treatise on the Devil and the four humoural complexions. Appended are poems on mastering one's passions, and a few very short essays attributed to Francis Bacon. Leeds cites that 'second Solomon', the (in)famous Heinrich Cornelius Agrippa, and is very concerned with distinguishing false magic and wicked lies from natural magic and divinity. While drawing on many sources, the work as a whole appears a cohesive synthesis.

Leeds' work at the end of the seventeenth century has been argued to mark an apogee of both popular and developed prophecy and magic; that 'although basic astrological information still appeared in almanacs, after about 1720 no almanac-makers promoted sophisticated occult ideas as Pennsylvania's Daniel Leeds'.[102] Leeds' son Titan continued the family tradition of advocating astrological timing for gathering herbs in his almanacs. He also continued prescribing herbal remedies based on astrological rulerships, treating astrology very much as a practical set of skills rather than a complex mathematical exercise.[103]

Titan also continued a broader almanac tradition of eschatological Christian astrology. His interpretation of a 1738 eclipse ('the Effects will not be bad to those that endeavor to avoid the Temptation of the great Red Dragon') derived from Revelation's twelfth chapter, and he also used the Saturn–Jupiter conjunctions of 1742 and 1762 to anticipate 'wonderful Changes and Revolutions in the World … perhaps then will be the beginning of the pouring forth of the Seven Vials, or last Plagues upon Babylon or Tyrus, i.e. the Papacy'.[104] This is entirely in keeping with the historicist method of interpreting prophecy.[105]

Thus historicist millenarians worked with Revelation by according numerological significances to various symbols in John's prophecy and using them to construct historical periodisations. Andrew Escobedo has argued John Foxe's *Acts and Monuments* amounted to 'one of the most thorough and detailed historical applications of the Apocalypse', noting that the initial book of the four volume set 'concludes with a numerological interpretation of the Book of Revelation and of recent events in European history'.[106] So we find in *The Bloody Almanack* for 1643 by astrologer John Booker (1602–1667) a periodised history of Christianity, beginning with the later life of Christ, based off the assertion that the seven seals mentioned therein mark seven-year periods by which 'you shall find the effect of every seale to be performed within the seven years of that seale; and so the harmony to be perfect betwixt those seales and the just history'.[107] Indeed, 'throughout the seventeenth century astrological, biblical and historical concepts were fused into a single "astro-historical-eschatological" analysis'.[108] More specifically, 'Revelation revealed the entire history of the Christian world, a history in which England played a crucial role, and the text made it possible to understand the past as a complete story in a way that antiquarian study alone could not do.'[109] Such a cosmic role played a large part in the expectations of and expeditions into the Americas, as well as a continuing line of apocalyptic astrology published and poured over by colonists.

Indeed, Gronim assesses 'the thread of Protestant millenarianism so prominent in England during the mid-seventeenth century, while more subdued, was still publicly acceptable in eighteenth-century New York'.[110] A parallel vein of Puritan predestinarian theology made divination as practical personal foreknowledge arguably more important in New England than this cosmological universal millenarianism; however, Euro-Americans in the British colonies were certainly very interested in the future and the occult means to apprehend and analyse it.[111]

7.2.2 Cunning-craft

The local magical practitioners broadly known as cunning-folk could be found offering their magical services across New England.[112] In some ways, especially given the lack of extant sacred Christian sites (or at least those familiar ruins and locales adopted by Christians),[113] 'the land militated against the occult', at least as it had been practised in England.[114] Yet at least one survey collected supposedly indigenous secrets of medicine and power, offering 'Remedies wherewith the Natives constantly use to Cure their Distempers, Wounds, and Sores'.[115] Native 'Priests' were known to serve their communities 'in stead of Physitions and Chirurgions' and 'they carry always about them a bag full of herbes and drugs to cure the sicke diseased'.[116] This work combined humoural assessment of New World botanicals, such as recommending watermelon for 'those sick of Feavers, and other hot diseases', with reports of indigenous practices, such as 'the Indians Cure their Wounds with [white hellebore], annointing the Wound first with Raccoons greese, or Wild-Cats greese, and strewing upon it the powder of the roots'.[117] There were both old and new ways to magically work with the flora and fauna of this New World.

Many settlers carried out various activities to 'predict the future, heal the sick, and protect themselves against witchcraft', and although colonists experimented with many of these techniques themselves, 'in times of need' people 'often turned to neighbours who had a reputation for occult expertise'.[118] While it is thus impossible to know how many people were experimenting in private, Godbeer considers that—especially given the sheer volume (not to mention apparent matter-of-fact tone) of the court records, Puritan sermons, and general correspondence concerning magic—'those who did turn to magical techniques were clearly members of a sizeable constituency'.[119] Godbeer further characterises this drive to magical solutions as 'pragmatic': not all traditions considered all occult forces as inherently evil, and 'when godly colonists turned to magic, they were not rejecting religious faith so much as turning to whatever supernatural resource seemed helpful at a given moment'.[120] Certainly, cunning-folk offered useful services. As in England, these were chiefly divination and unbewitching, along with various charms and spells to affect specific conditions.[121] Such magical activities transcended boundaries of class and education, for 'just as learned Puritans like Winthrop sought to achieve mastery over the occult through study and experiment, ordinary new Englanders sought the same kinds of controls over the unseen forces working in their lives through the application of a broad array of folk magic practices'.[122]

The most popular service, on both sides of the Atlantic, was undoubtedly divination—the telling of fortunes. This covered everything from describing a future spouse, to finding lost property, or even detecting thieves. Crucially, a fortune was not simply a futurological matter; divination pried workable data from the unknown present as well as from tracing the inertias of the underlying past. Coscinomancy—in which the diviner(s) balanced a sieve on a pair of scissors or shears and intoned names of suspects until the sieve wobbled, 'turned', or fell—seems a particularly popular activity in late-seventeenth-century New England, with three separate cases occurring in Andover alone.[123] Such activities were performed both by cunning experts and amateurs alike. Cunning-folk could also compel thieves to confess or return goods,[124] and seventeenth-century parliamentarian and legal scholar John Selden even remarked that such sorcerer-detectives 'kept thieves in awe, and did as much good in a country as a justice of peace'.[125]

An interesting distinction, or rather lack thereof, is highlighted when we consider folk magic to prevent theft rather than simply folk divination to detect it or its perpetrators. Along with identifying offenders, 'written charms were also used to afflict thieves and thereby force them into returning goods, and spirits could also be conjured up to do likewise'.[126] One anti-theft charm operated by bequeathing one's 'place and all my goods within and without to the Blessed Trinity', as well as to the Virgin Mary and various saints and angels, 'that no theeues away take'.[127] The actual affect on the prospective thief came when the operator charged 'you all [i.e. saints, Mary, God, etc.] to keepe him or them still... that they pass no foot ...'.[128] Significantly, these spiritual powers were themselves charged by the seven planets and twelve zodiacal signs. As I have argued elsewhere, the use of such astrological magical glyphs, inscribed onto a paper charm in their proper astrological order demonstrates how:

> the totality of the planetary and zodiacal governances could be employed to protect against every eventuality. A manageable astrological taxonomy of the complete mechanics of the universe allowed one to invoke and charge these forces with tasks and functions. This was the function of symbolising cosmic forces with glyphs—the extensive corresponding powers, responsibilities and influences of the planets and signs could be symbolised in their summarising glyphs. Hence 'there was also considerable use of overtly magical words and phrases, spirit names, occult symbols, planetary signs, and astrological terms'[129] in the various magical charms offered by astrological practitioners.[130]

The taxonomic divisions of astrology as a divination system—which after all posited the potential for a 'total coverage' epistemology in which any phenomena could be analysed—could also be employed to affect that which it described or appeal to that which it delineated as wielding powerful virtue in that matter. Divination and sorcery combined about a locus of need, anxiety, and hope. In this case, anxieties about theft were to a degree externalised, via resort to various magical techniques of compulsion (many with far more unpleasant results than simply not being able to move), to inflict such anxiety on the prospective theft. Thus 'the fear of magical reprisal itself was also hoped to induce enough of an effect to achieve a speedy recovery'.[131] That 'astrology could be a useful deterrent'[132] should also give us pause for thought. This potential deterrent utility is another instantiation of how divination did not merely describe or explain. This was not simply knowledge-at-a-distance. Such knowledge has consequences, and had real effects in the interpersonal world of the early modern period.

Of course, given that much thief-compelling involved magically torturing the suspect into confession or compliance, there was also a very real possibility that a magician-healer could end up suspected of witchcraft themselves.[133] This was also especially the case 'if their patients grew sicker instead of recovering'.[134] Most popular means of unbewitching involved 'causing the evil to return'[135] upon the suspected witch, that is, exploiting the magical link created by the bewitching to torture the suspect into defeat: most obviously with witch-bottles.[136] This essay cannot provide space for a detailed assessment of witchcraft in the British colonies, and certainly not for in-depth analysis of witch-trials or witch-hunting milieu or 'hysteria'. However, given the ease with which those considered experts in unbewitching could also be suspected of causing such harms, it should be briefly addressed as part of the contextual discussion of early American cunning-craft.

To Cotton Mather and his ilk, all folk magic customs were 'Little Witchcrafts' which allowed the Devil 'such Footing' in the New World.[137] However, witch-hunt documents also evidence some very specific accounts and accusations of *maleficium*. Crucially, we also return to texts, as 'evidence drawn from the Salem witchcraft trials suggests that the colonists' ownership of occult books and almanacs also betrays some real resort to malevolent occult practices'.[138] Perhaps the most iconic kinds of workings were those of poppets: dolls representative of victims which were stabbed, drowned or otherwise harmed, as when Mary Warrin accused Job Tookey of running 'a great pin into a poppets heart which killed'.[139] Goody Bishop was supposedly found to own ragdolls with pins stuck in them.[140] The fear of witchcraft could drive one to it, as when Abigall Hobbs reported she was convinced to stab a poppet with a thorn as 'She had better to afflict then be aflicted'.[141] Finally, animal familiars and the Devil in the shape of a beast—more common in England than elsewhere on the Continent— were reported in accounts of witchcraft, and conflated with indigenous concepts of animal spirits.[142]

As but one instance of how colonial American cunning-craft actually operated, let us examine a case from Butler's survey:

> Church and court records reveal deeply rooted occult practices in Chester County, Pennsylvania. In 1695 the county's Quaker leaders demanded that Phillip Roman, Jr. and his brother Robert stop using astrology, geomancy, and chiromancy 'in resolving questions Concerning Loss and gain with other vain Questions.' … Robert clung to his occult crafts … Chester County's Quaker leaders turned to the legal institutions they now commanded in America to stop the younger Roman's practices. Since many of them sat as county magistrates, they indicted Roman 'for practicing geomancy according to hidon [John Heydon] and divineing by a sticke' and for using occult means to take 'the wife of Henry Hastings away from her husband and

children.' To support their accusations, they named three books they found in Roman's possession: 'Hidon's Temple of Wisdom which teaches geomancy, and Scots Discovery of witchcraft, and Cornelias Agrippas Teaching negromancy.'[143]

Along with contextualising how local colonial authorities responded to magical, religious and political affairs, this report reveals much about seventeenth-century American magic itself. It confirms the popularity of palmistry: Massachusetts minister John Hale mentions meeting practitioners who claimed to tell a person's 'future Condition by looking into their hands', with one informing Hale she had learned the 'rules to knoe what should come to pass' from a 'book of Palmistry'.[144] Nor should the possible reference to necromancy be taken as mere scaremongering: Massachusetts governor John Winthrop noted in 1664 the arrival of a man from Virginia 'who professed himself to have skill in necromancy'.[145] Heinrich Agrippa had been developing a sinister reputation since his *Three Books* begun circulating in manuscript, demonologist Jean Bodin calling him 'the great doctor of the Diabolical Art'.[146] Books attributed to him—informally referred to simply as *Agrippas*—acquired demonic personalities of their own: in France these were frequently kept chained up under padlock, 'said to be a living book that hated to be consulted and hid its *characters* until it had been compelled, by beating it'.[147] Roman probably owned either the *Three Books* or, more likely, the *Fourth Book of Occult Philosophy* attributed to Agrippa, which did actually contain a magical system for conjuring spirits.[148]

While Butler's later comments suggest mild puzzlement at the appearance of Scot's anti-magical *Discovery* in a cunning-man's library, more recent scholarship has demonstrated that this tome was in fact popularly received as 'a treasure trove of magical information, providing spells, Catholic prayers, exorcisms, charms, talismans, and rituals on how to communicate with angels, demons, and the spirits of the dead'; that 'Scot produced what amounted to the first grimoire printed in the English language, and while he did so to prove the worthlessness of its contents he unwittingly ended up democratizing ritual magic rather than undermining it'.[149] Certainly it was used as a spell-book by cunning-folk in England, and it appears to have made the journey across the ocean to serve the same needs.[150]

John Heydon's *Theomagia*—like Leeds's *Temple of Wisdom*—taught 'Rosicrucian' geomancy via an idiosyncratic angelology. Heydon has been singled out as an exception to the general reformist empirical turn in late-seventeenth-century astrology for his thoroughly occult 'hodgepodge of alchemy, astrology and magic', with one commentator noting 'Heydon exemplifies the occult road that astrology failed to travel'.[151] That it was owned by Roman further vindicates Davies' opinion that 'cunning-folk would certainly have appreciated this detailed practical guide to astromantic and geomantic divination, and the diagrams showing the various signs and characters of the planets and their angels'.[152] It seems *Theomagia* and its geomancy had an appeal beyond the mere decade of novelty Monod suggests it enjoyed.[153]

The Roman case also highlights the use and apparent popularity of geomantic divination at the end of the seventeenth century. Certainly, the patient case-files of astrologer-physicians Simon Forman and Richard Napier show geomancy was being used across seventeenth-century England.[154] The Pennsylvania records show recognition not simply of the divination, but of the author of the handbook that taught it, which would certainly seem to indicate its popularity.

Geomancy deserves particular attention paid to its implicit relations to both prophecy and image magic. One of the most famous early modern authors on geomancy, Christopher Cattan, stated that this divination system was considered (by no less than Thomas Aquinas) to 'participate with Astrologie, and is called her daughter'.[155] Geomantic divination applies the 'use and rules of astrology'[156]—that is, astrological categories and correspondences as well as certain techniques—to data generated by making marks: originally in the earth or sand with a stick, although by the early modern period, often on paper with a pen. There were no ephemerides, no astronomical interest in the heavens at all, but rather in what the astrological bodies and forces represented here on earth. Geomantic divination thus relied upon discerning and analysing various guiding forces and inertias of the cosmos, not from detailed measurement of the relative positions of the stars, but in the fall of dice or the scratching and tallying of marks upon a page made 'without counting' and while 'pondering in your heart' the question about which you are inquiring.[157] In other words, rather than plotting the movements of sources or harbingers of particular influence and affect, one is directly communicating with an aspect of the divine. One of the most ardent proponents of geomancy was Robert Fludd, who 'saw the universe animated by a living soul and ruled by spiritual essences, angelic powers and a whole machinery of planetary intelligences'.[158] John Heydon more specifically insisted 'Rosie Crucians also judge the hand of the projector to be most powerfully moved and directed by the Idea's or Genii', that is, 'Invisible Created Spirits' that are 'incorporated into a figure'.[159] There was an inherent animism underlying many strains of geomancy.

Significantly, the image of a spirit of a particular force was thought to be a locus for that force, to allow that spirit some access to and affect in this world. This is a basic image magic axiom—manipulating the representation can affect the represented. Thus, geomantic figures—glyphs thought to encapsulate as well as merely signify astral potencies—existed as cosmological icons both of divination and something more sorcerous. Heydon begins his work on geomancy insisting the sixteen figures are the means by which we receive the virtues and influences of the zodiacal 'Ideas' and their planetary 'Lords' because 'God the Creator of all things, out of the Chaos, which was the bodies of wicked Angels made the Earth, which is divided into twelve equal parts ...'.[160] The figures are then explicitly considered as workable building blocks of the cosmos. Moreover, Agrippa notes that geomantic 'Figures, framed by the number and situation of the stars, and ascribed both to the Elements, and also to the Planets and Signs ... being engraven or imprinted under the dominion of their Planets and Signs, do conceive the vertue and power of images; and these Figures are *as a middle betwixt Images and Characters*'.[161] This overlap of pictographic representation and semeiotic letters is a further instance of the blurring of prophetic divination and operative sorcery, which we might think of as the engagement with (or even manipulation of) the energies and agents of an organic cosmos. The accusations of attempting to 'take' Henry Hastings' wife also highlight how a cunning-man's services could elide (either in reality or in suspicious imaginations) divination and enchantment, merging the decrypting of foreknowledge with modalities of influence or control. To an early modern worldview, the scratching of geomantic figures into the earth to divine on love could all too easily slip into casting and empowering those ideographic and pictographic magical 'hieroglyphs', which represented the actions of powerful spirits, in order to enchant people.

As a final note, if we are to take the charge of 'practicing geomancy according to hidon and divineing by a sticke' as accurately pertaining to a common practice, we may note a somewhat rustic character of casting geomantic figures in the American dirt—rather than with the pen and paper of an English study—suggesting a broader shift away from sedentary urban settings for colonial magic, and towards an older form of engagement with a new landscape.

7.3 Conclusion

The variety of people and religious practices mixing in the colonies produced heterodox conditions, at which 'even secular observers wondered at the number of settlers who ignored organized religious activity altogether'; indeed, 'colonial religious opinion embodied heterodoxy'.[162] This New World heterodoxy also fostered an apparent distrust of what might be called epistemological authority. Bringing both a history of science and socio-political class analysis to bear, Gronim attributes the

> reluctance of New Yorkers to accept British "learned opinion" on cosmology ... to the peculiarities of the local social structure, such as the marginality of the Anglican religion and the relative newness of the group claiming gentility ... the strong suspicion towards the pretentions of the elite meant that the middling sorts, the literate but not learned, were disinclined to substitute distant learned opinion for the evidence of their own senses.[163]

Similar trends appear present in British colonies further afield—especially Puritan rejection of growing 'Saduccist' scepticism over the powers of witchcraft and the Devil.[164]

Without a centralised 'Establishment epistemology', traditions that declined in England with the oncoming Enlightenment appear to have remained popular (or at least vehement) far longer in the colonies: chiefly astrological physic and prophecy, but not forgetting the relatively late and much-considered witch-hunts. The continuation of seventeenth-century English practices in eighteenth-century America can be observed in some very direct ways, such as when Nathaniel Ames reprinted a 1633 English almanac poem in his 1728 almanac, echoing the frustration at pressures from readership to print the Man of Signs, even from (apparently traditionalist) almanac-readers who practised no astrological physic.[165] Magical practices concerning the future—whether personal divination, millenarian analysis of the destiny of the world, or the astrology that bridged the two—were certainly popular.

Finally, proliferations of occult texts are well attested in the library records of the colonies. Library lists from Virginia estate inventories, for instance, show many collections containing books both decrying and defending occult philosophy and natural magic—which Butler takes as further evidence of 'the heterodox character of seventeenth-century Virginia Anglicanism'—with a preponderance of handbooks of astrological physic.[166] The library of Anglican minister Thomas Teackle even included further works by 'Rosicrucian' magus John Heydon.[167]

Such interest in the ideals of the Rosy Cross should not surprise us, given that Winthrop Jr. was 'one of the English alchemists who tried repeatedly to make contact with the Rosicrucians', and who 'found in alchemical culture an intellectual and Christian natural philosophy to which he could fully commit and through which he could seek knowledge and material gains while fulfilling his Christian duty to improve the world and serve others'.[168] By the time he joined his father in New England in 1631 he had already been collecting works from the library of John Dee, England's most (in)famous scholar and magus with ties to the Brotherhood. Indeed, Winthrop even 'adopted Dee's *monas hieroglyphica* as a personal mark inscribed next to his name within his alchemical texts and emblazoned on the crates of chemicals, instruments, and other supplies he transported to America'.[169] Alchemy was not merely a technology, but part of a general spiritual endeavour to perfect nature and the grammar and practice of a specific milieu amongst certain European intellectuals concerned with expressly eschatological ramifications of the Great Instauration.

As we have already seen, manuals on palmistry, geomancy, and a variety of other occult techniques were also available. These conditions appear to have allowed older occult traditions to sit alongside pluralist and empirical cosmology with a particularly pragmatic bent. Shorn of its 'elaborate and arcane calculations', Peter Eisenstadt has shown how transatlantic astrology began to (re)construct itself as collections of practical 'recipe knowledge', which 'characterized almanacs of the eighteenth century throughout the British colonies'.[170] Best exemplified in studies of New York's almanacs, but clearly a wider factor in colonial magic, 'astrology limited itself more closely to what an attentive observer could see in the actual night sky and practitioners consistently claimed that the correlation between the movements of the planets and the effects on earth were accessible to everyday experience'.[171] It seems this move away from computational astrology to a simpler, more quotidian and egalitarian practice may have kept it popular long after astrology lost its lustre back in England. American astrology, from observation to interpretation, seems to become less the preserve of authority and more an individual activity. These pragmatic recipes of self-reliance are also present in the assessment of cunning-craft services of 'sieve and shears … witch-bottles and little puppets' as 'self-help magic'.[172]

By taking stock of English occult knowledge and techniques brought from overseas, we are better situated to begin future studies on the extent and developments of English practitioners' relationships with other cultures' magics. This includes Euro-American (especially German

Pennsylvanian) settlers from across Lutheran, Pietist, and Quaker traditions,[173] and it seems reasonable to suggest Hermeticists and Kabbalists were talking to each other, albeit in their second languages. We also have scholarship on seventeenth-century interactions between Spanish and native Central Americans specifically addressing themes of magic and diabolism,[174] with which we can draw further comparative studies. Certainly by the late eighteenth century, American magic looked a lot more of a 'melting cauldron', as indigenous and then particularly African spiritual practices became incorporated—chiefly via the diasporic movements of enslaved people[175]—and this admixture continued birthing distinctly African-American conjure traditions throughout the nineteenth and twentieth centuries.[176]

Yet, given astrology's importance in early colonial occult texts and practice, it seems especially significant that Gronim notes:

> One of the striking silences in colonial New York records is the inattention to any Iroquois knowledge of the sky. If New Yorkers stood on the periphery of the British empire, they stood at the center of a crucial site of Indian-British relations, the border of Iroquoia. For all the volumes written about Iroquois war, trade, and society, New Yorkers noted only occasional instances of Iroquois knowledge of the natural world, and those were largely limited to the knowledge of territorial limits and of plants for food and healing. For New Yorkers, Iroquois knowledge of the sky was not 'Christian'. Their astronomy could not be the apprehension of a text of God, and so was worth no notice.[177]

When the natural world did not reflect the Almighty, it could all too easily become a further source of bedevilment. Native practices were framed in a sinister light by European onlookers casting shadows, as old World debates within occult moral philosophy were projected out—projections so strong, they often survived actual contact with othered peoples. As heterodoxy compounded at the colonial peripheries far from a centralised British establishment, so too did growing anxieties. Expectations of native devil-worship, idolatry, and human sacrifice had been apparently confirmed by eye-witnesses with little experience of indigenous rituals' emic cultural and theological meanings. Such fear of indigenous violence—magical or otherwise—contributed greatly to a sense of spiritual paranoia amongst many settlers, in which 'Indian raids, the authoritarian Dominion, Quaker evangelism, and the dramatic implications of the new charter … was equivalent to being assaulted by Satan', contextualising that 'the witch crisis of 1692 was not an isolated event but the climax of a devilish assault upon the region'.[178] Darkness stirred even within their midst, as a 'Puritan' emphasis on community and mutual support meant that arguments between neighbours became not only irritating in their own right but also a betrayal of social and moral values on which their practical and spiritual welfare depended.'[179] The (inter)personal was not merely the political, it was—as with prophetic eschatology—the moral and cosmological.

Notes

1. Jon Butler, 'Magic, astrology, and the early American religious heritage, 1600–1760', *American Historical Review* 84:2 (1979), p. 318. Butler contextualises that 'many people in English society simply did not clearly divorce Christianity from magic, astrology, and divination', and that this continued in the colonies (p. 323).
2. David D. Hall, *Worlds of wonder, Days of judgment: Popular religious belief in early New England* (Cambridge, MA, 1990), p. 7.
3. Zachary McLeod Hutchins, *Inventing Eden: Primitivism, millennialism, and the making of New England* (New York, and Oxford, 2014), p. 18.
4. Walter W. Woodward, *Prospero's America: John Winthrop, Jr., alchemy, and the creation of New England Culture, 1606–1676* (Williamsburg, NC, 2010), p. 27 [citing Charles Webster, *The great instauration: Science, medicine, and reform, 1626–1660* (New York, 1976), pp. 22–24, 326–329]; Stephen A. McKnight, 'The wisdom of the ancients and Francis Bacon's *New Atlantis*', in Allen G. Debus and Michael T. Walton (eds), *Reading the book of nature: The other side of the scientific revolution* (Kirksville, MO, 1998), pp. 111–132. See also Daniel 12:4.
5. Francis Bacon, *The novum organon; or, A true guide to the interpretation of nature*, ed. G.W. Kitchin (Oxford, 1855), p. 62.
6. For colonial witch-craze scholarship, see Richard Godbeer, *The Devil's dominion: Magic and religion in early New England* (New York, 1992); Carol F. Karlsen, *The Devil in the shape of a woman: Witchcraft in colonial New England* (London, 1998); David Harley, 'Explaining Salem: Calvinist psychology and the diagnosis of possession', *American Historical Review* 101:2 (1996), pp. 307–330; John Demos, *The enemy within: 2,000 years of witch-hunting in the western world* (New York, 2008), especially pp. 87–92; Richard Godbeer, 'Witchcraft in British America', in Brian Levack (ed.), *The Oxford handbook of witchcraft in early modern Europe and colonial America* (Oxford, 2013), pp. 393–411.
7. C.R. Boxer, *Women in Iberian expansion overseas, 1415–1815* (London, 1975), p. 108.

8. For example, treatises by Elias Ashmole, Nicholas Culpeper, John Heydon, and Henry Warren were advertised as for sale from Nathaniel Brooke's shop 'at the Angel in Cornehill', in Fernando Gorges, *America painted to the life* (London, 1658), ff. 121–123.
9. George Alsop, *A character of the province of Mary-land* (London, 1666), p. 56.
10. Ioseph Acosta, *The naturall and morall historie of the East and West Indies* (London, 1604), pp. 343, 342.
11. Acosta, *Naturall and morall*, 'The Authors advertisement to the Reader', f. 3.
12. See, for example, Kristina Bross, *Dry bones and Indian sermons: Praying Indians in colonial America* (Ithaca, NY, and London, 2004); Lee Ernest Huddleston, *Origins of the American Indians: European concepts, 1492–1729* (Austin, TX, and London, 1967); Karen Ordahl Kupperman, *Indians and English: Facing off in early America* (Ithaca, NY, 2000); Laura M. Stevens, *The poor Indians: British missionaries, Native Americans and colonial sensibility* (Philadelphia, PA, 2004); Sam White, '"Shewing the difference betweene their conjuration, and our invocation on the name of God for rayne": Weather, prayer, and magic in early American encounters', *William and Mary Quarterly* 72:1 (2015), pp. 33–56.
13. Keith Thomas, *Religion and the decline of magic* (London, 1971), pp. 367–368, 379, 777; Owen Davies, *Popular magic: Cunning-folk in English history* (London, 2007), p. 93; Nicholas Campion, *A history of western astrology volume II: The medieval and modern worlds* (London, 2009), p. 169; Paul Monod, *Solomon's secret art: The occult in the age of enlightenment* (New Haven, CT, 2013), p. 75.
14. Pierre d'Avity, *The estates, empires, & principallities of the world*, trans. Edward Grimstone (London, 1615), p. 253.
15. Acosta, *Naturall and morall*, p. 343.
16. Acosta, *Naturall and morall*, p. 345.
17. Acosta, *Naturall and morall*, p. 346.
18. Acosta, *Naturall and morall*, p. 347.
19. Sean Lovitt, 'The book, the mirror, and the living dead: Necromancy and the early modern period' (Unpublished MA thesis, Concordia University, 2009), p. 2.
20. Thomas Ady, *A candle in the dark* (London, 1656), p. 152.
21. Thomas Blout, *Glossographia* (London, 1661).
22. Ludwig Lavater, *Of ghostes and spirites walking by nyght* (London, 1572).
23. For a focused study on the contagion of witchcraft and notions of the European occult body, see Francesca Matteoni, 'Blood beliefs in early modern Europe' (Unpublished PhD thesis: University of Hertfordshire, 2009).

24. Stuart Clark, *Vanities of the eye* (Oxford, 2007) remains the seminal work on early modern European crises of images, sight, and the growing 'epistemology of doubt'. For some of the magical applications of these occult principles, see D.P. Walker, *Spiritual and demonic magic from Ficino to Campanella* (London, 1958).
25. George Lyman Kittredge, 'Image magic and the like', in Elaine G. Breslaw (ed.), *Witches of the Atlantic world* (New York, 2000), pp. 126–131; Stephen Wilson, *The magical universe: Everyday ritual and magic in pre-modern Europe* (London, 2000), pp. 80, 96, 97, 134, 143, 144, 158, 161, 174, 179, 180, 192, 241, 267, 322, 428–429, 439, 448.
26. See Anna Marie Roos, 'Israel Hiebner's astrological amulets and the English sigil war', *Culture and Cosmos* 6:2 (2002), pp. 17–43.
27. Acosta, *Naturall and morall*, pp. 332–333.
28. Acosta, *Naturall and morall*, p. 337. Plato, himself a pagan, was afforded by occult philosophers such as Robert Fludd a somewhat unique place in early modern Christian thought: while the works of the 'Greekish philosophers' was usually considered 'terrene, animal and diabolical', founded after all upon heathen lies propagated by 'the Prince of darknesse', Plato was exempt because he was believed to have 'read the Books of Moses'. Robert Fludd, *Mosiacall philosophy* (London, 1659), pp. 9, 13, 42.
29. Acosta, *Naturall and morall*, p. 336.
30. Chiefly, Paracelsus, *Of the supreme mysteries of nature*, trans. Robert Turner (London, 1655). See also Robin E. Cousins, 'Robert Turner of "Holshott"', in Robert Turner, Patricia Shore Turner, and Robin E. Cousins (eds), *Elizabethan magic: The art and the magus* (Shaftesbury, 1989), pp. 129–150.
31. Contemporary magicians and astrologer-physicians such as Richard Napier were certainly influenced by the *Picatrix*, and Simon Forman even transcribed a copy. Elias Ashmole and William Lilly shared a copy of the text, which was found referenced and copied in Ashmole's collection. Michael MacDonald, *Mystical Bedlam: Madness, anxiety, and healing in seventeenth-century England* (Cambridge, 1981), p. 17 (Napier); Lauren Kassell, *Medicine and magic in Elizabethan England* (Oxford, 2005), pp. 51–52, citing MS Ashm. 244, f. 97 (Forman); MS Ashm. 1136, f. 184; MS Ashm. 1437, 46; C.H. Josten, *Elias Ashmole (1617–1692)* (Oxford, 1966), pp. 466–467 (Ashmole and Lilly). For more on reception of the *Picatrix* in this period, see David Pingree (ed.), *Picatrix: The Latin version of the Ghayat al-hakim* (London, 1986), pp. xix, liii–lv.
32. To continue our shepherding comparison, an image of the twenty-fourth Mansion of the Moon was recommended 'for the multiplying of herds of cattle, they took the horn of... that sort of cattle which they would increase, and sealed in it burning with an iron seal, the image of a woman giving

suck to her son, an they hanged it on the neck of that cattle who was the leader of the flock, or they sealed it in his horn' Heinrich Agrippa, *Three books of occult philosophy*, trans. J.F. (London, 1651), p. 306.
33. William Lilly, *The world's catastrophe* (London, 1647), p. 42; citing 'John Tritemius, Abbot of Spanheim, of the heavenly Intelligencies, governing the Orbes under God'.
34. Acosta, *Naturall and morall*, p. 338.
35. Acosta, *Naturall and morall*, p. 338.
36. See Thomas, *Religion*, pp. 86–87, 113, 233, 280, 502, 520, 531, 569, 612–614, 649, 693, 721; Clark, *Vanities*, pp. 161–172, 283–284, 336; Nicholas Weill-Parot, 'Astral magic and intellectual changes (twelfth-fifteenth centuries): "astrological images" and the concept of "addressative" magic', in Jan M. Bremmer and Jan R. Veenstra (eds), *The metamorphosis of magic from late antiquity to the early modern period* (Leuven, 2002), pp. 167–187.
37. Thomas Tryon, *Friendly advice to the gentlemen-planters of the East and West Indies in three parts* (London, 1684), frontispiece.
38. See, for example, Henry Butts, *Diets dry diner* (London, 1599).
39. Stephen Pender considers 'diet was dominant' in terms of attention paid to non-natural principles. Stephen Pender, 'Subventing disease: Anger, passions, and the non-naturals', in Jennifer C. Vaught (ed.), *Rhetorics of bodily disease and health in medieval and early modern England* (Farnham, 2010), p. 198. Certainly, it was considered the most important for the 'constitution of body, and preparation of humours'. Robert Burton, *The anatomy of melancholy* (Oxford, 1621), 1.2.2.1.
40. Richard Hakluyt, *The principle nauigations* (London, 1600), p. 306.
41. For more on concerns over the Devil empowering even healing magic in America, see Godbeer, *The Devil's dominion*, 55–84.
42. Bauer develops this notion, pointing out such firsthand observations were subjected to 'the imposition upon experiential testimony of an authorial ideal that [Julie] Solomon calls "epistemic self-distancing" defined as "the effacement of the eye-witness's subjectivity in the delivery of facts".' Ralph Bauer, *The cultural geography of colonial American literatures* (New York, 2003), pp. 15–16.
43. Hutchins, *Inventing Eden*, p. 40.
44. Alfred Cave, 'Indian shamans and English witches', in Elaine G. Breslaw (ed.), *Witches of the Atlantic world* (New York, 2000), p. 197.
45. Edward Winslow, *Good nevvs from New England* (London, 1624), p. 55; Cave, 'Indian shamans', p. 197.
46. Roger Williams, *A key into the language of America* (London, 1643), pp. 119–120.
47. Alexander Whitaker, *Good nevves from Virginia* (London, 1613), 24. See also Samuel Purchas, *His pilgrimes in fiue bookes* (London, 1625); Samuel

Clarke, *A true and faithful account of the four chiefest plantations of the English in America* (London, 1670), p. 13.
48. 'No such allegations of the inflicting of personal injury through sorcery are to be found in early Puritan descriptions of Indian "witchcraft."' Cave, 'Indian shamans', p. 198.
49. Cave, 'Indian shamans', pp. 198, 199.
50. Cave, 'Indian shamans', pp. 201–202.
51. John Josselyn, *An account of two voyages to New-England* (London, 1674), p. 134.
52. Cave, 'Indian shamans', p. 202.
53. Allison Coudert, *Religion, magic, and science in early modern Europe and America* (Santa Barbara, CA, 2011), p. 144. Indeed, Coudert considers activism 'the most distinctive aspect of early modern millenarianism', its adherents 'did not sit back complacently and wait for the millennium to come to them; they sought to make it happen' (p. 138).
54. John Locke, *Two treatises of government* (London, 1690), 250.
55. Woodward, *Prospero's America*, p. 28.
56. Woodward, *Prospero's America*, pp. 29–30; citing *Fama fraternitatis*, trans. Thomas Vaughan (1652), in Francis A. Yates, *The Rosicrucian enlightenment* (London and New York, 1993), p. 238.
57. Woodward, *Prospero's America*, p. 28; citing Webster, *The great instauration*, pp. 24, 326.
58. Woodward, *Prospero's America*, p. 28; citing Miguel A. Granada, 'Kepler vs. Roeslin on the interpretation of Kepler's Nova: (1) 1604–1606', *Journal for the History of Astronomy* XXXVI (2005), pp. 299–319.
59. Butler, 'Magic, astrology', p. 325.
60. Cotton Mather, *The wonders of the invisible world* (Boston, 1693), pp. 66–67.
61. Robert C. Black III, *The younger John Winthrop* (New York, 1966), pp. 87–88; Harold Jantz, 'America's first cosmopolitan', *Proceedings of the Massachusetts Historical Society* 84 (1972), pp. 3–25; Ronald S. Wilkinson, '"Hermes Christianus": John Winthrop, Jr., and chemical medicine in seventeenth-century New England', in Allen G. Debus (ed.), *Science, medicine, and society in the Renaissance* (New York, 1972), pp. 222–241; Ronald S. Wilkinson, 'The alchemical library of John Winthrop, Jr. (1606–1676)', *Ambix* 11 (1963), pp. 33–51; Ronald S. Wilkinson, 'George Starkey, physician and alchemist', *Ambix* 11 (1963), pp. 121–152.
62. Butler, 'Magic, astrology', p. 325.
63. John L. Brooke, *The refiner's fire: The making of Mormon cosmology, 1644–1844* (Cambridge, 1994), p. 36 n. 20.
64. Woodward, *Prospero's America*, p. 30.
65. Peter Severinus, *Idea medicinae philosophiae* (Hague, 1660), p. 39; cited in Allen G. Debus, *The English Paracelsians* (New York, 1966), p. 20.

66. Woodward, *Prospero's America*, pp. 31–33.
67. Woodward, *Prospero's America*, p. 33.
68. Sara S. Gronim, 'At the sign of Newton's head: Astronomy and cosmology in British colonial New York', *Pennsylvania History* 66 (1999), p. 56.
69. Butler, 'Magic, astrology', pp. 329–330.
70. For instance, Nathaniel Chauncy, *Almanack* (Cambridg[e], 1662), frontispiece.
71. Samuel Atkins, *Kalendarium Pennsilvaniense, or, America's messenger* (Philadelphia, PA, 1686), 'December'.
72. For instance, William Williams, *Cambridge ephemeris: An almanac* (Cambridge, 1685), ff. 3–14.
73. Gronim, 'At the sign of Newton's head', p. 62.
74. Campion, *A history of western astrology* p. 182.
75. Thomas A. Horrocks, *Popular print and popular medicine: Almanacs and health advice in early America* (Amherst, MA, 2008), pp. 17–18.
76. 124 of 130 the almanacs printed in New York between 1694 and 1775 examined by Gronim included a Man of Signs or a substitute table. Gronim, 'At the sign of Newton's head', p. 79 n. 16.
77. Nogah Arikha, *Passions and tempers: A history of the humours* (New York, 2007), pp. 139–168.
78. Horrocks, *Popular print*, p. 22.
79. Butler, 'Magic, astrology', p. 330.
80. Gronim, 'At the sign of Newton's head', p. 69.
81. Gronim, 'At the sign of Newton's head', p. 58.
82. Butler, 'Magic, astrology', p. 339–345.
83. Gronim, 'At the sign of Newton's head', p. 63.
84. Thomas, *Religion*, pp. 128–130.
85. For more on this complex of issues see both Brooke, *Refiner's fire* and D. Michael Quinn, *Early Mormonism and the magic worldview* (Salt Lake City, UT, 1987). I am grateful to Professor Robert Mathiesen for bringing this topic to my attention.
86. Phyllis Mack, 'The unbounded self: Dreaming and identity in the British Enlightenment', in Ann Marie Plane and Leslie Tuttle (eds), *Dreams, dreamers, and visions: The early modern Atlantic world* (Philadelphia, PA, 2013), p. 216.
87. For an overview of this material, see Nigel Smith (ed.) *A collection of Ranter writings: Spiritual liberty and sexual freedom in the English revolution* (London, 2014). For more on scriptural hermeneutics and the Ranting prophetic voice, see Noam Flinker, 'The poetics of biblical prophecy: Abiezer Coppe's late converted midrash', in Ariel Hessayon and David Finnegan (eds), *Varieties of Seventeenth- and early eighteenth-century English radicalism in context* (Farnham, 2011), pp. 113–127. For more on occult philosophy in the Ranting milieu, see Ariel Hassayon, '*Gold tried in*

fire': *The prophet Theauraujohn Tany and the English revolution* (Aldershot, 2007).
88. Flinker, 'Poetics of biblical prophecy', p. 126.
89. William Perkins, *The Arte of Prophecying* (London, 1607), pp. 11–12.
90. Andrew Escobedo, 'The millennial border between tradition and innovation', in Richard Connors and Andrew Colin Gow (eds), *Anglo-American millennialism, from Milton to the Millerites* (London, 2004), p. 11.
91. Dorothy Partridge, *The woman's almanack, for the year 1694* (London, 1694), p. 5.
92. John Seller, *An almanack for the provinces of Virginia and Maryland* (London, 1685), f. 13. For more on dog days, see Thomas, *Religion*, p. 395.
93. Bernard Capp, *Astrology and the popular press: English almanacs 1500–1800* (London, 1979), pp. 118, 64–65, 120–121.
94. Gronim, 'At the sign of Newton's head', p. 58.
95. Butler, 'Magic, astrology', p. 331; Daniel Leeds, *The temple of wisdom for the little world* (Philadelphia, PA, 1688), pp. 1–125; *An almanack* (Philadelphia, PA, 1693); *An almanack* (Philadelphia, PA, 1695); *An almanack* (Philadelphia, PA, 1697).
96. Leeds, cited in Catherine L. Albanese, *A republic of mind and spirit: A cultural history of American metaphysical religion* (London, 2007), p. 78.
97. Nicholas Culpeper, *The English physician* (London, 1652), p. 8; Joseph Blagrave, *Astrological practice of physick* (London, 1671) sig. Bv; Israel Hiebner, *Mysterium sigillorum, herbarum & lapidum* (London, 1698), pp. 59–60.
98. Sara S. Gronim, *Everyday nature: Knowledge of the natural world in colonial New York* (New Brunswick, NJ, 2007), p. 48.
99. Daniel Leeds, *An almanack and ephemerides* (Philadelphia, PA, 1693), f. 22r.
100. Leeds, *An almanack and ephemerides* (1693), ff. 22–24.
101. Daniel Leeds, *An almanack and ephemerides* (Philadelphia, PA, 1696), ff. 17–20.
102. Butler, 'Magic, astrology', p. 337.
103. Titan Leeds, *The American almanack* (New York, 1715), f. 20.
104. Titan Leeds, *The American almanack* (New York, 1738), cited in Gronim, 'At the sign of Newton's head', p. 65.
105. Richard Bauckham, *Tudor apocalypse: Sixteenth century apocalypticism, millenarianism, and the English reformation* (Oxford, 1978), p. 15.
106. Escobedo, 'The millennial border', p. 13; citing John Foxe, *Acts and Monuments* (1570), sigs. m3v-m4v.
107. John Booker, *The bloody almanack* (London, 1642), p. 1.
108. Alexander Cummins, *The starry rubric: Seventeenth-century English astrology and magic* (Milton Keynes, 2012), p. 24.

109. Escobedo, 'The millennial border', p. 12.
110. Gronim, 'At the sign of Newton's head', p. 65.
111. Godbeer, *The Devil's dominion*, p. 52.
112. Godbeer, *The Devil's dominion*, p. 30.
113. See, for example, Lauren Kassell, '"All was this land full fill'd of faerie", or Magic and the past in early modern England', *Journal of the History of Ideas* 67:1 (2006), pp. 107–122.
114. Butler, 'Magic, astrology', p. 325.
115. John Josselyn, *New-Englands rarities discovered* (London, 1672), frontispiece.
116. Hakluyt, *The principle nauigations*, p. 306.
117. Josselyn, *New-Englands rarities*, pp. 57, 43.
118. Godbeer, 'Witchcraft in British America', p. 394.
119. Godbeer, *The Devil's dominion*, p. 31.
120. Godbeer, 'Witchcraft in British America', p. 395. Godbeer thus agrees with Butler, both challenging Richard Weisman's notions of 'competing cosmologies' between clergy and 'proponents of magic'. See Richard Weisman, *Witchcraft, magic, and religion in seventeenth-century Massachusetts* (Amherst, MA, 1984), pp. 54, 66.
121. See Davies, *Popular Magic*, especially Chaps. 4 and 6.
122. Woodward, *Prospero's America*, p. 217.
123. Paul Boyer and Stephen Nissenbaum (eds), *Salem witchcraft papers: Verbatim transcripts of the legal documents of the Salem witchcraft outbreak* (New York, 1977), II: 507, 387; III: 723.
124. Thomas, *Religion*, pp. 138, 143, 252–260, 357–359, 409–411.
125. Samuel Harvey Reynolds (ed.), *The table talk of John Selden* (Oxford, 1892), p. 130.
126. Davies, *Popular magic*, p. 101.
127. Moses Gaster, 'English charms of the seventeenth century', *Folklore* 21:3 (1910), p. 377.
128. Moses Gaster, 'English charms', p. 378.
129. Davies, *Popular magic*, p. 148 in Cummins, *Starry rubric*, p. 129.
130. Cummins, *Starry rubric*, p. 129.
131. 'The deterrent effect of their reputations was, in fact, the most important asset cunning-folk had in this respect.' Davies, *Popular magic*, p. 97.
132. Thomas, *Religion*, p. 410.
133. See Davies, *Popular magic*, pp. 75, 96–97, 109, 111, 192.
134. Godbeer, 'Witchcraft in British America', p. 395.
135. Blagrave, *Physick*, p. 154.
136. 'Knowledge of the witch-bottle and almost certainly the practice itself had crossed the Atlantic before the end of the [seventeenth] century.' Ralph Merrifield, *The archaeology of ritual and magic* (New York, 1988), p. 174.

137. Mather, *The wonders of the invisible world*, pp. 67–68.
138. Butler, 'Magic, astrology', p. 331.
139. 'Examination of Job Tookey 7 June 1692', *Massachusetts Archives*, Vol. 135—Witchcraft, 1692–1759, No. 32, p. 31.
140. Chadwick Hansen, *Witchcraft at Salem* (New York, 1969), pp. 93–103.
141. 'Examination of Abigail Hobbs, June 29, 1692', *Essex County Court Archives* I: 156.
142. Virginia DeJohn Anderson, *Creatures of empire: How domestic animals transformed early America* (Oxford, 2004), pp. 49–51.
143. Butler, 'Magic, astrology', p. 333.
144. John Hale, *A modest enquiry* (Boston, MA, 1697), p. 144; *Salem Witchcraft Papers*, II: 397, 400.
145. John Winthrop, *Journal*, ed. James Hosmer (New York, 1908), II: 156.
146. Jean Bodin, *De la démonomancie des sorciers* (Paris, 1580), f. 51r.
147. Claude Lacouteux, *High magic of amulets and talismans*, trans. Jon E. Graham (Rochester, NY, 2014), pp. 43–44.
148. As opposed to the theoretical occult philosophy of his *Three books*, the *Fourth* was a collection of treatises on geomancy and planetary angel summoning, as well as aphorisms for magical practice and a discourse on the nature of spirits. *Fourth book of occult philosophy*, trans. Robert Turner (London, 1655).
149. Owen Davies, *Grimoires: A history of magic books* (Oxford, 2009), p. 70.
150. Davies, *Popular magic*, pp. 125–133; S.F. Davies, 'The reception of Reginald Scot's *Discovery of witchcraft*: Witchcraft, magic, and radical religion', *Journal of the History of Ideas* 74:3 (2013), pp. 381–401.
151. Monod, *Solomon's secret art*, p. 69.
152. Davies, *Popular magic*, p. 124.
153. Monod, *Solomon's secret art*, pp. 70–75.
154. For example, between July 1597 and November 1601, Simon Forman made 158 geomantic readings for which we have records. See the Casebooks Project online archive: Lauren Kassell (ed.) with Michael Hawkins, Robert Ralley and John Young, 'Welcome | Casebooks Project', *Casebooks Project*, http://www.magicandmedicine.hps.cam.ac.uk. Last accessed 4 May 2015. See also Kassell, *Medicine and magic*, pp. 45, 52, 67, 136.
155. Stephen Skinner, *Terrestrial astrology: Divination by geomancy* (London, 1980), p. 129.
156. Agrippa, *Three books*, p. 412.
157. John Heydon, *Theomagia, or The temple of wisdom* (London, 1664), p. 2.
158. Skinner, *Terrestrial astrology*, p. 132.
159. Heydon, *Theomagia*, p. 2.
160. Heydon, *Theomagia*, p. 1.
161. Agrippa, *Three books*, p. 397.

162. Butler, 'Magic, astrology', p. 317.
163. Gronim, 'At the sign of Newton's head', p. 75.
164. For example, Cotton Mather, *Memorable providences relating to witchcrafts and possessions* (Boston, MA, 1689), 'To The Reader'; 'Introduction', p. 41; 'A Discourse on the Power of Devils', p. 2; 'A Discourse on Witchcraft', pp. 14–15.
165. Nathaniel Ames, *An astronomical Diary: Or, An almanack* (Boston, MA, 1728).
166. Butler, 'Magic, astrology', pp. 326–328.
167. Frances Yates, *Giordano Bruno and the Hermetic tradition* (Chicago, IL, 1964), pp. 416–423; Philip A. Bruce, *Institutional history of Virginia in the seventeenth century*, I (New York, 1910), pp. 150, 175–176, 182–183, 211.
168. Woodward, *Prospero's America*, p. 30. Woodward also notes 'Winthrop's interest in the medical aspects of alchemy, which became central to his service to New England's Puritan colonies...'
169. Woodward, *Prospero's America*, p. 35; citing Ronald S. Wilkinson, 'The Alchemical Library of John Winthrop, Jr. (1606–1676) and His Descendants in Colonial America, Parts I–III', *Ambix* XI (1963), pp. 33–51.
170. Peter Eisenstadt, 'Almanacs and the Disenchantment of Early America', *Pennsylvania History* 65 (1998), pp. 143–169; Gronim, 'At the sign of Newton's head', p. 61.
171. Gronim, 'At the sign of Newton's head', p. 61.
172. W.R. Jones, '"Hill-diggers and hell-raisers": Treasure hunting and the supernatural in Old and New England', in Peter Benes and Jane Montague Benes (eds), *Wonders of the invisible world: 1600–1900* (Boston, MA, 1995), p. 105.
173. Elizabeth W. Fisher, '"Prophecies and revelations": German cabbalists in early Pennsylvania', *The Pennsylvania Magazine of History and Biography* 109:3 (1985), p. 301.
174. See Fernando Cervantes, *The Devil in the New World: The impact of diabolism in New Spain* (New Haven, CT, 1994); Nicholas Griffith and Fernando Cervantes (eds), *Spiritual encounters: Interactions between Christianity and native religions in colonial America* (Birmingham, 1999); Iris Gareis, 'Merging magical traditions: Sorcery and witchcraft in Spanish and Portuguese America', in Brian Levack (ed.), *The Oxford handbook of witchcraft in early modern Europe and colonial America* (Oxford, 2013), pp. 412–428.
175. See William D. Piersen, *Black Yankees: The development of an Afro-American subculture in eighteenth-century New England* (Amherst, MA, 1988); Philip D. Morgan, *Slave counterpoint: Black culture in the*

eighteenth-century Chesapeake and Lowcountry (Chapel Hill, NC, 1998); M. Drake Patten, 'African American spiritual beliefs: An archaeological testimony from the slave quarter', in Peter Benes and Jane Montague Benes (eds), *Wonders of the invisible world: 1600–1900* (Boston, MA, 1995), pp. 44–52.
176. The most popular archival collection of such conjure and hoodoo traditions arguably remains Harry M. Hyatt, *Hoodoo—conjuration—witchcraft—rootwork*, 5 vols. (Hannibal, MO, 1970). See also Owen Davies, *America bewitched: The story of witchcraft after Salem* (Oxford, 2013).
177. Gronim, 'At the sign of Newton's head', p. 73.
178. Godbeer, 'Witchcraft in British America', p. 406.
179. Godbeer, 'Witchcraft in British America', p. 400.

CHAPTER 8

Eschatology and Radicalism after the Restoration: The English Context

Warren Johnston

On 6 January 1661 the streets of London became the site of an unusual disturbance: that evening, inspired by their belief that the millennial kingdom of Christ was at hand, a group of about fifty Fifth Monarchy Men, led by the preacher Thomas Venner, marched on St Paul's Cathedral and fought with the men of the city's trained bands. On 9 January, in a continuation of their uprising, the group moved to kidnap the Lord Mayor of London. However, this time government soldiers defeated the group, wounding and capturing a number of its members. Venner and a dozen of his followers were executed for their involvement in the insurrection.

For historians, Venner's rebellion might be seen to signal several things: it could be characterised as the last gasp of apocalyptic convictions that had such significance in the 1640s and 1650s; it might also be interpreted as a demonstration of the continuing importance of radical apocalypticism, which historians have traditionally seen as the principal avenue of that thought throughout the late medieval and early modern period.[1] However, as I have written elsewhere, neither of these assessments represents the whole story of later seventeenth-century apocalyptic thought. Significant forms of such beliefs lasted long after the Restoration put an

W. Johnston (✉)
Department of History, Algoma University, Algoma, Ontario, Canada
e-mail: warren.johnston@algomau.ca

© The Author(s) 2016
A. Crome (ed.), *Prophecy and Eschatology in the Transatlantic World, 1550–1800*, Christianities in the Trans-Atlantic World, 1500–1800, DOI 10.1057/978-1-137-52055-5_8

end to the experiments in godly government that had punctuated the period of the civil wars and Interregnum, and they continued to appear in a variety of ways, including especially more moderate manifestations.[2] Despite that broader interest in and use of apocalyptic ideas, it is true they also remained a powerful means of expression for those who wanted to give voice to more radical views. For the purposes of this chapter, then, I will concentrate on radical apocalyptic thought, showing it as one stream of a vibrant political, religious, and social eschatology that continued into the last decades of the seventeenth century.

It is also useful to discuss how 'radical' will be applied in this chapter. I have previously defined apocalyptic radicalism rather strictly as the attempt 'to bring about the prophetic climax by instigating political and military events of the apocalyptic last days through active, violent political militancy'.[3] Here, this definition will be expanded slightly. Though some of the works discussed below clearly demonstrate such active militant thought, some other expressions of religious ideas are also included that contain only the suggestion of an eventual necessary violent human participation in the advent of Christ's millennial kingdom. In their aggressive criticism of existing authorities and their assertive encouragements of disobedience, these can also be seen as radical.[4] Yet even with this expanded definition, it will be apparent that radical apocalyptic thought appears prominently only in several periods of the later seventeenth century in England. This is because such ideas were moderated and absorbed into other lines of expression, especially Restoration religious nonconformity. However, as a whole, apocalyptic writings from the 1660s to the 1690s do show that radical apocalypticism did survive the last four decades of the seventeenth century.

8.1 Venner's Rising: A Radical Apocalyptic Response to the Restoration

The apocalyptic origins of Venner's rebellion are found in a pamphlet called *A Door of Hope* (1661). Summoning the saints 'to become Souldiers in the Lambs Army', this work described the newly restored Charles II as 'a profest Enemy, a Rebel and Traytor to Christ' and compared the king to the beast, the scarlet whore, and the mother of harlots.[5] It determined that the current year saw 'the sweet harmony and agreement' of the prophecies of the death and raising of the two witnesses (Rev. 11:3–11), based on chronological calculations that placed the onset of the 1290 days

(Dan. 12:11) in 366 CE, during the reign of Julian the Apostate. This period finished in 1656 with the death of the witnesses, and their rise three and a half (prophetic) days later would come at the end of the year 1660, leading to their resurrection in early 1661.[6]

Beyond its apocalyptic chronology, Venner's instauration of Christ's millennial kingdom would also bring about fundamental political and social change: good men would become judges and magistrates, and they would institute 'justice irrespective of wealth'. The laws concerning debt, as well as other commercial and agricultural legislation, would be reformed, and taxes, customs and excise, and tithes would be abolished. In this way, 'all the poor of the Land might be set to work, and we might have no beggars'.[7] Some of the language resonated with Leveller and Digger overtones, harkening back to the radical ideas of the previous decades:

> the chief of the Spoil which shall be taken in Battell, and all the Estates which shall be forfeited through Treason and Rebellion [against Christ's kingdom], shall be brought into one common Treasury … [to] carry on the Work of God with the Army of the Lamb, in which every Souldier shall be sufficiently provided for, by a certain honourable constant Revenue, issuing out of the said Treasury, according to his Place, Degree, Services, and Family.[8]

Christ himself would hold sovereign political authority, the laws in England would originate from the Bible, and the saints 'shall be the Administrators thereof, or shall have the executive Power'. Any national church and ministry were Antichristian, and thus would be abolished in this millennial kingdom, making way for congregational self-government.[9] Thus Venner's efforts were intended to instigate a new apocalyptic order, fundamentally displacing the existing political, social, legal, and religious institutions of England.

With such an extreme and militant intent, it is no surprise that Venner's rebellion and the doctrine that accompanied it received an immediate reaction. The responses demonstrated how seriously such radical ideas were taken and the threat they were seen to embody. A group of Baptists published their *Humble Apology of Some Commonly Called Anabaptists* at the end of January in order to distance and differentiate their beliefs from those who had led the rebellion. This pamphlet described the motivations behind the Fifth Monarchist rising as 'evil opinions and practices … through the wicked Treason, Rebellion and Murder, of a few heady and distempered persons, pretending to introduce a Civil and temporal reign and Government of Jesus Christ'. These Baptists also noted that, because of their submission to civil authority and their challenges to 'conceited, wild interpretations of dark Prophecies', they themselves had been attacked as 'worshippers of the Beast' at Fifth Monarchist meetings.[10] Interestingly, another group of Baptists had sent out a statement six months earlier that strongly asserted that the saints would inherit the kingdoms of the world after Christ's reappearance on earth.[11] Clearly such beliefs from the early weeks of the Restoration were not now conducive to the spirit of rapprochement the leaders of the group sought in the aftermath of Venner's revolt.

Quakers also felt the need to dissociate themselves from radical apocalypticsm. Like the Baptists, in later January 1661 a group of Quaker leaders released a declaration criticising militant millenarian convictions. It affirmed 'that the Spirit of Christ ... will never move us to fight and war against any man with outward Weapons, neither for the Kingdom of Christ, nor for any Kingdoms of this World', as well as denying any Quaker involvement in the recent plot.[12] Again, however, other Quaker writings had belied such moderate apocalyptic convictions. In 1660 John Braithwaite had decried Anglican bishops, along with Presbyterians and Baptists, as Antichristian, and saw the Restoration as a return to 'the Whore, and the Merchants of Babylon' to drink from 'the Whores Cup of Abomination'. Similarly, Richard Crane characterised his previous membership in the Church of England as feeding 'upon the Whore's Flesh'; its clergy were ministers of Antichrist whom he likened to reptiles creeping out of their holes at the dawn of the restored monarchy. Also in 1660 the emerging leader of the Quakers, George Fox (who prominently signed the January 1661 *Declaration*), had associated Babylon and the beast from the Book of Revelation with 'Pulpits, Tythes, Churches with crosses in the Church-yards and ... making Ministers by the will of men, by their Schooles and Colledges'.[13] This language suggested a very critical and vocal opposition to the restored church, even before the official legislative re-establishment of the Church of England and its proscription of alternate forms of worship in 1662 and afterwards.

London leaders of the Congregational movement responded with their own denunciation of Venner's millenarian rising. They drew a direct connection between militant apocalypticism in their time and the radical Anabaptist millenarian political and social experiment attempted in Münster during the early Reformation.[14] These Congregational ministers denied the dangerous assumption that the saints could 'in the Name of Jesus Christ ... take to themselves, the Titles of all the Kingdoms of the world', or that humans could choose the time and place for founding Christ's kingdom on earth and then invite him to enter it.[15]

The presence of radical religious and political apocalyptic ideas in the early Restoration also saw other responses that were not necessarily concerned with sectarian face-saving. Edward Bagshaw, a Congregational minister, developed a fuller argument denouncing the conviction that saw godliness as a valid justification for challenging existing civil authority. Like his Congregational brethren, for Bagshaw the results of the events in Germany in the mid-1530s warned against such beliefs. Even 125 years later, the consequences of Münster were 'so fatall and horrid, ... so fresh, and recent, that it might almost seem needless to endeavour any other confutation, then a bare relating of the Story'.[16] Also published in 1660, *A Breife Description ... of the Phanatiques* used reference to Münster as a cautionary reminder of the disorder and bloodshed caused by radical millenarian ideas. It condemned the conceit in the saints' claims of their ability 'to pry into the third Heaven in Apocalyptick Revelations, to all which in word and fancy they pretend ... that they have speciall visions'. Once more alluding to Münster, this time mentioning one of the leaders of that rebellion, the pamphlet saw such claims 'to set up (as Iohn of Leyden did) ... the Throne and Scepter of *King Jesus*' as 'but a decoy to intrap the vulgar'.[17]

In direct response to Venner's rebellion, other works continued to use such comparisons and criticisms to great effect. A tract entitled *Hell Broke Loose* (1661) noted John of Leiden and another of the Münster leaders, Bernhard Knipperdoling, as examples of where the 'folly' of the 'Quinto Monarchian' led. Turning the apocalyptic tables, it called the rebels in London 'regicides' with the 'Beasts-mark' on their own foreheads,[18] also a pointed reference to the all-too-recent political turmoil of the civil wars and Interregnum. Similarly, *Munster Paralleld* (1661) placed the origins of the Fifth Monarchy movement in the year 1641, thus associating it with the beginning of the Civil Wars and 'the ruine of the Church and Religion of England'. As its title suggested, it included comparisons between the motivations and leaders of Münster and of Venner's rebellion, along with an account of events and the subsequent trial of Venner and his followers.[19] *The Phanatiques Creed* attacked the Fifth Monarchist manifesto, disparaging its prophetic interpretations as 'Nauseous Calculations ... Delusion ... setting Daniel and the Revelation together by the Ears, about the Number of the Beast'. Another pamphlet referred to the 'great pretensions of the Fifth-Monarchy-Men' and their 'violent impulse', which led them to the opinion that the saints should oppose all civil authority and impose their own tyranny in place of 'the Consent of the People'. Still another blamed the supposed sectarian hybrid of 'Anabaptistical Quakers' whose intent was to level society's social and property distinctions.[20] Each of these works attacked the belief that Christ's kingdom would be brought about by human means, drew connections between previous radical events and those in January 1661, condemned fanatical compulsions, and censured the claim to special apocalyptic insight that provided the motivation behind this revolt. The virulence of the reaction illustrated the feared destructive potential of radical millenarianism. It is also interesting to see how deeply the radical millenarianism of the early Reformation still resonated in England in the later seventeenth century. Over a century after they had ended, the Anabaptist political and social experiments of Münster continued to be used as symbols of the dangerous effects and consequences of militant apocalyptic beliefs.

8.2   Radical Apocalypticism in the 1660s and 1670s

Despite this response to the January 1661 insurrection, Venner's attempt was not the only manifestation of radical apocalyptic thought in the early Restoration, nor did its failure signal the end of such ideas. The restoration of the monarchy also brought the prospect of the reimposition of Church of England worship and a threat to end the relative religious liberty of the 1650s. In 1660 the Baptist and seventh-day sabbatarian preacher Thomas Tillam equated the Dragon (that pursued the woman clothed in the sun in Rev. 12) to the revived episcopacy and Prayer Book, calling them a 'mean image of the decayed Papacie'. Believing that he was living in the time of the sounding of the seventh trumpet (Rev. 11:15), Tillam found in his sectarian denomination 'a small remnant of the Womans seed in these Islands ... who by their intire separation, are become Victors over the Beast, his Image, his Mark, and the number of his Name' that were found in the revived Church of England. Tillam reinforced these assertions by outlining Anglican practices that he characterised as Antichristian and the mark of the beast.[21] Tillam's radicalism was noted and he was arrested in the early Restoration, though he escaped and fled to the Netherlands.[22] He returned to England at least once in the 1660s, and established a sabbatarian colony on the Continent, in the Palatinate, for the followers he recruited.[23] Tillam's story is instructive, demonstrating links between England and the Continent for radical apocalyptic ideas and believers in the 1660s and afterwards.[24]

Lodowick Muggleton provides another example of radical millenarian convictions that attracted a small but devoted group of adherents. For Muggleton, his form of radical religious belief placed himself and his cousin John Reeve in prominent apocalyptic roles. Muggleton believed that he and Reeve were actually the two witnesses who were killed by the beast in Revelation 11. In a number of publications in the 1660s, Muggleton attacked not only the established church, but also other nonconforming denominations, including the Baptists, Presbyterians, and Congregationalists, as well as more radical sects like the Quakers and Ranters. Muggleton's writings were heavily punctuated by condemnations of other religious groups and beliefs through the application of apocalyptic imagery.[25] The attraction of Muggletonian beliefs to a certain audience is attested to by the fact that survivors of the sect remained into the twentieth century.[26]

The religious settlement of 1662 and re-establishment of the Church of England's monopoly on legal worship was a further instigation to strong apocalyptic expressions of discontent. The anonymous pamphlet *Antichrist Unhooded* (1664) was written in verse, but this did not dull its scathing critique of the practices of the established church. The long poem denounced the episcopal hierarchy, clerical dress, sacramental practice, and church music, among other things, and characterised all of these as Antichristian, spiritual Babylon, and representative of the beast.[27] In 1667 the Baptist minister Hanserd Knollys used interpretation of apocalyptic prophecy to criticise the suppression of non-Anglican religious worship. He encouraged the saints not to obey 'the Roman-Antichristian-Politick and Ecclesiastick-Power, Authority, Dominion, and Government of the Beast', implying that resistance to the government of England was justified in prophetic terms.[28] While such criticisms of Anglican religious policies later moderated and became absorbed within a more general nonconformist stance of patient waiting for God to act, especially in the 1670s, it is clear that some of these more forceful apocalyptic denunciations toed the line of militancy.

Quaker authors continued their criticisms as well. Edward Burrough described any kind of imposition of religious worship, laws, or authority as Antichristian, noting that secular government was also complicit in

'Antichrist's Power and Rule'. In a similar vein, Francis Howgill decried the 'Ministers of Antichrist' for convincing 'Kings and Rulers that God hath required of them to enforce and injoyn all people unto a Worship'.[29] An interesting variant of the Quaker response came from the missionary John Philly. Departing from England in 1662, Philly travelled to Hungary and Austria, and was imprisoned and tortured by the Inquisition.[30] During his time on the Continent, Philly published *The Arrainment of Christendom* (1664), which he wrote using a simplified 'Orthografy' that would allow non-native English speakers, as well as children and those with lower levels of literacy, to read his prophetic exegesis.[31] Though he advised his readers not to rebel against them, Philly did identify 'Kings, Prinses, Heds, & Rulers throughout Christendom' as being the fourth beast of Daniel 7:19 and the beast with seven heads and ten horns (Rev. 12:3; 13:1).[32] He went on to accuse the clergy of having convinced rulers to impose 'Antichristian & cruel laws', which forced the people into allegiance and to pay for their livings. In this way, Philly saw 'the lamb … [being] crucified afresh' between 'the Beast, & fals[e] Profet, the Civil & Ecclesiastical Power'.[33] In a reference to specifically English circumstances, Philly criticised the Church of England for hypocrisy because they had sworn allegaince to Charles II, who they would follow back again 'to their mother … the whor of Rome' rather than 'indanger their Persons, or loos their provision for their Bellys'.[34] Not surprisingly, when he returned to England in 1670, Philly was imprisoned in Dover for refusing to take the Oath of Allegiance.[35]

Even two decades later, Thomas Lawson warned Quakers and 'Nonconformists of what denomination soever' not to comply with prescribed public worship, as it was the weapon of the beast from the bottomless pit (Rev. 11:7; 17:8) which persecuted the witnesses. In a reference to the images coinciding with the sounding of the fifth trumpet, Lawson described 'Man-made Ministers' as locusts emerging from the 'smoke of Earthly Wisdom', and advised that 'when Civil Authority usurps the Power of Christ … and imposes Laws and Ordinances contrary to Truth and Conscience', passive disobedience was the appropriate response.[36] These Quaker assertions demonstrate how the line between religious and political, dividing ecclesiastical and civil authority in seventeenth-century England, was not clearly drawn, and that pointed critique in one sphere could lead to radical challenges in the other.

Though religious nonconformity and radical doctrinal criticisms were taken as significant antagonisms to authority in Restoration England, radical political challenges were seen as far more serious. As noted above, Venner's rising showed how dangerous such apocalyptic ideas and activities could be, and others followed in the footsteps of such radical challenges in the years following. Already in 1662 a socially and politically radical text called *The Panther-Prophesy* appeared. In thinly veiled symbolism and allusion, it described the abandonment of godly principles by magistrates, the clergy, and citizens who became supporters of the Restoration government. The panther, a reference to the restored monarchy, transforms its newfound supporters into nobles and churchmen, while the poor move off, saying 'Come out of her, lest ye partake of her Plagues' (a paraphrase of the condemnation of spiritual Babylon found in Revelation 18:4). Watching over all of this, Christ intervenes by killing the panther and its supporters, while the poor people emerge from hiding to inherit the kingdom.[37] Though purportedly composed late in 1653 in response to Cromwell's Lord Protectorship,[38] the work clearly contained a powerful millenarian message for the early 1660s. Its concluding result, of social inversion through Christ's intervention in earthly affairs, along with the violent way in which it was to be achieved, clearly contained a warning to those who conformed to the political and religious settlements of the Restoration.

Another work, published in the same year as the *Panther-Prophesy*, also connected back to the political struggles of the previous decades. *Two Treatises* by Henry Vane was reported to have been written during his imprisonment and appeared in print only after his execution in June 1662.[39] Vane, a prominent parliamentarian in the 1640s and 1650s, noted that the saints had been fighting for a good cause but, in fulfilment of apocalyptic prophecy, had been defeated by the beast. Yet he assured his readers that 'the time is coming, yea is even at the very door … to depend on God, for the avenging of his people'. Though stating that people should not rush out to apply 'humane ability' to overcome Antichrist's kingdom, Vane went on to denounce 'all the visible Rule and Authority, whether Civil or Ecclesiastical, that is exercised on Earth, and is supported by humane Wisdom and Power'. This civil and ecclesiastical power was represented by the beast rising from sea (Rev. 13:1) and the beast rising from the earth (Rev. 13:11) respectively. Vane concluded that the time for such regimes was nearing its end, signalled by the rising of the witnesses (Rev. 11:11) 'which shall be as a necessary dispensation for Christ's Personal Manifestation and Rule on the Earth a thousand years'.[40] Despite his caution against using human power to bring about this millennial kingdom, Vane's affirmation of divine vengeance and his depiction of the corrupted basis of worldly temporal and spiritual governments was a powerful and radical censure of existing political authorities.

In 1663 a tract entitled *Mene Tekel; or, the Downfal of Tyranny* contained a much more direct assertion of what constituted proper (and improper) government. The title is a reference to the prophecy in Daniel 5 that predicted the fall of the impious king Belshazzar, and much of the treatise concentrates on delineating the responsibilities of a godly magistrate. However, the work's characterisation of the 'tyrannous Kings of the Fourth Monarchy' being given their power by the beast, and its justification of resistance to such kings, shows the author's affinity with Fifth Monarchist militant principles.[41] Two other pamphlets appeared in the same year and developed the same themes. *The Mysterie of Magistracy Unvailed* also outlined the attributes of good rulers, contrasting these with those of 'evil' ones. Though stopping just short of endorsing rebellion, the work does state that an absolute prohibition of resistance against bad magistrates 'would utterly make void all the Prophecies that fore-told the coming of Anti-Christ' and 'would for ever keep him upon the stage'.[42] Its condemnation of false rulers as rising 'out of the Bottomless pit' to seize power by 'force & tyrannous usurpation, fraud or Antichristian intrusion' and its recommendation that the saints should 'yield most unwilling subjection' to those rulers suggest a radical differentiation between subjects' responsibilities to godly and ungodly magistrates. *A Treatise of the Execution of Justice* continues along the same lines. Along with its general criticism of bad rulers, this pamphlet justifies rebellion against wicked rulers under certain circumstances. It identifies the re-established Prayer Book as the whore's cup (Rev. 17:4) and places the struggles of English nonconformists in the context of the saints' war against the beast.[43] As in the works mentioned above, the *Treatise* also uses prophetic evidence to refute arguments that godly citizens should not resist earthly rulers, claiming instead that 'Christ doth not mean to forbid the Saints to take a two-edged Sword in their hands, to execute the Judgements written in the Law of God upon wicked Kings, which the Lord hath foretold his Saints shall do.'[44]

The appearance of these radical ideas challenging temporal authorities was not a coincidence. A rising against the government was planned to take place in northern England in the autumn of 1663.[45] Clear echoes of Venner's efforts several years earlier can be found in the title of 'A Door of Hope Opened in the Valley of Achor', which was written to coincide with this planned rebellion.[46] With its full title referring to the rise of the witnesses and judgements against spiritual Babylon and the whore, this manifesto declared that 'several thousands of us, poor low worms' had searched scripture and prophecy 'to understand the Lord's mind, and our own duties'.[47] Equating the imprisonment of nonconformists in England with souls slain for God's word at the sounding of the fifth trumpet (Rev. 9:1), the tract criticised the heavy taxation of the poor and the silencing of godly ministers under the Restoration settlement. In response, 'the use of Temporal Weapons of War' was deemed lawful for the saints as 'one means' by which they could bring about the fall of the kingdoms of the world so that they might 'become the Kingdoms of our Lord & of his Christ'. This radical millenarian militancy was punctuated by a pronouncement of the revival of 'the Good Old Cause' eliciting support to renew the conflicts of the 1640s, and with its references to the rise of the witnesses having chronological significance (Rev. 11:11) in the timing of the rebellion three and a half years after the restoration of the monarchy in the spring of 1660.[48]

Opposition to the Restoration government continued into the later 1660s. *The Saints Freedom From Tyranny Vindicated* (1667) opened with a reminder of God's promise to 'Restore his Political Government … in the Earth, under the Peaceable Kingdom and Rule of Jesus the Christ'.[49] Though acknowledging that magistrates were 'Polittical Fathers' of God's people to whom obedience (or only passive disobedience in cases of conscience) was owed, the author asserted that Antichristian kings were not ordained by God and that any king who did not rule by God's laws was 'no Magistrate, or Minister of God' and did not have to be obeyed. The tract argued that Christ's temporal and ecclesiastical jurisdiction had been usurped by the papacy and by other worldly rulers, which caused 'the great Body of Protestants' to 'own Antichrist (in his Civil Power) for the Ordinance of God' by adhering to false authorities.[50] This argument was supported by the interpretation of the beast in Revelation 13:11–12, and it was further concluded that in England Henry VIII had seized power by similarly usurping 'absolute Jurisdiction Civil and Ecclesiastical'.[51] Having previously contended that 'a People Opposing or Deposing a wicked or oppressing King or Ruler, is not Opposition to Magistracy', the author declared that England had not been part of the four monarchies identified in Daniel's prophecies (2:31–43, 7:1–25), and it was the English people who had discovered the true nature of Antichrist. English political power was instead properly founded upon 'The people [who] are the first seat of Power', and kings were bound 'to govern by Law'.[52] The constitutional theories found here were not only provocative politically, but were also validated through apocalyptic rhetoric and meaning, linking them again to Fifth Monarchist principles.

Though beyond the scope of this chapter, it is important to note that themes similar to those in radical English apocalyptic thought were apparent in the American colonies after 1660. As Avihu Zakai has shown, after the Restoration Puritans in New England were also disappointed with the failure of the attempts at godly reform of the church and government of England. Ministers such as John Davenport, John Norton, and Increase Mather described these circumstances using apocalyptic prophecy, and likened their situation to that of the pure church in the wilderness preserving itself against the efforts of the dragon and the beast.[53] Such language and beliefs corresponded nicely to the apocalyptic sentiments and discontent of nonconformists in England during the 1660s. There are also several more direct associations between the New England colonies and the radical millenarianism of the early Restoration that can be traced through Thomas Tillam and Thomas Venner.

Tillam's efforts to establish a sabbatarian colony in the Palatinate in the 1660s were noted above, but several decades prior to this he had joined a different migration, leaving England for the American colonies in the late 1630s. Landing in New England in June 1638, he marked his arrival with a poem expressing his hopefulness for the Puritan project in the New World.[54] Though little is known of his time in America, Tillam was back in England in the 1640s. There is evidence that he may have kept some contact with the colonies, perhaps exchanging letters with Samuel Hutchinson of Boston in 1659 or after about Fifth Monarchist ideas, where Hutchinson expressed his disagreement with the militant millenarian actions endorsed by his correspondent.[55]

Thomas Venner's time in New England is somewhat better documented. He settled in Salem early in 1638, working as a cooper and becoming a member of the church there.[56] Venner served as a juryman and a constable in Salem before moving to Boston in 1644, where he joined the Artillery Company, formed a guild of coopers, and likely became a member of John Cotton's congregation.[57] Though Venner returned to England in 1651, his colonial experience was recalled in the aftermath of his rebellious activities a decade later. At his trial, Venner mentioned his 'having had a testimony of above twenty years in New England'.[58] This suggestive association with the colonies prompted John Clarke, Rhode Island's representative in London, to write a tract entitled *The Plotters*

Unmasked, Murderers No Saints (London, 1661) repudiating Venner's rebellion, and the General Court of Massachusetts to later declare in an address to Charles II that 'Venner ... went out from us because he was not of us' in an effort to distance the colony from such radical activities.[59] These efforts in dissociation from militant English apocalypticism again reveal the threat it continued to maintain during the early Restoration.

Nothing in the 1670s quite rose to the level of challenges to the Restoration government found in the early and mid-1660s. However, ideas about the role of the godly in prophetic fulfilment, along with the limitations upon temporal authority, continued to be found in apocalyptic interpretations throughout the decade. For example, the sum of various statements made in *Theopolis, or the City of God New Jerusalem* (1672) equated to a militant apocalyptic belief. This work began with a statement that the millennial reign would be inaugurated without Christ's presence on earth, going on to assert that the kingdom would be established through warfare. The anonymous author then suggested that the godly saints would carry out the work of defeating and then keeping Christ's enemies at bay.[60] The work of the saints is later more clearly articulated as 'fighting' against the Antichristian 'Powers and Potentates' of the world to defeat the 'Dragon, Beast and False Prophet'. Though some kings of the earth would submit to the power of the millennial New Jerusalem, the 'others are broken to pieces in their opposition'.[61] Taking a similar stance, Hanserd Knollys affirmed that Christ's enemies would be defeated by the saints 'who shall bind kings in Chains and Nobles in Fetters of Iron', resulting in their victory over the kings of the fourth monarchy.[62] The descriptions found in such works, of the active role of the saints in bringing down earthly power, shared much with the militant viewpoints that characterised radical apocalyptic beliefs of an earlier period.

8.3   The Apocalypse and Radicalism in the Late Restoration

The late 1670s and the early 1680s were marked by an increase in anti-Catholic discourse, along with its accompanying apocalyptic rhetoric. The anxiety and concerns raised by the 'Popish Plot', with its supposed plan to assassinate the king and overthrow Protestantism in England, saw attacks in the press against perceived papal machinations, which were often placed in the context of prophetic fulfilment. In his account of the Plot, William Bedloe warned 'Protestant Dissenters ... to abhor all Conspiracies' against the government 'lest they shall by indirect means ... do the Jesuits Drudgery, and really be found diligent Instruments to advance that Scarlet Whore whom they so loudly declaim against'.[63] Hanserd Knollys was heard from again, quickly placing the Plot in apocalyptic context, asserting that no other kingdom had as much reason as England 'to hate, and to be Avenged on Mysterie Babylon the great, the Mother of Harlots, that great Whore, the Church of Rome, and her head the Pope, that Beast, ... the false Prophet', especially because of 'this late bloody traiterous design ... this damnable and Hellish Plot'.[64]

In all of this, however, it becomes difficult effectively to distinguish radical voices, as the general tone of the political language had become so heightened and shrill. A few authors did find prophetic correspondence with their critique of existing ecclesiastical and civil authorities in the early 1680s. For example, *Of the Two Last Things* (1682), likely written by the Presbyterian divine William Sherwin, outlined a number of events that would signal and accompany Christ's return to earth. The tract identified the pouring of the fifth vial (Rev. 16:10) as being directed against imposed human authority over people's consciences, and stated that this apocalyptic event had been carried out by parliament in 1642 in its actions against William Laud.[65] Contemporaries would clearly have seen this association between apocalyptic retribution against religious authority, the imprisonment and execution of Laud, and the justifying of Parliament's rebellion against Charles I as having serious radical implications, especially in the context of the debate over a Catholic successor and parliamentary demands for his exclusion that were playing out in the early 1680s. Attacks on Rome could also be used to make a point within the English political context. Christopher Ness's *Signs of the Times* (1681) connected the kings of the earth with the Whore of Babylon and described 'prerogative' as a dragon, as well as associating the 'beastly Religion of that monstrous Beast of Rome' with 'Monstrous Tyranny', a clear reference to the possibility of a Catholic successor to the throne.[66] The Baptist minister Benjamin Keach, in turn, noted that 'Rome or Mystery Babylon, hath made the worst of Men rulers', with the mark of the beast on their foreheads.[67] While such pronouncements could be seen as a challenge to temporal authorities, most criticism was directed against perceived doctrinal errors of Catholicism and papal influence over rulers, and only indirectly against ruling powers in England.

Though the last years of Charles II's reign and the brief reign of the Catholic James II did not generate a tremendous volume of the kind of radical apocalyptic response that had been prominent in the period of political transition of the 1660s, the events of 1688–1689 and the decade that followed did allow for the re-emergence of radical apocalyptic ideas. However, many of these appear to have been constructed in hindsight in response to the accomplishment of the Revolution of 1688–1689. These were part of a changed political and religious context: what had been radical from 1660 through much of the 1680s was now reinterpreted in light of the transformations that began with William and Mary's reign. For example, the Anglican minister Drue Cressener's apocalyptic critique of earlier government policies provides a useful example of this changing environment. Cressener's two volumes of apocalyptic exegesis found significance in policies of oppression directed towards and within early Christianity. Though couching his analysis in terms of the Roman Empire and the church founded upon its collapse, Cressener's concerns obviously applied to the suppression of nonconforming groups by the English government during the Restoration.[68] Cressener described the 'power of giving Law to the Consciences of Men in disputable things' as tyranny, and he identified the worship of the beast and his image as 'the Acknowledgement of an Universal Arbitrary Jurisdiction over the Consciences of all Men'.[69] Similarly, the Congregational minister Thomas Beverley equated the silencing and exclusion of nonconforming churches with the 'synagogue of Satan' mentioned in Revelation 2:9 and 3:9 and went on to suggest that such activities had led to the bringing down of the Church of England in the mid-seventeenth century.[70] Two years on, Beverley repeated this criticism of the Church of England, asserting that it was 'under Prophetic Censure' and intimating that, in its hierarchical structure, it mirrored some of the 'Horrid Antic[h]ristianisms of Popery'.[71] While such assertions would have appeared as blatant and threatening attacks on the Restoration church and state, the results of 1689 made them much less dangerous. Indeed, Cressener believed that William and Mary's success in England was a sign of the approach of the millennium.[72]

Yet there were some who remained more strident in their expressions of concern. Hanserd Knollys' pointed condemnation of the ecclesiastical policies of the Restoration church and state did not disappear with the downfall of James II. He continued to assert the coming power of the saints over earthly kingdoms, as well as his criticisms of the 'lukewarmness' (see Rev. 3:16) and 'formality' of the Church of England, for which it would be rejected by Christ.[73] Though the nonconformist Israel

Morland celebrated the inception of William and Mary's reign, he did place the Church of England among those 'Nations which solace themselves with the Harlot Church of Rome' and pronounce it 'the body of Antichrist'.[74] The Quaker Henry Mollineaux condemned a number of the practices of the Church of England, including the sign of the cross at baptism and receiving the bread and wine of communion, as accepting the mark of the beast.[75] The anonymous author of *An Enquiry Into the Vision of the Slaying and Rising of the Witnesses* (1692) condemned Anglican Protestantism from its origins, stating that the English Reformation 'made no Alteration in the Civil Government and therefore [was]... continuing a Part or a Member of the Ten-horned-beast'. Its political commentary was even more radical, locating the pouring of the third vial as the execution of Charles I, whose government was 'Ruinous to True Religion, and the Rights and Priviledges of the Subject, and therein obstructive to the Advancement of Christ's Kingdom'. The Restoration itself had continued in the same spirit, with the beast's war against the witnesses found in its policies against Protestant nonconformity.[76] The work went on to criticise 'the despotick dominion of worldly Rulers' as 'the Empire of the Devil'. Yet, in spite of all this, the changed circumstances in England were laying the foundations of the New Jerusalem and would bring about the pouring of the fifth vial and the sounding of the seventh trumpet.[77] This pamphlet's equating of the results of the Civil Wars with the Revolution of 1688–1689, declaring both 'Works of Providence for promoting the ruine of Antichrist',[78] demonstrated an opinion that was more radical than most arguments concerning recent political events. Most contemporaries would have balked at the inference that the revolt against Charles I and the overthrow of his youngest son could be equated as episodes of appropriate resistance to invalid civil authority.

Though not necessarily as harsh in its denunciation of existing authorities in church and state, Thomas Brookhouse's *The Temple Opened* (1696) was radical in several ways. This work also looked back to the mid seventeenth-century conflicts as a time of apocalyptic accomplishment. Brookhouse characterised Oliver Cromwell as a herald sent by Christ and credited the destruction of both monarchy and the Church of England as progress towards apocalyptic fulfilment, with the recent overthrow of James by William III revealing further movement towards that accomplishment.[79] Brookhouse declared that the 'Millennium Commences ... At the Expiration of the Whores Lease, when all the Kingdoms of the

World devolve to Christ'. This process had begun in Cromwell's time but would advance as Christ carried out the conquest of the world. He makes clear that the millennial government would not be a monarchy, and that only the saints would reign with Christ.[80] For Brookhouse, the harvest of the earth (Rev. 14:14–20) was the 'cutting down' of 'Constitutions Civil and Ecclesiastical', which had begun to occur already in England when established political and religious authorities had been overthrown during the 1640s and 1650s; more vividly, Brookhouse described how 'the head of Monarchy was Cut off, and the Head of Episcopacy too; and the Head of Republick and Presbytery'. The time of the witnesses lying dead had been the period of the Restoration, until they began to rise with the implementation of liberty of conscience in the later 1680s.[81] Brookhouse proposed that the millennial government would be based in ecclesiastical authority, with preachers being sent out on monthly circuits from the New Jerusalem 'to heal the Nations'. Thus the millennial reign would be a kind of spiritual and 'Priestly', not 'Imperial', rule.[82] Brookhouse made it clear that the advent of this kingdom was imminent, stating that the 'whole Civil and Ecclesiastical World is now in the Crucible, and the Fire of Gods Wrath will quickly melt it down, and make it ready for a new Impression'.[83] Though this work did not threaten militant action against the government, it is clear that its endorsement of the political and ecclesiastical results of the Civil Wars, and its revolutionary realignment of millennial temporal and spiritual authority, envisioned an impending apocalyptic accomplishment that would initiate a radical upheaval of earthly society.

Two tracts published in 1699 provide a last glimpse of the remnants of radical apocalypticism in England from the Restoration, in their echoing of the concerns of the previous decades. *The Mysteries of God Finished* characterised the two witnesses' testimony as 'bearing witness to the Kingly Office of Christ' that had 'lately been contested for, even to blood, in the late Wars in England'. In these struggles, the oppression of the witnesses had become political as well as religious, with 'the Beast taking it upon himself to persecute them as Rebels, and not as Hereticks only'.[84] The author lamented the spread of superstition and popish traditions in the English church, as well as the decline in morals, the rise of 'Debauchery', and the growth of 'Antichristian Abominations', and he expected the pouring of the seventh vial to come quickly.[85] Again casting its view back to the 1640s and 1650s, the pamphlet also had a parting shot for the more radical sects, suggesting that the beast's war against the witnesses was also seen in Satan sowing 'those abominable Errors of the Ranters, Adamites, and Quakers, misleading Men both in Principle and Practice from the Purity and Truth of the Gospel'.[86] *A Short Survey of the Kingdom of Christ* found the battle between Michael and the dragon (Rev. 12:7–9) fought 'in the late wars in England', where 'Popery and Hierarchy' in the Church of England succumbed to 'the Gospel-light'.[87] This struggle continued into the 'late Revolution' where the episcopal hierarchy had actually helped to defeat the dragon. Yet the tract concluded with the continued concern that England would not achieve the 'utter destruction of Antichrist, and all of Antichrist in the midst of thee' because it was failing to respond properly to the call of the witnesses to rise.[88] These two final pamphlets demonstrate that, even at the end of the seventeenth century, the struggles over political and ecclesiastical authority that had animated the previous decades had not completely disappeared, and, for some, a radical overturning of the temporal and spiritual order remained a distinct, and not necessarily unwelcome, possibility.

Much of the radical tone that can be found in apocalyptic writings from the 1690s comes from their acclamation of the militant political and religious stances from the past, as well as some remaining concern with the (mostly ecclesiastical) policies unresolved by the Revolution settlement. However, for many, the results of 1689 provided a solution to issues that had been principal areas of apocalyptic focus over the preceding decades, bringing to an end the threats of a revived Roman Catholic monarchy, arbitrary government, and continued religious persecution of Protestant denominations and sects. These complaints had been the primary motivation behind Restoration radical thought in general, and radical apocalyptic interpretation in particular. Even radical voices of the 1690s applauded William and Mary's overthrow of James II's short-lived regime, seeing this as a happening of great prophetic significance. That the new reign, and subsequent ones, did not bring about the anticipated millennial kingdom allowed for the emergence of other concerns and radical platforms in the eighteenth century. However, it is interesting to note that, a century after the extraordinary events of the late 1680s and early 1690s, English apocalyptic thought would be used to condemn the even more earth-shaking achievements of the French Revolution. In that context, prophetic interpretation became a weapon for defenders of the political status quo in the face of radical movements and change.

Notes

1. See for example: Norman Cohn, *The pursuit of the millennium: Revolutionary millenarians and mystical anarchists of the middle ages* (London, 1993); Christopher Hill, *Antichrist in seventeenth-century England* (Oxford, 1971).
2. See for example: Warren Johnston, *Revelation restored: The apocalypse in later seventeenth-century England* (Woodbridge, 2011); Warren Johnston, 'The patience of the saints, the apocalypse, and moderate nonconformity in Restoration England', *Canadian Journal of History/Annales canadiennes d'histoire* 38:3 (2003), pp. 505–520; Warren Johnston, 'The Anglican apocalypse in Restoration England', *Journal of Ecclesiastical History* 44:3 (2004), pp. 467–501.
3. Johnston, *Revelation restored*, p. 69.
4. For some further considerations of ways in which radicalism can be defined in consideration of later seventeenth-century ideas and activities, see for example: Ariel Hessayon and David Finnegan, 'Introduction: Reappraising early modern radicals and radicalisms', in Ariel Hessayon and David Finnegan (eds), *Varieties of seventeenth- and early eighteenth-century English radicalism in context* (Farnham, 2011), pp. 1–13; Richard L. Greaves, *Deliver us from evil: The radical underground in Britain, 1660–1663* (Oxford, 1986), pp. 3–20; Richard L. Greaves, *Enemies under his feet: Radicals and nonconformists in Britain 1664–1677* (Stanford, CA, 1990), p. viii; Melinda Zook, *Radical Whigs and conspiratorial politics in late Stuart England* (University Park, PA, 1990), p. xiii; Gary S. De Krey, *Restoration and revolution in Britain: A political history of the era of Charles II and the Glorious Revolution* (New York, 2007), p. 86.
5. Anonymous, *A door of hope; or, A call and declaration for the gathering together of the first fruits unto the standard of our lord Jesus* [London, 1661], pp. 5, 3, 1–2.
6. *Door of hope*, pp. 2, 12–14.
7. *Door of hope*, pp. 4–5, 10 (quotations on p. 5).
8. *Door of hope*, p. 10.
9. *Door of hope*, p. 9.
10. William Kiffen et al., *The humble apology of some commonly called Anabaptists, on behalf of themselves and others of the same judgement with them: With their protestation against the late wicked and most horrid treasonable insurrection and rebellion acted in the city of London* (London, 1661), pp. 7–8.
11. Jospeh Wright et al., *A brief confession or declaration of faith (Lately presented to King Charles the Second) Set forth by many of us, who are (falsely) called Ana-Baptists* (London, 1660).
12. George Fox et al., *A declaration from the harmles & innocent people of God, called Quakers, against all plotters and fighters in the world* (n.p., 1661), pp. 2, 5, 7.

13. John Braithwaite, *The ministers of England which are called, the ministers of the gospel, weighed in the ballance of equity ... Whereby it plainly appears, whether they be ministers of Christ or Antichrist* (London, 1660), pp. 11–12; Richard Crane, *A short, but strict account taken of Babylons merchants who are now forcing the sale of their rusty, cankered ware, upon the people of these nations* (London, 1660), title page, pp. 6, 8–9; George Fox, *The pearle found in England* (London, 1660), p. 8.
14. Located in northwestern Germany, Münster was seized by radical Anabaptists in 1534. Believing that Christ's return to the world to establish his millennial kingdom was imminent, the leaders of the movement introduced new laws for the city, including polygamy and communal ownership of property. Ecclesiastical and imperial forces recaptured the city in 1535, and the Anabaptists leaders were tortured and executed.
15. Joseph Carlyll, George Griffiths, Richard Kentish, et al., *A renuntiation and declaration of the ministers of congregational churches and publick preachers of the same judgement, living in, and about the city of London; Against the late horrid insurrection and rebellion acted in the said city* (London, 1661), pp. 2, 3, 4.
16. Edward Bagshaw, *Saintship no ground of soveraignty: Or a treatise tending to prove, that the Saints, barely considered as such, ought not to govern* (Oxford, 1660), sig. A3r.
17. Anonymous, *A breife description or character of the religion and manners of phanatiques in generall* (London, 1660), pp. 16, 40–41 (quotations at 16 and 40).
18. Anonymous, *Hell broke loose: Or, an answer to the late bloody and rebellious declaration of the phanatiques entituled A Door of Hope, &c.* (London, 1661), pp. 5, 21.
19. Anonymous, *Munster paralleld in the late massacres committed by the Fifth Monarchists* (London, 1661), sig. 2r and *passim*.
20. Anonymous, *The phanatiques creed, or A door of safety; In answer to a bloody pamphlet Intituled A Door of Hope* (London, 1661), p. 3; Anonymous, *A judgement & condemnation of the Fifth-Monarchy-Men, their late insurrection* (London, 1661), pp. 3, 7; Anonymous, *An advertisement as touching the fanaticks late conspiracy and outrage attempted and acted partly in the city* (London, 1661), pp. 3, 5.
21. Thomas Tillam, *The temple of lively stones* (London, 1660), 'Epistle to the reader' (no pag.), pp. 2, [174–175], and *passim*.
22. David S. Katz, 'Tillam, Thomas (*d.* in or before 1674)', in *Oxford dictionary of national biography* (online edition), January 2009, http://www.oxforddnb.com/view/article/69134. Last accessed 3 May 2015.
23. Katz, 'Tillam, Thomas'; David S. Katz, *Sabbath and sectarianism in seventeenth-century England* (Leiden, 1988), pp. 39–40; Bernard

S. Capp, *The Fifth Monarchy Men: A study in seventeenth-century English millenariainism* (London, 1972), pp. 201–202; Mark R. Bell, *Apocalypse how? Baptist movements during the English Revolution* (Macon, GA, 2000), pp. 244–246, 249, 252–253; J.F. Maclear, 'New England and the Fifth Monarchy: The quest for the millennium in early American Puritanism', *William and Mary Quarterly* 32:2 (1975), pp. 259–260; Ernest A. Payne, 'Thomas Tillam', *Baptist Quarterly* 17:2 (1957–1958), pp. 65–66.

24. For demonstrations of these links, see for example: Greaves, *Enemies under his feet*, pp. 199–200; Greaves, *Deliver us from evil*, pp. 187, 204; Richard L. Greaves 'The tangled careers of two Stuart radicals: Henry and Robert Danvers', *Baptist Quarterly* 29 (1981), pp. 38–39; David S. Katz, 'Menasseh ben Israel's Christian Connection: Henry Jessey and the Jews', in Yosef Kaplan, Henry Méchoulan, and Richard H. Popkin (eds), *Menasseh ben Israel and his world* (Leiden, 1989), pp. 133–134; Richard H. Popkin, 'Hartlib, Dury and the Jews', in Mark Greengrass, Michael Leslie, and Timothy Raylor (eds), *Samuel Hartlib and universal reformation: Studies in intellectual communications* (Cambridge, 1994), pp. 133–134; Richard H. Popkin, 'The end of the career of a great 17th Century millenarian: John Dury', *Pietismus und Neuzeit* 14 (1988), p. 209; Richard H. Popkin, 'The third force in seventeenth-century thought: Scepticism, science and millenarianism', in Richard H. Popkin (ed.), *The third force in seventeenth-century thought* (Leiden, 1992), p. 94; Ernestine van der Wall, 'The Amsterdam millenarian Petrus Serrarius (1600–1669) and the Anglo Dutch circle of philo-Judaists', in Johannes van den Berg and Ernestine van der Wall (eds), *Jewish-Christian relations in the seventeenth century* (Dordrecht, 1988), pp. 73–94; Ernestine van der Wall '"Antichrist stormed": The Glorious Revolution and the Dutch prophetic tradition', in Dale Hoak and Mordecai Feingold (eds), *The world of William and Mary: Anglo-Dutch perspectives on the revolution of 1688–89* (Stanford, CA, 1996), pp. 154–155.

25. Lodowick Muggleton and John Reeve, *A divine looking glass: Or, the third and last testament of our lord Jesus Christ* (London, 1661 [reprint of 1656 edition]); Lodowick Muggleton, *A true interpretation of the eleventh chapter of the Revelation of St. John, and other texts in that book* (n.p., 1662); Lodowick Muggleton, *The neck of the Quakers broken; or, cut in sunder by the two-edged sword of the Spirit which is put into my mouth* (Amsterdam, 1663); Lodowick Muggleton, *A true interpretation of all the chief texts, and mysterious sayings and visions opened, of the whole book of the Revelation of St. John* (London, 1665).

26. See William Lamont, 'Muggleton, Lodowicke (1609–1698)', in *Oxford dictionary of national biography*, online edition, May 2008, http://www.oxforddnb.com/view/article/19496. Last accessed 3 May 2015.

27. Anonymous, *Antichrist unhooded; or, an explanation of the names and titles by which the scripture exhibits Antichrist to the world* (London, 1664), pp. 3–5.

28. Hanserd Knollys, *Apocalyptical mysteries, touching the two witnesses, the seven vials, and the two kingdoms, to wit, of Christ and of Antichrist expounded* (London, 1667), p. 9.
29. Edward Burrough, *Antichrist's government justly detected* (London, 161), see for example pp. 1, 37, 46; Francis Howgill, *The glory of the true church discovered, as it was in its purity in the primitive time* (London, 1661), p. 108.
30. Anonymous, 'A narrative of the sufferings of John Philly and William Moore in Hungary and Austria', in William Evans and Thomas Evans (eds), *The Friends' library: Comprising journals, doctrinal treatieses, and other writings of members of the religious society of Friends*, Vol. IV (Philadelphia, PA, 1840), pp. 469–479.
31. John Philly *The arrainment of Christendom, containing a revelation of the rys, growth & fulnes of the great whor, man of sin or mistery of iniquity* (n.p., 1664), p. 2. The place of publication identified on the title page is 'Europ' [*sic*].
32. Philly, *Arrainment*, pp. 17, 9–10, quote at p. 9.
33. Philly, *Arrainment*, pp. 44, 52.
34. Philly, *Arrainment*, pp. 33–34.
35. 'Narrative of the sufferings of John Philly', p. 469.
36. Thomas Lawson, *A treatise relating to the call, work & wages of the ministers of Christ; as also to the call, work and wages of the ministers of Antichrist* (London, 1680), pp. 48, 36, 110.
37. Anonymous, *The panther-prophesy, or, a premonition to all people, of sad calamities and miseries like to befall these islands* (London, 1662), pp. 1–6.
38. *Panther-prophesy*, sig. A2r.
39. Henry Vane, *Two treatises: viz. I. An epistle general, to the mystical body of Christ on earth the Church universal in Babylon. II. The face of the times* (London, 1662), title page, sig. A2r.
40. Vane, *Two treatises*, pp. 3, 43, 45, 53.
41. Anonymous, *Mene tekel; or, the downfal of tyranny* (London, 1663), p. 72.
42. Anonymous, *The mysterie of magistracy unvailed: Or, Gods ordinance of magistracy asserted, cleared, and vindicated, from heathenish domination, tyranous and antichristian usurpation* (London, 1663), p. 44.
43. Anonymous, *A treatise of the execution of justice, wherein is clearly proved, that the execution of judgement and justice, is as well the peoples as the magistrates duty* (n.p., 1663), pp. 17, 29. Copies of this work were found in a raid on the shop of the printer John Twyn in 1663, and Twyn himself was executed for treason: Lois G. Schwoerer 'Liberty of the press and public opinion: 1660–1695', in James R. Jones (ed.), *Liberty secured? Britain before and after 1688* (Stanford, CA, 1992), pp. 207–208; Neil H. Keeble, *The literary culture of nonconformity in later seventeenth-century England* (Leicester, 1987), pp. 99–100.
44. *Treatise of the execution of justice*, p. 29.

45. Richard Greaves provides a full analysis of the plotting of this rebellion in *Deliver us from evil*, pp. 159–206.
46. Greaves, *Deliver us from evil*, pp. 178–179; Capp, *Fifth Monarchy Men*, p. 184 and n. 8.
47. Anonymous, 'A door of hope opened in the Valley of Achor, for the mourners of Sion out of the north' (1663), in Evan Price, *Eye-salve for England: Or, the grand trappan detected* (London, 1667), p. 4. Price transcribes the declaration in full on pp. 4–6 of his account.
48. 'A door of hope', pp. 4, 5, 6.
49. Anonymous, *The saints freedom from tyranny vindicated: Or, the power of pagan Caesars, and antichristian kings examined* (London, 1667), sig. A2v.
50. *Saints freedom*, pp. 9, 10, 11.
51. *Saints freedom*, p. 28.
52. *Saints Freedom*, pp. 23, 29.
53. Avihu Zakai, *Exile and kingdom: History and apocalypse in the Puritan migration to America* (Cambridge, 1992), pp. 195–206.
54. Katz, *Sabbath and Sabbatarianism*, p. 23; Katz, 'Tillam, Thomas'; Bell, *Apocalypse how?*, p. 235; Zakai, *Exile and kingdom*, p. 230; Maclear, 'New England and the Fifth Monarchy', p. 230.
55. Maclear, 'New England and the Fifth Monarchy', pp. 259–260 and n. 83.
56. Charles Edward Banks, 'Thomas Venner. The Boston Wine-Cooper and Fifth-Monarchy Man', *The New-England Historical and Geneological Register* 47 (1893), pp. 437–438; Maclear, 'New England and the Fifth Monarchy', pp. 255–256.
57. Banks, 'Thomas Venner', p. 438; Maclear, 'New England and the Fifth Monarchy', p. 255, 256. See also Capp, *Fifth Monarchy Men*, pp. 114–115, 267; David S. Katz and Richard H. Popkin, *Messianic revolution: Radical religious politics to the end of the second millennium* (New York, 1998), p. 72.
58. *A relation of the arraignment and trial of those who made the late rebellious insurrections in London* (London, 1661), as quoted in Banks, 'Thomas Venner', p. 442. See also Maclear, 'New England and the Fifth Monarchy', pp. 255, 257.
59. Maclear, 'New England and the Fifth Monarchy', 257, 255; Banks, 'Thomas Venner', p. 439; Owen Stanwood, 'Crisis and opportunity: The Restoration Church Settlement and New England', in N.H. Keeble (ed.), *'Settling the Peace of the Church': 1662 Revisited* (Oxford, 2014), p. 198 and n. 22.
60. Anonymous, *Theopolis, or the city of God New Jerusalem, in opposition to the city of the nations great Babylon* (London, 1672), pp. 1 (see also 83–84), 25, 33.
61. *Theopolis*, pp. 115, 176.
62. Hanserd Knollys, *The parable of the kingdom of heaven expounded* (London, 1674), pp. 75, 88.
63. William Bedloe, *A narrative and impartial discovery of the horrid popish plot* (London, 1679), p. 14.

64. Hanserd Knollys, *Mystical Babylon unvailed* (n.p., 1679), p. 31.
65. [William Sherwin], *Of the two last things, viz. resurrections and judgments at last revealed by Christ himself* (n.p., 1682), pp. 7–8. Sherwin wrote over ten other millenarian works in the later 1660s and 1670s. For a discussion of evidence supporting Sherwin's authorship of this work, see Johnston, *Revelation restored*, p. 118 n. 126.
66. Christopher Ness, *The signs of the times: Or, wonderful signs of wonderful times. Being a faithful collection and impartial relation of several signs and wonders, call'd properly prodigies* (London, 1681), pp. 29–30.
67. Benjamin Keach, ΤΡΟΠΟΣΧΗΜΑΛΟΓΙΑ: *Tropes and figures; or, a treatise of the metaphors, allegories and express similtudes, &c.* (London, 1682), pp. 324–325.
68. See for example: Drue Cressener, *The judgments of God upon the Roman-Catholick church, from its first rigid laws for universal conformity to it, unto its last end* (London, 1689), pp. 54–58; Drue Cressener, *A demonstration of the first principles of the Protestant application of the apocalypse* (London, 1689), pp. 249–254.
69. Cressener, *Judgments of God*, p. 57; Cressener, *Demonstration*, p. 254.
70. Thomas Beverley, *The prophetical history of the Reformation; or the Reformation to be reform'd; in that great re-reformation: That is to be 1697* (n.p., 1689), sig a4v.
71. Thomas Beverley, *The thousand years kingdom of Christ, in its full scripture-state: Answering Mr. Baxter's new treatise, in opposition to it* (London, 1691), p. 4; Thomas Beverley, *The universal Christian doctrine of the Day of Judgment: Applied to the doctrine of the thousand years Kingdom of Christ* (London, 1691), pp. 35–36.
72. Cressener, *Judgments of God*, sig. A2v; Cressener, *Demonstration of the first principles*, sigs. A3r–v.
73. Hanserd Knollys, *An exposition of the whole book of Revelation* (London, 1689), pp. 40, 57–58.
74. Israel Morland, *A short description of Sion's inhabitants from the days of Abel the righteous; as also of the inhabitants of the bloody city and harlot-church, from the days of Cain the murderer* (London, 1690), sigs. A3r, B1r.
75. Henry Mollineaux, *Antichrist unvailed, by the finger of Gods power; and his visage discovered by the light of Christ Jesus* (London, 1695), pp. 200–201.
76. Anonymous, *An enquiry into the vision of the slaying and rising of the witnesses, and falling of the tenth part of the city* (London, 1692), pp. 11, 13, 14 (quotations at 11 and 13).
77. *Enquiry into the vision*, pp. 31, 15.
78. *Enquiry into the vision*, p. 30.
79. Thomas Brookhouse, *The temple opened: Or, the great mystery of the millennium, and the first resurrection, revealed* (London, 1696), sigs. A2r–v.

80. Brookhouse, *Temple opened*, sigs. A4r, A4v.
81. Brookhouse, *Temple opened*, pp. 23, 25.
82. Brookhouse, *Temple opened*, pp. 33, 46.
83. Brookhouse, *Temple opened*, p. 56.
84. Anonymous, *The mysteries of God finished: Or, an essay toward the opening of the mystery of the mystical numbers in the scriptures* (London, 1699), p. 28.
85. *Mysteries of God finished*, pp. 40, 42, 26.
86. *Mysteries of God finished*, pp. 41–42.
87. Anonymous, *A short survey of the kingdom of Christ here on earth with his saints* (London, 1699), p. 52.
88. *Short survey*, p. 56.

CHAPTER 9

Reading Canticles in the Tradition of New England Millennialism: John Cotton and Cotton Mather's Commentaries on the Song of Songs

Jan Stievermann

John Cotton (1584–1652) and Cotton Mather (1663–1728) are widely recognised as key figures in the evolution of American Puritanism. John Cotton was one of the theological leaders in the founding of the Massachusetts Bay Colony and a principal architect and apologist of the New England Way. His grandson Cotton Mather rose to be a highly influential religious thinker and organiser in the phase when the Puritan social order was starting to collapse in the early eighteenth century. He helped New England Congregationalism adjust to the dramatic changes in the wake of the Glorious Revolution and make the transition into the age of the early Enlightenment, revivalism, and voluntary religion.

Both men were ardent millennialists and deeply convinced of the imminence of the final age. A number of John Cotton's most significant writings

---

J. Stievermann (✉)
Department of History, Universität Heidelberg, Heidelberg, Germany
e-mail: jstievermann@hca.uni-heidelberg.de

© The Author(s) 2016
A. Crome (ed.), *Prophecy and Eschatology in the Transatlantic World, 1550–1800*, Christianities in the Trans-Atlantic World, 1500–1800,
DOI 10.1057/978-1-137-52055-5_9

were concerned with end time prophecies, including *The Churches Resurrection, or the Opening of the Fift and Sixt verses of the 20th Chap. Of the Revelation* (1642), *Powring Out of the Seven Vials* (1655), and *Exposition upon the Thirteenth Chapter of the Revelation* (1655). Cotton Mather published more than fifty titles on the subject, and devoted the largest section of his last major work of systematic theology, the *Triparadisus* (written 1726/27), to millennialism.

However, grandfather and grandson strongly diverged in how they interpreted the prophecies pertaining to the latter-day events and Christ's kingdom. These differences have been perceived as reflecting larger changes in the development of New England millennialism and as being indicative of a significant bifurcation.[1] First formulated during a period of heightened Puritan expectancy for a radical transformation of the church, John Cotton's vision of the millennium was more spiritualist-progressivist in nature and has been identified as an important fountainhead of the strand of eschatology in America that later came to be called postmillennialism. Together with his father Increase (1639–1723), Cotton Mather has been described, in contrast, as a founding father of American premillennialism, *avant la lettre*. Mather's eschatology bespeaks a fundamentally altered outlook on the state of religion at home and abroad, as well as the changing intellectual climate of the early Enlightenment.

In this essay I seek to shed some new light on the important differences between the millennialism of John Cotton and Cotton Mather and on the hermeneutical debates and socio-political and ecclesial contexts in which they emerged. I will do so by looking at the two men's interpretations of Canticles,[2] which have never been read side by side. The existing comparative scholarship on Cotton's and Mather's millennialism has focused on their respective explications of the traditional core prophecies in Christian apocalypticism, in particular those from the Book of Revelation. However, during the seventeenth century, a historico-prophetic mode of reading Canticles gained popularity, which also made a considerable contribution to contemporary millennialist discourse in the Atlantic world, especially as it pertained to ecclesiology. Turning our attention from the studies of Revelation to these studies of Canticles allows for a fuller understanding of hermeneutical and cultural issues at stake in the developments and shifts of Puritan millennialism.

John Cotton's *A Brief Exposition of the whole Book of Canticles, or, Song of Solomon* (first ed. 1642; second ed. 1655) has received a good measure of scholarly attention.[3] So far, however, it is virtually unknown that Cotton

Mather also wrote extensive annotations on Canticles. They are part of his unpublished *opus magnum*, the 'Biblia Americana' (1693–1728), which only now is being made accessible through a ten-volume scholarly edition.[4] For his historico-prophetic reading of Canticles, Mather leans primarily on the exegetical authority of the German-Dutch Pietist Johannes Coccerius (Koch, Coch, 1603–1669). He widely departs from his grandfather, not only in how he maps details of church history onto the Song but also and especially in how he envisions the establishment and nature of the millennial church. These discrepancies reveal much about the trajectory of New England millennialism between the founding generation and the third generation of Puritan divines.

9.1 John Cotton's Reading of Canticles

The first edition of Cotton's *Brief Exposition*, based on a series of sermons preached in the 1620s, was published some nine years after he had decided to relocate to the Massachusetts Bay Colony in 1633. He had been pushed out of England by Laudian persecution of non-conformists, at the same time that he was pulled to the New World by the possibility of building a church establishment based upon what he and his fellow Puritans regarded as true scriptural principles. By 1642, however, the conflict with Roger Williams and the Antinomian crisis had revealed the fragility of this experiment and the need to define more precisely the polity of the new church. Cotton clearly wished to address this need with his commentary on Canticles. He read the Song not only as a 'divine Abridgment of the Acts and Monuments of the Church' from the days of Solomon to the millennial age[5]; but also found in the bridal imagery of Canticles important prophetic pointers for those who 'endeavour and thirst after the settling of Church and State, according to the Rule and Pattern of the Word of God'.[6]

As scholars have pointed out, Cotton's approach to Canticles as 'an Historical prophecie or proheticall history'[7] was most immediately indebted to the *Commentary on Canticles* by Thomas Brightman (1562–1607),[8] which was itself part of a larger seventeenth-century trend. Over the course of the century some 500 exegetical works on Canticles were published in England alone, making it one of the most frequently interpreted biblical texts that served as an important medium for religious and political debates. During the middle decades, historico-prophetic interpretations of the Song gained considerable traction among Pietistically-inclined

Reformed exegetes in Europe and were especially popular with Puritan theologians of the Civil War era, who often read the Song in close correlation with Revelation.[9]

In Cotton's understanding, King Solomon had composed Canticles on the occasion of his marriage with Pharaoh's daughter. Through the inspiration of the Holy Spirit, however, the imagery of the royal wedding song constituted an allegorical sequence, which predicted in amazing detail the relation between Christ (the Bridegroom) and his Bride (the church) over the course of history. At the same time, Cotton read the descriptions of Bridegroom and Bride and of their amorous exchanges in a typological manner. They prefigure the qualities of Christ's true church, its rightful government, ordinances, and legitimate relation to the state.

Like Brightman, Cotton found the great turning point of church history in Cant. 4:6. The breaking of the new day here spoken of marked the transition from the legal to the evangelical dispensation, made fully effective by Christ's incarnation and redemptive work. Following the substitution of old Israel, the New Israel of the gentile church experienced a brief period of apostolic purity. However, pollutions began creeping into the main body of the church soon after the Constantinian turn. To Cotton, the image of the slumbering Bride of Cant. 5:2 thus foretells the latter part of the reign of Constantine, when the newly established church in its hunger for worldly power first 'neglected the purity and power both of doctrine and worship, and received corruptions'.[10] According to Cotton, the actual reign of the Antichrist and the period of the Babylonian captivity of the church began with the death of Theodosius I in 395. Like so many millennialists, Cotton understood Rev. 12:4–6 as predicting that this period would last for 1260 years. He therefore expected the eventual downfall of the Antichrist to occur around 1655, ushering in the millennial age of the church.[11]

For Cotton, though, the overthrow of the Antichrist, like the regeneration of the church, was a gradual process. While the popish corruptions had grown throughout Late Antiquity and the Middle Ages, there always had been witnesses of the true gospel faith. They represented the true invisible body of Christ on earth during the reign of the Antichrist and pressed for reforms of the visible church. These efforts led to the Reformation age, when the primitive ideal of the church was powerfully revived and Antichrist's stranglehold began to weaken. This crucial juncture was marked by Cant. 6:2–9, where the Bridegroom delights in how his beloved 'has gone down to his garden ... to gather lilies', visits her in the garden, and praises her excellency.[12] These images for Cotton signified Christ's happiness at the successes of the great Reformers on the Continent and in England and his renewed fellowship with the church. To Cotton and his fellow Puritans, the Reformation was, of course, still incomplete. He believed that it would only be fully accomplished over the course of the millennial age, when the church would increasingly triumph over its enemies and be restored to unity and purity. Thus Cotton's reading of Canticles was directly tied into his radical politics.

Like many other Pietist and Puritan millennialists, Cotton expected the conversion of the Jewish people to play an important part in the millennial transformations of the church. God had not permanently cast off old Israel, but would gradually bring the diasporic Jews to the true faith and call them home from exile. The Jews would be instrumental in the reconquest of the Holy Land and the ultimate defeat of the Antichrist, after he had been ousted from his seat of power by Protestant forces. Thus, to Cotton, Cant. 6:10 foretold how, 'The Armies of the Jewes shall bee terrible to the Turkes and Tartars, and to the false Prophet then driven from Rome by ten Christian Princes, and associating himselfe to the Turke for succor.'[13] After this victory, the converted Jews would 'assemble for the establishment of the Kingdome and throne of Christ among them', as Cotton interpreted Cant. 6:13.[14] God's ancient *peculium* would thus be reinstituted into a position of primacy within the millennial kingdom.

In the last two chapters of Canticles, Cotton found detailed visions of Christ's kingdom and church, healed of all its schisms and defects. Especially noteworthy are Cotton's explications of the Bride's beautiful features, praised in Cant. 7:1–9, in terms of ecclesial polity. Together these explications amount to a concrete blueprint of church government and discipline that looks like an ideal version of the Congregational establishment that Cotton was attempting to build in the Bay colony. Consider, for instance, his note on Cant. 7:5: 'The head of the Church under Christ is the Civill Magistrate. The meaning then is, that the Magistrate of this church shall yield store of sound and sweet nourishment to the people, by giving and maintaining free passage to each holy Ordinance of God, and also by wholesome Lawes, and lastly by good example of godly life.'[15] However, as protectors of the church, magistrates (and even kings) were to have no authority over ecclesial affairs and were also to be 'bee bound with the censure of the Church'.[16] Most importantly, Cotton derived from these verses the two-tier model of church membership that the founders sought to implement in New England. In line with a long Christian tradition, Cotton understood Cant. 7:2 ('Thy navel is like a round goblet ... thy belly is like an heap of wheat set about with lilies') to speak of the administration of the two sacraments in the millennial church. On the one hand, Cotton interpreted this verse to support infant baptism and thus to uphold the ideal of a comprehensive church: 'The Navell, serving for the nourishing of the Infant in the wombe, resembleth Baptisme, nourishing Infants, and new borne babes in the wombe of the Church.' On the other hand, he took this verse to confirm the practice of restricting access to the Lord's Table, and thus full church membership, to the truly faithful, who could attest to their new birth by a demonstrable conversion experience: '[T]he Lord's Supper, it is as an heape of wheat, for store of excellent, and sweet, and fine nourishment, set about with lilies; because onely the faithfull pure Christians shall bee admitted to partake in that Sacrament.'[17] Fencing the Table and even the excommunication of offending church members would be necessary means of discipline even in the millennial church.

The church's progressive regeneration and expansion would not be completed until the very end of the thousand years. In his *The Churches Resurrection* and *An Exposition*, Cotton spelled out this model of an inchoate millennium. Taking an allegorical-spiritualist perspective on the prophecies of the Second Coming, he did not expect Christ to return in person before the millennium to establish a state of sinless perfection. The Lord Jesus, he wrote, 'doth not come down in his owne presence but in his instruments and Members'.[18] The binding of the dragon in Rev. 20:2–3 to Cotton signified the restraining of Satan's activities and the growth of Christ's power on earth through the extension of a purified Christendom under the rule of the saints. Just as the church would remain a *corpus mixtum* until the conclusion of the millennial age, the world more generally would continue to be plagued by conflict, illness, and death. Likewise, Cotton expounded the resurrection of the true witnesses in Rev. 20 in an allegorical-spiritualist fashion. These prophecies, as he explained, spoke of both an individual, spiritual resurrection through the regeneration of more and more believers, and of a corporate resurrection of particular churches. Churches not thus transformed would be vanquished with the Antichrist in the coming apocalyptic stand-off. The Bridegroom would physically return for the Last Judgement only at the end of the millennium.

Convinced that the onset of the millennium was near, Cotton thought it of utmost importance for the churches of the Reformation to realise as fully as possible the scriptural model of church government prophetically laid out in Canticles. By God's providence, the New England colonies had been given a unique opportunity to do this and thereby serve as an example for co-religionists across the Atlantic. 'In reading the biblical characters, their physical description, and their actions as prophetic types of the evolving church, its members, polity, and governance,' as Reiner Smolinski points out, 'Cotton derived clear instructions for New England's churches. Built on the prophetic model, they could anticipate Christ's pure church in theory even before his Second Coming would fully actualize them in practice.'[19] The most pressing issue for him and the other architects of the New England Way as later encoded in the Cambridge Platform (1648) was to ensure as much as possible by rigid tests and discipline that none but those grafted into Christ by a saving faith would be full members. Only then could the American churches expect to partake in the glory of Christ's coming reign. While Cotton in the 1640s obviously hoped that the Puritans could create something like an exemplary anticipation of the millennial church in the colonies, he never assumed that New England as such would occupy any special place in Christ's coming kingdom. Its centre would be the Holy Land, with New Jerusalem as the capital of the restored 'Church of the Jewes' to which all Christendom would look for leadership.[20]

9.2 Cotton Mather's Interpretations of Canticles in 'Biblia Americana'

About half a century later, in 1693, Cotton Mather started the most ambitious intellectual project of his career, the 'Biblia Americana'. He would work on this project, on and off, until his death in 1728, without ever mustering the necessary patronage or subscriptions to publish the mammoth manuscript in London. Covering all the canonical books of scripture, the 'Biblia' was intended to be a digest of the best critical and devotional commentaries in Mather's reach. Interestingly enough, Mather from the beginning all but totally ignored his grandfather's commentary in his work on Canticles. Indeed, in his first round of annotations on Canticles, Mather stayed entirely clear of the historico-prophetic approach to the Song of Songs, even though he used it with notable enthusiasm for other sections of the Old Testament.[21] Several factors might explain this reticence.

Already during Cotton's lifetime, his commentary had received sharp criticism, even among Puritans and fellow-millennialists. In 1655, the very year Cotton had expected the dawn of the millennium, a second, expanded version of his Canticles commentary was published posthumously by Cotton's friend Anthony Tuckney (1599–1670).[22] The revisions that Cotton had made before his death in 1652 did not fundamentally alter his scheme of redemptive church history, though. They sought to balance it out by the inclusion of less controversial, practical-devotional observations. In his preface, Tuckney noted that Cotton's annotations, like those of Brightman, were still filled with 'seeming uncouth expounding' of historical correspondences and 'particular Expositions and Applications' regarding church government.[23] After the Civil War, Cotton's work seemed even more of an oddity.

In post-Restoration England, as Alexander has pointed out, historico-prophetic readings of Canticles more generally started to go out of fashion.[24] One reason for this trend would have been the defeat of Puritanism and the rise of latitudinarian Anglicanism that generally frowned upon such perceived eschatological fancies, even though millennialism continued to have appeal, especially in dissenting circles.[25] Another reason was the emergence of a new paradigm of historical hermeneutics, which gave priority to the *mens auctoris* and the reconstruction of original contexts. Building on earlier 'heterodox' literalist interpreters, including Theodore of Mopsuestia (ca. 350–428) and Sebastian Castellio (Castalio; Chatillon; 1515–1563) in Calvin's Geneva, critics like Hugo Grotius (Huig de Groot; 1583–1645) and Jean LeClerc (Johannes Clericus; 1657–1736) argued that Canticles had been composed by Solomon as his wedding song and spoke of human erotic, not divine, love.[26] Only very few scholars in England would have followed Grotius and LeClerc all the way. Many, however, became more cautious in their interpretations of Canticles, and restored the more traditional devotional approach with its focus on pious individualistic applications.

One of the last post-Restoration exegetes to embrace the Brightman–Cotton tradition was Thomas Beverley in his *An exposition of the divinely prophetick Song of Songs which is Solomons* (1687). Toward the end of the seventeenth century, critics in the English-speaking world regularly charged that instead of solving the difficulties of the Song, attempting to read it as a detailed prophetic prediction of church history had only increased them. It had also led to dangerous political appropriations. For instance, the Scottish Presbyterian theologian James Durham (1622–1658), whose posthumously published commentary on Canticles was quite influential, complained in his preface that the method led: 'wholly to uncertainty, or mens pleasure, or their invention, and groundless conjectures'.[27] Closer to Mather's day, another Scottish divine, Robert Fleming the Younger (ca. 1660–1716), whose works on eschatology Mather greatly appreciated, sounded an even sharper note in the introduction to his poetical paraphrase of the Song. Fleming wrote that prophetic readings threatened to 'turn the whole Scripture into a meer Nose of Wax, or the Schools Materia prima, that can admit of what sense we please'.[28]

The most popular English commentaries in Mather's day, Matthew Poole's (1624–1679) *Annotations upon the Holy Bible* (2 vols., 1683–1685) and *An Exposition of all the Books of the Old and New Testaments* (1708–1710) by Matthew Henry (1662–1714), also reflect these concerns. On the one hand, both authors emphatically deny that the Song ought to be read in a literalist, non-spiritual sense. Poole's preface asserts 'that this Book is to be understood mystically or Allegorically concerning the spiritual Love and marriage which is between God or Christ, and his Church, or every believing Soul'.[29] On the other hand, both Dissenter exegetes eschew any historico-prophetic speculations with their baggage of radical politics.[30] Only in his gloss on Cant. 8:14 did Henry allow for a very muted millennialist perspective: 'Thou *Jesus Christ* be now retired, he will return ... [and] every Eye shall see him in all the Pomp and Power of the upper and better World; the Mystery of God being fulfilled, and the Mystical Body completed'.[31]

Poole and Henry hark back to the more contemplative-devotional Christian approach, fully developed from patristic sources by medieval mystical commentators such as Bernard of Clairvaux, which had remained vital through the Reformation period and was adopted by many early seventeenth-century English commentators, including the Puritan Henry Ainsworth (1571–1622).[32] In this approach, the emphasis was less on the ecclesial or collective and more on the individual dimension, that is, on the spiritual love between Christ and the souls of his faithful followers. Of course, this model of allegorising Canticles did have some historical dimension in that the interaction between bride and bridegroom, church and Christ, was thought to develop through the main stages of redemption history. But no attempts were made to find any particulars of church history predicted. It deserves mention here that Jonathan Edwards (1703–1758), the most important colonial exegete in the generation after Mather and one of the founding fathers of American postmillennialism, largely followed Poole and Henry in his approach to Canticles. He, too, took the Song above all else as the poetic dramatisation of an intimate colloquy between Christ and the individual soul. In the exchanges of

Bride and Bridegroom the text mapped out the steps of a spiritual journey toward the desired unification.[33]

Although fully aware of these trends, Cotton Mather did not in principle become disinclined toward a historico-prophetic reading of Canticles. He also held on to his literalist expectation of a future millennium. Still, John Cotton's specific interpretation of the Song would have appeared to him as outmoded and vulnerable to attack in the scholarly debates of the early Enlightenment. Its fixation on a Congregational polity seemed somewhat embarrassing by the early 1700s. Moreover, Cotton's commentary on Canticles was very closely tied into a spiritualist-progressivist version of millennialism that had high-flying expectations for a regeneration of the church before the actual return of Christ. Increase and Cotton Mather had come to reject this outlook. All their hopes were invested in Christ's supernatural transformation of the world at his Second Coming. Already in Cotton Mather's earliest systematic treatment of the subject, the 'Problema Theologicum' (ca. 1695–1703), he embraced the premillennialist model of his father, which also included a literalist-corporeal understanding of the Petrine conflagration, the saints' resurrection, and the coming kingdom. To the Mathers, a key concern was to identify the signs that still needed to be fulfilled before the imminent parousia. For a long time, Cotton agreed with his father that a regeneration of the church and the Christianisation of the Jews was to be expected before the Second Coming. During the 1710s, however, Cotton Mather's doubts about this eschatological conversion grew.[34]

At the same time, Cotton Mather's expectations for the renewal of the church moved away from what both his grandfather and his father had imagined. His ecclesiology became increasingly less corporate, more individualistic, pietistic, and ecumenical. At least within the Protestant spectrum, the differences in ecclesial polity appeared less important to Mather than the sincerity of personal faith. He stopped ascribing any eschatological significance to the New England Way. At the turn of the eighteenth century, the colonies were much more fully assimilated into the British Empire and its cultural and religious life. The New Charter of 1691 had created an ecclesial environment in which the Congregational churches were still privileged but had to accept inter-Protestant toleration and limited religious diversity.

On the one hand, Mather, like most of the Congregational clergy, bemoaned these changes and castigated the perceived decline of piety among an increasingly heterogeneous population. On the other hand, he, after a phase of initial shock, adjusted to this new reality better than others. He gave up on the founders' establishment ideal, no longer believing that Christ's true church would or could be realised in a specific territory through the agency of princes and magistrates. On this side of the millennium, the primary means to further unity and purity was revivalism and reform. Perfection, however, was only to be expected for the time after Christ's return. Until then, Protestants of all stripes were to work together under the common principles of their faith. Mather engaged in interdenominational cooperation both at home, where he reached out to Anglicans and Baptists, and across the Atlantic. His connections to Reformed and Lutheran Pietists are especially noteworthy.[35] Mather hoped that what he called an 'American Pietism' might play a role in the desired Protestant awakening.[36] However, the idea that New England Congregationalism was to provide a blueprint for church reform in the Old World, as his grandfather had believed, was no longer plausible to him.

Adapting Cotton's *A brief Exposition* for the 'Biblia' was therefore out of the question. And it seems that initially no other, more convincing, historico-prophetic reading suggested itself to Mather. Completed in the early years of the eighteenth century, Mather composed a first commentary on Canticles for the 'Biblia' that took a different route. It sought to update in the light of recent scholarship the venerable tradition which primarily viewed the Song as an intimate colloquy between Christ and the individual soul to be contemplated for devotional purposes. For this first commentary Mather drew on a variety of patristic, medieval, and early modern sources. It is somewhat surprising that he relied on *A Paraphrase upon the Books of Ecclesiastes and the Song of Solomon* (first ed. 1685) by the Latitudinarian churchman and outspoken critic of dissenting theology and exegesis, Bishop of Ely and biblical scholar, Simon Patrick (1625–1707), most heavily. With the help of Patrick, Mather's commentary also addressed critical issues concerning the original communicative context of the Song and the historicity of Solomon's wedding. Cotton had maintained that the king had indeed composed Canticles on the occasion of his wedding. Given the radical conclusions drawn by Grotius or LeClerc, it would have seemed dangerous to Cotton Mather to admit any such historical background for Canticles. With Patrick, Mather thus argued that Canticles was not at all an epithalamium but had been written by Solomon in the tradition of the messianic psalms of David. These had also employed bridal imagery to speak of Christ and his faithful.[37]

In many ways similar to those of Poole and Henry, Patrick's commentary can be characterised as a compromise between an individualistic-meditative and an ecclesiological interpretation. While the first perspective dominates, Patrick also reads the Song as a historical allegory of the church's relation with Christ. However, he consciously avoids the level of specificity and chronological systematisation, as well as any correlations with the Book of Revelation, which were typical of the seventeenth-century historico-prophetic model. Thus Mather might have looked at Patrick's work as a thoroughly christocentric but also safe alternative. Like his fellow-Dissenter Matthew Henry, Mather might have wished to distance himself 'from the history of radical interpretations of the Song of Songs' and, seeking integration into the religious life of the Empire, concentrate more 'on a spiritual reading disengaged from contemporary politics'.[38]

Apparently Mather was not fully satisfied with the solution worked out in his first commentary, however. Lacking an overarching interpretative scheme, the first commentary seemed to ultimately fail to integrate the Song's complex web of images into a meaningful whole and provide a convincing eschatological perspective. Mather was also not ready to give up on Canticles as a prophetic book. He thus penned a second, completely independent commentary, roughly the same length as the first.

In his prefatory remarks to the second commentary, Mather noted he was venturing 'to make a trial' of uncovering the prophetic intent of Canticles after all. In this experiment, he continued, 'I will sett aside all Interpreters ... confining myself to none but the famous *Cocceius*; [and his] Commentaries on this mystical Book'.[39] The reference is to the *Cogitationes de Cantico Canticorum Salomonis*, by the Reformed theologian and exegete Johannes Cocceius (1603–1669), who held chairs at the universities of Franeker and Leiden. *Cogitationes* was originally printed as a stand-alone work in 1665, before being subsequently included in the three different *Opera Omnia* editions of Cocceius's work that appeared in Mather's lifetime (1673–1675; 1689; 1701).[40] The exact date when Mather composed this second commentary cannot be determined with certainty. Circumstantial evidence and a few hints in the manuscript seem to point to 1715, though.

While Cocceius's basic approach was the same as Brightman and Cotton, Mather obviously found Cocceius's execution much more compelling, both in terms of its exegetical sophistication and its historical correlations. It was also free from entanglements with radical English politics. Like Mather, Cocceius was an advocate of ecumenism based on Protestant core principles and personal piety. While Mather certainly thought that the 'Illustrations' proposed by the *Cogitationes* were most worthy of consideration and, as he wrote in a concluding paragraph, 'perhaps, as near the Mark as any that have been yett offered', he did not regard them as authoritative. Mather made it clear that he was not providing 'a Formal Translation of *Cocceius's* Commentary', but had merely selected for his English version 'such Passages as give me most of Satisfaction' from the more than two hundred pages of Latin annotations.[41]

Indeed, Mather was not just being highly selective. He substantially modified Cocceius's overall hermeneutical scheme, so as to make it less determinate and rigid. Mather also altered Cocceius's interpretation of the millennium, mostly by means of silent omission. Like Cotton, Cocceius's understanding of the church's final age of triumph was spiritualistic-progressivist. It did not include a belief in the personal return of Christ or a bodily resurrection before Judgement Day. In contrast to Cotton, however, Cocceius, for the most part, kept his representation of these latter-day events relatively short and vague. He also refrained from proposing any specific date for the onset of the millennium. This made Cocceius's vision of the final age quite easy to adjust to Mather's own eschatology.

Cocceius divided the historical allegory of the Song into seven periods that he correlated with the Book of Revelation, specifically the historical events signified by the letters to the seven churches (Rev. 1–3), the seven seals (Rev. 5–8), and seven trumpets (Rev. 8–11). Mather did not take on this systematic correlation with Revelation. Presumably this had to do with the fact that Mather had developed in his own commentary on Revelation a different historical interpretation of these cycles of vision. While he basically accepted Cocceius's historical timeline, Mather in his commentary on Canticles chose not to make explicit the periodisation of his source or draw clear-cut divisions between them. Instead, Mather simply followed the structure of the biblical book, though he did adopt Cocceius's subdivisions of the individual verses.

Whereas Cotton understood Canticles to predict the history of the church from the reign of Solomon to the millennial age, Cocceius assumed a more narrow temporal scope. A brief prologue (Cant. 1:1–4) looked back to 'the Church, before & until the Incarnation of our Lord, longing for the Accomplishment, of what had been foretold about His Coming',[42] the appearance of the Messiah, and the actualisation of the gospel covenant. The subsequent verses, in Cocceius's interpretation, prefigured the history of the church from the time after Christ's ascension and exaltation to his Second Coming. Thus Cocceius assumed that Canticles was only tangentially concerned with the history of old Israel and that Solomon's prophetic foresight had been very much set on the new Israel of the gospel church. Following Cocceius, Mather therefore made the Song a thoroughly Christocentric prophecy.

Guided by Cocceius, Mather assumes Cant. 1:5 marks the actual beginning of the Song's prophetic history of the church after Christ's ascension. For Cocceius, the first period of this history ran until chapter 3 of the Song, covering the epoch of spreading the gospel among Jews and gentiles before the increasing persecutions and the destruction of the temple in 70 CE. Although Mather here and elsewhere avoids speaking of a fixed period, he nevertheless follows Cocceius's basic chronology.[43] In his subsequent annotations on Cant. 1:5 to Cant. 2:17, Mather, like Cocceius, finds allegorical prefigurations of the planting and wondrous growth of the Apostolic Church, first among Jewish and then also the gentile communities, of the great hardships that antagonistic Jews caused these early Christian congregations, and of the mutual delight they and their exalted Lord messiah took in each other. In this section, Mather adopts passages from Cocceius that support his changing theology of substitution, and also that reflect his ideal of the primitive church and of the apostolic ministry. Up until Cant. 2:8, Mather sees predictions of the time when considerable numbers of Jewish converts (the 'remnant') in and around Jerusalem will join the new covenant. However, the majority of Jews continue in their rejection of Christ and old Israel is finally replaced as God's *peculium*: 'Here,' Mather notes on Cant. 2:8, 'is the Departure of the Church unto the *Gentiles*, from the *Jewes* who allowed no Rest unto it.'[44]

The imagery of spring, budding flowers, and singing birds in Cant. 2:11–13 is then taken to foreshadow the way in which 'The Success of the Gospel among the *Gentiles*, afforded incredible Delights unto the Church of God.'[45] The gentile church begins to slowly spread across the Roman Empire. Even in these splendid visions, however, Cocceius and Mather identify the first harbingers of trouble not just in the form of persecutions but also of heresy, represented by the 'little foxes' of Cant. 2:15, which 'are styled, *little*, because they were Fore-runners of the *greater* ones, & præparatory to the Introduction of *Antichrist*'.[46]

Mather also accepts Cocceius's proposal here that chapters 3 and 4 form the second act in the Song's visionary bridal drama, containing predictions about the history of the early church, up to and including the reign of Constantine. Thus, with Cocceius's help, Mather decodes the images of these two chapters as predicting the terrible sufferings and trials of the early Christians, first in the wake of the disastrous Jewish uprising and the destruction of Jerusalem (read as divine punishments for the obduracy of natural Israel), and then under the various Roman persecutions. Both exegetes see these first three centuries to be at once the darkest, most desperate and the brightest, most glorious time of the church on this side of the millennium. The primitive Christians were, after the destruction of the temple and the Jewish state, for the first time fully free from the yoke of legalism. Not fearing martyrdom, they were amazingly active and successfully expanded the gospel kingdom. 'The Beauty of the Church appears under the Cross'; as Mather summarises his interpretation of this time at Cant. 4:2. "Tis then *twice Fair*, in both active & passive Obedience. The *Eyes* of the Church, are then, like those of the *Dove*, directed & confined unto the Messiah alone."[47] The 'day-break' at which 'shadows flee away', and the Bride ascends to the mountains of myrrh and frankincense in Cant. 4:6 is then read as a prophecy of the Constantinian turn in the first decades of the fourth century.

In Cant. 5:1 to 6:9 Mather, after Cocceius, identifies the third act of the bridal drama. Here, the ambiguous results of the establishment of Christianity as the official religion of the Roman Empire were adumbrated. The Constantinian church is given increasing might to subdue the external enemies of God in this time, and a growing number of pagan peoples are Christianised. At Cant. 5:2, however, Mather points to the first signs of internal 'Deformity' that are 'coming upon the Church, after *Peace* granted unto it'.[48] The ecclesial hierarchy becomes dangerously enamoured with fruitless learning and its privileges and worldly power. As more and more lose sight of the pure gospel, heresies such as Arianism begin to endanger the church.

The Bridegroom's attributes of physical beauty in Cant. 5:10–16 are taken as allegorical representations of Christ's true nature, his relation to the other persons of the Trinity, and his majesty as sole head of the church. Although these positions were defended by the early ecumenical councils, and enshrined in the Nicene-Constantinopolitan Creed, the councils also strengthened the Roman claims to power. Heterodoxy and divisions continued to plague the church as the Roman Empire descended into chaos.[49] The fifth chapter, according to Cocceius's and Mather's scheme, also contained the prediction of a momentous turning point in the history of the church. When the pope was established as the head of an ever more expansive and powerful church, after the final collapse of the Empire in the early fifth century, the Antichrist, though still restricted in his power, raised his head. Under this growing influence of the Antichrist, the Church of Rome would enter into its Babylonian captivity step by step.[50] This assumption dovetailed with Mather's calculations that the 1260 years of Antichrist's reign would end at some point in the eighteenth century. For a long time, he had set his sights on 1716 but when that year came and went, he restricted himself instead to announcing that the downfall of the Antichrist was to be expected very soon—sometime between 1736 and the end of the century.[51]

Rome's claim to absolute authority would, in the long run, also lead to the great schism of 1054, which both interpreters saw prefigured in Cant. 6:1–4. All the while, true witnesses of Christ would persist within the increasingly corrupt papal church. 'As, *Omni tempore supersunt in Ecclesia, in quibus Vita Christi cernatur*,'[52] Mather noted on Cant. 5:8–9, 'so the Lord continually stirs up some or other, from what they see and hear in His Faithful Servants, to enquire further after Him.'[53] The appellation of the Bride as an undefiled dove and only daughter in Cant. 6:9 provides Cocceius and Mather with the occasion to develop from their exegesis of Canticles the basics of an ecumenical ecclesiology with characteristically primitivist and pietist inflections. 'The Church is a *Dove* in regard of her Chastity; and an *undefiled one*, in regard of a *Dove-like Simplicity*', Mather propounds. And, 'All things in the True Church, have a Tendency to *Unity*. And the *True Church* ha's [*sic*] a Resemblance alwayes to the *First Church*; her Endeavour is to Resemble the Primitive Church, that was *her Mother*, & she *that bare he*.'[54] In contrast to Cotton, however, no specific model of ecclesial polity is defined for the '*True Church*', which is constituted by the community of witnesses across times, nations, and denominations.

Cocceius and Mather find in the remaining verses of Canticles predictions of the ongoing historical struggle between the faithful witnesses of Christ and the Antichrist, who distorts the true teachings of the gospel and puts himself as Lord in the place of Christ. Mather follows Cocceius in marking off Cant. 6:9 to 7:11 as a separate fourth act in this drama, which reaches from the ninth century to the Reformation of the sixteenth century. This framework allows Cocceius and Mather to incorporate a great number of medieval and late-medieval church critics and reform movements into an apologetic pre-history of Protestantism. Hincmar, archbishop of Reims, Berengar of Tours, Bernard of Clairvaux, the Waldensians, the Albingensians, John Wycliff, and Jan Hus are all prefigured in the poetic images of Solomon's Song. They become forerunners of Luther and Calvin in their supposed fight against the Beast of Rome. Cant. 7:4, then, is taken to encapsulate a prophecy of the time when this 'pressing after a Reformation' finally culminated in open ecclesial conflict and divisions, as the critics found the church unresponsive to their arguments, and '*Luther* particularly, now coming upon the Stage, found it so, as well as his Predecessors'.[55] The Reformers lead their churches out of the Babylonian captivity. However, the power of the Antichrist is not yet broken and he strikes back with a vengeance. Cant. 7:5–13, according to Cocceius and Mather, contains a historical allegory of the bloody persecution and wars of religion in the sixteenth century. Amidst all this new trouble and suffering, the Bridegroom still sustains his Bride with acts of kindness, including 'The Peace of Religion, established in *Germany*, about the Middle of the sixteenth Century' foreshadowed by Cant. 7:10.[56]

In Cocceius's historical scheme, Cant. 7:11 to 8:3 comprised the fifth period. Here, the schism becomes permanent after the Peace of Augsburg and the anathemas of the Council of Trent. The churches of the Reformation consolidate, and find increasing acceptance among the common people. At the same time, the *ecclesia reformata* is still far from being the true church of God. It is internally divided along territorial and confessional lines, disturbed by dangerous enthusiasts and full of unregenerate members lacking a genuine *praxis pietatis*. As a Pietist of irenic-ecumenical orientation, Cocceius was also highly critical of the polemical tendencies among the scholars of that age of confessionalisation.

Mather found this criticism congenial. He noted on Cant. 8:2 that this was to be read as a regretful confession of the church to her Bridegroom that she had been 'so taken up in Managing Disputations and Controversies with her Adversaries, upon the Truth already advanced, that she had not the Liesure [*sic*] to make a due Progress in the Knowledge of the Lord'.[57] But she now assures her Lord that she would commit herself to 'The Introduction of His True Doctrine' only, that is, to the unadulterated teaching of the gospel, which 'would be the Introduction of the Lord Himself. She thereupon promises to herself, a fuller Instruction from Him, whereto she would ingeniously Resign herself.'[58] Mather attempted to contribute to such a 'fuller Instruction' and thereby to Protestant unity by his famous project of defining the fundamental 'Maxims of Piety' to which all sincere Christians could agree.[59]

Mather's annotations give virtually no indication that Cocceius believed Cant. 8:3–7 to contain the prophecy of a separate epoch in church history of unprecedented suffering. For Cocceius, these verses spoke in detail of the horrors of the seventeenth-century religious wars and persecutions across Europe, especially of the Thirty Years' War, which he himself had experienced. In this sixth period, the Beast was raging against the church with terrible power, until at last the first signs of Christ's victorious approach were beginning to show when open warfare came to an end. The final defeat of the Antichrist, however, and the moment when the Beast would be cast into the lake of fire, were still pending. This was the point in the course of history where Cocceius located himself when he wrote the commentary in 1665. In the *Cogitationes*, no precise date is given for the end of this sixth period of suffering. However, Cocceius was convinced that it was practically over and that the church was on the threshold to the last age.[60]

Mather chose to remain much less concrete on these verses. Half a century after the publication of Cocceius's commentary, it was apparent to him that the earlier commentator's hopes had been premature. The Beast was still on its throne at Rome. The wars and the suffering of the Reformation churches continued as much as their internal divisions and corruptions. Also, in contrast to both Cotton and Cocceius, Mather did not think these realities would change without the direct and personal interference of Christ, whose Second Coming would soon bring down the Antichrist and usher in the millennium. Through revival, reform, and supplications, the saints everywhere could prepare for the parousia and save as many in their reach as possible. But the millennium would not come about through the activities of the church. In Mather's entry on Cant. 8:5–6, he thus merely has the Bride attempting to stir up the Bridegroom with her cries and expressing her hope, 'That the *Love* and Zeal of her Lord, for her, break forth as a *Fire*, to torment the Powers of Darkness, that have sought her Destruction.'[61] This prophecy of a great fire that would torment 'the Powers of Darkness', did, of course, agree well with Mather's belief in a literal Petrine conflagration. But he seems to have made a decision to not spell out any of his own expectations about the *diluvium ignis* in the context of the Canticles commentary and to remain silent on his differences with Cocceius.

This was also Mather's strategy in adopting the annotations on the last four verses of Canticles (Cant. 8:10–14). In Cocceius's scheme, these predicted the seventh period and treated the church's final triumph in realising the kingdom of Christ on earth. Cocceius's vision of this final age was in many respects quite unlike Mather's. As Cocceius imagined it, the final period would begin with the defeat of the Beast through the forces in league with Christ's church, but not as Mather imagined it, through Christ's direct intervention. With the great adversary gone, the *ecclesia reformata* would flourish inwardly and outwardly. It would progress to glorious unity and holiness, as the lives of its members became ever more thoroughly reformed. The pure gospel would be spread across the globe. All the heathen nations would come into the church and serve it. For the most part, Coccejus remained quite general on how these things were to play out. He was very explicit, however, on one significant point: the total triumph of the church also implied that God would not only miraculously cause the Christianisation of all the Muslim nations, but also that he would have mercy on his erstwhile chosen people and lead all the natural children of Israel home into the true faith, as promised in Rom. 11.

Coccejus also connected the seventh age of church history to the 'New Heavens and New Earth' predicted by Isaiah and Revelation. In sharp contrast to Mather's hyperliteralist understanding, Coccejus thought the new life on earth was to be understood in ecclesiological and spiritual terms as the regeneration of those who had been dead in faith (both individuals and nations), and thus signified the same renewal and global expansion of the church foreseen in the last verses of Canticles. This renewal and global expansion of the church would be the fulfilment of Christ's spiritual rule on earth. Coccejus expected Christ's return in the body only for the Last Judgement at the end of the seventh age, which would also bring a general bodily resurrection. Overall, then, Coccejus's interpretation of the final verses of Canticles was informed by a highly spiritualised form of chiliasm characterised by a great optimism for the future of the church, which was expected to soon enter a time of wondrous spiritual progress.

Mather went along with Coccejus's proposal to set apart the last four verses of Canticles as a prophecy of the happy times that were also promised to the church elsewhere in the Bible. He also accepted the legitimacy of some very general hints to the glories that lay in store. Otherwise, however, he ignored the spiritualist-progressivist glosses of his famous colleague. For example, on the images of the vineyard of Cant. 8:11–12, which were key to Coccejus's eschatological vision, Mather wrote in very unspecific terms that they foreshadowed a better future of the church when 'another State is to be expected', as it is going to be 'delivered from the Hands of Oppressors, & because there is that *Communion of Saints* in the Church, by which they all belong to one another .... The whole Revenue of this *Vineyard*, is to be rendred unto the *Lord-Messiah*. And yett He grants a Share of it, unto those faithful Servants of His, who do their Part for the Præservation & Fructification of the Vineyard.'[62]

Mather also omitted Cocceius's reference to the 'New Heavens and New Earth' of Isa. 66, which he understood in a dramatically different way to the Dutch scholar, who interpreted them as signifying the truly reformed *regimen Ecclesiæ* and the *novam conditionem populi*.[63] Mather, moreover, made no mention of when and how this happy day would come about, where 'the Lord-Messiah' would reside, about how He might 'possess Himself, of all the *Kingdomes* of the World', who might be included in his kingdom, or of the physical state of the saints. Likewise, in his conspicuously terse gloss on Cant. 8:14, Mather completely edited out Cocceius's lengthy predictions about the evangelisation of the world in the last age. All that Mather found in this verse 'is the Answer of the Faithful', expressing 'A Desire that the Lord would with a singular Celerity and Expedition, possess Himself, of all the *Kingdomes* of the World; especially such as ever have been the *Mountains of Spices*, in regard of His having been entertained with the Graces of His Faithful People there.'[64] The reader is not informed of the fact that Cocceius had established a direct correspondence between how the Bridegroom is envisioned on top of the 'mountains of spice' and Paul's prophecy of Rom. 11. Cocceius stated emphatically in his entry on Cant. 8:14 that the verse predicted the conversion of the Jews and the heathen peoples of the world.[65]

Mather also makes no mention of a *conversionem Judæorum*. This shows that by the time he wrote his second commentary on Canticles he no longer believed the diasporic Jews had to be collectively brought to Christ before His return. Mather thought the prophecies concerning the saving of the 'remnant' of Israel had already found their literal *primum implementum* in the Christianisation of Jewish communities during the Apostolic Age. The higher eschatological fulfilment of these prophecies referred to the New Israel of the church. All the necessary signs pointing to the parousia had already been fulfilled. The world stood ready for judgement and re-creation at the hands of the Lord.

By truncating and modifying Cocceius's speculations on the seventh age, Mather made them compatible with his own hyperliteralist and intensely supernaturalist version of the coming latter-day events, as spelled out in his 'Biblia'-commentaries on Isaiah and Revelation, and summarised in the *Triparadisus*. Upon the Lord's personal coming in the clouds of heaven with his heavenly host, there would occur:

The *Raising* of the Dead Saints, and the *Changing* of the Living Ones, to a State of *Sinless Immortality*; and the Purifying of this Polluted World with a tremendous CONFLAGRATION; and thereupon the Succession of *New Heavens* and a *New Earth*, wherein *shall dwell Righteousness*; and there shall be a *Restitution of all things* to *Paradisaic* Circumstances; and a Glorious Kingdome of GOD maintained by the *New Heavens* reigning over the *New Earth*, and the *Raised*, made *Equal to the Angels*, continually descending from the *Holy City* in the *New Heavens*, to teach & rule the *Changed* who on the *New Earth* shall *build Houses and Inhabit them, & Plant Vineyards & Eat the Fruit of them, and have Offspring that shall be the Blessed of the Lord*.[66]

It is important to emphasise that Mather expected the conflagration to be global. From among the sinful nations and churches, only the faithful few would be caught up in the air and transfigured by the power of Christ for a new and flawless existence. These changed saints would then enjoy the blessings of the New Earth, which would have its centre in the Holy Land. Above it, in the upper parts of the atmosphere (the New Heavens), the heavenly city of New Jerusalem would hover in the air. From here, Christ would rule together with the resurrected saints of former times (including the Jewish patriarchs and prophets), 'made *Equal to the Angels*'. Mather thus envisioned the millennium as a second, sinless and deathless paradise under immediate divine governance. Herein lay the true meaning of the heavenly country spoken of in the Old Testament and the happy times promised to the church. This dispensation would continue at least for a thousand years, during which the changed saints would eventually all be translated to the heavenly city as well. Then would follow the final assault of the Devil and his legions of Gog and Magog, who would be destroyed and sent to the eternal torments of Hell in the completion of the Last Judgement, while the saints would continue forever in their state of beatitude.

Even as the exegetical tide turned against it, Cotton Mather thus defended and continued the Puritan tradition of reading Canticles as a prophetic history of the church, but de-politicised it considerably. In accordance with his distinct eschatology and ecclesiology as well as his chastened view of New England, Mather nevertheless widely departed from John Cotton's interpretation in adopting Cocceius's *Cogitationes*. Mather's commentary on Canticles thus illustrates how much New England millennialism changed and diversified within three generations. His grandfather had found in the Song prophetic signs pointing to an inchoate, spiritual millennium of the church and a building plan for its true polity, which he hoped could be prefigured in the colonies. Mather arrived at a reading in which the Bride at the end of the Song had no expectation for making any progress in history. She rather called upon the Bridegroom to 'make haste' (Cant. 8:14) with returning and bringing this world to an end. While John Cotton thus anticipated many characteristics of a full-fledged postmillennialism, Mather in many ways was a precursor of modern premillennialism. However, in contrast to many later American premillennialists, the New World, in his mind, had no special part to play in the grand revolution to come. Most of the saints to be raptured, Mather wrote in the *Triparadisus*, would likely reside in 'the *European* Parts of the World. [M]y poor *American* Countrey, Lett me pray and hope, for thy adding some unto the Number!'[67]

NOTES

1. For good surveys, see Reiner Smolinski, 'Apocalypticism in colonial North America', in Stephen J. Stein (ed.), *The encyclopedia of apocalypticism, Vol. 3: Apocalypticism in the modern period and the contemporary age* (New York, 1998), pp. 36–72; Jeffrey K. Jue, 'Puritan millennialism in old and New England', in John Coffey and Paul C.H. Lim (eds), *The Cambridge companion to puritanism* (Cambridge, 2008), pp. 259–276.
2. Also known as the 'Song of Songs' or 'Song of Solomon'.
3. See, for instance, Jeffrey A. Hammond '"The bride in redemptive time": John Cotton and the Canticles controversy', *New England Quarterly* 56:1 (1983), pp. 78–102; On the ecclesiological and political conflicts in the background of Cotton's commentary, see Jesper Rosenmeier, 'Eaters and non-eaters: John Cotton's *A Brief Exposition of Canticles* (1642) in light of Boston's (Linc.) religious and civil conflicts, 1619–1622', *Early American Literature* 36:2 (2001), pp. 149–181. On Cotton's millennialism, see Theodore Dwight Bozeman, *To live ancient lives: The primitivist dimension in Puritanism* (Chapel Hill, NC, 1988), pp. 237–262, and J.F. Mclear, 'New England and the fifth monarchy: The quest for the millennium in early American puritanism', *New England Quarterly* 32:1 (1975), pp. 223–260, on this see pp. 229–238.
4. The section on Canticles is part of the recently edited volume, *Biblia Americana*, Vol. 5, *Proverbs–Jeremiah*, ed. Jan Stievermann (Tübingen, 2015).
5. John Cotton, *A briefe exposition of the whole book of Canticles, or Song of Solomon; Lively describing the estate of the Church in all ages thereof*, (London, 1642), p. 10.
6. Cotton, *A brief exposition*, title page.
7. Cotton, *A brief exposition*, p. 10.

8. Brightman's commentary was first published in Latin in 1617. In 1644 it was published twice in English, once as part of his *Works* and once as a stand-alone volume that was produced in Amsterdam. On Brightman's millennialism and his concern with the eschatological conversion of the Jews, see Andrew Crome, *The restoration of the Jews: Early modern hermeneutics, eschatology, and national identity in the works of Thomas Brightman* (Cham, 2014).
9. The understanding of Canticles as a prophetic history of the church was, simplistically speaking, a Christianisation of early midrashic exegesis, the Targum of Songs, and many subsequent rabbinic interpretations, which saw in the Song a parabolic account of God's relationship with his covenanted people. On this, see Philip S. Alexander, 'The Song of Songs as historical allegory: Notes on the development of an exegetical tradition', in Kevin J. Cathcart and Michael Mather (eds), *Targumic and cognate studies: Essays in honour of Martin McNamara* (Sheffield, 1996), pp. 14–29. Other English commentaries in this vein were written during this period by, among others, Nathanael Homes, John Davenport, Edmund Hall, and George Wither. For the larger exegetical and political debates surrounding these prophetical and political readings of Canticles, see Elizabeth Clarke, *Politics, religion and the Song of Songs in seventeenth-century England* (London, 2011), esp. pp. 123–133.
10. Cotton, *A brief exposition*, p. 144.
11. Cotton, *Exposition upon the thirteenth chapter*, p. 93; John Cotton, *The Churches resurrection or the opening of the fift and sixt verses of the 20th chapter of the Revelation* (London, 1642), pp. 4–5.
12. Cotton, *A brief exposition*, p. 169.
13. Cotton, *A brief exposition*, p. 195.
14. Cotton, *A brief exposition*, p. 198.
15. Cotton, *A brief exposition*, p. 213.
16. Cotton, *A brief exposition*, p. 214.
17. Cotton, *A brief exposition*, p. 209.
18. Cotton, *Churches resurrection*, p. 4.
19. Reiner Smolinski, '"The way to lost Zion": The Cotton–Williams debate on the separation of church and state in millenarian perspective', in Bernd Engler, Joerg O. Fichte, and Oliver Scheiding (eds), *Millennial thought in America: Historical and intellectual contexts, 1630–1860* (Trier, 2002), pp. 61–96, 70.
20. Cotton, *A brief exposition*, pp. 227–228.
21. For general information on the 'Biblia', see my 'General introduction', in Reiner Smolinski and Jan Stievermann (eds), *Cotton Mather and Biblia Americana—America's first bible commentary: Essays in Reappraisal* (Tübingen, 2010), pp. 1–58; and the first two parts of Jan Stievermann,

Prophecy, piety, and the problem of historicity: Interpreting the Hebrew scriptures in Cotton Mather's Biblia Americana (Tübingen, 2016).

22. John Cotton, *A brief exposition with practical observations upon the whole Book of Canticles, or, Song of Solomon* (2nd edition, 1655).
23. From Tuckney's unpaginated preface, 'To the Reader', Cotton, *A brief exposition* (1655).
24. Alexander, 'The Song of Songs as historical allegory', p. 18.
25. See Warren Johnston, *Revelation restored: The apocalypse in later seventeenth-century England* (Woodbridge, 2011).
26. Compare the section on Canticles in Grotius's *Annotationes ad Vetus Testamentum* (1644), contained in volume one of the 1679 *Opera omnia theologica* (esp. 1:267), and Jean Le Clerc, *The five letters concerning inspiration* (London, 1690), third letter, pp. 93–99. For a detailed discussion, see chapter II.2 of my *Prophecy, piety, and the problem of historicity*.
27. James Durham, *Clavis Canticis; or, an Exposition of the Song of Solomon* (1668), p. 12.
28. From the unpaginated preface to Robert Fleming, *The Mirrour of divine Love unvail'd, in a poetical Paraphrase of the high and mysterious Song of Solomon* (London, 1691).
29. Matthew Poole, *Annotations upon the Holy Bible*, Vol. 1, no pag. In his preface to Canticles Henry makes the same claim but gives it a slightly more covenantal twist that reflects his dissenting theology. The Song, he writes, should be read as an allegory by which is 'illustrated the mutual Affections that pass between God and a distinguished Remnant of Mankind'. Thus, 'Experienced Christians here find a Counterpart of their Experiences, and to them 'tis intelligible, while they neither understand it, nor relish it who have no Part or Lot in the Matter.' *An Exposition of all the Books of the Old and New Testaments*, Third edition (London, 1721–1725), 3:613 (613).
30. Poole had already done so in the learned Latin commentary, on which his English annotations were based. See Matthew Poole, *Synopsis criticorum aliorumque S. Scripturae interpretum*, 6 vols. (London, 1669), 2: 1969.
31. Poole, *An Exposition*, 3:642.
32. See Henry Ainsworth, *Annotations upon the five Bookes of Moses; the Booke of the Psalmes, and the Song of Songs, or, Canticles* (1627).
33. On this, see Chap. 6 in Douglas A. Sweeney, *Edwards the exegete: Biblical interpretation and Anglo-Protestant culture on the edge of the Enlightenment* (New York, 2015).
34. On the development of Mather's eschatology, see Reiner Smolinski, 'Introduction', in *The threefold paradise of Cotton Mather: An edition of 'Triparadisus'* (Athens, GA, and London, 1995), pp. 3–78, this pp. 39–78.
35. On this, see Robert Middlekauff, *The Mathers: Three generations of puritan intellectuals, 1596–1728* (New York, 1976), pp. 209–230, 305–349.

36. Richard Lovelace, *The American pietism of Cotton Mather: Origins of American evangelicalism* (Grand Rapids, MI, 1979).
37. Cotton Mather, *Biblia Americana*, Vol. 5, *Proverbs-Jeremiah*, ed. Jan Stievermann (Tübingen, 2015), pp. 461–463. Hereafter *BA*.
38. Clarke, *Politics, religion, and the Song of Songs*, p. 132.
39. *BA* 5: 523.
40. The best recent comprehensive treatment of Cocceius's theology is Willem J. Van Asselt, *The federal theology of Johannes Cocceius (1603–1669)*, trans. Raymond A. Blacketer (Leiden, 2001).
41. *BA* 5: 523.
42. *BA* 5: 524.
43. *BA* 5: 526.
44. *BA* 5: 532.
45. *BA* 5: 533.
46. *BA* 5: 534.
47. *BA* 5: 539.
48. *BA* 5: 544–545.
49. *BA* 5: 548–549.
50. In his commentary on Revelation, Cocceius explained that he understood the rise of Antichrist to have been completed with Luis IV (1282–1347), the last Emperor to resist the claim of papal supremacy. For Cocceius, the thousand years from Constantine to Luis were in fact the millennial age of the church spoken of in Rev. 20:2. He assumed that Christ's eschatological reign would be of an indeterminate length. See Gottlob Schrenk, *Gottesreich und bund im Älteren Protestantismus, vornehmlich bei Johannes Coccejus: Zugleich ein Beitrag zur geschichte des Pietismus und der Heilsgeschichtlichen Theologie* (Gütersloh, 1923), p. 223. It is not clear whether Mather was aware of Cocceius's preterist interpretation of the millennium; if he was, he chose to ignore it.
51. Smolinski,'Introduction', *Triparadisus*, p. 64.
52. 'In all times they remain in the church, in whom the life of Christ is discerned.' Johannes Cocceius, *Cogitationes de Cantico Canticorum* (Leiden, 1665), p. 89.
53. *BA* 5: 548.
54. *BA* 5: 552.
55. *BA* 5: 557.
56. *BA* 5: 558–559.
57. *BA* 5: 560.
58. *BA* 5: 560.
59. Mather first worked out his 'MAXIMS of PIETY' in his *Things to be more thought upon* (1713). Subsequently he revised them then in *The stone cut out of the mountain* (1716), and then in *Malachi: Or, the everlasting gospel,*

preached unto the nations (1717). The maxims were supposed to serve as the basis for ecumenical cooperation or even union among the Protestant churches of Europe and North America. In *Malachi* Mather proposes '[t]hat there should be formed SOCIETIES of Good Men, who can own some such Instrument of PIETY, and make it their most inviolate Law, to bear with Differences in one another upon the Lower and Lesser points of Religion, and still at their Meetings have their Prayers for the growth of the People, who being Established on the Grand MAXIMS of Christianity are to become a Great Mountain and fill the whole Earth, accompanied with Projections of the most unexceptionable Methods to accomplish it' (pp. 92–93). Mather's *Three letters from New-England, relating to the controversy of the present time* (p. 9), and his *Manuductio ad ministerium* (p. 119) also contain reflections on church union on the basis of a vital, christocentric piety. On this, see Middlekauff, *The Mathers*, pp. 305–319.
60. As Schrenk has shown, Cocceius expected this eschatological turn for the better to occur around 1667. See his *Gottesreich und bund im Älteren Protestantismus*, p. 234.
61. *BA* 5: 561.
62. *BA* 5: 563.
63. Cocceius, *Cogitationes*, p. 198.
64. *BA* 5: 563–564.
65. Cocceius, *Cogitationes*, pp. 199–200.
66. Mather, *Triparadisus*, pp. 180–181.
67. Mather, *Triparadisus*, p. 189.

CHAPTER 10

Prophecy and Revivalism in the Transatlantic World 1734–1745

Jonathan Downing

> But then I rais'd up Whitefield, Palambron raised up Westley [*sic*],
> And these are the cries of the Churches before the two Witnesses
> Faith in God the dear Saviour who took on the likeness of men:
> Becoming obedient to death, even the death of the Cross
> The Witnesses lie dead in the Street of the Great City
> No Faith is in all the Earth: the Book of God is trodden under Foot:
> He sent his two Servants Whitefield and Westley; were they Prophets
> Or were they Idiots or Madmen? shew us Miracles!
> Can you have greater Miracles than these? Men who devote
> Their lives whole comfort to intire scorn & injury & death[1]

Writing in the early nineteenth century, decades after the deaths of John Wesley (1703–1791) and George Whitefield (1714–1770), William Blake invoked their memory to present them as the two witnesses of Revelation 11:1–13. He cast the two preachers as God's emissaries, who are given permission to 'shut heaven', 'smite the earth with plagues', and emit fire from their mouths for the duration of 'the days of their prophecy' (Rev. 11:5–6).[2] Blake thus depicted these pre-eminent figures of the transatlantic evangelical

J. Downing (✉)
Department of History, University of Bristol, Bristol, UK
e-mail: jd15739@bristol.ac.uk

revival of the early eighteenth century as prophets. Indeed, for Blake, they were prophets *par excellence*, the prophets who would be resurrected and translated to heaven ahead of the 'great earthquake' that would level a tenth of 'the great city' (Rev. 11:11–13). As Michael Farrell states, Blake in *Milton: A Poem* presented the religious revival wrought by Whitefield and Wesley as a prophetic mission, and an important precursor to the eventual establishment of the New Jerusalem.[3]

Wesley and Whitefield were important British preachers and writers, who, in the late 1730s and early 1740s, were key figures in a religious movement termed by later scholars as the 'evangelical revival', or the 'great awakening'.[4] In colonial communities in New England, and in cities and towns across England, Scotland, and Wales, individuals recounted powerful experiences of conversion and repentance. Occasionally, these conversions were spontaneous, but often they were a response to the ardent and emotional preaching of early evangelical leaders.

Blake's depiction of these revivalist preachers as divisive prophetic figures echoes important questions asked about many of the key figures involved in early eighteenth-century evangelicalism. Were these preachers, with their capacity to whip their audiences into ecstatic frenzies, genuine agents of the Spirit of God? Or were they intoxicated with religious 'enthusiasm'? Were the dramatic swathes of conversions recorded by preachers such as Wesley, Whitefield, and Jonathan Edwards (1703–1758) in Britain and America the start of the fulfilment of the Bible's end-time prophecies? Or were these conversions inauthentic by-products of a dangerous cult of personality? Crucially, how did these figures themselves see their ministries and activities fitting into the Bible's prophetic-historical schema? What were their own attitudes to the prophetic claimants that emerged out of their own converted congregations?

In this essay, I propose to look at these questions by exploring the evangelical revival's relationship with prophecy under three different, but overlapping, modes of interpretation. By drawing on writings from—and about—early evangelical revivalist communities, I examine the ways that preachers and leaders encountered prophetic activity in their respective congregations and missions. First, I explore accounts of prophetic activities amongst evangelical converts, and how pre-eminent evangelical figureheads reacted to them. Second, I look at the ways that key revivalist leaders interpreted biblical prophecy, and their attitudes towards the possibility of prophetic activity in their own ages. Finally, I look at the reception of Edwards's, Wesley's, and Whitefield's ministries in contemporary print culture, and probe the extent to which these three figures were thought of as prophetic, and whether they might have seen themselves in a similar light.

10.1 Encountering Revivalist Prophecy

In his journal of Wednesday 24 May 1738, John Wesley narrated a powerful experience of conversion, feeling his heart 'strangely warmed' whilst attending a Moravian meeting in Aldersgate Street, London.[5] Two years later, Wesley encountered two women in Bristol, Susan Peck and Betty Bush. Wesley found that after their conversions, the women had begun to claim that they were receiving 'private revelations' from God:

> I met with one who, having been lifted up with the abundance of joy which God had given her, had fallen into such blasphemies and vain imaginations as are not common to men. In the afternoon I found another instance, nearly, I fear, of the same kind: one who, after much of the love of God shed abroad in her heart, was become wise, far above what is written, and set her *private revelations* (so called) on the self-same foot with the written Word.[6]

Jonathan Edwards, reflecting back upon the conversions he witnessed in his parish in Northampton, recounted an incident involving a man in nearby South Hadley, Massachusetts, who thought he was 'divinely instructed' to encourage a 'poor man in melancholy and despairing circumstances' to recite the words of Psalm 116:4 in prayer. Edwards gave a précis of the man's reasoning:

> in short he was exceedingly rejoiced and elevated with this extraordinary work, so carried on in this part of the country; and was possessed with an opinion that it was the beginning of the glorious times of the church spoken of in Scripture: and had read it as the opinion of some divines, that there would be many in these times that should be endued with extraordinary gifts of the Holy Ghost ... But he since exceedingly laments the dishonor he has done to God, and the wound he has given religion in it, and has lain low before God and man for it.[7]

These accounts point towards an important issue in early revivalist theology. The key appeal in early modern evangelicalism was emotional and personal. In exchange for their recognition of their sinfulness before Christ, evangelical converts could expect to experience the blessing and 'indwelling' of God's spirit. In his 1746 *A Treatise Concerning Religious Affections*, Edwards wrote:

> The inheritance that Christ has purchased for the elect, is the Spirit of God; not in any extraordinary gifts, but in his vital indwelling in the heart, exerting and communicating himself there, in his own proper, holy or divine nature.[8]

The direct experience of 'divine nature' envisaged by revivalist leaders, ensured that early evangelical leaders had to navigate carefully between two poles of early modern religious experience. Ann Taves demonstrates that early evangelical experience was commonly depicted as reacting against 'formalism' (where religious activity was purely external, with no internal effect on the believer), but often careering dangerously towards 'enthusiasm', where believers became convinced of their own divine power in the light of their experience of the Spirit. She notes that enthusiasm was an extremely loaded term in early eighteenth-century discourse, carrying with it overtones of religious and political insurgency, the rise of Puritanism, Civil War, and regicide.[9] The behaviours exhibited by some evangelical converts, including claims to visionary experience and direct divine revelation, veered dangerously close to enthusiasm for some critics, leading converts into the kinds of over-zealous radicalism that had led to political and religious catastrophe in recent memory. George Lavington, then Bishop of Exeter and vehement opponent of the early Methodist movement, linked Methodist 'enthusiasm' both to prominent Roman Catholic saints and to the second-century heretics, the Montanists: Lavington was particularly critical of a shared inclination towards '*Ecstasies and Raptures, Apparitions and Visions*'.[10]

An example from George Whitefield's letters demonstrates the problem acutely. Writing to a colleague in London in 1739, Whitefield expressed concern that a prominent member of the community was claiming prophetic inspiration, but becoming aggressive when his claims were challenged. Whitefield lamented 'I would all the Lord's servants were prophets, but then I would not have people think themselves prophets of the Lord, when they are only enthusiasts.'[11] A pivotal claim of early evangelicals was that conversions were intense and personal; the danger was that converts may believe themselves to be uniquely inspired.

As demonstrated above, revivalist leaders such as Wesley and Edwards came into direct contact with converts who claimed that they had been given prophetic authority at an early stage in their respective evangelical preaching careers. Their strategies for dealing with such instances demonstrate an ambivalence in their attitudes towards such apparently enthusiastic activities. In both their accounts, Wesley and Edwards concede that the unacceptable prophetic outbursts from the converts are a direct result of their experiences of conversion. What started as being 'lifted up with the abundance of joy' evolved into 'blasphemies and vain imaginations'; becoming 'rejoiced and elevated' at the success of the revival lapsed into the belief that one may be blessed 'with extraordinary gifts of the Holy Ghost'. In these specific instances, Wesley and Edwards were united in their condemnation of these prophetic pretensions. For Wesley, it was the fact that one of the prophets placed their utterances on the same level as God's word that made her activities unacceptable. Edwards, in his account, is careful to note the South Hadley prophet's eventual repentance at the 'wound' given to the evangelical cause. Later in his career, Edwards had to work to calm his congregation after they had experienced unprecedented raptures whilst under the stewardship of a preacher called Samuel Buell in 1742. Reflecting on events in a letter the following year, Edwards wrote:

> many in their religious affections being raised far beyond what they ever had been before: and there were some instances of persons lying in a sort of trance, remaining for perhaps a whole twenty-four hours motionless, and with their senses locked up; but in the meantime under strong imaginations, as though they went to heaven, and had there a vision of glorious and delightful objects. But when the people were raised to this height, Satan took the advantage and his interposition in many instances soon became very apparent: and a great deal of caution and pains were found necessary to keep the people, many of them, from running wild.[12]

The ambivalence of Edwards' attitude towards such ecstatic, visionary experiences is clear. There is, perhaps, a cautious scepticism towards his congregation's claims: they were under 'strong imaginations', and it was 'as though' they ascended to heaven. Nonetheless, Edwards did not offer a straightforward denial that the experiences took place. 'Many' cases, but perhaps implicitly not all, were attributed to diabolical imposition. The crucial issue was the behaviour of these converts after their experiences. Whether their visionary experiences were genuine divine revelations or not, Edwards claimed that his duty as a pastor was to prevent these visionaries from becoming too over-exuberant in their subsequent proclamations.

These kinds of prophetic behaviours which early evangelical leaders had to contend with were a frequent feature of early revivalist experience. Methodist conversion narratives, which became widely disseminated in the transatlantic print culture of the eighteenth century, frequently depicted believers falling into trances, portraying an overwhelming sense of divine indwelling, and spontaneous outbursts of joy or despair.[13] Ronald Knox notes that John Wesley consistently encountered such behaviours throughout his preaching career, particularly when visiting new areas, and invariably attributed them to God's activity.[14] In Edwards' account of the early conversions in Northampton he accepted such responses as inevitable, given the powerful emotional experience of conversion:

> When persons have been exercised with extreme terrors, and there is a sudden change to light and joy, the imagination seems more susceptive of strong ideas, and the inferior powers, and even the frame of the body, is much more affected and wrought upon ...[15]

Douglas Winiarski, in his study of religious experiences amongst early revivalist communities in New England, identifies 17 separate cases of visions or trances reported between 1741 and 1742.[16] Dramatic physiological manifestations of conversion experiences, claims to prophetic inspiration, and visionary experiences, were thus frequent accompaniments to the preaching activities of early revivalist ministers.

The need to account for such experiences emerges as a consistent theme in the writings of prominent early evangelical leaders. In a journal entry in May 1739, Wesley appended a letter responding to a critic of the claims to visionary experiences amongst early converts. In his response, Wesley affirmed his belief that such behaviours could be signs of God's work: 'The question between us turns chiefly, if not wholly, on matter of fact. You deny that God does now work these effects; at least, that He works them in this manner. I affirm both.'[17] For Wesley, conversions which were wrought as a result of visionary experiences should not, in and of themselves, be considered inauthentic. These experiences and symptoms of conversion, however, ought to be judged as secondary to the long term changes in the convert's life:

> And that such a change was then wrought appears (not from their shedding tears only, or falling into fits, or crying out: these are not the fruits, as you seem to suppose, whereby I judge, but) from the whole tenor of their life, till then many ways wicked; from that time holy, just and good.[18]

Wesley's openness to the possibility of prophetic inspiration is perhaps best demonstrated in his account of a meeting with a French Camisard prophet in 1739. Wesley described how the prophet 'seemed to have strong workings in her breast' and that 'every part of her body, seemed also to be in a kind of compulsive motion', before speaking of 'the fulfilling of the prophecies, the coming of Christ now at hand, and the spreading of the gospel all over the earth'. Wesley was not totally convinced that the woman spoke from genuine spiritual inspiration. He suggested that the prophet's reliance on scriptural phrases may mean she had committed them to memory. However, he refused to explicitly rule out the possibility that her prophetic utterances were genuine: 'I let the matter alone; knowing this, that if it be not of God, it will come to nought.'[19] Wesley's response indicates his agnosticism towards the possibility that communication between God and humanity had been opened up amidst the extraordinary revival of religion in the early eighteenth century. The possibility of prophetic inspiration could not be immediately ruled out, but instead needed to be evaluated in terms of the long-term impact on the convert's behaviour.

For Edwards too, the presence of prophetic claimants and reports of visionary experiences amongst revivalists did not necessarily tell against interpreting the awakening as the work of the Spirit:

> It is no argument that a work is not the work of the Spirit of God, that some that are the subjects of it, have in some extraordinary frames been in a kind of ecstasy, wherein they have been carried beyond themselves, and have had their minds transported into a train of strong and pleasing imaginations, and kind of visions, as though they were wrapped up even to heaven, and there saw glorious sights.[20]

Edwards's approach was to demonstrate that ecstatic behaviour, or claims of prophetic inspiration, were not proof either way of the authenticity of spiritual activity.[21] They were the kinds of reactions one might expect to an unprecedented and personal experience of divine activity. We can see at work here in Edwards's thinking a pathological and psychological approach to prophetic behaviour. Edwards frequently concerned himself with interrogating the likely mental effects of conversion experiences. He concluded that many of the behaviours labelled by the opponents of revival as 'enthusiasm' were explicable as the result of converts' conversion experiences:

> 'Tis no wonder that in such a case, the brain in particular (especially in some constitutions) … should be overborne and affected, so that its strength and spirits should for a season be diverted … and wholly employed in a train of pleasing delightful imaginations.[22]

Crucially, however, would-be prophets were expected to exercise extreme caution before acting on their prophetic impulses. Wesley, whilst remaining open to the possibility of direct divine inspiration, employed a clear test to determine whether an individual had slipped into enthusiasm: inspiration is imaginary if 'it contradicts the Law and the Prophets'.[23] Edwards, whilst not definitively ruling out the possibility of prophetic inspiration amongst members of his congregation, counselled that 'I have known such impressions to fail, and prove vain by the event', even when apparently being faithful to scriptural texts.[24] Like Wesley, Edwards argued that the biblical text, rather than any contemporary prophecies, should be the true 'light shining in a dark place'. For both revivalist writers, prophecy should remain subordinate to scripture if it was to be an acceptable component of the revivalist experience.

10.2 Revivalism as/and the Fulfilment of Biblical Prophecy

For many revivalist figures, the swathes of successful conversions throughout the transatlantic world called to mind the workings of the Spirit in the early church. In his preaching, George Whitefield placed a strong emphasis on the Spirit as an essential component of Christian experience—to the extent that he acknowledged that it invited the criticism of 'enthusiasm' from those outside of the movement. In a 1739 sermon preached in Kent, Whitefield lamented 'we no sooner mention the necessity of our receiving the *Holy Ghost* in these last days as well as formerly; but we are look'd upon by some, as enthusiasts and madmen'.[25] Jonathan Edwards speculated that the readiness of many American converts to claim prophetic status was due to the belief that 'the glory of the approaching happy days of the church would partly consist in restoring those extraordinary gifts of the Spirit' as experienced by the Corinthian church (1 Corinthians 12–13).[26] Many early revivalist leaders thus found that converts' experience of the Spirit stood in continuity with the experience of the early church, and this contributed to the expectation that they would be able to wield the same spiritual powers, including the power of prophecy and visionary experience.

The responses to such expectations by leading revivalist preachers is noteworthy. George Whitefield's strategy was to argue that the experiences of the early church were exceptional, and not akin to the contemporary context. He argued that supernatural spiritual activities only occurred at the establishment of a 'new Revelation' of God, such as the 'first settling of the mosaic and gospel dispensation'. In the 'nominally Christian' transatlantic world of the eighteenth century, however, Whitefield argued 'there need not [be] outward miracles, but only an inward cooperation of the *Holy Spirit* with the *word*, to prove that *Jesus* is the *Messiah*'.[27] Edwards's approach was similar, as he argued it was more likely that 'God should give immediate revelations to his saints in the dark times of popery, than now in the approach of the most glorious and perfect state of his church on earth'.[28] He also invited his readers to pay attention to 1 Corinthians 12:31: 'covet earnestly the best gifts: and yet shew I unto you a more excellent way'. For Edwards, this verse indicated that the experience of the Spirit would be mediated through the more subtle 'grace of the spirit, which summarily consists in charity and divine love'.[29] Whitefield's and Edwards' careers coincided with what David Bebbington has depicted as an 'uniformally postmillennial' eschatological culture in transatlantic evangelicalism.[30] That is to say, for many prominent revivalist authors, the millennial age would not coincide with a radical break within history. As Crawford Gribben has suggested, Edwards's writings show a consistent belief in the improvement of life on earth, culminating in the eventual overthrow of the antichristian papacy.[31] For both Whitefield and Edwards, then, the apparent emergence of miraculous and ecstatic religious experiences within their congregations, needed to be carefully managed so as not to incite the hope that the transatlantic revivals were themselves the inauguration of a blessed, and distinct, eschatological age. In these authors' responses to the expectation of prophetic gifts within their communities of converts, we can see how preachers across the Atlantic employed similar rhetorical strategies to manage expectations, place the revival in an appropriate context within salvation history, and to defend their activities from external critics. In encouraging a revival of the experience of the Spirit of the early church, early evangelical revivalists had to be careful not to encourage a revival of early Christian charismatic prophecy: an activity which was inappropriate, and indeed damaging, in an eighteenth-century context.

One of Whitefield's strategies in *The Indwelling of the Spirit* was to underplay the idea that the evangelical revival constituted a new and distinct epoch of revelation in world history, akin to God's revelation to Moses and in Jesus. Yet it is clear that, at times, other authors felt that the revival was in fact the precursor of a new dispensation, and a key stage in the fulfilment of the Bible's prophetic hopes for the future. In 1742, Jonathan Edwards offered his reflections on the evangelical revival, and argued:

'Tis not unlikely that this work of God's Spirit, that is so extraordinary and wonderful, is the dawning, or at least a prelude, of that glorious work of God, so often foretold in Scripture, which in the progress and issue of it, shall renew the world of mankind. If we consider... how long this event has been expected by the church of God, and ... consider what the state of things now is, and has for a considerable time been, in the church of God and world of mankind, we can't reasonably think otherwise, than that the beginning of this great work of God must be near.[32]

Edwards's language here, with its optimism that the experience of the Spirit amongst the congregations of New England was perhaps the start of the eschatological upheavals envisaged by prophetic texts such as Revelation 21 and Isaiah 65:17, was echoed by a number of other revivalist leaders. In 1742, upon witnessing conversions in Cambuslang and Kilsyth in Scotland, John Erskine wrote a tract in which he argued that the success of George Whitefield's preaching, and the international scope of the revival, pointed to the conclusion that 'we have Ground to expect a speedy Implement of these prophecies relative to the latter ages of the Church'.[33]

This eschatological interpretation of the revival is perhaps unsurprising when we consider the interest that key figures such as Edwards and Wesley had in the interpretation of biblical prophecy. Edwards wrote at length on the Apocalypse, and demonstrated a clear interest in periodising history against the scenes presented in the text. In a tract published in 1747, Edwards attempted to argue that Zechariah 8:22—which in the King James Version states 'many people and strong nations shall come to seek the Lord of hosts in Jerusalem, and to pray before the Lord'—was an unfulfilled prophecy which would be fulfilled through an ambitious coordinated prayer programme with evangelical communities across the world, of which the inception of prayer societies on both sides of the Atlantic from October 1744 to November 1746 was an important precursor.[34] In this work, Edwards supported his claim that history was approaching a climactic moment by linking events in the Book of Revelation to events in the history of the church. Turning his eye to the contemporary Jacobite rebellion in Britain in 1745–1746, Edwards depicted the era as one which represented an intensification of 'Antichristian powers against the Protestant interest'. He argued, however, that the 'extensive awakening of many thousands in England, Wales and Scotland, and almost all the British provinces in North America' indicated that 'God was about to do something more glorious ... and that these unusual commotions are the forerunners of something exceeding glorious approaching'.[35] For Edwards, evangelicals' experiences of persecution and revival—across the transatlantic world—pointed forward to the inception of God's kingdom on earth, the promises of texts such as Revelation 11:15–7 inaugurated through the united prayers of God's evangelical 'saints' in America, England, Scotland, and Wales.[36] John Wesley also, in his *Explanatory Notes on the New Testament*, printed a schema presenting scenes from Revelation alongside events in world history which fulfilled John's visions which predicted the destruction of the beast (Revelation 19–20) in 1836.[37] For Edwards and Wesley, the Bible provided a clear means of decoding world history, and thus evangelicals could—to a degree—find their own role in human history mapped out through the exposition of biblical prophecy.

Interpretations of the revival as the fulfilment of biblical prophecy, however, were rich fodder for the evangelicals' critics. Charles Chauncy, an ardent censurer of the revival in New England, lamented Edwards's intimations of millennial speculation. Chauncy affirmed his own expectation of a 'glorious state of things in the last days', but argued 'for the *particular Time* when this will be, it *is not for us to know it, the Father having put it in his own Power*'.[38] As for Edwards's specific suggestion that the revival would lead to the renewal of the world, Chauncy replied:

> what are such Suggestions but the Fruit of Imagination? Or at best, uncertain Conjecture? And can any good End be answered in endeavouring, upon Evidence absolutely precarious, to instill into the Minds of People a Notion of the *millennium* State, as what is now going to be introduced; yea, and of AMERICA, as that Part of the World... where this glorious Scene of Things 'will, probably, first begin?'[39]

Edwards repudiated Chauncy's claim that he had predicted the specific onset of the millennium. In a letter to William McColloch in Cambuslang, Edwards assured his revivalist colleague that:

> I looked upon the late wonderful revivals of religion as forerunners of those glorious times so often prophesied of in the Scripture ... But there are many that know that I have from time to time added, that there would probably be many sore conflicts and terrible convulsions ... before this work shall have subdued the world, and Christ's kingdom shall be everywhere established and settled in peace, which will be the beginning of the millennium ...[40]

When pushed, Edwards would not unequivocally equate the awakenings of the 1730s and 1740s with the onset of the millennium in Revelation 20. However, it is clear that Edwards, as well as many other revivalist leaders in Britain, saw their activities as evidence that the revival was a prelude to the eventual establishment of Christ's kingdom on earth. Additionally, leaders like Edwards, Erskine, and Wesley, set great store in the ability of biblical prophecy to give shape to human history. To this end, we can discern a keen interest in going back to the Bible—and, in particular, texts concerned with prophecy and prophetic acts—in order to account for the experience of evangelical conversion and revival. Whitefield, Edwards, Erskine, and Wesley looked to biblical prophecy to see how converts' experience of prophetic inspiration squared with the experiences of the early church, and to discern how the revival may have fitted in to God's plan for the future of the church.

10.3 Revivalists as Prophets

Thus far, we have examined the connections between prophecy and early revivalism by looking at how pre-eminent figures within the movement reacted to prophetic claimants, and how they interpreted their movements in the light of biblical prophecy. Is it possible, however, to see intimations of prophecy in the writings and actions of revivalist leaders? That is to say, were key preachers and leaders such as Wesley, Whitefield, and Edwards seen as prophets in their own right? We have noted how, in their writings, these figures attempted to dampen down the expectation that converts would share in the early church's ability to prophesy. How far, however, did these writers draw upon prophetic language and ideas to account for their own experiences of conversion and of subsequent evangelical ministry?

When George Whitefield preached in America at the end of 1739, the *New England Weekly Journal* gave an account of him preaching in New York. At the onset, the reporter claimed that he felt Whitefield was a 'good man' but that 'some *Enthusiasm* might have mix'd itself with his Piety'. Seeing the energy which greeted Whitefield when he saw him preach in a field did not entirely dispel the reporter's doubts, 'But as I tho't I saw a visible Presence of God with Mr. *Whitefield*, I kept my Doubts to myself.' It was witnessing Whitefield preaching at the local Presbyterian church that evening, however, that changed the correspondent's mind:

I never in my Life saw so attentive an Audience: Mr. *Whitefield* spake as one having Authority: All he said was *Demonstration, Life* and *Power*! The People's Eyes and Ears hung on his Lips. They greedily devour'd every Word. I came Home astonished! Every Scruple vanished. I never saw nor heard the like, and I said within my self, *Surely God is with this Man of a Truth*.[41]

The depiction of Whitefield preaching as 'one having Authority' is a clear allusion to the reaction given to Jesus's teaching in the Sermon on the Mount in Matthew 7:29, and in Mark 1:22, as the author presents Whitefield as Christ-like in his preaching.[42] The language of the reporter's letter was also used, albeit more sardonically, in a letter by Charles Chauncy to a minister in Edinburgh, published in 1742, who claimed:

The Minds of People in this Part of the World, had been greatly prepossest in Favour of Mr. *Whitefield*, from the Accounts transmitted of him ... as a *Wonder of Piety, a Man of God*, so as *no one was like him*: Accordingly, when he came to *Town* ... he was received as though he has been an *Angel of God*; yea, *a God come down in the Likeness of Man*.[43]

The elevated presentations of Whitefield's preaching in print culture during the revival underscore the fervour with which his ministry was greeted in America. Yet, more than this, Whitefield's supporters could describe him in terms which echoed the presentation of Jesus in the gospels: a teacher whose supreme authority was marked by God's very presence.

Undoubtedly, the description of Whitefield in the *New England Weekly Journal* is embellished for rhetorical effect. Yet, when we probe Whitefield's own journals, we can see that the preacher uses language to describe his experience in terms which strongly echo the biblical prophetic tradition. In an entry from 1735, Whitefield wrote:

How often have I been carried out beyond myself when sweetly meditating in the fields! How assuredly have I felt that Christ dwelt in me, and I in him! ... Not that I was always upon the mount; sometimes a cloud would overshadow me; but the Sun of Righteousness quickly arose and dispelled it, and I knew it was Jesus Christ that revealed Himself to my soul.[44]

Whitefield's language of being 'upon the mount'—notable throughout the biblical tradition as being a place of revelation (see Exodus 19:20;

Matthew 5–7; the transfiguration narratives of Mark 9:2–13 and parallels; Revelation 21:10)—and being 'carried out beyond myself', present his experiences of spiritual inspiration in a prophetic mode. When Whitefield felt Christ's presence, he was carried out of himself to a place of prophetic inspiration and revelatory insight. The fact that no content of these ostensibly revelatory experiences is revealed is perhaps indicative that Whitefield is using rhetoric imbued with prophetic language to convey the intensity of his experiences to his readers, rather than making prophetic claims for himself. Nonetheless, his recourse to prophetic language indicates how applicable prophecy was as an interpretative category for understanding and expressing early evangelical experiences.

We have also seen how Jonathan Edwards's own strategies for accounting for prophetic claimants in New England had two goals: quelling the enthusiastic tendencies of those who claimed they had received prophetic insight, and drawing upon the experience of the Corinthian church to argue for the superiority of other, more benign, effects of spiritual inspiration. Yet Douglas Winiarski has suggested that Edwards himself may have contributed to the prophetic fervour that broke out amongst the early evangelical revivals. Drawing upon a manuscript which recounted Edwards's preaching in the town of Suffield in July 1741, Winiarski argues that Edwards as a preacher was 'a fervent revival promoter who had fully embraced the radical spirit of the Awakening, seemingly without reservation'.[45] In the light of testimony about the power of Edwards's own preaching, and the effects it had on certain New England audiences, we should perhaps hold in tension Edwards's keenness to decouple evangelical conversion and prophetic experience in his writings, with his apparent capacity to elicit ecstatic experiences in his congregations through his emotive preaching.

John Wesley also, in his journal entry outlining his conversion in 1738, presents his experience as akin to a divine revelation. Despairing at his sinful state, Wesley lamented that he felt condemned by God for his unholiness before writing 'Yet I hear a voice (and is it not the voice of God?) saying, "Believe and thou shalt be saved. He that believeth is passed from death unto life…"'[46] The catena of biblical quotations which came to Wesley's mind in his despair are described as an auditory experience: Wesley hearing the 'voice of God'. Whether or not Wesley's words were purely for literary or rhetorical effect, we find here another early revivalist leader presenting his experience of conversion in terms which suggest a revelatory experience: as communication from God to human sinner.

We have seen how Wesley's own encounters with evangelical prophetic claimants showed an ambivalence towards their specific claims of inspiration, rather than the concept itself. Furthermore, in his journals, we can see that Wesley himself was occasionally greeted as a prophet by converts. When preaching in Bristol in May 1739, Wesley and his colleagues oversaw a number of ecstatic conversion experiences amidst the crowd of onlookers. One amongst the crowd, a Quaker, looked on disapprovingly at Wesley's and the crowd's actions, before he 'dropped down as if thunderstruck'. As Wesley and his colleagues witnessed the man's agony, the man eventually came out of his catatonic state, 'lifted up his head, and cried aloud, "Now I know thou art a prophet of the Lord."'[47] Wesley offered no evaluative comment of this experience and simply moved on to talk about the rest of the meeting and his further experiences in Bristol. Yet Wesley's silence in response to being called a 'prophet of the Lord' is intriguing. Can his silence be taken as a tacit assent to the man's claims? Was Wesley untroubled at the idea of his successful preaching being described through the idiom of prophecy?

In any case, Wesley's stark presentation of this event, and his lack of explicit renunciation of the man's cry, is indicative of the ways in which the evangelical conversions could be presented as manifestations of prophetic authority. In their preaching ministries, in their writings, and in the testimonies of witnesses to the evangelical revival, we can consistently see prophecy and revelation used as interpretative lenses to account for the actions and experiences of important leaders of the eighteenth-century revival movement. Whitefield, Edwards, and Wesley were all seen as—and occasionally perhaps saw themselves as—taking on prophetic authority as they became figureheads of a transatlantic communion of evangelical converts.

10.4 Conclusion

Looking back on the careers of the revivalist figureheads Whitefield and Wesley, William Blake asked 'were they prophets/Or were they Idiots or Madmen?' Blake's question is one which we can see asked repeatedly of evangelical converts and leaders in the early eighteenth century. The Spirit-centred and emotionally intense nature of the evangelical conversion experience frequently gave rise to revelatory visions, catatonic ecstatic states, and claims of prophetic insight. Across a thriving transatlantic print culture, leaders of the revival were forced to defend their movement from the loaded charge of 'enthusiasm'. They employed a range of strategies to account for, and to placate, would-be prophets within their communities.

Yet, at the same time, these leaders placed great store in biblical prophecy as a method for interpreting history, and many evangelical writers saw the apparently international work of God's Spirit as an important stage in the fulfilment of the Bible's future hopes. Furthermore, they frequently depicted their own experiences of God's Spirit using language which suggested they saw them as revelatory in nature, and they were often depicted by others as having prophetic authority.

The evangelical revival did not mean that 'all the Lord's people' were to become prophets, but its leaders did affirm that converts' lives could be dramatically altered by their experience of the Spirit, which had vitiated and guaranteed the authenticity of prophets in ages past. As the outline above has demonstrated, we can see writers on both sides of the Atlantic wrestling with the consequences of this evangelical theology of prophecy from the very onset of the revival. Prophecy had a prominent, yet precarious, position in the life, thought, and experience of early eighteenth-century evangelicals. It is therefore perhaps unsurprising that the prophetic credentials of the revival's leaders could still be a subject of speculation even after their death.

Notes

1. William Blake, 'Milton: A poem', plate 22:56–23:2, in David V. Erdman (ed.), *The complete poetry and prose of William Blake*, rev. ed. (New York, 1988), p. 118.
2. All biblical quotations are from the King James Version unless otherwise indicated.
3. Michael Farrell, *Blake and the Methodists* (Basingstoke, 2014), pp. 9–10. For a further study of Blake's affinity with Methodist thought see Jennifer G. Jesse, *William Blake's religious vision: There's a Methodism in his madness* (Lanham, MD, 2013).
4. The literature on the so-called 'Great Awakening' of the early eighteenth century is vast. Questions can be raised as to whether the concurrent emergence of evangelical congregations and preachers in England, Wales, Scotland, and America (to say nothing of the broader European context of early eighteenth-century Pietism) should be seen as a unified phenomenon (*the* Evangelical Revival; *the* Great Awakening), or as a series of localised flourishings of religious fervour. Useful historical overviews of Evangelicalism in this period can be found in Mark Noll, *The rise of Evangelicalism: The age of Edwards, Whitefield and the Wesleys* (Leicester, 2004) and W.R. Ward, *The Protestant Evangelical awakening* (Cambridge, 1992).

An influential study by David Bebbington attempted to identify key theological commonalities between British evangelical groups, including conversionism, activism, biblicism, and crucicentrism. See David W. Bebbington, *Evangelicalism in modern Britain: A history from the 1730s to the 1980s* (London, 1989), pp. 2–3. For an additional study which focuses on the Revival in Britain see G.M. Ditchfield, *The Evangelical Revival* (London, 1998). For a study which offers insight into the American context of the Evangelical Revival see Thomas S. Kidd, *The Great Awakening: The roots of Evangelical Christianity in colonial America* (New Haven, CT, 2007).
Jon Butler questioned the extent to which a unified term such as '*the* Great Awakening' (italics my own) should be used when it did not feature in contemporary accounts to describe concurrent conversions in America. He argued that the term tendentiously presents a series of (in his view) localised and divergent conversion experiences as a single homogeneous movement; Jon Butler, 'Enthusiasm described and decried: The Great Awakening as interpretative fiction', *Journal of American History* 69:2 (1982), pp. 305–325. For the argument that the concept of a 'Great Awakening' was a category 'invented' through the networks of correspondence and publications forged by key figures in transatlantic revival movements see Frank Lambert, *Inventing the 'Great Awakening'* (Princeton, NJ, 1999). By contrast, Susan O'Brien saw the correspondences between Enlightenment figures on both signs of the Atlantic as a sign that revivalists saw themselves as part of an international movement with manifestations in local contexts: Susan O'Brien, 'A transatlantic community of saints: The Great Awakening and the first Evangelical network, 1735–1755', *American Historical Review* 91:4 (1986), pp. 811–832.

5. John Wesley, 24 May 1738, *Journals and diaries I (1735–38)*, ed. W.R. Ward and Richard P. Heitzenrater, Vol. 18 of *The bicentennial edition of the works of John Wesley* (Nashville, TN, 1976–), p. 249.
6. Wesley, 3 September 1740, *Journals and diaries II (1738–43)*, in *Works*, 19:166.
7. Jonathan Edwards, *A faithful narrative of the surprizing work of God in the conversion of many hundred souls in Northampton* in Perry Miller, John E. Smith, and Harry Stout (eds), *The works of Jonathan Edwards*, 26 vols. (New Haven, CT, 1957–2008), 4:207. Electronic editions of Edwards' collected works (in addition to further digital volumes of sermons) are available at http://edwards.yale.edu
8. Edwards, *A treatise concerning religious affections*, in *Works*, 2:236.
9. See Ann Taves, *Fits, trances, & visions: Explaining religion and explaining experience from Wesley to James* (Princeton, 1999), pp. 15–19.
10. George Lavington, *The enthusiasm of Methodists and Papists compared*, Second edition (London, 1749), p. 89. Italics in original.

11. George Whitefield, 'Letter 48', 12 June 1739, in *A select collection of the letters of the late Reverend George Whitefield*, 3 vols. (London, 1772), 1:52.
12. Edwards, 'Letter to the Reverend Thomas Prince', 12 December 1743, in *Works*, 16:115–126.
13. On the popularity of the conversion narrative as a genre in eighteenth-century culture, see D. Bruce Hindmarsh, *The Evangelical conversion narrative: Spiritual autobiography in early modern England* (Oxford, 2005). On his account of ecstatic experiences amongst early Methodist converts see pp. 133–135.
14. Ronald A. Knox, *Enthusiasm: A chapter in the history of religion with special reference to the XVII and XVIII Centuries* (Oxford, 1950), pp. 528–535.
15. Edwards, *A faithful narrative*, in *Works*, 4:189.
16. Douglas L. Winiarski, 'Souls filled with ravishing transport: Heavenly visions and the radical awakening of New England', *William and Mary Quarterly* 61:1 (2004), pp. 3–46. See especially p. 18.
17. Wesley, 20 May 1739, *Journals and diaries II (1738–43)*, in *Works*, 19:59.
18. Wesley, 20 May 1739, *Journals and diaries II (1738–43)*, in *Works* 19:59–60.
19. Wesley, 28 January 1739, *Journals and diaries II (1738–43)*, in *Works*, pp. 33–34.
20. Edwards, *Distinguishing marks of the work of a work of the Spirit of God*, in *Works*, 4:236–237.
21. So David S. Lovejoy, *Religious enthusiasm in the New World: Heresy to revolution* (Cambridge, MA, 1985), p. 190.
22. Edwards, *Distinguishing marks*, in *Works*, 4:237.
23. Wesley, 17 January 1739, *Journals and diaries II (1738–43)*, in *Works*, p. 32.
24. Edwards, *Distinguishing marks*, in *Works*, 4:282.
25. Whitefield, *The indwelling of the Spirit, The common privilege of all believers* (London, 1739), p. 4.
26. Edwards, *Distinguishing marks*, in *Works*, 4:278.
27. Whitefield, *Indwelling of the Spirit*, p. 7.
28. Edwards, *Distinguishing marks*, in *Works*, 4:281.
29. Edwards, *Distinguishing marks*, in *Works*, 4:278.
30. Bebbington, *Evangelicalism in modern Britain*, p. 61.
31. Crawford Gribben, *Evangelical millennialism in the trans-Atlantic world, 1500–2000* (Basingstoke, 2011), pp. 58–62.
32. Edwards, *Some thoughts concerning the revival*, in *Works* 4:353.
33. John Erskine, *The sign of the times consider'd or, the high probability, that the present appearances in New-England, and the west of Scotland, are a prelude of the glorious things promised to the church in the latter ages* (Edinburgh, 1742), pp. 9, 10–13. Erskine's role as a disseminator of evangelical literature and ideas is particularly noted by Jonathan Yeager, *Enlightened Evangelicalism:*

The life and thought of John Erskine (Oxford, 2011). For further examples of eschatological interpretations of the revival among European writers, see O'Brien, 'Transatlantic community of saints', pp. 817–818.
34. Edwards, *An humble attempt to promote agreement and visible union of God's people in extraordinary prayer*, in *Works*, 5:321–328.
35. Edwards, *Humble attempt*, in *Works*, 5:362–364, 358.
36. Edwards, *Humble attempt*, in *Works*, 5:353.
37. John Wesley, *Explanatory notes on the New Testament* (London, 1755), pp. 756–757.
38. Charles Chauncy, *Seasonable thoughts on the state of religion in New England* (Boston, MA, 1743), p. 371 (Chauncy's italics).
39. Chauncy, *Seasonable thoughts*, pp. 372–373. For an account of the debate between Chauncy and Edwards on the nature of the events surrounding the conversions in New England see Taves, *Fits, trances & visions*, pp. 20–46 and Edward M. Griffin, *Old brick: Charles Chauncy of Boston 1705–1787* (Minneapolis, MN, 1980), pp. 71–94.
40. Edwards, Letter to the Reverend William McColloch, 5 March 1744, in *Works*, 16:136.
41. Anonymous, *The New England Weekly Journal*, 4 December 1739, in Richard L. Bushman (ed.), *The Great Awakening: Documents on the revival of Religion, 1740–1745* (New York, 1970), pp. 22–23.
42. We could push this still further. If Jesus's reception after the Sermon on the Mount is the intended allusion, we may note the strong prophetic themes which pervade this section of Matthew's gospel, particularly the echoes of Moses delivering God's commands from Mount Sinai. See further, Dale C. Alison, *The new Moses: A Matthean typology* (Edinburgh, 1993), pp. 172–180.
43. Charles Chauncy, *A letter from a gentleman in Boston, to Mr. George Wishart, one of the ministers in Edinburgh, concerning the state of religion in New-England*, in Bushman, *Documents*, p. 116.
44. George Whitefield, *George Whitefield's journals* (London, 1960), p. 61.
45. Douglas L. Winiarski, 'Jonathan Edwards, enthusiast? Radical revivalism and the Great Awakening in the Connecticut Valley', *Church History* 74:4 (2005), p. 728.
46. Wesley, 22–24 May 1738, *Journals and diaries I (1735–38)*, in *Works*, 18:242.
47. Wesley, 1 May 1739, *Journals and diaries (1738–43)*, in *Works*, 19:53.

CHAPTER 11

Prophecy in the Age of Revolution

Deborah Madden

Protestant interpretations of biblical prophecy, its imagery, language, and structure, have inspired multiple re-enactments of the Bible's archetypes in numerous subcultures and geographical contexts.[1] More generally, this tradition has produced dissenters, missionaries, prophets, radicals, writers, artists, and composers, who, from Mede, Milton, and Bunyan, through to Handel and Blake, have created many different millennial visions. Metaphorical appropriations of Jerusalem and the 'Promised Land' have featured heavily in the Anglo-American cultural and literary imagination, where the 'homeland' has also been visualised in golden utopian hues.[2] More controversially, perhaps, is where covenantal Protestantism has literally built 'moral geographies' and 'elect' communities, thereby providing a materialist rationale for prophetic, millennial, mystical, or republican ways of life on both sides of the Atlantic.

This chapter has been re-worked from my earlier monograph on Richard Brothers, *The Paddington prophet: Richard Brothers's journey to Jerusalem* (Manchester, 2010). My thanks to the commissioning editor for granting permission to re-use the monograph for this chapter.

D. Madden (✉)
Department of History and Cultural Studies, University of Brighton, Brighton, UK
e-mail: d.madden2@brighton.ac.uk

Perhaps the most prominent example of trans-Atlantic prophetic millenarianism can be seen in the Shakers under Mother Ann Lee, who, in 1774, set sail for colonial America with a small group of believers. Flourishing under the spiritual outpouring of the evangelical Great Awakening, this group was one of the earliest amongst many other Protestant sects to settle in what would later become known as the 'burned over district' of New York state. It is this deeper history of trans-Atlantic millenarianism, which was harboured by Anglo-American Protestantism, that gave impetus to the so-called 'Southcottian' and Christian-Israelite millenarian prophets, where attempts were made to actualise biblical prophecy in both Britain and the United States. Broadly speaking, the 'Southcottian' framework contains a series of 'Visitations', or visionary prophets, between 1790 and 1950.[3] By 1821, under the spiritual direction of John Wroe (1782–1863), distinctive features of the Southcottian 'Visitation' scheme were systematised and consciously repeated in a number of geographical contexts, giving it a transnational identity that was rooted in trans-Atlantic millennialism.

This chapter will map out the distinct, but interconnected, prophetic narratives set down by the first three 'Visitations' within the Southcottian scheme: Richard Brothers (1757–1824), Joanna Southcott (1750–1814), and George Turner (d. 1821). Taken together, these early prophets form an interesting constellation of theological ideas that can tell us a lot about the political, intellectual, and cultural shifts taking place in Britain during the 1790s and 1800s. Their respective theologies capture Britain's emerging sense of national purpose and burgeoning empire following the loss of its American colonies and in the aftermath of the Napoleonic wars. Furthermore, each of these prophets continued to exert influence over the development of Christian Israelite theology within the broader context of Anglo-American Protestantism well beyond their own lifetime. For example, following directly on from George Turner after his death in 1821, John Wroe offered a coherent Christian Israelite movement that was more pragmatic and workable whilst promising a global pre-millennial foretaste of what they could expect at the end of time. This enabled him, unlike Brothers, Southcott or Turner, to implement and make concrete, in microscopic form, his vision of a Christian Israelite future—a groundplan—that could be repeated around the Anglosphere world in America, Australia, and New Zealand. In this sense, despite substantial differences in their theology, Wroe's Christian Israelite movement shared many of the same material features that marked Shaker, Mormon, and Millerite communities that had grown out of the age of democratic revolutions.

We will see how the prophetic narratives of Richard Brothers and Joanna Southcott interpreted different passages from Revelation within this context. Moving from a relationship of peaceful co-existence to competitive rivalry, Brothers and Southcott mined the profoundly eschatological possibilities of Revelation, believing that they alone were God's chosen instrument. Following a pre-ordained period of apocalyptic destruction, their prophetic ministry would usher in the new millennium on earth. The millenarian expectations of George Turner interacted powerfully between these competing prophets, as he oscillated from being Richard Brothers's chief conduit, to Joanna Southcott's most trusted supporter. It was Turner, in fact, who took leadership and steered the Southcottian movement after her death in 1814. Furthermore, it was Turner who would incorporate Christian Hebraic themes that would be institutionalised by later Southcottian prophets across the Atlantic world.

11.1 Protestant Biblical Prophecy: Millenarianism and Sacred Geography

A yearning for the Promised Land is a well-established tradition that is as old as the Bible itself; a recurring motif in the scriptures, it can be seen in the nomadic religious practices of Abraham and the ancient Israelites, who, devoted and obedient to Yahweh, separated themselves by living on the fringes of civilisation. Recent scholarship has attested well to the renewing power of this yearning in terms of Protestant covenantal theology and its seemingly limitless capacity in the Atlantic world to visualise, imagine, create, and re-create the Promised Land and the New Jerusalem.[4] A specifically Protestant tradition of internalising, re-enacting and actualising biblical archetypes has ensured that both its literal and metaphorical significance forms part of Anglo-American religious, cultural, national, and even racial identity.[5]

A providential framework for this national identity in Britain was initially secured by the Church of England's independence from Rome during the Elizabethan Settlement and vernacular translations of the scriptures, namely the King James Bible of 1611. With its 'true' reformed Church—as opposed to Roman Catholicism—Britain was God's 'elect' nation with a sacred mission in the story of global salvation. In its earliest usage, the 'nation' articulated the notion of divine election and a 'covenanted' people who retained an exalted role distinct from the rest of humanity. The message of salvation therefore becomes the responsibility of God's chosen, though, significantly, what Reformation theologies revealed to many, was that God's Covenant of Grace with one set of people could be claimed over and above another.

Orthodox Christianity posits that Christ's incarnation, death, and resurrection heralded the New Covenant. This was instigated by the Last Supper, but continues to be accessed by Christians through baptism, faith, and the Eucharist. During the end times, or Christ's 'Second Coming', the living and the dead are judged before his New Covenant inaugurates the new heaven and new earth. Christian nations, communities, groups, and even individuals could thus claim for themselves authentic witness over other claimants to the Covenant of Grace, evidenced most powerfully in the 'Godly' communities established during the 1620s and 1640s by Puritan settlers in the New World. As newly democratised polities, these settler communities eschewed the Church of England's ecclesiastical power, with some separatist Puritans rejecting it altogether.

Biblical typologies and prophetic narratives revolving around a covenantal faith in the newly restored Jerusalem and Holy Land were harvested by many Reformation theologies. In England and America this type of covenantal Protestantism found its fullest expression in Puritan congregationalism, though its currency within Calvinism meant that its reach was interdenominational and included Presbyterians and Baptists, as well as a plethora of millennialist sects and individuals 'dissenting' or breaking away from the Anglican fold. Accordingly, the relationship between God and humanity becomes formulated as a distinct Covenant of Grace originally set down in the Old Testament and fulfilled by Christ. This covenant carried its own 'signs' for God's chosen or elect in a myriad of contexts. Thus, for Brothers, but also Southcott and Turner, the Old Testament was not simply a series of Christological pre-figurations, but a history of how God's covenant was revealed to those specifically chosen.[6]

For Southcottian millenarians this elect status is further evidenced by the Book of Revelation which foretells Christ's Second Coming and the 'sealing' of God's 144,000 elect into the millennial kingdom (Rev. 7:1, 14:1). This number pertains to an 'ingathering' of Israel's 'lost tribes' in the Old Testament, which are also referred to in Revelation 7:1–8—hence an insistence by the more literal-minded millenarians like Richard Brothers that only 144,000 of God's elect could claim salvation.[7] Brothers held that this elect was Britain's 'hidden' Jews who had descended from Israel's lost tribes. These tribes, which he believed had settled mainly in Northern Europe, would be gathered together at the appointed time for one final journey to the Promised Land. Emphasis here on Britain's 'hidden' or 'invisible' Jews means that Brothers continues to be regarded as father of the British-Israelites, though he was by no means a straightforward Anglo-Israelite and, in fact, it was George Turner who provided a more exacting mechanical framework for these ideas. Furthermore, modern British-Israelites have been particularly testy about this repeated assertion, which they rightly say is based on historical ignorance.[8]

Brothers proclaimed that he was 'Nephew of the Almighty' with a genealogical lineage that could be traced through the biblical line of Judah. This was taken as revealed evidence of his prophetic mission to fulfil the covenant during Christ's Second Coming. To undertake this mission, Brothers would be revealed in 1795 as 'Prince of the Hebrews': Shiloh, the man-child of Revelation (Rev. 12:5), who would literally take the Jews back to rebuild Jerusalem. Brothers's unique interpretation of human redemption during the end times is clearly some distance from orthodox Christianity, which makes no 'prediction' about when Christ's return will take place and finesses the literal number of 144,000 in terms of a universal message of salvation—open to Jew and Gentile alike.

Millenarians claiming elect status believed that spiritual transformation during the end times would take as its starting point their 'authentic' apperception of the New Jerusalem, which is situated where they, as God's chosen, were dwelling. This is why some millennial groups make no claim for a literal location of Jerusalem, whilst others insist upon a physical migration to the Holy Land during the millennium. The specific location of the restored Jerusalem was therefore open to contestation between different millennialist sects or individuals. This rich history of millenarianism within the wider Protestant tradition has thus created competing visions of Jerusalem, simultaneously mystical, republican, and patriotic. The varied appropriations of Revelation, but also the scriptures in general, thus makes Protestant Christianity inherently divisive—an aspect that was, of course, anticipated, feared, and condemned by the papacy.

Whilst Protestantism was certainly an important factor in the construction of a distinctively British identity, the nature of this was open to interpretation. The sheer variety of denominations on the Protestant spectrum created innumerable sectarian divides, which, though rooted in the Reformation, continued to affect British political life up until the nineteenth century when religious tests and legal restrictions barring nonconformists and dissenters from public life were finally removed. Sectarian division was most apparent between Anglicans and nonconformists. This was notable in Britain's colonies, where Protestant migrants, travellers, and settlers carried with them highly individualised variants of a much larger Protestant culture.[9] For many Protestant settlers and missionaries, the New World offered the same millennial promise as the sacred geography of the Holy Land and was quite literally 'the land of milk and honey'.

When tackling the complicated issue of national identity and sectarian difference, the reciprocal influences of religion and politics over migratory habits and cultural practice are difficult to determine. An example of this can be seen in the case of Brothers, who was himself a product of the colonial New World. His prophetic ministry was an intricate matrix of theological commitment, patriotic loyalty, and colonial superiority, which nevertheless did not preclude a searing political and moral criticism of Britain's imperial expansion and slave trade. Brothers, as the first prophet in the so-called Southcottian 'Visitation' scheme, used the bloody and apocalyptic images of Revelation to denounce Britain's colonial trade in slaves and her imperial ambitions in the aftermath of the French Revolution.

In this, he shared much in common with the radicalism of Blake—both men had been forged in the fires of revolutionary ferment created by American Independence and French Jacobinism. Brothers criticised Britain's sin of slavery, though he also imbibed its maritime colonial confidence when explicating detailed plans literally to conquer the Holy Land. Undoubtedly, this confidence was determined by a successful career as an officer in the British Navy, but also his childhood in Newfoundland, which was an established British colony; Newfoundland was, of course, England's first step into the New World in 1583. Brothers's prophetic ministry was premised on an unshakeable faith in the spiritual enlightenment of elect followers and the fulfilment of biblical prophecy as divined by him acting as God's instrument. The note of Jacobin radicalism sounded in his early prophecies should not obscure the strong assumption of religious, cultural, and colonial authority implied by his desire to literally rebuild Jerusalem in Palestine.

The global spread of Judeo-Christianity has meant that the sacred territory of the Holy Land has been imagined, envisioned, and actualised in a range of historical, social, and geographical contexts.[10] Given Britain's strong tradition of providential history of election and divine covenant, it should come as no surprise that use of such biblical typologies can be discerned amongst a more marginal group of millenarian prophets gathered together under the aegis of the 'Southcottian Visitation'. This Visitation scheme is a retrospectively applied theological system of belief in the prophetic gifts held by specific messengers such as Brothers,

Southcott, and Turner, who, so it was believed, were typologies related to the trumpeting angels in Revelation (Rev. 8–11).[11] The scheme was first devised by John Wroe, though utilised again by subsequent prophets and believers. All of the messengers, or prophets in the scheme, were thought to signal the latter days before God's promise of restoration for his elect.

The prophets listed in the Southcottian Visitation disseminated their own individualised message, though, after Brothers, this was rooted in the larger corpus of Joanna Southcott's millennial texts and substantially added to by later prophets following in her tradition. Dissemination was achieved primarily through biblically inspired writings and divine 'communications', but often supplemented by poetic verse, songs, architectural designs, domestic interior spaces, sacred objects, clothing, and religious rites.[12] The recurring use of poetry and song amongst Southcottian prophets might usefully be regarded as what Benedict Anderson refers to as 'unisonance': 'the echoed physical realisation of the imagined community', where members are brought together in a vision which seeks to extend its reach over thousands of years.[13] Evidence of this can be seen in Brothers's poetry, which he used to imagine the rebuilding of Jerusalem and its extended territory. For Brothers, Jerusalem would literally represent an act of shared faith that was vivid and tangible. His printed descriptions thus sustained a clear sense of collective purpose, irrespective of any empirical evidence to the contrary. This is perhaps pertinent, given that his detailed descriptions of Jerusalem were written from the punishing confines of an asylum.

Taken together, Brothers, Southcott, and Turner cover an important phase of British history; these prophets believed that they were witness to the apocalyptic age foretold in Revelation. Political ferment at home and abroad ignited apocalyptic expectations amongst English Jacobins and reformers, as well as artists, poets, and writers. Drawing on a rich tradition of millenarian exegesis, those with an apocalyptic cast of mind turned to the prophetic books of Daniel and Revelation to make sense of contemporary events, whilst nourishing an expectation for great transformation. The line between political agitation and millenarian anticipation was by no means clear cut and, in fact, the language of prophecy was scrutinised by government authorities during the 1790s to seek out its revolutionary inflection. This conflation had the potential, as Jon Mee has amply demonstrated, to breed a virulent form of 'dangerous enthusiasm'.[14] The king-killing visions that led to Brothers's arrest in 1795 were regarded as highly symbolic because they excited in the public a desire for radical change. To 'imagine' the King's death, as John Barrell reminds us, was an act of treason itself.[15]

Brothers and Southcott believed that it was through their prophetic declarations that Britain would be saved from the danger of home-grown radicalism and Napoleon's invading troops. As Britain struggled to foster national purpose following the erosion of its American colonies and the upsurge of Jacobinism inspired by the French Revolution, prophets like Brothers, Southcott, and Turner occupied a contradictory place between millenarianism, radicalism, national identity, and colonialism during the 1790s.

11.2 REVELATION RE-ALIGNED: THE PROPHETIC NARRATIVES OF RICHARD BROTHERS, JOANNA SOUTHCOTT, AND GEORGE TURNER, 1790–1820

All of the prophets listed in the Southcottian Visitation scheme started out as Anglicans before they took a dramatic shift towards millenarianism. Their route through to biblical prophecy, however, was informed by very different forms of religious dissent. Richard Brothers came under the mystical sway of Emanuel Swedenborg during the 1780s, when London was awash with cheaply printed visionary texts.[16] Meanwhile, Joanna Southcott's millenarianism was informed by Methodist dissent, though Methodism had not yet separated from the Church of England and was still nominally Anglican. Similarly, Turner's attraction to Brothers's prophetic declarations in 1794 was motivated by his involvement with Methodism in Manchester, Leeds, and Lancaster.

Brothers's prophetic call promised spiritual enlightenment and a differently ordered reality for those who believed. From this perspective, his messianic and damning indictment of George III in his first published work, *Revealed Knowledge of the Prophecies and Times* (1794), threatened to carry revolutionary implications. One month after the second volume of *Revealed Knowledge* was published in 1795 the government arrested Brothers for 'treasonable practices'. Broadsheet commentary and pamphlet debates were intensified by the fact that *Revealed Knowledge* elicited the support of prominent MP and renowned scholar, Nathaniel Brassey Halhed.[17] Yet although Brothers utilised the rhetoric of radicalism for these early prophetic works, he was operating from a completely different basis. Like Tom Paine, Brothers believed that Britain was teetering on the brink of destruction and penned a powerful commentary on what was taking place in the aftermath of the French Revolution. Unlike Paine, however, he was not convinced that parliamentary or radical politics could provide a satisfactory and thoroughgoing solution to the problems facing Britons.[18]

In his appearance and demeanour Brothers did not conform to expectations of what a religious 'enthusiast' should look like—usually 'enthusiasts' who conflated reason and revelation bore the marks of such madness in their physical appearance.[19] Observers were troubled by the fact that this 'prophet' was disarmingly handsome, well-spoken, mild mannered, and even 'polite'. As an ex-Lieutenant who had served in the British Navy, he impressed those quick to brand him an enthusiast, which served only to arouse further curiosity and comment. He became a fashionable topic of conversation in salons and drawing rooms, which is how Joanna Southcott first came to hear about the 'Paddington prophet' whilst working as a servant in Exeter. In April 1795 *Harrison's Lady Pocket Magazine* carried a portrait of the Prince of Wales, Richard Brothers, and the Italian Opera House in the Haymarket.[20]

William Sharp, a renowned engraver, pledged his support for 'the Man whom God has appointed' by producing a handsome engraving, which stood in stark contrast to James Gillray's famous caricature of Brothers as 'Prophet of the Hebrews', printed on 5 March 1795, the day after he was arrested for treason. His gentlemanly attire, admired by many, convinced others that, if not an 'enthusiast', Brothers must certainly be a very clever and designing 'impostor'—someone who deliberately set out to exploit the credulity of those with a weak or superstitious mind. Set against the backdrop of 'dangerous enthusiasm' stoked up by the French Revolution, the visionary quality of Brothers's writings, combined with its anti-war rhetoric and quasi-republican idiom, produced palpable fear. This fear, real or imagined, was nevertheless used with expedient political efficiency to strengthen William Pitt's resolve when attempting to quash radicalism in London, potently illustrated by the introduction of repressive legislation between 1794 and 1795. Brothers's arrest served as a useful public example; following a Privy Council hearing and medical inquiry, he was deemed criminally insane and in May 1795 confined to Fisher House, a private asylum, for eleven years.[21]

Brothers's startling claim to be 'Nephew of the Almighty', with his promise to literally restore the Jews to their homeland and visionary hopes for a renewed Jerusalem, formed part of an effective riposte to the Babylonian London of Pitt's administration. This rhetoric was channelled into perfecting an alternative 'plan of the estate': God's own city. His obsession with sacred Hebraic imagery and poetry saw him set down a vivid topography of the Promised Land in his *Address to the Members of his Britannic Majesty's Council* (1798) and *Description of Jerusalem* (1801), both of which were written from the confines of Fisher House. When depicting his detailed architectural vision of Jerusalem, Brothers adopted an almost static neo-classical form of prose and poetry to convey specific Hebraic themes. In this, his style was more intellectually grounded and controlled than the formless, mystical, visionary, and deeply personal communications of Joanna Southcott or George Turner. His theological, intellectual, and literary interests drew from a deep well of Protestant piety, a tradition that could also find itself aligned during this period with 'Hasidism', a compelling force within European Judaism, which privileged the charismatic, primitive faith of the Jewish homeland over and above a legalistic framework developed by *Haskalah* Enlightenment scholars or learned Rabbis.[22]

Like Blake, Jerusalem offered Brothers a 'discursive space' where spiritual, religious, political, intellectual, and creative liberty could flourish. Blake created a mythic congruence between London and Jerusalem to envisage a 'prelapsarian' and druidic past, where humanity was free once more. Importantly, his city was located in both Britain and Israel. Blake's Jerusalem, which was an emanation of Albion, exposed the multi-layered nature of redemption that was simultaneously personal and collective. His concept is suggestive of a spiritual state of existence, which will be re-established in England's 'green and pleasant land'. This vision, which was in no way metaphorical—it was visionary—nevertheless turned away from the literal site of Jerusalem in a move that was the complete reversal of Brothers's colonial expansion.[23] Here, Blake shared with Joanna Southcott an 'inward' and spiritual vision of Jerusalem. Southcott, the Devon-born prophetess, came to national prominence in 1801 when she claimed to be the 'woman Clothed with the sun' in the Book of Revelation.

Morton Paley has suggested that Blake can hardly have been unaware of Brothers's description of Jerusalem, which was published as work on his own Jerusalem was getting under way.[24] Brothers's intention, on the other hand, was to literally rebuild Jerusalem as another London in a specific geographic space, reconstructing its neo-classical buildings and thoroughfares on a correspondingly postmillennial scale. For Brothers, London was located in Jerusalem and functioned as its municipal desideratum. The extent to which Brothers was influenced by the scale of neo-classical architectural works being undertaken in London at this time, such as John Soane's Bank of England, can be seen in his plans.[25]

As was the case for Southcott and Turner, Brothers claimed a burden of responsibility for the Jews, whose rejection of Christ had brought salvation to the Gentiles. The Jews were owed a debt of gratitude, but their conversion to Christianity would finally rid the world of evil, thereby completing salvation for the elect.[26] To undertake this mission, Brothers would literally take the Jews back to Jerusalem to expedite the millennium. On this, he shared something in common with Napoleon who developed a similar interest in the Holy Land and Jewish repatriation.

The overtly Hebraic themes deployed by Brothers were less important to Joanna Southcott, who was concerned to emphasise the pivotal role played by a woman—herself as second Eve—in the same eschatological story. It was Turner who provided a framework for these Christian Hebraic ideas, though his views were inconsistent and subject to revision. For example, under Southcott's influence, he believed that Jewish Restoration was more symbolic than real, stating in July 1812 that Israel merely represented the community of those faithful she had already sealed, as opposed to the actual Promised Land envisaged by Brothers.[27] As Turner's prophetic ministry began to gather its own momentum in 1818, he found himself reverting to a more literalist position, which closely resembled that set down in Brothers's *Description of Jerusalem*.[28]

Brothers believed that the Jews were symbolic carriers or signs but, unlike Southcott who engaged with the Jewish community living in the East End of London, he did not believe that direct involvement with contemporary Judaism was necessary. In addition to this, Brothers thought there was a greater preponderance of Israel's lost tribes amongst the British population. This type of speculative genealogy was already popular from the late eighteenth-century onwards in Britain,[29] but where he parted company with other Anglo-Israelites was his insistence that England was not the Jewish homeland. He also suggested that individuals of high rank and status selected by him had descended from the tribe of Judah, which, of course, was not amongst those tribes that were lost.[30]

Brothers's writings post-1795 retain the same anger and heightened sense of injustice concerning the corruption and immorality of modernity as he sees it, though the self-consciously marginal, displaced, and millenarian prophet of *Revealed Knowledge* becomes God's powerful agent: the appointed king and ruler of a new 'Hebrew Constitution' in postmillennial Jerusalem. In this context, Brothers is presented adorned with imperial robes, as seen in an engraved image printed by another disciple and supporter, John Finleyson [Finlayson], and included in the posthumously published *New Covenant Between God and His People* (1830). The culmination of Brothers's prophetic journey is presented as being consummated in the strange birth-marriage to his 'woman clothed with the sun' and 'Queen of Israel'. Brothers is the bridegroom prophesied in Revelation (19:7) and his marriage represents a new covenant promised by God. It was this interpretation of Revelation that first embroiled Brothers in a theological and eschatological conflict with the prophetess and 'woman clothed with the sun', Joanna Southcott.

Turner's spiritual orientation towards Brothers had come to him as he experimented with devotional and ecstatic forms of Methodism in Manchester, Yorkshire, and Lancashire. An examination of Turner's journals for those years between 1795 and 1801 shows that many of his divine 'communications' came to him via Methodist ministers. This theological and social context provided him with much needed spiritual nourishment, and, having seen John Wesley some years before in Leeds, Turner firmly believed that 'the Lord shone' upon the people called Methodists. At a Methodist Conference in Manchester during July 1795 he watched in both awe and adoration as the preachers, some of whom he knew personally, lifted their faces 'up towards heaven ... their eyes wide open, intensely praying ...'[31]

This image stayed with Turner and he recalled it in 1801 during a vision or 'apparition' in which Wesley himself appeared.[32] Turner eventually spoke out against Methodist preachers when, despite his best efforts, they refused to acknowledge the prophecies of Richard Brothers and, later, Joanna Southcott. Nevertheless, his close connection with Methodism attracted many rank-and-file members to Southcott's cause in the years following 1802 when he ceased being Brothers's supporter. Later, Turner would adopt the Methodist model of Conference and centrally organised bureaucracy when structuring his own Southcottian movement in 1814.

It was Brothers's move from being a simple prophet or instrument carrying God's message to the self-fashioning cultivation of a Solomonic personality which led Southcott and, eventually, Turner, to denounce him as an angel of light who had become like Napoleon and Satan's puppet. The conflation Southcott made between Brothers and Napoleon was particularly apposite; calling as they did on the powers of darkness, these men were in league with the Antichrist. They had come at this tumultuous time to challenge God's authority and keep humanity in spiritual bondage. In the eschatological war between good and evil, Satan was making his presence felt in the work of Brothers and Napoleon.[33]

For Southcott, the age-old battle between God and Satan, which had its origins in Genesis, was now drawing to a dramatic close, as prophesied powerfully in Revelation. Southcott's apocalyptic vision of how God would defeat Satan, and his judgement on Man's disobedience since the Fall, involved a role that was assigned to her alone. She penned a letter to Nathaniel Brassey Halhed in 1802, shortly after her move from Exeter to London, explaining Revelation in terms of Genesis, stating that the scriptures have been revealed in their perfect form to one who was 'ordered to begin at the last and go back to the first'.[34] As the bride prophesied in Revelation (19:7), Southcott was making herself 'ready to declare unto all men the coming of the Lord', who would place a crown of twelve stars upon her head and place the moon at her feet.[35]

Genesis was the *fons et origo* around which the competing hermeneutics of Revelation offered by Brothers and Southcott revolved. In *Revealed Knowledge* Brothers had dismissed the idea that the 'woman clothed with the sun' represented a second Eve, believing instead that she was birth mother and consort to him as King of Israel.[36] The patriarchal nature of this theology, present in his first published work, was restated in his *Dissertation on the Fall of Eve* (1802). This was Brothers's public riposte to a private letter that had been sent to him at Fisher House by Southcott. On 7 June 1802 Southcott wrote to Brothers expressing serious doubts about the authenticity of his revealed knowledge. *Dissertation on the Fall of Eve*, an exegesis of Gen. 3:13, was written specifically to correct this rival and nemesis. Keen to make a distinction between his divinely ordained mission and the claims of a woman displaying defective learning and reasoning, the *Dissertation* deploys every marker of rational, Lockean language against his 'enthusiastic' opponent.

Southcott's primary concern with the complicating issue of gender remained within a theologically orthodox interpretation of the serpent as Satan in the Creation story. For Southcott the Devil was in the detail of Man's mischief, hell-bent on offending God with pride and vanity—characteristics that had seen Adam wrongfully blame Eve for their exile from Paradise. As the second Eve, Southcott would absorb this injustice in the form of bodily salvation by giving birth to the man-child, Shiloh. By contrast, Brothers took a more global perspective by locating the root of evil, Original Sin, in human institutions.[37]

Brothers saw how the relationship between Man and God was expressed as a structural formation in Genesis. He did not see Genesis purely in terms of an allegory. Rather than apportioning blame to Adam, Eve or, in fact, Satan, Brothers believed that it was the very conjunction of finite and infinite, humanity and divinity, which produced the evil of temptation, disobedience, and pride.[38] Like Blake, Brothers saw evil, not as some original act of disobedience, but as a naïve misuse of very human faculties.[39] He regarded the serpent as merely acting as a powerful place-marker for Original Sin. In this sense, the viper had been retrospectively personified by man-made theological and cultural histories of the demonic. His solution was to clear layers of corruption that had accrued since the Fall by rebuilding Jerusalem from its foundations.

Before her move from Exeter to the metropolis in May 1802 Southcott had expressed only a passing interest in Brothers, claiming, in fact, that she had not read any of his work.[40] On arrival, she found his ever-faithful but much depleted circle of supporters lacking in organisation, bereft as they were of practical leadership: Brothers was incarcerated indefinitely and his supporter Halhed lived as a recluse. Southcott immediately took matters in hand by throwing herself into obtaining Brothers's liberty. One week after her arrival, she gathered together the so-called 'Seven Stars' to help petition for Brothers's release. The 'Seven Stars', most of whom were Brothers's supporters, met the prophetess when they travelled to Exeter in December 1801 to authenticate Southcott's communications and prophecies. These men, who felt called by God to judge her prophetic works, included George Turner, Peter Morrison, Thomas Foley, Stanhope Bruce, Thomas Webster, William Sharp, and John Wilson.[41]

Much of the groundwork for her support in London had already been laid in the correspondence that took place between Southcott and these men in 1801. Indeed, Brothers's supporters actually believed that Southcott had been providentially sent to them. Through her, God would vindicate and liberate their leader. For Southcott, adroit management of this discipleship worked in tandem with a private correspondence to Brothers in which she questioned the authenticity of his revelations and theology.[42] Southcott's machinations effectively put an end to Brothers's mission well before his release in 1806; by 1808 she had gained a very sizeable following of her own and continued to exert influence over those she 'sealed'. Brothers never regained his credibility as a prophet and, with the exception of Scottish lawyer John Finleyson, lost all of his followers to Southcott.

Before 1801 Turner remained confident that those prophecies declared by Richard Brothers in 1794 would come to pass. By 1802 the picture had changed with Southcott's arrival and Turner was soon gravitating towards her camp.[43] It could be said that Turner understood better than either Brothers or Southcott how the spirit of prophecy functioned theologically. This was how he could remain faithful to Southcott's prophetic promises in December 1814 when followers struggled to comprehend the failure of her predictions following her unexpected death. Southcott astonished her contemporaries in February of that year with an announcement that, at the age of 64, she was going to give birth to a baby: Shiloh, the man-child prophesied in Revelation. A post-mortem conducted by physicians established with clinical certainty that Southcott had not, in fact, been pregnant or due to give birth before her death. Following this bitter disappointment amongst her followers, Turner gave reassurance, direction, and prophetic continuity to her flock by telling them that God's word and promise would stand: the birth of Shiloh, Southcott's spiritual child, would come to pass during his prophetic ministry.[44]

In January 1815 Turner declared that he, as God's newly appointed servant, could 'reveal' the mystery of Southcott's spiritual vocation and legacy, whilst providing some clues about her death. Turner suggested that both Richard Brothers and Joanna Southcott were instruments through which the Spirit of prophecy had worked. Now God was utilising a new instrument, George Turner, to carry forward his covenant. With this message, Turner initiated an umbrella organisation under which Southcottians, Turnerites, and followers of Brothers gathered. He managed to win over a large proportion of her followers in the North and South-West of England, though it was also the case that key members of Southcott's inner circle regarded his bid for leadership as opportunistic. This division became even more acrimonious when Turner claimed to have experienced a spiritual encounter with the prophetess in February 1815.[45]

Following Southcott's death, Turner revisited and reintroduced particular Hebraic themes that had been set down by Brothers, though he placed much heavier emphasis upon tracing Jewish lines of descent and sought to identify exactly what distinguished Southcottian followers from the profane multitude. He carried this out in a fairly rigorous fashion; 'speaking in the Spirit', these origins were divined by Rebecca Woods, a Southcottian follower from the West-Country, but transcribed by her amanuensis, Ann Searle. The transcripts were authenticated in London by a 'witness', Samuel Gompertz, who was Secretary and Treasurer to Turner's committee, which was based in Granby Gardens, Lambeth.[46] Gompertz, a converted Jew from London's East End, had served as assistant preacher at one of Southcott's chapels in the city.[47] He sent a number of lists or rolls with the names of Turner's followers to Searle and Woods for clarification. These genealogies were underpinned by Turner's austere directive for followers to observe the Mosaic Law. Turner's ministry made selective use of Brothers's Christian-Hebraic ideas, though these were subverted into a prophetic narrative that further enhanced Southcott's legacy as the 'Woman clothed with the sun'.[48]

11.3 Conclusion

It is in the crevices between millenarian Protestantism and political radicalism that the theological narratives offered by Brothers, Southcott, and Turner intersect so powerfully. The appropriation of a female redemptrix by Turner in 1802, for example, took place at a time when discussions about the moral influence of a specifically feminine sensibility reached its height in the late eighteenth and early nineteenth centuries. When Southcott claimed that only woman could do the work of deliverer where man had so miserably failed—and here she had Brothers clearly within her sights—this tonal register chimed in with a much broader evangelical religious and literary culture. The pious redemptive female was frequently invoked and envisioned to heal those violent revolutionary forces wrought by political, economic, and social turmoil. Both community and nation could entrust women with familial, domestic, moral, and spiritual affairs, matters of the heart which would yield positive results beyond the confines of her feminine sphere, seen most notably in philanthropic campaigns revolving around the transatlantic slave trade, missionary work and, at a more localised level, Anti-Corn Law Leagues. It has been observed that this configuration of gender politics worked its influence over artisans and factory workers to such an extent that socialist radicalism amongst the British working class was noticeably 'muted' as a result.[49] Southcott, who disliked political radicalism, nevertheless utilised popular discourses around political agitation to formulate a specifically feminine piety by way of galvanising her prophetic mission in the public sphere.

The prevalence of this domestic ideology remains difficult to gauge with any degree of accuracy, though many of Southcott's followers felt reassured by a prophetic narrative which orientated itself towards local concerns and grievances felt by ordinary folk—as opposed to any ambitious restorationist claims literally to rebuild Jerusalem. In this, Southcott's moral critique blended millenarianism with an incipient British patriotism that contrasted markedly with the global covenantal theology of Brothers.[50] Her interest in operating at a more parochial level has led Eitan Bar-Yosef to suggest that Southcott, like Blake, envisaged the New Jerusalem residing, not in the literal Holy Lands, but at the very heart of England. For this reason, he says, Southcott might easily be regarded as 'a prophetess against Empire'.[51] Whilst the tenor of this argument can be taken in good faith, it is also true that Southcott's metaphorical and literal figurations of Jerusalem are not so easily determined. Nor were her concerns purely local, and Southcott's millennial perspective ultimately offered a global mission for her elect.[52]

The prophetic narratives and moral geographies envisioned by Brothers, Southcott, and Turner fitted within a much larger context of Protestant millennialism and biblical prophecy located within Britain and America. Key factors can account for the continued global reach and appeal of Southcottian theology on both sides of the Atlantic, such as the legacy of Puritan covenantal theology, combined with the democratic revolutions in America and France. These latter cataclysmic upheavals were regarded by prophets and millennialists living through the age of democratic revolution as signs that Revelation was unravelling.

The backdrop of Evangelical revivalism and development of industrial capitalism also played a major role in the spread of nineteenth- and twentieth-century Southcottianism, but specifically the emergence of Southcottian Christian Israelite theology.[53] In the context of Britain's expanding empire, the confluence of Evangelicalism and industrialisation had a profound impact on the formation of identities that were more sharply defined in terms of class and gender. The eschatological and Christian Israelite theologies enacted by later Southcottian prophets like John Wroe reflect this, as well as an individualist desire for self-discipline, improvement, and cleanliness, which sought, in an ideal earthly world, to express religious commitment through thrift and hard work. In other words, good Protestant values. When blended with the spiritual renewal of millennialism, this extended into an eschatological belief in the salvation of the elect promised by Christ's Second Coming—a missionary message spread by later Christian Israelites right across Britain's colonies.[54]

Richard Brothers, Joanna Southcott, and George Turner each attempted to negotiate and renegotiate changing conceptions about self, class, and gender during the 1790s and 1800s. To be sure, they did so within a prophetic narrative that now seems bizarre, idiosyncratic, and self-willed. Yet the prophetic narratives bequeathed by these Southcottian prophets stood at the nexus of an inherited discourse about the divine purpose of a covenantal religion in national and global terms. Their theological ideas were put forward at a time when many in the Anglo-American world wanted to explore, either literally or metaphorically, a restored Jerusalem.

Evidence of this can be seen in the growth of travel literature concerned with the Holy Land during the eighteenth and early nineteenth centuries. This popular genre offered a vivid sense of what Hilton Obenzinger refers to as 'sacred theatricality', where the traveller imagines they are re-enacting biblical scenes.[55] Clarke Garrett has also noted the important place of 'sacred theatre' in terms of creating quasi-ritualistic activities that could produce a public space for collective conversion experiences— amply tried and tested by evangelical revivalism.[56] Undoubtedly, the popularity of this genre attests well to the biblical literacy of Britain's Protestant print culture. Like the Bible itself, such travelogues created vivid imaginary spaces where readers could engage with both the metaphorical and literal Holy Land. These popular texts evinced and confirmed scriptural authority and, as Jacques Le Goff has observed, the Bible was an extremely effective instrument for the production of sacred memories with profound historical consequences.[57] The intersection between scripture, memory, and history, frequently ritualised as sacred memories, produced an extended network of religious, colonial, and cultural codes common to the Protestant tradition. When combined with ideas of eschatological missionary purpose, these codes continued to extend their influence across the Anglo-American world during the nineteenth and twentieth centuries.

As the first prophet in the Southcottian scheme, it was Richard Brothers's topography of the Holy Land that instigated a cartography of belonging. His physical and moral geography created a sacred space which, because of its alleged divine provenance, inspired loyalties that were much stronger than those historically situated in his own day. Thus an examination of Southcottian biblical prophecy, with its associated sacred geography, demonstrates the extent to which the Holy Land paradigm offered western Protestant culture an origin around which various rhetorical, metaphorical, and literal figurations of Jerusalem were envisaged. These figurations saw a convergence of national, political, cultural, and religious interests, which were linked to Jerusalem functioning as a literal or spiritual space and where Judeo-Christian prophecy would ultimately be fulfilled at the end of time. The rich religious and literary soil in which this paradigm is rooted yields particularly fruitful results in terms of investigating the relationship between millenarianism, nationalism, and imperial expansion in the years following the American and French revolutions.

Richard Brothers and Joanna Southcott utilised specific biblical archetypes from Revelation to enact different prophetic narratives against a background of eschatological expectation during the 1790s. Southcott was the female prophet and 'woman clothed with the sun' bursting onto the metropolitan scene from the provinces. Brothers was Shiloh and would-be King of Jerusalem, established in London but desperately working to retain his wavering followers whilst confined to an asylum. Their different roles and expectations of exactly how Revelation would unfold translated into a series of interconnected conflicts, which were theological, political, and gendered—though never personal. George Turner attempted to mollify these differences by synthesising the characteristic features of Brothers's Christian Hebraism.[58]

In so doing, Turner hoped to create an organisation that paid due acknowledgement to its spiritual mother, thus providing much needed continuity to Southcottians, whilst incorporating significant changes of his own. Brothers's role as the singular, romantic, and heroic prophet, writing his own future with a creative, rhetorical, and inseminating power, was a narrative no longer available to Turner. This was largely due to Southcott's highly effective strategy for emasculating Brothers by demolishing his patriarchal interpretation of Revelation, thereby retaining woman's place in the story of redemption. It was a move that insulated Southcott's prophetic claims and protected her legacy amongst those who subsequently joined the movement after her death. Turner's response was to revive the millenarian urgency of Southcott's cause by deriving practical efficiency from those available structures of Methodist bureaucracy, with its committee-led forms and procedures that had influenced his early dalliances with prophecy.

Their interpretative strategies, harvested by Protestant covenantal theology, gave Brothers, Southcott, and Turner an unstinting conviction that Revelation offered humanity a narrative of liberation and salvation. Each believed that the prophetic parts of scripture could only be understood, at God's command, through the interpretative facilities of his chosen prophet. For this reason, despite sometimes deploying the rhetoric of political radicalism, all three were inherently autocratic, seeking to establish an authority that was based exclusively on their strong, charismatic leadership. With their potent blend of prophetic freedom, which they blended seamlessly with restriction and autocracy, it might very well be said that Brothers, Southcott, and Turner were authentic prophets of the Napoleonic era.

NOTES

1. Elizabeth Elbourne, *Blood ground: Colonialism, missions and the contest for Christianity in the Cape Colony and Britain, 1799–1853* (Montreal and Kingston, 2002), p. 18.
2. The utopian tradition differs significantly to millenarian and millennialist uses of Jerusalem and the Holy Land. The distinctions between millenarian, millennial, and millennialist go beyond the scope of this chapter. For a fuller discussion of this, see Deborah Madden, *The Paddington prophet: Richard Brothers's journey to Jerusalem* (Manchester, 2010), pp. 193–194.
3. For full details about all of Southcottian prophets in the 'Visitation', see Gordon Allan, 'Southcottian sects from 1790 to the present day', in Kenneth G.C. Newport and Crawford Gribben (eds), *Expecting the end: Millennialism in social and historical context* (Waco, TX, 2006), pp. 213–236; Philip Lockley, *Visionary religion and radicalism in early industrial England: From Southcott to Socialism* (Oxford, 2013), and Philip Lockley and Jane Shaw (eds), *The Southcottians: A modern millennial movement*, forthcoming with I.B. Tauris.
4. Stephen Spector, *Evangelicals and Israel: The story of American Christian Zionism* (New York, and Oxford, 2008); Victoria Clark, *Allies for Armageddon: The rise of Christian Zionism* (New Haven, CT, 2007); Eitan Bar-Yosef, *The Holy Land in English culture 1799–1917* (Oxford, 2005); Stephen Sizer, *Christian Zionism: Road map to Armageddon?* (Leicester, 2004); Burke O. Long, *Imagining the Holy Land* (Indiana, IN, 2002).
5. Bar-Yosef, *Holy Land in English culture*, p. 11; Anthony D. Smith, *Chosen peoples: Sacred sources of national identity* (Oxford, 2003); Colin Kidd, *The forging of races: Race and scripture in the Protestant Atlantic world 1600–2000* (Cambridge, 2006); Linda Colley, *Britons: Forging the nation, 1707–1837* (New Haven, CT, 1992).
6. Murray Roston, *Prophet and poet: The Bible and the growth of Romanticism* (London, 1965), pp. 47–48.
7. This figure refers to Israel's twelve tribes in the Old Testament, though in Revelation (7:1–8) the tribes of Ephraim and Dan are replaced by Joseph and Levi.
8. Madden, *The Paddington prophet*, pp. 297–298.
9. Elbourne, *Blood ground*, p. 26.
10. This reach has been captured in Newport and Gribben (eds), *Expecting the end* and Crawford Gribben, *Evangelical millennialism in the trans-Atlantic world, 1500–2000* (Basingstoke, 2011).
11. See Lockley and Shaw (eds), *The Southcottians*.
12. The cultural materialist features of Southcottianism were most apparent in the movement initiated by prophets listed later in the scheme, John Wroe

(1782–1863) and James Jezreel (1851–1885), but were clearly influenced by Richard Brothers. See, Lockley, *Visionary religion*.
13. Benedict Anderson, *Imagined communities: Reflections on the origins and spread of nationalism* (London, 1983), p. 145; Smith, *Chosen peoples*, p. 19.
14. Jon Mee, *Dangerous enthusiasm: William Blake and the culture of radicalism in the 1790s* (Oxford, 1992) and Jon Mee, *Romanticism, enthusiasm and regulation: Poetics and the policing of culture in the romantic period* (Oxford, 2003).
15. John Barrell, *Imagining the king's death: Figurative treason, fantasies of regicide 1793–1796* (Oxford, 2000), pp. 504–550.
16. Madden, *The Paddington prophet*, pp. 48–49; Iain McCalman, *Radical underworld: Prophets, revolutionaries and pornographers in London, 1794–1840* (Cambridge, 1988); Mee, *Dangerous enthusiasm* and *Romanticism, enthusiasm and regulation*; Christopher Burdon, *The Apocalypse in England: Revelation unravelling, 1700–1834* (Basingstoke, 1997); Barrell, *Imagining the king's death*; Susan Juster, *Doomsayers: Anglo-American prophecy in the Age of Revolution* (Philadelphia, PA, 2003).
17. Madden, *The Paddington prophet*, p. 18.
18. Madden, *The Paddington prophet*, p. 19.
19. Madden, *The Paddington prophet*, p. 74.
20. Clarke Garrett, *Respectable folly: Millenarians and the French Revolution in France and England* (Baltimore, MD, 1975), p. 199; Madden, *The Paddington prophet*, p. 74.
21. Madden, *The Paddington prophet*, pp. 143–147.
22. Madden, *The Paddington prophet*, p. 65.
23. Madden, *The Paddington prophet*, pp. 194–196.
24. Morton Paley, 'William Blake, the Prince of the Hebrews and the woman clothed with the Sun', in Morton Paley and Michael Phillips (eds), *William Blake: Essays in honour of Geoffrey Keynes* (Oxford, 1973), pp. 260–293.
25. For how Brothers's vision was linked to contemporary architecture and culture, see Madden, *The Paddington prophet*, pp. 191–217.
26. Nabil I. Matar, 'Milton and the idea of the restoration of the Jews', *Studies in English Literature, 1500–1900*, 27 (1987), pp. 109–124 at 110.
27. George Turner, *A Book of wonders; Revealed to George Turner, the servant of God* (London, 1817), p. 69.
28. George Turner, *Wonderful prophecies by George Turner, the servant of God, being a call to the Jews to return* (London, 1818–20), 2 vols. 1:pp. 6–9.
29. Madden, *The Paddington prophet*, pp. 57–62.
30. Madden, *The Paddington prophet*, pp. 57–60.
31. George Turner, *Communications of the Holy Spirit of God* (Leeds, 1817–18).

32. MS. 'Letter from George Turner, Regarding the Rev. John Wesley's apparition' (3 December 1801), Panacea Society [PS], PN.103, 75.
33. Madden, *The Paddington prophet*, p. 269.
34. MS. Southcott, 'Communication given to Joanna Southcott with a Letter to Mr. Halhed concerning Richard Brothers' (2 June 1802), [PS], PN. 222, 340–346 at 344; Madden, *The Paddington prophet*, p. 255.
35. MS. Southcott, 'Communication given to Joanna Southcott with a Letter to Mr. Halhed', 342, 343.
36. Brothers, *Revealed knowledge*, ii. p. 55.
37. Madden, *The Paddington prophet*, pp. 249–260.
38. Madden, *The Paddington prophet*, pp. 249–260.
39. John Beer, 'Blake, Coleridge, and Wordsworth, Some cross-currents and parallels 1789–1805', in Morton Paley and Michael Phillips (eds), *William Blake: Essays in honour of Geoffrey Keynes* (Oxford, 1973), pp. 231–259, at 246.
40. Frances Brown, *Joanna Southcott: The woman clothed with the sun* (Cambridge, 2002), p. 109.
41. Brown, *Joanna Southcott*, pp. 117–126, 174–190.
42. Madden, *The Paddington prophet*, pp. 249–260.
43. George Turner, *Communications of the Holy Spirit of God* (Leeds, 1795), p. 19.
44. Turner, *A book of wonders*, p. 102; Deborah Madden, 'A Southcottian Methodist: The prophetic odyssey of George Turner', forthcoming in Lockley and Shaw (eds), *The Southcottians*.
45. Turner, *A book of wonders*, pp. 110–111; Madden, 'A Southcottian Methodist'.
46. This can be seen in letters from Ann Searle addressed to Samuel Gompertz. See, MS. [PS], PN. 237, 241, 243; Madden, 'A Southcottian Methodist'.
47. John Fletcher Clews Harrison, *The Second Coming: Popular Millenarianism 1780–1850* (London, 1979), p. 250 n. 24.
48. Madden, 'A Southcottian Methodist'.
49. Catherine Hall, *White, male and middle class: Explorations in feminism and history* (Cambridge, 1992); Anna Clark, *The struggle for the breeches and the making of the British working class* (Berkeley, CA, 1995); Leonore Davidoff and Catherine Hall, *Family fortunes: Men and women of the English middle class, 1780–1850*, Revised edition (London, 2002), p. 117. See Lockley's *Visionary religion* for a full synthesis of the secondary sources concerned with the discussion amongst feminist social historians here.
50. Kevin Binfield, 'The French, the 'long-wished for revolution', and the just war in Joanna Southcott', in Adriana Craciun and Kari E. Lokke (eds), *Rebellious Hearts* (New York, 2001), pp. 135–159; Madden, *The Paddington prophet*, pp. 194–195.

51. Bar-Yosef, *The Holy Land in English culture*, p. 60.
52. Madden, *The Paddington prophet*, pp. 194–195.
53. Lockley, *Visionary Religion*; Deborah Madden, 'The emergence of Southcottian Israelite theology', forthcoming in Lockley and Shaw (eds), *The Southcottians*.
54. Lockley and Shaw (eds), *The Southcottians*.
55. Hilton Obenzinger, *American Palestine: Melville, Twain and the Holy Land mania* (Princeton, NJ, 1999).
56. Clarke Garrett, *Spirit possession and popular religion from the Camisards to the Shakers* (Baltimore, MD, 1987).
57. Jacques Le Goff, *History and memory*, trans. Steven Rendall and Elizabeth Claman (New York, 1992), pp. 68–71; Hilary M. Carey, 'The vanished kingdoms of Patrick O'Farrell: Religion, memory and migration in religious history', *Journal of Religious History* 31:1 (2007), pp. 40–58.
58. Madden, *The Paddington prophet*, pp. 288–291.

BIBLIOGRAPHY

Alexander, Philip S., 'The Song of Songs as historical allegory: Notes on the development of an exegetical tradition', in Kevin J. Cathcart and Michael Mather (eds), *Targumic and cognate studies: Essays in honour of Martin McNamara* (Sheffield, 1996), pp. 14–29.

Allan, Gordon, 'Southcottian sects from 1790 to the present day', in Kenneth G.C. Newport and Crawford Gribben (eds), *Expecting the end: Millennialism in social and historical context* (Waco, TX, 2006), pp. 213–236.

Angell, Stephen W. and Pink Dandelion (eds), *Early Quakers and their theological thought 1647–1723* (Cambridge, 2015).

Armitage, David and Michael J. Braddick (eds), *The British Atlantic world 1500–1800*, Second Edition (Basingstoke, 2009).

Bailyn, Bernard and Patricia L. Denault (eds), *Soundings in Atlantic History: Latent structures and intellectual currents, 1500–1830* (Cambridge, MA and London, 2009), pp. 1–43.

Ball, Bryan W., *A great expectation: Eschatological thought in English Protestantism to 1660* (Leiden, 1975).

Barrell, John, *Imagining the king's death: Figurative treason, fantasies of regicide 1793–1796* (Oxford, 2000).

Bar-Yosef, Eitan, *The Holy Land in English culture 1799–1917* (Oxford, 2005).

Bauckham, Richard, *Tudor apocalypse: Sixteenth century apocalypticism, millenarianism, and the English Reformation* (Oxford, 1978).

Beer, John, 'Blake, Coleridge, and Wordsworth, Some cross-currents and parallels 1789–1805', in Morton Paley and Michael Phillips (eds), *William Blake: Essays in honour of Geoffrey Keynes* (Oxford, 1973), pp. 231–259.

Belserak, Jan, *John Calvin as sixteenth-century prophet* (Oxford, 2014).
Ben-Dor Benite, Zvi, *The ten tribes: A world history* (Oxford, 2009).
Bercovitch, Sacvan, *The American jeremiad* (Madison, WI, 1978).
Bethencourt, Francisco, 'Le millénarisme: idéologie de l'impérialisme eurasiatique?', *Annales. Histoire, Sciences Sociales* 57 (2002), pp. 189–194.
Binfield, Kevin, 'The French, the "long-wished for revolution", and the just war in Joanna Southcott', in Adriana Craciun and Kari E. Lokke (eds), *Rebellious Hearts* (New York, 2001), pp. 135–159.
Black, Robert C. III, *The younger John Winthrop* (New York, 1966).
Bloch, Ruth, *Visionary Republic: Millennial themes in American thought* (Cambridge, 1985).
Boys, Jayne E.E., *London's news press and the Thirty Years War* (Woodbridge, 2014).
Bozeman, Theodore Dwight, *The precisianist strain* (Chapel Hill, NC, 2004).
Bozeman, Theodore Dwight, *To live ancient lives: The primitivist dimension in Puritanism* (Chapel Hill, NC, and London, 1988).
Bradstock, Andrew, *Radical religion in Cromwell's England: A concise history from the English Civil War to the end of the Commonwealth* (London, 2012).
Braga-Pinto, César, *As promessas da história. Discursos proféticos e assimilação no Brasil Colonial (1500–1700)* (São Paulo, 2003).
Bremer, Francis J., *John Winthrop: America's forgotten founding father* (Oxford, 2005).
Bremmer, Jan M. and Jan R. Veenstra (eds), *The metamorphosis of magic from late antiquity to the early modern period* (Leuven, 2002).
Brooke, John L., *The refiner's fire: The making of Mormon cosmology, 1644–1844* (Cambridge, 1994).
Bross, Kristina, *Dry bones and Indian sermons: Praying Indians in colonial America* (Ithaca, NY, and London, 2004).
Brown, Francis, *Joanna Southcott: The woman clothed in the sun* (Cambridge, 2002).
Bruyneel, Sally, *Margaret Fell and the end of time: The theology of the mother of Quakerism* (Waco, TX, 2010).
Burdon, Christopher, *The Apocalypse in England: Revelation unravelling, 1700–1834* (Basingstoke, 1997).
Butler, Jon, 'Magic, astrology, and the early American religious heritage, 1600–176', *American Historical Review* 84:2 (1979), pp. 317–346.
Byrd, James P., *Sacred scripture, sacred war: The Bible and the American Revolution* (Oxford, 2013).
Campion, Nicholas, *A history of western astrology Volume II: The medieval and modern worlds* (London, 2009).
Cañizares-Esguerra, Jose, *Puritan Conquistadors: Iberianizing the Atlantic* (Stanford, CA, 2006).

Canny, Nicholas and Philip Morgan (eds), *The Oxford handbook of the Atlantic World* (Oxford, 2011).
Capp, Bernard, *Astrology and the popular press: English almanacs 1500–1800* (London, 1979).
Capp, Bernard, *The Fifth Monarchy Men: A study in seventeenth-century English Millenarianism* (London, 1972).
Carey, Hilary M., 'The vanished kingdoms of Patrick O'Farrell: Religion, memory and migration in religious history', *Journal of Religious History* 31:1 (2007), pp. 40–58.
Castro, Daniel, *Another face of empire: Bartolomé de Las Casas, indigenous rights, and ecclesiastical imperialism* (Durham, NC, 2007).
Cervantes, Fernando, *The Devil in the New World: The impact of diabolism in New Spain* (New Haven, CT, 1994).
Christianson, Paul, *Reformers and Babylon: English apocalyptic visions from the Reformation to the eve of the Civil War* (Toronto, 1978).
Clark, Anna, 'The sexual crisis and popular religion in London, 1770–1820', *International Labor and Working-Class History* 34 (1988), pp. 56–69.
Clarke, Elizabeth, *Politics, religion and the Song of Songs in seventeenth-century England* (London, 2011).
Clarke Garrett, *Respectable folly: Millenarians and the French Revolution in France and England* (Baltimore, MD, 1975), p. 199.
Connors, Richard and Andrew Colin Gow (eds), *Anglo-American millennialism, from Milton to the Millerites* (Leiden, 2004).
Coclanis, Peter A., 'Atlantic World or Atlantic/World?', *William and Mary Quarterly*, 3rd Series 63:4 (2006), pp. 725–742.
Cohn, Norman, *The pursuit of the millennium: Revolutionary millenarians and mystical anarchists of the Middle Ages* (London, 1993).
Cogley, Richard W., 'The fall of the Ottoman Empire and the restoration of Israel in the "Judeo-Centric" strand of Puritan millenarianism', *Church History* 72 (2003), pp. 304–322.
Cogley, Richard W., '"The most vile and barbarous nation of all the world": Giles Fletcher the Elder's *The Tartars Or, Ten Tribes* (ca. 1610)', *Renaissance Quarterly* 58:3 (2005), pp. 781–814.
Colley, Linda, *Britons: Forging the nation, 1707–1837* (New Haven, CT, 1992).
Como, David R., *Blown by the Spirit: Puritanism and the emergence of an Antinomian underground in pre-Civil War England* (Stanford, CA, 2004).
Coudert, Allison, *Religion, magic, and science in early modern Europe and America* (Santa Barbara, CA, 2011).
Crome, Andrew, 'English national identity and the readmission of the Jews, 1650–1656', *Journal of Ecclesiastical History* 66:2 (2015a), pp. 280–301.
Crome, Andrew, 'The Jewish Indian theory and Protestant use of Catholic thought in the early modern Atlantic', in Crawford Gribben and Scott Spurlock (eds),

Puritans and Catholics in the trans-Atlantic world 1600–1800 (Basingstoke, 2015b), pp. 112–130.

Crome, Andrew, *The restoration of the Jews: Early modern hermeneutics, eschatology, and national identity in the works of Thomas Brightman* (Cham, 2014).

Cummins, Alexander, *The starry rubric: Seventeenth-century English astrology and magic* (Milton Keynes, 2012).

Davies, Owen, *Grimoires: A history of magic books* (Oxford, 2009).

Davies, Owen, *Popular magic: Cunning-folk in English history* (London, 2007).

Debus, Allen G., *The English Paracelsians* (New York, 1966).

De Krey, Gary S., *Restoration and revolution in Britain: A political history of the era of Charles II and the Glorious Revolution* (New York, 2007).

Demos, John, *The enemy within: 2,000 years of witch-hunting in the western world* (New York, 2008).

Dobranski, Stephen, 'Principle and politics in Milton's *Areopagitica*', in Laura Lunger Knoppers (ed.), *The Oxford handbook of literature and the English revolution* (Oxford, 2012), pp. 190–205.

Dolle, Raymond F., 'The new Canaan, the old canon, and the new world in American literature anthologies', *College Literature* 17:2/3 (1990), pp. 196–208.

Eire, Carlos M.N., *War against the idols: The reformation of worship from Erasmus to Calvin* (Cambridge, 1986).

Eisenstadt, Peter, 'Almanacs and the disenchantment of early America', *Pennsylvania History* 65 (1998), pp. 143–169.

Elbourne, Elizabeth, *Blood ground: Colonialism, missions and the contest for Christianity in the Cape Colony and Britain, 1799–1853* (Montreal and Kingston, 2002).

Elliott, John, *Empires of the Atlantic world: Britain and Spain in America 1492–1830* (New Haven, CT, 2006).

Endelman, Todd M., *The Jews of Britain, 1656–2000* (Berkeley, CA, 2002).

Endy, Melvin B., 'Just war, holy war, and millennialism in Revolutionary America', *William and Mary Quarterly*, 3rd series 42:1 (1985), pp. 3–25.

Escobedo, Andrew, 'The millennial border between tradition and innovation: Foxe, Milton, and the idea of historical progress', in Richard Connors and Andrew Colin Gow (eds), *Anglo-American millennialism, from Milton to the Millerites* (Leiden, 2004), pp. 1–42.

Farr, David, *Major-General Thomas Harrison: Millenarianism, Fifth Monarchism and the English Revolution 1616–1660* (Farnham, 2014).

Farrell, Michael, *Blake and the Methodists* (Basingstoke, 2014).

Firth, Katherine, *The apocalyptic tradition in Reformation Britain 1530–1645* (Oxford, 1979).

Force, James E. and Richard H. Popkin (eds), *Millenarianism and messianism in early modern European culture. Vol. III: The millenarian turn: Millenarian contexts of science, politics, and everyday Anglo-American life in the seventeenth and eighteenth centuries* (Dordrecht, 2001).

França, Eduardo d'Oliveira, *Portugal na época da Restauração* (São Paulo, 1997).

Francis A. Yates, *The Rosicrucian enlightenment* (London and New York, 1993), p. 238.

Goldish, Matt, *The Sabbatean prophets* (Cambridge, 2004).

Godbeer, Richard, *The Devil's dominion: Magic and religion in early New England* (New York, 1992).

Godbeer, Richard, 'Witchcraft in British America', in Brian Levack (ed.), *The Oxford handbook of witchcraft in early modern Europe and colonial America* (Oxford, 2013), pp. 393–411.

Greenblatt, Stephen, *Marvellous possessions: The wonder of the New World* (Oxford, 1992).

Gregerson, Linda and Susan Juster (eds), *Empires of God: Religious encounters in the early modern Atlantic* (Philadelphia, PA, 2011).

Gregory, Jeremy, 'Transforming the "age of reason" into "An age of faiths": Or, putting religions and beliefs (back) into the eighteenth century', *Journal for Eighteenth Century Studies* 32:3 (2009), pp. 287–305.

Gregory, Jeremy, 'Transatlantic Anglican networks c.1680-c.1770: Transplanting, translating and transforming the Church of England', in Jeremy Gregory and Hugh McLeod (eds), *International religious networks* (Woodbridge, 2012), pp. 127–142.

Gribben, Crawford, *Evangelical millennialism in the trans-Atlantic World, 1500–2000* (Basingstoke, 2011).

Gribben, Crawford, *The Puritan millennium: Literature and theology, 1550–1682*, Second Edition (Milton Keynes, 2008).

Griffith, Nicholas and Fernando Cervantes (eds), *Spiritual encounters: Interactions between Christianity and native religions in colonial America* (Birmingham, 1999).

Gareis, Iris, 'Merging magical traditions: Sorcery and witchcraft in Spanish and Portuguese America', in Brian Levack (ed.), *The Oxford handbook of witchcraft in early modern Europe and colonial America* (Oxford, 2013), pp. 412–428.

Garrett, Clarke, *Spirit possession and popular religion from the Camisards to the Shakers* (Baltimore, MD, 1987).

Garrett, Clarke, *Respectable folly: Millenarians and the French Revolution in France and England* (Baltimore, MD, 1975), p. 199.

Greaves, Richard L., *Deliver us from evil: The radical underground in Britain, 1660–1663* (Oxford, 1986).

Greaves, Richard L., *Enemies under his feet: Radicals and nonconformists in Britain 1664–1677* (Stanford, CA, 1990).

Griffin, Edward M., *Old brick: Charles Chauncy of Boston 1705–1787* (Minneapolis, MN, 1980),

Gronim, Sara S., 'At the sign of Newton's head: Astronomy and cosmology in British colonial New York', *Pennsylvania History* 66 (1999), pp. 55–85.

Gronim, Sara S., *Everyday nature: Knowledge of the natural world in colonial New York* (New Brunswick, NJ, 2007).
Gura, Philip, *A glimpse of Sion's glory: Puritan radicalism in New England, 1620–1660* (Middletown, CT, 1984).
Guyatt, Nicholas, *Providence and the invention of the United States, 1607–1876* (New York, and Cambridge, 2007).
Gwyn, Douglas, 'Quakers, eschatology, and time', in Stephen W. Angell and Pink Dandelion (eds), *The Oxford handbook of Quaker studies* (Oxford, 2013), pp. 202–217.
Hall, David D., *Worlds of wonder, Days of judgment: Popular religious belief in early New England* (Cambridge, MA, 1990).
Haller, William, *Foxe's Book of Martyrs and the elect nation* (London, 1963).
Hammond, Jeffrey A., '"The bride in redemptive time": John Cotton and the Canticles controversy', *New England Quarterly* 56:1 (1983), pp. 78–102.
Hansen, João Adolfo, 'Vieira: Tempo, alegoria, história', *Broteria* 145 (1997), pp. 541–556.
Harley, David, 'Explaining Salem: Calvinist psychology and the diagnosis of possession', *American Historical Review* 101:2 (1996), pp. 307–330.
Harrison, John Fletcher Clews, *The second coming: Popular millenarianism 1780–1850* (London, 1979), p. 250 n. 24.
Hatch, Nathan O., *The sacred cause of liberty: Republican thought and the millennium in revolutionary New England* (New Haven, CT, 1977).
Herbert, Amanda, 'Companions in preaching and suffering: Itinerant female Quakers in the seventeenth- and eighteenth-century British Atlantic world', *Early American Studies* 1 (2011), pp. 73–113.
Hessayon, Ariel, *'Gold tried in fire': The prophet Theaurau John Tany and the English Revolution* (Aldershot, 2007).
Hessayon, Ariel and David Finnegan (eds), *Varieties of seventeenth- and early eighteenth-century English radicalism in context* (Burlington, VT, 2011).
Hill, Christopher, *Antichrist in seventeenth-century England* (Oxford, 1971).
Hill, Christopher, *The world turned upside down* (New York, 1984).
Hindmarsh, D. Bruce, *The Evangelical conversion narrative: Spiritual autobiography in early modern England* (Oxford, 2005).
Hodgkins, Christopher, *Reforming empire: Protestant colonialism and conscience in British literature* (Columbia, MI, 2002).
Holmberg, Eva Johanna, *Jews in the early modern English Imagination* (Aldershot, 2011).
Horrocks, Thomas A., *Popular print and popular medicine: Almanacs and health advice in early America* (Amherst, MA, 2008).
Hutchins, Zachary McLeod, *Inventing Eden: Primitivism, millennialism, and the making of New England* (Oxford and New York, 2014).
Hutton, Sarah, 'More, Newton and the language of biblical prophecy', in James E. Force and Richard H. Popkin (eds), *The books of nature and scripture: Recent*

essays on natural philosophy, theology and biblical criticism in the Netherlands of Spinoza's time and the British Isles of Newton's time (Dordrecht, Boston, MA, and London, 1994), pp. 39–54.

Hutton, Sarah, 'The seven trumpets and the seven vials: Apocalypticism and Christology in Newton's theological writings', in James E. Force and Richard H. Popkin (eds), *Newton and religion: Context, nature and influence* (Dordrecht, 1999), pp. 165–178.

Iliffe, Rob, '"Making a shew": Apocalyptic hermeneutics and the sociology of Christian idolatry in the work of Isaac Newton and Henry More', in James E. Force and Richard H. Popkin (eds), *The books of nature and scripture: Recent essays on natural philosophy, theology and biblical criticism in the Netherlands of Spinoza's time and the British Isles of Newton's time* (Dordrecht, Boston, MA, and London, 1994), pp. 55–88.

Jesse, Jennifer G., *William Blake's religious vision: There's a Methodism in his madness* (Lanham, MD, 2013).

John Fletcher Clews Harrison, *The Second Coming: Popular Millenarianism 1780-1850* (London, 1979), p. 250 n. 24.

Johnston, Warren, *Revelation restored: The apocalypse in later seventeenth-century England* (Woodbridge, 2011).

Johnston, Warren, 'The Anglican apocalypse in Restoration England', *Journal of Ecclesiastical History* 44:3 (2004), pp. 467–501.

Johnston, Warren, 'The patience of the saints, the apocalypse, and moderate nonconformity in Restoration England', *Canadian Journal of History/Annales canadiennes d'histoire* 38:3 (2003), pp. 505–520.

Jowitt, Claire, 'Radical identities? Native Americans, Jews and the English Commonwealth', *Seventeenth Century* 10:1 (1995), pp. 101–119.

Jue, Jeffrey K., *Heaven upon earth: Joseph Mede (1586–1638) and the legacy of millenarianism* (Dordrecht, 2006).

Jue, Jeffrey K., 'Puritan Millennialism in old and New England', in John Coffey and Paul C.H. Lim (eds), *The Cambridge Companion to Puritanism* (Cambridge, 2008), pp. 259–276.

Juster, Susan, *Doomsayers: Anglo-American prophecy in the Age of revolution* (Philadelphia, PA, 2003).

Karlsen, Carol F., *The Devil in the shape of a woman: Witchcraft in colonial New England* (London, 1998).

Kassell, Lauren, '"All was this land full fill'd of faerie", or Magic and the past in early modern England', *Journal of the History of Ideas* 67:1 (2006), pp. 107–122.

Kassell, Lauren, *Medicine and magic in Elizabethan England* (Oxford, 2005), pp. 51–52.

Katz, David S., 'Menasseh ben Israel's Christian Connection: Henry Jessey and the Jews', in Yosef Kaplan, Henry Méchoulan, and Richard H. Popkin (eds), *Menasseh ben Israel and his world* (Leiden, 1989), pp. 117–138.

Katz, David S., *Philo-Semitism and the readmission of the Jews to England 1603–1655* (Oxford, 1982).

Katz, David S., *The Jews in the history of England* (Oxford, 1994).
Katz, David S. and Richard H. Popkin, *Messianic revolution* (New York, 1999).
Keeble, Neil H., *The literary culture of nonconformity in later seventeenth-century England* (Leicester, 1987).
Kidd, Colin, *Identities before nationalism: Ethnicity and nationhood in the Atlantic world, 1600–1800* (Cambridge, 2006a).
Kidd, Colin, *The forging of races: Race and scripture in the Protestant Atlantic world 1600–2000* (Cambridge, 2006b).
Kidd, Thomas S., *The Great Awakening: The roots of Evangelical Christianity in colonial America* (New Haven, CT, 2007).
Knox, Ronald A., *Enthusiasm: A chapter in the history of religion with special reference to the XVII and XVIII Centuries* (Oxford, 1950).
Laborie, Lionel, *Enlightening enthusiasm: Prophecy and religious experience in early eighteenth-century England* (Manchester, 2015).
Lambert, Frank, *Inventing the 'Great Awakening'* (Princeton, NJ, 1999).
Lamont, William, *Richard Baxter and the millennium: Protestant imperialism and the English Revolution* (London, 1979).
Lauren Kassell, *The witch-hunt in early modern Europe* (Oxford, 2005).
Levack, Brian, *Medicine and magic in Elizabethan England* (London, 2006).
Lima, Luís Filipe Silvério, *Império dos sonhos: Narrativas Oníricas, Sebastianismo e Messianismo Brigantino* (São Paulo, 2010).
Liu, Tai, *Discord in Zion: The Puritan divines and the Puritan revolution 1640–1660* (The Hague, 1973).
Lockley, Philip, *Visionary religion and radicalism in early industrial England: From Southcott to socialism* (Oxford, 2013).
Lovejoy, David S., *Religious enthusiasm in the New World: Heresy to revolution* (Cambridge, MA, 1985).
Lovelace, Richard, *The American pietism of Cotton Mather: Origins of American evangelicalism* (Grand Rapids, MI, 1979).
MacDonald, Michael, *Mystical Bedlam: Madness, anxiety, and healing in seventeenth-century England* (Cambridge, 1981).
Mack, Phyllis, *Heart religion in the British Enlightenment: Gender and emotion in early Methodism* (Cambridge, 2008).
Mack, Phyllis, 'The unbounded self: Dreaming and identity in the British Enlightenment', in Ann Marie Plane and Leslie Tuttle (eds), *Dreams, dreamers, and visions: The early modern Atlantic world* (Philadelphia, PA, 2013), pp. 207–225.
Mack, Phyllis, *Visionary women: Ecstatic prophecy in seventeenth-century England* (Berkley, CA, 1992).
Mackay, Ruth, *The baker who pretended to be King of Portugal* (Chicago, IL, 2012).
Maclear, J.F., 'New England and the Fifth Monarchy: The Quest for the Millennium in Early American Puritanism', *William and Mary Quarterly*, 3rd Series 32:2 (1975), pp. 223–260.

Madden, Deborah, *The Paddington prophet: Richard Brothers's journey to Jerusalem* (Manchester, 2010).
Magro, Maria, 'Spiritual biography and radical sectarian women's discourse: Anna Trapnel and the bad girls of the English revolution', *Journal of Medieval and Early Modern Studies* 34:2 (2004), pp. 405–437.
Marini, Stephen A., 'Uncertain dawn: Millennialism and political theology in revolutionary America', in Richard Connors and Andrew Colin Gow (eds), *Anglo-American millennialism, from Milton to the Millerites* (Leiden, 2004), pp. 159–176.
Marriott, Brandon, *Transnational networks and cross-religious exchange in the seventeenth-century Mediterranean and Atlantic Worlds: Sabbatai Sevi and the lost tribes of Israel* (Farnham, 2015).
Matar, Nabil I., 'George Herbert, Henry Vaughan, and the conversion of the Jews', *Studies in English Literature* 30:1 (1990), pp. 79–92.
Matar, Nabil I., 'Milton and the idea of the restoration of the Jews', *Studies in English Literature, 1500–1900* 27:1 (1987), pp. 109–124.
Matar, Nabil, *Islam in Britain 1558–1685* (Cambridge, 1998).
McCalman, Iain, *Radical underground: Prophets, revolutionaries and pornographers in London, 1794–1840* (Cambridge, 1988).
Mee, Jon, *Dangerous enthusiasm: William Blake and the culture of radicalism in the 1790s* (Oxford, 1992).
Middlekauff, Robert, *The Mathers: Three generations of puritan intellectuals, 1596–1728* (New York, 1976).
Miller, Perry, *Errand into the wilderness* (Cambridge, MA, 1956).
Miller, Perry, *The New England mind: The seventeenth century* (Cambridge, MA, 1983).
Monod, Paul, *Solomon's secret art: The occult in the age of enlightenment* (New Haven, CT, 2013).
Moore, Susan Hardman, *Pilgrims: New World settlers and the call of home* (New Haven, CT, and London, 2007).
Morgan, Philip D. and Jack P. Greene (eds), *Atlantic History: A critical appraisal* (New York and Oxford, 2009).
Muchnik, Natalia, 'Antonio Vieira y la diáspora sefardí en el siglo XVII', in Pedro Cardim and Gaetano Sabatini (eds), *António Vieira, Roma e o Universalismo das Monarquias Portuguesa e Espanhola* (Lisbon, 2011), pp. 97–120.
Murrin, Michael, 'Newton's Apocalypse', in James E. Force and Richard H. Popkin (eds), *Newton and religion: Context, nature and influence* (Dordrecht, 1999), pp. 203–220.
Nalle, Sarah, 'El Encubierto revisited: Navigating between visions of Heaven and Hell on earth', in Kathryn A. Edwards (ed.), *Werewolves, witches, and wandering spirits* (Kirksville, MO, 2002), pp. 77–92.
Nalle, Sarah, 'The millennial moment: Revolution and radical religion in sixteenth-century Spain', in Peter Schäfer and Mark Cohens (eds), *Toward the Millennium: Messianic Expectations from the Bible to Waco* (Leiden, 1998), pp. 153–173.

Newport, Kenneth G.C., *Apocalypse and millennium: Studies in biblical eisegesis* (Cambridge, 2000).
Newport, Kenneth G.C., 'George Bell, prophet and enthusiast', *Methodist History* 35:2 (1997), pp. 95–105.
Niblett, Matthew, *Prophecy and the politics of salvation in late Georgian England: The theology and apocalyptic vision of Joanna Southcott* (London, 2015).
Nordholt, Jan Willem Schulte, *The myth of the west: America as the last empire* (Grand Rapids, MI, 1995).
O'Brien, Susan, 'A transatlantic community of saints: The Great Awakening and the first Evangelical network, 1735–1755', *American Historical Review* 91:4 (1986), pp. 811–832.
Obenzinger, Hilton, *American Palestine: Melville, Twain and the Holy Land mania* (Princeton, NJ, 1999).
Olsen, Eric, *The Calabrian charlatan, 1580–1603: Messianic nationalism in early modern Europe* (New York, 2003).
Pagden, Anthony, *Lords of all the world: Ideologies of empire in Spain, Britain and France c.1500–c.1800* (New Haven, CT, 1998).
Paley, Morton, 'William Blake, the Prince of the Hebrews and the woman clothed with the Sun', in Morton Paley and Michael Phillips (eds), *William Blake: Essays in honour of Geoffrey Keynes* (Oxford, 1973), pp. 260–293.
Pestana, Carla Gardina, *Protestant Empire: Religion and the Making of the British Atlantic World* (Philadelphia, PA, 2009).
Phelan, John Leddy, *The Millennial kingdom of the Franciscans in the New World: A study of the writings of Gerónimo de Mendieta (1525–1604)*, Revised Edition (Los Angeles, CA, 1970).
Pompa, Cristina, 'O lugar da utopia: os jesuítas e a catequese indígena', *Novos Estudos (Cebrap)* 64 (2002), pp. 84–90.
Popkin, Richard, *Isaac La Peyrère (1596–1676): His life, work, and influence* (Leiden, 1987).
Quitslund, Beth, 'The Virginia Company, 1606–1624: Anglicanism's millennial adventure', in Richard Connors and Andrew Colin Gow (eds), *Anglo-American millennialism, from Milton to the Millerites* (Leiden, 2004), pp. 43–114.
Roos, Anna Marie, 'Israel Hiebner's astrological amulets and the English sigil war', *Culture and Cosmos* 6:2 (2002), pp. 17–43.
Rosenmeier, Jesper, 'Eaters and non-eaters: John Cotton's *A Brief Exposition of Canticles* (1642) in light of Boston's (Linc.) religious and civil conflicts, 1619–22', *Early American Literature* 36:2 (2001), pp. 149–181.
Roston, Murray, *Prophet and poet: The Bible and the growth of Romanticism* (London, 1965).
Schrenk, Gottlob, *Gottesreich und bund im Älteren Protestantismus, vornehmlich bei Johannes Coccejus: Zugleich ein Beitrag zur geschichte des Pietismus und der Heilsgeschichtlichen Theologie* (Gütersloh, 1923).

Schwartz, Hillel, *The French Prophets: The history of a millenarian group in eighteenth-century England* (Berkley, CA, 1980).
Shapiro, James, *Shakespeare and the Jews* (New York, 1996).
Sharpe, Kevin, 'Reading revelations: Prophecy, hermeneutics and politics in early modern Britain', in Kevin Sharpe and Steven N. Zwicker (eds), *Reading, society and politics in early modern England* (Cambridge, 2003), pp. 122–163.
Shaw, Jane, *Miracles in Enlightenment England* (New Haven, CT, and London, 2006).
Smith, Anthony D., *Chosen peoples: Sacred sources of national identity* (Oxford, 2003).
Smith, Nigel (ed.), *A collection of Ranter writings: Spiritual liberty and sexual freedom in the English revolution* (London, 2014).
Smith, Nigel, *Literature and revolution in England, 1640–1660* (New Haven, CT, 1987).
Smith, Robert O., *More desired than our owne salvation: The roots of Christian Zionism* (Oxford, 2013).
Smolinski, Reiner, 'Apocalypticism in colonial North America', in Stephen J. Stein (ed.), *The encyclopedia of apocalypticism, Vol. 3: Apocalypticism in the modern Period and the contemporary Age* (New York, 1998), pp. 36–72.
Smolinski, Reiner, 'Introduction', in *The threefold paradise of Cotton Mather: An edition of 'Triparadisus'* (Athens, GA, and London, 1995), pp. 3–78.
Smolinski, Reiner, 'Israel redivivus: The eschatological limits of typology in New England', *New England Quarterly* 63:3 (1990), pp. 357–395.
Smolinski, Reiner, '"The way to lost Zion": The Cotton-Williams debate on the separation of church and state in millenarian perspective', in Bernd Engler, Joerg O. Fichte, and Oliver Scheiding (eds), *Millennial thought in America: Historical and intellectual contexts, 1630–1860* (Trier, 2002), pp. 61–96.
Stanwood, Owen, 'Crisis and opportunity: The Restoration Church Settlement and New England', in N.H. Keeble (ed.), *'Settling the Peace of the Church': 1662 Revisited* (Oxford, 2014), pp. 190–208.
Stievermann, Jan, 'General introduction', in Reiner Smolinski and Jan Stievermann (eds), *Cotton Mather and Biblia Americana—America's first bible commentary: Essays in Reappraisal* (Tübingen, 2010), pp. 1–58.
Stievermann, Jan, *Prophecy, piety, and the problem of historicity: Interpreting the Hebrew scriptures in Cotton Mather's Biblia Americana* (Tübingen, 2016).
Subrahmanyam, Sanjay, 'Du Tage au Gange au XVIe siècle: une conjoncture millénariste à l'échelle eurasiatique', *Annales. Histoire, Sciences Sociales* 56 (2001), pp. 51–84.
Sutton, Matthew Avery, *American apocalypse: A history of modern Evangelicalism* (Cambridge, MA, and London, 2014).
Sweeney, Douglas A., *Edwards the exegete: Biblical interpretation and Anglo-Protestant culture on the edge of the Enlightenment* (New York, 2015).

Taithe, Bertrand and Tim Thornton (eds), *Prophecy: The power of inspired language in history 1300–2000* (Stroud, 1997).
Tavares, Maria Ferro, 'O messianismo judaico em Portugal (la metade do seculo XVI)', *Luso-Brazilian Review* 28 (1991), pp. 141–151.
Taves, Ann, *Fits, trances, & visions: Explaining religion and explaining experience from Wesley to James* (Princeton, NJ, 1999).
Thomas, Keith, *Religion and the decline of magic* (London, 1971).
Toon, Peter (ed.), *The Puritans, the millennium, and the future of Israel* (Cambridge, 2002 [1970]).
Valdez, Maria Ana, *Historical interpretations of the 'fifth empire'* (Leiden, 2011).
van der Wall, Ernestine, 'The Amsterdam millenarian Petrus Serrarius (1600–1669) and the Anglo Dutch circle of philo-Judaists', in Johannes van den Berg and Ernestine van der Wall (eds), *Jewish-Christian relations in the seventeenth century* (Dordrecht, 1988), pp. 73–94.
Voigt, Lisa, *Writing captivity in the early modern Atlantic: Circulations of knowledge and authority in the Iberian and English imperial worlds* (Chapel Hill, NC, 2009).
Walsham, Alexandra, *Charitable hatred: Tolerance and intolerance in England, 1500–1700* (Manchester, 2006).
Walsham, Alexandra, *The reformation of the landscape: Religion, identity and memory in early modern Britain and Ireland* (Oxford, 2011).
Ward, W.R., *Early evangelicalism: A global intellectual history, 1670–1789* (Cambridge, 2010).
Ward, W.R., *The Protestant Evangelical awakening* (Cambridge, 1992).
White, Sam, '"Shewing the difference betweene their conjuration, and our invocation on the name of God for rayne": Weather, prayer, and magic in early American encounters', *William and Mary Quarterly*, 3rd Series 72:1 (2015), pp. 33–56.
Wilkinson, Ronald S., 'George Starkey, physician and alchemist', *Ambix* 11 (1963a), pp. 121–152.
Wilkinson, Ronald S., '"Hermes Christianus": John Winthrop, Jr., and chemical medicine in seventeenth-century New England', in Allen G. Debus (ed.), *Science, medicine, and society in the Renaissance* (New York, 1972), pp. 222–241.
Wilkinson, Ronald S., 'The alchemical library of John Winthrop, Jr. (1606–1676)' *Ambix* 11 (1963b), pp. 33–51.
Williamson, Arthur H., 'An Empire to end empire: The dynamic of early modern British expansion', *Huntington Library Quarterly* 68 (2005), pp. 227–256.
Williamson, Arthur, *Apocalypse then: Prophecy and the making of the modern world* (Westport, CT, 2008).
Winiarski, Douglas L., 'Jonathan Edwards, enthusiast? Radical revivalism and the Great Awakening in the Connecticut Valley', *Church History* 74:4 (2005), pp. 683–739.

Winiarski, Douglas L., 'Souls filled with ravishing transport: Heavenly visions and the radical awakening of New England', *William and Mary Quarterly*, 3rd Series 61:1 (2004), pp. 3–46.

Woodward, Walter W., *Prospero's America: John Winthrop, Jr., alchemy, and the creation of New England Culture, 1606–1676* (Williamsburg, NC, 2010).

Yates, Francis A., *The Rosicrucian enlightenment* (London and New York, 1993), p. 238.

Zakai, Avihu, *Exile and kingdom: History and apocalypse in the Puritan migration to America* (Cambridge, 1992).

Zook, Melinda, *Radical Whigs and conspiratorial politics in late Stuart England* (University Park, PN, 1990).

INDEX

A

Acosta, José de, 43–45, 56, 60n34, 71, 80n16, 153, 155
Africa, 7, 8, 35, 36, 39, 47
Alchemy, 14, 158, 160, 171, 174, 176n4, 184n168
Almanacs, 22, 159, 161–166, 169, 174, 181n76
Alsop, George, 153
Anabaptists, 14, 103n46, 189, 205n10, 206n14
Antichrist
  Catholic Church as, 109–111, 113, 118
  Ottoman Empire as, 21
Antinomianism, 107, 111, 113, 114, 115, 120
Astrology, 14, 22, 151, 155, 156, 162, 164–166, 168, 169, 171, 173–175, 176n1
Atlantic history, 6, 7, 9, 26n23, 26n31, 27n40
Augustine, 38, 58n15, 129, 154

Austin, Ann, 15, 117
Austin, David, 1, 3

B

Bacon, Francis, 152, 156, 165, 176n4
Bagshaw, Edward, 191, 206n16
Baillie, Robert, 110, 112, 115, 122n19
Bale, John, 129
Bandarra, Gonçalo Annes, 50, 51, 53, 62n65
Baptists, 18, 86, 189, 190, 193, 223, 262
Baxter, Richard, 113, 115, 122n24, 133, 136, 139
ben Israel, Menasseh, 52, 63n75, 131, 207n24
Bercovitch, Sacvan, 12, 28n48, 103n45
Beverley, Thomas, 136, 147n57, 201, 210n70, 210n71, 220
Black legend, 11
Blake, William, 32n88, 239, 240, 253, 259, 264, 268, 271, 274, 279n14
Booker, John, 165

Bradstreet, Anne, 21, 84–98, 99n10, 100n11, 100n17, 101n18, 101n21, 101n28, 101n30, 103n41, 103n48, 104n49
Brazil, 34, 39, 43, 44, 47, 50, 52, 54, 55, 58n20, 63n81
Bridge, William, 109, 121n14
Brightman, Thomas, 13, 25n14, 79n14, 80n17, 103n46, 129, 130, 134, 136, 139, 141, 145n14, 215, 216, 220, 224, 235n8
Brookhouse, Thomas, 202, 203, 210n79
Brothers, Richard, 2, 3, 19, 23, 24, 32n88, 39, 260–277
Bulkeley, Peter, 111, 130, 135, 141
Burgess, Anthony, 110, 112, 115, 122n23, 124n37
Burrough, Edward, 117, 125n74, 193, 208n29
Burroughs, Jeremiah, 112, 124n35, 130, 134
Burton, Henry, 109, 121n11, 121n12

C
Calamy, Edmund, 109, 112, 122n16, 122n17, 124n36
Camisard prophets. *See* French Prophets
Campanella, Tommaso, 48, 61n49, 61n58
Canticle of canticles. *See* Song of Songs
Casas, Bartolomé de las, 10, 41, 42, 44
Cattan, Christopher, 171
Charles I (of England), 13, 106, 200, 202
Charles I (of Spain), 46
Charles II (of England), 188, 194, 199, 205n4
Charles V (Holy Roman Emperor), 36, 46, 47
Chauncy, Charles, 249, 251, 257n39, 257n43

Christian Israelites, 275
Civil wars. *See* English revolution
Clapham, Henoch, 129, 145n13
Cocceius, Johannes, 23, 215, 224–232, 237n50
Columbus, Christopher, 3, 5, 10, 25n15, 34, 42
Congregationalism, 213, 223, 262
Coppe, Abiezer, 163
Cotton, John, 13, 23, 85, 111, 112, 121n7, 130, 134, 143, 213–238
Cradock, Walter, 113, 114
Crane, Richard, 190, 206n13
Cressener, Drue, 201, 210n68
Cromwell, Oliver, 83, 84, 106, 119, 120, 140, 202, 1206n90

D
Daniel, Book of, 92
Davenport, John, 198, 235n9
de Castro, João, 50, 62n67
Dee, John, 129, 160, 174
Dell, William, 124n45, 124n46, 124n48, 124n49
Downing, Emmanuel, 71
Draxe, Thomas, 127, 128, 134
Durán, Diego, 41, 59n25
Durham, James, 71, 220
Dury, John, 80n17, 131, 137, 207n24
Dyer, Mary, 15, 117

E
Eden
  In America, 25, 158
  In millennial imagination, 25n16, 176n3
Edwards, Jonathan, 16, 17, 23, 30n70, 31n75, 144, 221, 240–250, 252, 253, 255n7, 257n39
Edwards, Roger, 129
Eliot, John, 131, 143

Elizabeth I, 1
Empire, 7, 9, 13, 20, 21, 30n70, 31n76, 31n79, 34–36, 40, 42, 47, 48, 51, 53–56, 57n7, 62n72, 63n78, 63n81, 73, 79, 96, 102n36, 102n37, 137, 146n19, 175, 201, 202, 222, 224, 226, 227, 260, 275
Encubertismo/ Encobertismo, 46
English revolution, 28n58, 29n61, 98n1, 99n6, 99n7, 102n31, 126n89, 145n2, 181n87, 206n23
Enthusiasm, 17, 19, 23, 30n68, 30n69, 32n88, 75, 99n10, 140, 219, 240, 242, 245, 246, 250, 253, 255n4, 265, 267, 279n16
Erskine, John, 248, 250, 256n33
Evangelicalism, 16, 20, 30n70, 31n71, 32n93, 240, 241, 247, 254n4, 256n33, 275
  and revival, 249, 250
Everard, John, 115, 116, 118, 125n63

F
Farnworth, Richard, 125n73
Ferrar, Nicholas, 68, 73
Fifth Monarchists, 14, 21, 29n60, 98, 104n49, 112, 131, 206n19
Fifth Monarchy Men. *See* Fifth Monarchists
Fisher, Edward, 119, 267, 268, 271
Fisher, Mary, 15, 117
Fox, George, 15, 106, 118, 126n77, 190, 205n12
Foxe, John, 124n34, 129, 145n9
Franciscan order, 42
French Prophets, 30n68
Fuller, Thomas, 81n20, 133, 134, 147n37, 191, 214, 229, 278n2

G
Gender
  and the prophetic office, 2, 19, 85, 117, 272, 274, 275, 277

George III, 2, 19, 266
Gog and Magog, 70, 71, 138, 233
Goodwin, Thomas, 109, 112, 122n18, 124n34
Gookin, Daniel, 157
Gouge, William, 134

H
Hackett, William, 1–4, 28n59
Hakluyt, Richard, 153
Halhed, Nathaniel Brassey, 24n7, 266, 271, 272, 280n34
Hall, Edmund, 135, 140, 148n78, 235
Hartlib, Samuel, 80n17, 160, 207n24
Henequim, Pedro de Rates, 54–56
Henry, Matthew, 221, 223, 224, 236n29
Herbert, George, 65–81
Herbert, Magdalen, 68, 77
Heydon, John, 170–173
Hill, Christopher, 79n14, 113
Hill, Thomas, 110, 122n21
Historicism, 23, 88, 139–140, 152, 165
Huit, Ephraim, 130, 135, 137
Hutchinson, Anne, 111
Hutchinson, Samuel, 198

I
Indians. *See* Native Americans
Islam, 13
Israel, lost tribes of, 3, 22, 27n41, 28n56, 39, 129, 138

J
Jacobite Rebellion, 248
James I of England, VI of Scotland, 109
James II of England, VII of Scotland, 200, 201, 204

Jerusalem, 5, 19, 22, 24, 40, 65, 68–75, 78, 80n20, 81, 130, 133, 135–139, 142–144, 202, 203, 219, 226, 227, 233, 240, 248, 259, 261–265, 267–269, 272, 274–277, 278n2
Jews
 conversion of, 39, 50, 73–75, 78, 97, 128–131, 134, 135, 139, 141, 144, 217, 226, 232, 234n8, 269, 273
 native Americans as, 39, 41, 71, 143, 144, 149n95
 restoration to Palestine, 2, 14, 19, 24, 128–131, 133, 134, 137, 139–141, 143
Joachim of Fiore
 Joachimite ideas, 11
John IV of Portugal, 52–54, 61n47

K
Keach, Benjamin, 200
Knollys, Hanserd, 193, 199, 200, 201

L
La Cruz, Francisco de, 44, 48, 60n39
Las Casas, Bartolomé de, 10, 41, 42, 44
Laud, William, 200
Lavington, George, 242
Lawson, Thomas, 194
Lead, Jane, 87, 89
Lee, Ann, 260
Leeds, Daniel, 163–165
Leeke, Jacob, 71
Lightfoot, John, 110, 122n20, 123n26
Lowman, Moses, 16

M
Mather, Cotton, 23, 87, 159, 169, 213–234
Mather, Increase, 15, 130, 135–137, 141–144, 146n21, 198
Mede, Joseph, 13, 70, 71, 79n14, 80n15, 80n16, 80n17, 80n20, 134, 138, 139, 259
Mendieta, Gerónimo de, 42, 43, 45, 53, 54, 63n81
Methodism, 30n69, 266, 270
Millennialism
 amillennialism, 5
 postmillennialism, 5, 214, 221, 234
 premillennialism, 5, 19, 23, 214, 234
Miller, Perry, 11, 18, 81, 144
Milton, John, 108, 109, 121n8
Mollineaux, Henry, 202, 210n75
Moravianism, 241
More, Henry, 15, 29n66
Morland, Israel2, 202, 210n74
Muggleton, Lodowick, 15, 193, 207n25
Muggletonianism, 86, 193
Münster, 14, 29, 190, 191, 192, 206n14

N
National identity
 in America, 12, 18, 95
 in England, 12, 92, 94, 146n30, 261, 264
 in Spain, 46–56
Native Americans
 as lost tribes, 35, 39, 41, 139
 conversion of, 35, 38, 39, 41, 58n18, 68, 71, 144
 magic and native prophecy, 38, 41, 143, 144, 151–153, 156, 177n12

Nayler, James, 15
Necromancy, 153, 154, 155, 170
Ness, Christopher, 200, 210n66
New England Way, 12, 213, 219, 222
New Jerusalem, 65, 69–73, 78, 80n20, 133, 138, 144, 199, 202, 203, 219, 233, 240, 261, 263, 274
Newton, Isaac, 15, 29n66
Nóbrega, Manoel da, 39, 45, 58n20
Norton, John, 198

O
Owen, John, 106, 107, 113, 121, 122n24, 123n27, 130

P
Parker, Robert, 141, 142
Patrick, Simon, 223, 224
Perkins, William, 2, 3, 24n4, 24n9, 108, 121n7
Phillip II of Spain, I of Portugal, 35, 36, 47
Philly, John, 194, 208n29, 208n31
Poole, Matthew, 221, 223, 236n29, 236n30
Popish Plot, 199, 203, 216
Presbyterianism, 81n27, 108
Preterism, 237n50
Priestley, Joseph, 18
Prophecy
 and gender, 2, 19, 24, 117, 275, 277
 definitions of, 89, 106
 links to revolution, 3, 15, 18, 19, 23, 88n32, 106, 163–165, 259–281
Providentialism, 35
Publick Universal Friend, 2
Purchas, Samuel, 133, 147n41
Puritanism, 11, 28n54, 69, 86, 87, 96, 107, 110, 213, 220, 242

Q
Quakerism, 105, 106

R
Radicalism, 21–23, 32n90, 86, 93, 97, 106, 117, 187–211, 242, 264, 266, 267, 274, 277
Ranters, 86, 163, 193, 204
Reeve, John, 14, 193
Reubeni, David, 34
Revelation, book of, 1, 17, 40, 144, 165, 190, 214, 224, 225, 248, 262, 268
Revivals(s), 16, 17, 30n70, 31n71, 197, 230, 240, 243, 245, 247–249, 250, 251–254, 252, 253, 254, 254n4
Rutherford, Samuel, 113, 115, 122n24

S
Salem, 169, 198
Saltmarsh, John, 114
Santidade do Jaguaripe, 20, 45, 48, 60n41
Satan, 5, 22, 70, 71, 110, 115, 122n19, 138, 139, 158, 175, 201, 204, 218, 243, 270, 271
Sebastian I, 36, 49
Sebastianism, 49, 50, 51, 52, 56, 61n49
Severinus, Peter, 160
Shakerism, 18, 260
Sherwin, William, 200, 210n65
Song of Songs, 23, 129, 130, 213–238
Southcott, Joanna, 19, 23, 24, 260–262, 265– 275, 277, 280n34
Southcottian Visitation, 23, 264–266
Stansby, Robert, 111
Star Chamber, 106, 108, 130
Strong, William, 122n24, 130, 133, 135, 137, 146n24

T

Tany, TheaurauJohn, 14, 99n6, 131
Teate, Faithful, 112, 124n38
Thorowgood, Thomas, 27n41, 138, 140, 143, 149n94
Tillam, Thomas, 192, 193, 198
Tillinghast, John, 131
Tompkins, Mary, 117
Torquemada, Juan de, 58n19, 138
Totney, Thomas. *See* Tany, TheaurauJohn
Translatio Studii et Imperii, 91, 92, 102n36
Trapnel, Anna, 21, 83–87, 89, 97, 98, 99n6
Tuckney, Anthony, 220
Turner, George, 23, 260–263, 265–275, 277
Twisse, William, 70, 72, 81, 138, 144

U

Ussher, James, 112, 113

V

Vane, Henry, 195, 208n39
Vaughan, Henry, 67, 76
Venner, Thomas, 14, 22, 29n60, 187–192, 195, 196, 198, 199
Vieira, Antônio, 40, 41, 52–54, 56, 59n21, 63n81
Virginia, 11, 68, 69, 77, 79n10, 85, 128, 145n4, 157, 163, 170, 173
Virginia company, 11, 59, 68, 79n10, 145n4

W

Walton, Izaak, 69
Ward, Samuel, 69, 70, 72, 78
Wesley, Charles, 31n77
Wesley, John, 17, 23, 30n70, 31n77, 239–246, 248–250, 252, 253, 254n4, 270
Westminster Assembly, 109, 110, 113, 114, 119, 120
Whitefield, George, 16, 23, 30n70, 239, 240, 242, 246–248, 250–253, 254n4
Wilkinson, Jemima, 2, 4, 18. *See also* Publick Universal Friend
William III, 202
Williams, Roger, 123n26, 157, 215
Winslow, Edward, 157
Winstanley, Gerrard, 15, 92
Winthrop Jr., John, 86, 160, 174
Winthrop, John, 11, 71, 80n20, 95, 170
Witchcraft, 151, 154, 159, 166, 168–170, 173, 177n23, 179n48, 183n120
Woodbridge, John, 84
Wroe, John, 260, 265, 275, 278n12

The manufacturer's authorised representative in the EU is Springer Nature Customer Service Centre GmbH, Europaplatz 3, 69115 Heidelberg, Germany. If you have any concerns regarding our products, please contact ProductSafety@springernature.com

Printed and bound by CPI Group (UK) Ltd, Croydon, CR0 4YY

23/03/2026

02076673-0005